The
Fin-de-Siècle
Poem

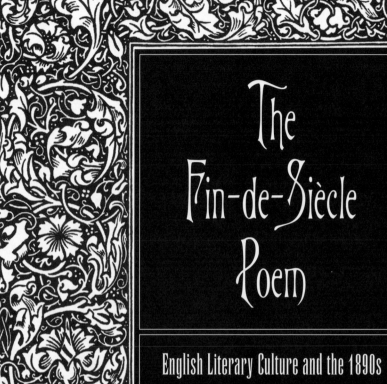

The Fin-de-Siècle Poem

English Literary Culture and the 1890s

edited by
Joseph Bristow

Ohio University Press　Athens

Ohio University Press, Athens, Ohio 45701

www.ohio.edu/oupress

© 2005 by Ohio University Press

Printed in the United States of America

All rights reserved

12 11 10 09 08 07 06 05   5 4 3 2 1

LIBRARY OF CONGRESS CATALOGING-IN-PUBLICATION DATA

The fin-de-siècle poem : English literary culture and the 1890s / edited by
Joseph Bristow.
   p. cm.
   Includes bibliographical references (p.) and index
   ISBN 0-8214-1627-8 (acid-free paper)—ISBN 0-8214-1628-6 (pbk. : acid-
free paper)
     1. English poetry—19th century—History and criticism. 2. Great
Britain—Intellectual life—19th century. 3. Modernism (Literature)—Great
Britain. I. Bristow, Joseph.

PR583.F55 2005
821'.809112—dc22

2005047708

CONTENTS

ILLUSTRATIONS

PREFACE

In *The Fin-de-Siècle Poem: English Literary Culture and the 1890s* the contributors address a field of study that has for years been subject to extensive misrepresentation in widely circulated literary-historical accounts of the era. In my introduction, I show readers how and why poetry of the 1890s has seldom been well served by the trio of critical terms—"aestheticism," "Decadence," and "fin-de-siècle"—that have for the most part cast such leading figures as Ernest Dowson, Arthur Symons, Lionel Johnson, and Oscar Wilde in unfavorable critical light. I reveal, too, how the traditional overconcentration on these male writers as representatives of a seemingly declining age has by and large occluded the recently acknowledged achievements of distinguished women writers such as Michael Field (Katharine Bradley and Edith Cooper), Amy Levy, Dollie Radford, A. Mary F. Robinson, and Graham R. Tomson (later Rosamund Marriott Watson). As the present volume makes plain, fresh inquiries into this period bear witness to the fact that women poets were central to London's literary circles. Likewise, this was an era that saw remarkable innovations in literary publishing, since it was during the 1890s that the aesthetic book came into its own. Further, as the lists of such pioneering publishers as Elkin Mathews and John Lane reveal, some of the finest binding and printing of literary works at this time took place in the sphere of poetry.

But, as I also make clear, if we take some modernist accounts of the literary 1890s on trust, then it becomes extremely difficult to draw anything but the discouraging conclusion that this was in no respect a poetically fertile era. To this day the engaging but negative perspectives of W. B. Yeats and the funny but misleading caricatures of Max Beerbohm (both men are closely linked with this decade) have done an untold amount of damage to the received, mostly dispiriting understandings of the poetic fin de siècle. In their influential view the intoxicating self-destructiveness of this era's characteristic male protagonists expressed a depressive purposelessness of the age, often in antiquated forms and pretentious rhetoric whose excesses supposedly accentuated the superficiality of the fin-de-siècle poet's art.

Jerusha McCormack's chapter develops this line of inquiry into critical estimations of the period by exploring how a "drastic narrowing of the 1890s poets came about." McCormack's main focus is how certain biographical myths served to create a sexual division of labor in the poetic marketplace. Where the male poets cultivated a rather theatrical manner in the presentation of their Decadent work (much of which, in any case, showed a strong interest in performance, whether by famous actresses, female dancers, or women on the music-hall stage), well-regarded women poets such as Alice Meynell did the opposite by fostering a rather private, angelic persona that hardly squared with the supposed irresponsibility of her male peers. Meynell was considered by many members of the literary establishment to be a strong candidate for the laureateship, which became vacant upon Tennyson's death in 1892. (The post, owing to much wrangling over who should succeed him, remained open for four years.) But Meynell's life of devotion to her family of seven children and her faith (she had converted to Catholicism in 1864) for decades made it difficult for historians to acknowledge that by the 1890s she had come to attention as one of the foremost essayists and poets published by Mathews and Lane's imprint, the Bodley Head. As McCormack discloses, in the case of Rosamund Marriott Watson—one of the most widely published English poets of the 1880s and 1890s—the fact that this accomplished writer endured two divorces, losing in the process custody of three children, in many ways accounted for her unwillingness to develop a public persona in later life.

In the second chapter, Holly Laird turns attention on how and why biographical accounts of leading male fin-de-siècle poets such as Davidson, Dowson, and Johnson (as well as the somewhat older James Thomson) have been intent to view these writers' achievements, even in their own time, as built on self-murder. Laird observes that these life myths tend to ignore the significance of suicide as a pressing topic that absorbed these poets' imaginations. Rather than assume that these writers' interest in self-murder inspired their untimely deaths, she urges readers to consider how and why their aesthetics remained enduringly fascinated with formal and stylistic structures of fragmentation and destruction. By broadening her analysis to include the suicidal subject matter of three women poets—Amy Levy, Charlotte Mew, Adela Cory Nicolson—Laird reveals how tricky it has proved for scholars to imagine that the topic of hopelessness might be understood as separate from these authors' decision to end their lives.

Linda K. Hughes, in the third chapter, maintains the focus on fin-de-siècle poets' enduring interest in fragmentariness by returning our attention to Rosamund Marriott Watson, whose oeuvre dramatizes an almost unmatched fracturing of identity. But, like Laird, Hughes is aware of the pitfalls of relying on biographical events in order to explain this poet's formal and thematic preoccupations. While it was the case that Marriott Watson's changing marital circumstances resulted in changes of name (she emerged as R. Armytage, then wrote as Graham R. Tomson, and then took the family name of her common-law husband), such information scarcely accounts for this writer's fascination with a range of poetic forms and styles—from ballades, rondeaus, and villanelles to impressionist nocturnes—that provided her with various masks behind which she enjoyed the freedom to articulate forthright sexual passion. The fact that poetic masks worked in Marriott Watson's favor in part accounts for her outstanding success in placing her work in a wide variety of journals. Hughes also makes a special point of showing how the print media in which Marriott Watson appeared in her transforming guises—whether an ostensibly conservative periodical such as W. E. Henley's *Scots Observer* or a finely bound and illustrated volume issued by John Lane—discloses some of the connections between what have been conventionally viewed as discrete, if not antipathetic, sections of the 1890s literary world.

The next two chapters accentuate the frequent emergence of fin-de-siècle poetry in volumes that exemplify decisive trends in the history of the book. Nicholas Frankel draws detailed attention to the Rhymers' decision not to present their collective poems as the kind of aesthetic artifact that John Gray's *Silverpoints* (1893) most emphatically was. As I point out in the introduction, Charles Ricketts's distinctive designs for the lizard-green binding and unusual page layout ensured that Gray's first book of poetry became one of the most visually arresting volumes of the 1890s. The Rhymers' two books looked comparatively plain, with running headers stating "The Rhymers' Club" at the top of pages printed in a uniform style. The typographic reiteration of "The Rhymers' Club" certainly makes sense in volumes in which the identity of a single author remains far less significant than the topics that absorb the authors' works. Their books, rather than relate individual poets to groups of poems, insist that it is the subject matter of the contributions that has decided the order in which their works appear, and such themes of course have implicitly arisen from the exchanges among members of the club. On this view, it becomes possible to see how Yeats's famous lyric "The Lake Isle of Innisfree" forms part of a dialogue with a lyric by Ernest Radford, a link that shows the depth of Yeats's involvement in a grouping whose camaraderie taught him his trade. Frankel contends that the typographic uniformity of the Rhymers' books anticipates the designs that influential publishers such as Faber and Faber (in Britain) and New Directions (in the United States) would adopt in order to present their stable of poets.

Jerome McGann, in the next chapter, looks closely at the neglected but gifted writer whose expertise in other arts—notably architecture—made a decisive contribution to the *Century Guild Hobby Horse,* the avant-garde periodical that fostered vital critical debate at this time. In his study of Herbert P. Horne's compact volume *Diversi Colores* (1891), printed to perfection at the Chiswick Press, McGann discusses the poet's "bibliographical aesthetics." In a series of adept readings, McGann shows that when Horne pays homage to earlier forms—whether Christian devotional works or Robert Herrick's lyrics—his dedication is neither to orthodox religion nor to a seventeenth-century forbear. Instead, Horne's commitment lies in the kind of pastiche that discloses that each poetic articulation stands as a typographical performance. McGann's point is that Horne's volume should not be read in a solely vehicular or referential mode, since the words on the page possess a decidedly material significance. Thus, as readers, we need to observe not so much what the language of the poem signifies as the beautiful medium through which the printed word creates such significations. "Horne devotes himself to glorifying Beauty by making a beautiful thing," McGann writes, and in the process of such glorification the poet requires us to consider the non-semantic aspects of poetic textuality.

In chapter 6, Julia Saville considers how two coauthors explored the fin-de-siècle interest in the unity of the arts through the development of highly accomplished ekphrasis. In *Sight and Song* (1892), Michael Field's third collection of poetry, the aunt and niece Bradley and Cooper responded to Walter Pater's call to respond to the Old Masters in a manner of self-restraint, thus enabling such artworks to speak for themselves. Saville shows how Bradley and Cooper drew upon this Paterian perspective, first developed in his *Studies in the History of the Renaissance* (1873) and amplified in later essays such as "Prosper Merimée" (1890), when they took lessons from the young art historian Bernard Berenson, whose critical engagement with physical detail and color in Renaissance art intersected with Pater's emphasis on the viewer's self-discipline. The result of such withholding of any subjective interpretation is that Michael Field's ekphrastic poems permit each artwork to produce lyrical significations that complicate how an otherwise small detail might be interpreted. For example, in Giorgione's *Sleeping Venus*, the position of Venus's left hand covering her genitals might not be seen, as some viewers have thought, solely as a token of modesty. In their poem, Bradley and Cooper suggest that, in this painting, "Universal pleasure sex / Must unto itself annex"— a gesture of self-pleasuring that gives the somnolent Venus a previously unacknowledged agency. Through their particular adaptation of Paterian ascesis, the coauthors suggest that such restraint on their part enables them to engage in what Saville calls a "playful erotic allusiveness." Bradley and Cooper's finely wrought ekphrasis was probably too advanced even for their teacher, and, sadly, like so much of the ambitious poetry that they produced during the 1890s, *Sight and Song* went largely unnoticed.

The seventh chapter, by Linda Hunt Beckman, turns attention to another woman poet, Amy Levy. Beckman maintains that Levy, who took her life in 1889, stood at the forefront of British poets who absorbed *Symboliste* poetics in the name of producing a decidedly urban poetry. Until recently scholarship has suggested that the poetic interest in the metropolitan scene was the preserve of volumes such as Symons's *London Nights*, Henley's *London Voluntaries* (1893), and John Davidson's "London" (1894), which memorably celebrates "[t]he heart of London beating warm" (John Davidson, "London," in *John Davidson: A Selection of His Poems*, ed. Maurice Lindsay [London: Hutchinson, 1961], 69). Beckman's argument is that Levy's city poems, which appeared in the poet's final volume, *A London Plane-Tree and Other Verse* (1889), reveal that this exceptional writer was deeply acquainted with the urban poetics of Baudelaire and Mallarmé. Levy's fascination with the city's modernity, as Beckman shows, predates the writings of the 1890s male poets, who are usually credited as the progenitors of a distinctly new poetry that confronts the fracturing experiences of modern London. Beckman also makes it clear that Levy draws on *Symboliste* sources in a manner that anticipates Eliot's and Pound's engagement with Baudelaire's *Les Fleurs du mal* (1857, expanded in 1861) and Mallarmé's *Poésies* (1887).

In the chapter that follows, Ana Parejo Vadillo explores the haunting poetry of A. Mary F. Robinson, who, like Levy, came to notice prior to 1890, and whose writings absorbed aspects of avant-garde French poetry well in advance of Symons's influential essay, "The Decadent Movement in Literature" (1893). Robinson's earliest collections share with Levy's slightly later writing an interest in the *Symboliste* poetics of the city. Vadillo contends that Robinson's wide reading in the work of French poets such as Verlaine and her responsiveness to Pater's aestheticism resulted in an experimental type of writing in which the cityscape could supply figures that intensified particular states of mind. Thus in "London Studies" Robinson's poetic voice attempts to integrate the bleak, darkened urban scene with acute feelings of helplessness. In Vadillo's view, such evocative, abstract writing results in an "immaterial poetics," one that negates physical experience by stressing the kind of disembodied soul that Symons would later perceive as a defining aspect of the Decadent movement in literature.

In chapter 9, Yopie Prins sustains the focus on poetics in a close study of Alice Meynell's enduring fascination with another abstract phenomenon—the metrical measure. As Prins explains, Meynell proved immensely responsive to the New Prosody that had its origins in Coventry Patmore's path-breaking "Essay on Metrical Law" (1857). As Patmore saw it, the craving for metrical measure is not just characteristic of poets; it defines the very movements of the human mind. In light of Patmore's and (much later) George Saintsbury's research on meter, the study of prosody became interested in identifying, counting, and then quantifying the spaces that operated within English systems of accentual-syllabic verse. As she reflected on Patmore's essay, Meynell drew a number of intriguing conclusions about the ways in which this new engagement with the measuring of meter disclosed that systems of rhythm structure almost every aspect of our lives. Meynell, as Prins shows, became particularly fascinated by the intervals or pauses between beats. It was in these unspoken metrical spaces that Meynell realized a universal rule. In her view, the orbit of the sun, the pangs of motherhood, and the reappearance of disease and subsequent recovery are governed by patterns of silent but powerful recurrence. She asserted that poetry, which is based on intervallic principles, has an unrivalled capacity to celebrate the all-pervasive but otherwise unnoticed metrics that govern our diurnal lives.

The tenth chapter, by Tricia Lootens, considers another frequently sidelined but fundamental aspect of fin-de-siècle poetry. Lootens draws a comparison between two writers whose movement from the colonial periphery of India to London suggested that the preoccupations of much fin-de-siècle poetry, no matter how avant-garde its claims, belonged firmly to the metropolitan heart of empire. By comparing the works of Anglo-Indian Rudyard Kipling with those of Indo-Anglian Toru Dutt, Lootens shows how these authors, in very different ways, put the spotlight on the "alien homelands" of an increasingly burdensome empire whose conflicts during this period would result in the brutal Second Anglo-Boer War. In poems such as Kipling's "Chant-Pagan," Lootens identifies how the raw, "pagan" vernacular of an irregular soldier serving in South Africa affronts the elevated poetic diction consecrated by the English literary tradition. Combining urban and military slang, snatches of Afrikaans, and Cockney dialect, the speaker of this "chant" wonders, in light of his wartime life, whether he can remain a patriot to the old country. It would seem that this speaker's home has become instead the South African landscape where he has witnessed so much bloodshed. By comparison, Toru Dutt—who died at the age of twenty-one in 1877, and whose works London critics continued to discuss extensively in the 1880s—produced poems that relocated, in productively questioning ways, her deep knowledge of the English Romantics to her Bengal birthplace. Dutt, who received part of her education in Europe, was in many respects an Indian cosmopolitan; her cross-cultural experiences encouraged her to absorb and honor England's poetic heritage while exposing, in the far reaches of empire, some of its national—if not nationalist—limitations.

In the final chapter, Marion Thain moves beyond the turn of the century to consider the later, largely forgotten poetry of Katharine Bradley and Edith Cooper. In the early stages of their collaboration as Michael Field, Bradley and Cooper swore themselves to paganism. Their later poetry, however, records their conversion to Rome, which occurred when their reputation had long suffered serious decline, making them arguably the obscurest of those poets who had first tried to win an audience during the fin de siècle. In her pioneering discussion, Thain shows that the coauthors' decision to embrace Catholicism does not mark a break in

Michael Field's prolific output but in fact reveals continuity with the aestheticism that they espoused in their first book of poetry—based in part on
Sappho's fragments—titled *Long Ago* (1889). In order to secure their conversion, Bradley and Cooper turned to John Gray, author of *Silverpoints*,
for guidance, and in the process they developed a series of poems that
drew on the imagery of St. John of the Cross, whose own poetic writings
Gray had explored in his second volume, *Spiritual Poems* (1896): a volume, designed by Ricketts, that defined Gray's developing identity as a
Catholic aesthete. Many of the most significant poems about their faith
appear in one of the most hard-to-obtain volumes among Michael Field's
extensive but rare editions. Published by Lucien Pissarro's monument to
fine woodblock printing, the Eragny Press, in 1914, *Whym Chow: Flame of
Love* was issued in only twenty-seven copies. The fact that the poems in
this inaccessible book focus on the death of Michael Field's Chow dog,
and their eventual belief that their beloved pet embodied the Holy Spirit,
may well deepen the impression that the coauthors' eccentricities knew
no bounds. But, as Thain clarifies, the poems in *Whym Chow*, like the
posthumously published works that focus on Bradley's and Cooper's conversions, derive from a highly developed system of personal myth: one
that shows that these coauthors—aunt and niece, as well as lovers—carefully reflected on how their earlier paganism prefaced their turn to Rome.
By showing that such idiosyncratic writings should not be summarily dismissed but seriously reassessed, Thain's study provides a fitting conclusion to *The Fin-de-Siècle Poem*.

*

Since this collection of essays refers to a great many fin-de-siècle poets, it
includes an alphabetical list of writers who established their reputation either just before or during the 1890s. In addition, there is a chronology
that lists the most notable works of all of these poets; this list, while it
cannot include each and every volume published during this era, aims to
help readers understand the widening scope of the field. The select bibliography and the notes to the chapters that follow refer readers to the
most noteworthy essays and books that have assisted in positively reshap-
ing our knowledge of the poetry of the time. (The select bibliography does
not include single-author studies. Instead, it lists anthologies and critical
sources that touch on the work of a range of fin-de-siècle poets.)

For the sake of clarity, in each chapter readers will find the dates of publication of each work that is mentioned. In the main, the contributors to the present collection agree that the term "fin-de-siècle" should be viewed as a periodizing (rather than valuational) one that focuses on the cultural life of the 1890s (the term, after all, made its earliest appearances in the British press in 1890). It is, however, the case that a number of writers who established their careers in the mid-1880s—such as Amy Levy and A. Mary F. Robinson—bear significant connections, whether in style or subject matter, with the writers more conventionally associated with this era. In a similar manner, the chronology of poetical works extends through the outbreak of World War I, since several writers who became prominent during this period continued to produce noteworthy volumes long after the *siècle* reached its end.

JEB
June 2004

ACKNOWLEDGMENTS

This collection of essays in part originates in the conference titled "The Fin-de-Siècle Poem" that was held on February 22–23, 2002, at the William Andrews Clark Memorial Library, University of California, Los Angeles (UCLA). The editor would like to thank the staff of the Center for Seventeenth- and Eighteenth-Century Studies, which administers all of the symposia arranged at the Clark Library. In particular, Peter Reill, Marina Romani, Candis Snoddy, and Elizabeth Krown Spellman gave generously of their time. Anne Sheehan, under the auspices of the center, provided invaluable research assistance. At the Clark Library, Scott Jacobs, Suzanne Tatian, Jennifer Schaffner, and Bruce Whiteman gave extensive help in locating materials from the large archive devoted to Oscar Wilde and fin-de-siècle literature. At the Department of Reference and Maps, Young Research Library, UCLA, Miki Goral provided sustained help and guidance in identifying sources. Reprographics Services at the Office of Instructional Development, UCLA, prepared a number of the figures. I am grateful to Adreanna Adler for processing photographic orders and to Reed Hutchinson for shooting the images. At the UCLA English Department, Alison Harvey alerted me to some of W. B. Yeats's reviews.

The editor and the contributors would like to thank all of the collectors, copyright holders, librarians, and publishers who have made it possible to reproduce the illustrations in this volume.

Figures 1, 2, 3, and 18 are reproduced courtesy of the William Andrews Clark Memorial Library, UCLA. Suzanne Tatian processed the order. Reed Hutchinson of the Office of Instructional Development photographed these images. Figure 4 is reproduced by permission of the Bodleian Library, University of Oxford. Figures 5 and 8 are reproduced by permission of the British Library. Figures 6 and 7 are reproduced by permission of the Trustees of the National Library of Scotland. Figures 9, 10, 11, and 12 are reproduced by permission of the Harry Ransom Humanities Research Center, University of Texas, Austin. Figures 13, 14, and 15 have been provided from the collection of Linda K. Hughes. Figures 16, 17, and 19 have been provided from the collection of Nicholas Frankel. Figures 20, 21, 22, and 23 are reproduced by permission of the University of Virginia. Figure 24 has been provided by Réunion des Musées Nationaux/Art Resource, NY, and is reproduced by permission of the Louvre, Paris. Figures 25, 26, and 28 are reproduced by permission of the Gemäldegalerie Alte Meister, Staatliche Kunstsammlungen, Dresden. Figure 27 is reproduced by permission of the Städelsches Kunstinstitut, Frankfurt am Main. Figure 29 is reproduced by permission of Special Collections, Miller Library, Colby College, Waterville, Maine; our thanks to Patricia Burdick for making this image available. Figure 30 is reproduced by permission of the Institut Pasteur, Paris. Figure 31 is reproduced by permission of Adelson Galleries Inc., New York. Figure 32 is reproduced by permission of the Tate Gallery, London. We have not been able to trace the copyright holder of figure 33.

The publisher would like to thank the Johns Hopkins University Press for granting kind permission to reprint Jerome McGann's "Herbert Horne's *Diversi Colores:* Incarnating the Religion of Beauty" (*New Literary History* 34 [2002]: 535–52) in chapter 5 of this volume.

The editor is especially grateful to the contributors for their patience, cooperation, and support during the time that it has taken to bring this volume together. In particular, Nicholas Frankel and Yopie Prins engaged in helpful discussion about a number of points raised in the introduction. Finally, William T. Hendel provided invaluable assistance with checking some last-minute queries.

JEB
September 2004

FIN-DE-SIÈCLE POETS
A Chronology

Alfred Austin (1835–1913)
John Barlas ("Evelyn Douglas") (1860–1914)
Aubrey Beardsley (1872–98)
Louisa S. Bevington (1845–95)
Mathilde Blind (1841–96)
Katharine Bradley (1846–1914)
Robert Bridges (1844–1930)
Horatio F. Brown (1854–1926)
T. E. Brown (1830–97)
Edward Carpenter (1844–1929)
Elizabeth Rachel Chapman (1850–post-1897)
Mary E. Coleridge (1861–1907)
Edith Cooper (1862–1913)
Aleister Crowley (1875–1947)
Olive Custance (1874–1944)
John Davidson (1857–1909)
Austin Dobson (1840–1921)
Alfred Douglas (1870–1945)
Ernest Dowson (1867–1900)
Toru Dutt (1856–77)
Violet Fane (Mary Montgomerie Lamb Singleton Currie)
   (1843–1905)
Michael Field (see Katharine Bradley and Edith Cooper)
May Clarissa Gillington (later Byron) (d. 1936)
Eva Gore-Booth (1870–1926)
Edmund Gosse (1849–1928)
John Gray (1866–1934)
G. A. Greene (b. 1853)
W. E. Henley (1849–1903)
Emily Hickey (1845–1924)
Laurence Hope (Adela Cory Nicolson) (1865–1904)

Nora Hopper (1871–1906)

Herbert P. Horne (1864–1916)

A. E. Housman (1859–1936)

Lionel Johnson (1867–1902)

May Kendall (1861–1943)

Rudyard Kipling (1865–1936)

Andrew Lang (1844–1912)

Edward Cracroft Lefroy (1855–91)

Richard Le Gallienne (1866–1947)

Amy Levy (1861–89)

Charlotte Mew (1869–1928)

Alice Meynell (1847–1922)

Lewis Morris (1833–1907)

Constance Naden (1858–89)

E. Nesbit (1858–1924)

Henry Newbolt (1862–1938)

John Gambril Nicholson (1861–1931)

Roden Noel (1834–94)

Victor Plarr (1863–1929)

May Probyn ([1856?]–1909)

Dollie Radford (1858–1920)

Ernest Radford (1857–1919)

Marc-André Raffalovich (1864–1934)

Ernest Rhys (1859–1946)

A. Mary F. Robinson (1857–1944)

T. W. Rolleston (1857–1920)

William Sharp (1855–1905)

Dora Sigerson Shorter (1816–1918)

Eric Stanislaus Stenbock ("Count Stenbock") (1860–95)

Robert Louis Stevenson (1850–94)

Arthur Symons (1865–1945)

Francis Thompson (1859–1907)

James Thomson ("B. V.") (1834–82)

John Todhunter (1839–1916)

Graham R. Tomson (later Rosamund Marriott Watson)
    (1860–1911)

Katharine Tynan (1861–1931)
Margaret Veley (1843–87)
William Watson (1858–1935)
Oscar Wilde (1854–1900)
Theodore Wratislaw (1871–1933)
W. B. Yeats (1865–1939)

FIN-DE-SIÈCLE POETRY
A Chronology

1885   Alfred Austin, *At the Gate of the Convent, and Other Poems*

John Barlas ("Evelyn Douglas"), *The Bloody Heart*

Robert Bridges, *Eros and Psyche*

Austin Dobson, *At the Sign of the Lyre*

Andrew Lang, *Rhymes à la mode*

Edward Cracroft Lefroy, *Echoes from Theocritus and Other Poems*

Roden Noel, *Songs of the Heights and the Deeps*

Marc-André Raffalovich, *Tuberose and Meadowsweet*

Katherine Tynan, *Louise de la Vallière and Other Poems*

1886   Mathilde Blind, *The Heather on Fire: A Tale of the Highland Clearances*

Rudyard Kipling, *Departmental Ditties and Other Verses*

E. Nesbit, *Lays and Legends*

Marc-André Raffalovich, *In Fancy Dress*

A. Mary F. Robinson, *An Italian Garden: A Book of Songs*

1887   John Barlas ("Evelyn Douglas"), *Bird-Notes*

John Barlas ("Evelyn Douglas"), *Phantasmagoria: "Dream-Fugues"*

T. E. Brown, *The Doctor, and Other Poems*

May Kendall, *Dreams to Sell*

Lewis Morris, *Songs of Britain*

Constance Naden, *A Modern Apostle, The Elixir of Life, and Other Poems*

Robert Louis Stevenson, *Underwoods*

Katharine Tynan, *Shamrocks*

1888   Edward Carpenter, *Chants of Labour*

William Ernest Henley, *A Book of Verses*

Andrew Lang, *Grass of Parnassus: Rhymes Old and New*

E. Nesbit, *The Better Part, and Other Poems*

Roden Noel, *A Modern Faust and Other Poems*

A. Mary F. Robinson, *Songs, Ballads, and a Garden Play*

William Sharp, *Romantic Ballads and Poems of Phantasy*

1889   Alfred Austin, *Love's Widowhood, and Other Poems*
John Barlas ("Evelyn Douglas"), *Love-Sonnets*
Mathilde Blind, *The Ascent of Man*
T. E. Brown, *The Manx Witch, and Other Poems*
Austin Dobson, *Poems on Several Occasions*
Michael Field, *Long Ago*
Emily Hickey, *Verse-Tales, Lyrics, and Translations*
Richard Le Gallienne, *Volumes in Folio*
Amy Levy, *A London Plane-Tree, and Other Verse*
Marc-André Raffalovich, *It Is Thyself*
Arthur Symons, *Days and Nights*
Graham R. Tomson (later Rosamund Marriott Watson), *The Bird-Bride: A Volume of Ballads and Sonnets*
Margaret Veley, *A Marriage of Shadows and Other Poems*
W. B. Yeats, *The Wanderings of Oisin and Other Poems*

1890   Alfred Austin, *English Lyrics*
Robert Bridges, *The Shorter Poems*
Ernest Radford, *Chambers Twain*
Robert Louis Stevenson, *Ballads*

1891   Alfred Austin, *Lyrical Poems*
Alfred Austin, *Narrative Poems*
Mathilde Blind, *Dramas in Miniature*
John Davidson, *In a Music-Hall and Other Poems*
Emily Hickey, *Michael Villiers, Idealist, and Other Poems*
Herbert P. Horne, *Diversi Colores*
Rudyard Kipling, *Departmental Ditties, Barrack-Room Ballads, and Other Verses*
Dollie Radford, *A Light Load*
Graham R. Tomson (later Rosamund Marriott Watson), *A Summer Night, and Other Poems*
William Watson, *Wordsworth's Grave, and Other Poems*
W. B. Yeats, *The Countess Kathleen and Various Legends and Lyrics*

1892   Alfred Austin, *Fortunatus the Pessimist: A Dramatic Poem*
Austin Dobson, *The Ballad of Beau Brocade and Other Poems of the XVIIIth Century*
Michael Field, *Sight and Song*
M[ay]. C[larissa]. Gillington and A[lice]. E. Gillington, *Poems*

William Ernest Henley, *The Song of the Sword and Other Verses*
Rudyard Kipling, *Barrack-Room Ballads and Other Verses*
Richard Le Gallienne, *English Poems*
E. Nesbit, *Lays and Legends (Second Series)*
John Gambril Nicholson, *Love in Earnest: Sonnets, Ballades, and Lyrics*
William Sharp, *Romantic Ballads and Sospiri di Roma*
Arthur Symons, *Silhouettes*
Katharine Tynan, *Ballads and Lyrics*
William Watson, *Lachrymae Musarum*
Oscar Wilde, *Poems*

1893   John Barlas ("Evelyn Douglas"), *Selections from Songs of a Bayadere and Songs of a Troubadour*
Mathilde Blind, *Songs and Sonnets*
T. E. Brown, *Old John, and Other Poems*
John Davidson, *Fleet Street Eclogues*
Michael Field, *Underneath the Bough*
John Gray, *Silverpoints*
Alice Meynell, *Poems*
Lewis Morris, *Love and Sleep, and Other Poems*
Lewis Morris, *Ode on the Marriage of H. R. H. the Duke of York and H. S. H. Princess Victoria Mary of Teck, July 6th 1893*
A. Mary F. Robinson, *Retrospect, and Other Poems*
Dora Sigerson Shorter, *Verses*
Count Eric Stanislaus Stenbock, *The Shadow of Death: A Collection of Poems, Songs, and Sonnets*
Francis Thompson, *Poems*
William Watson, *The Prince's Quest and Other Poems*
Oscar Wilde, *The Sphinx*
Theodore Wratislaw, *Caprices*

1894   Elizabeth Rachel Chapman, *A Little Child's Wreath*
John Davidson, *Ballads and Songs*
Lewis Morris, *Songs without Notes*
Ernest Rhys, *A London Rose, and Other Rhymes*
Katharine Tynan, *Cuckoo Songs*
William Watson, *Odes and Other Poems*
Oscar Wilde, *The Sphinx*

1895   Louisa S. Bevington, *Liberty Lyrics*
        Mathilde Blind, *Birds of Passage: Songs of the Orient and Occident*
        John Davidson, *The Ballad of a Nun*
        Lionel Johnson, *Poems*
        May Kendall, *Songs from Dreamland*
        Fiona Macleod (William Sharp), *From the Hills of Dream: Mountain Songs and Island Runes*
        E. Nesbit, *A Pomander of Verse*
        May Probyn, *Pansies: A Book of Poems*
        Dollie Radford, *Songs and Other Verses*
        Ernest Radford, *Old and New: A Collection of Poems*
        Marc-André Raffalovich, *The Thread and the Path*
        Arthur Symons, *London Nights*
        Francis Thompson, *Sister Songs*
        Rosamund Marriott Watson, *Vespertilia, and Other Verses*
        William Watson, *The Father of the Forest, and Other Poems*

1896   Mary E. Coleridge, *Fancy's Following*
        John Davidson, *A Second Series of Fleet Street Eclogues*
        Alfred Douglas, *Poems*
        John Gray, *Spiritual Poems*
        Emily Hickey, *Poems*
        Nora Hopper, *Under Quicken Boughs*
        A. E. Housman, *A Shropshire Lad*
        Rudyard Kipling, *The Seven Seas*
        Lewis Morris, *Idylls and Lyrics*
        Victor Plarr, *In the Dorian Mood*
        Robert Louis Stevenson, *Songs of Travel and Other Verses*
        Katharine Tynan, *A Lover's Breast-Knot*
        William Watson, *The Purple East: A Series of Sonnets on England's Desertion of Armenia*
        Theodore Wratislaw, *Orchids*

1897   Alfred Austin, *Victoria: June 20 1837–June 20 1897*
        Olive Custance, *Opals*
        John Davidson, *New Ballads*
        Lionel Johnson, *Ireland, with Other Poems*
        Lewis Morris, *The Diamond Jubilee*
        Henry Newbolt, *Admirals All and Other Verses*

Henry Newbolt, *The Sailing of the Long Ships, and Other Poems*

Dora Sigerson Shorter, *The Woman Who Went to Hell, and Other Ballads and Lyrics*

William Watson, *Ode on the Day of the Coronation of King Edward VII*

1903   Laurence Hope (Adela Cory Nicolson), *Stars of the Desert*

Rudyard Kipling, *The Five Nations*

William Watson, *For England: Poems Written during Estrangement*

W. B. Yeats, *In the Seven Woods: Being Poems Chiefly of the Irish Heroic Age*

1904   Aleister Crowley, *The Argonauts*

Aleister Crowley, *The Sword of Song*

John Davidson, *The Testament of a Prime Minister*

Katharine Tynan, *Innocencies: A Book of Verse*

Rosamund Marriott Watson, *After Sunset*

1905   Olive Custance, *The Blue Bird*

Andrew Lang, *New and Collected Rhymes*

E. Nesbit, *The Rainbow and the Rose*

Ernest Rhys, *Lays of the Round Table, and Other Lyric Romances*

Arthur Symons, *A Book of Twenty Songs*

1906   John Davidson, *Holiday and Other Poems*

Ernest Radford, *A Collection of Poems*

Arthur Symons, *The Fool of the World and Other Poems*

W. B. Yeats, *Poems, 1899–1905*

1907   Rudyard Kipling, *Collected Verse*

Dollie Radford, *A Ballad of Victory and Other Poems*

1908   Mary E. Coleridge, *Poems*

Michael Field, *Wild Honey from Various Thyme*

E. Nesbit, *Ballads and Lyrics of Socialism, 1883–1908*

Henry Newbolt, *Clifton Chapel and Other School Poems*

Katharine Tynan, *Experiences: Poems*

1909   John Davidson, *Fleet Street and Other Poems*

Henry Newbolt, *Songs of Memory and Hope*

T. W. Rolleston, *Sea Spray: Verses and Translations*

Katharine Tynan, *Lauds*

William Watson, *New Poems*

1910   Richard Le Gallienne, *New Poems*
       Dollie Radford, *Poems*
       Dora Sigerson Shorter, *The Troubadour and Other Poems*
       William Watson, *Sable and Purple, with Other Poems*
       W. B. Yeats, *The Green Helmet and Other Poems*
1911   Olive Custance, *The Inn of Dreams*
       E. Nesbit, *Ballads and Verses of the Spiritual Life*
       Katharine Tynan, *New Poems*
1912   Michael Field, *Poems of Adoration*
       Dora Sigerson Shorter, *New Poems*
       Rosamund Marriott Watson, *The Poems of Rosamund Marriott
         Watson*
1913   Michael Field, *Mystic Trees*
       Emily Hickey, *Later Poems*
       Alice Meynell, *Poems*
       Dora Sigerson Shorter, *Madge Linsey and Other Poems*
       Arthur Symons, *Knave of Hearts, 1894–1908*
       William Watson, *The Muse in Exile*
       W. B. Yeats, *Poems Written in Discouragement, 1912–1913*
1914   Michael Field, *Dedicated*
       Michael Field, *Whym Chow: Flame of Love*
       Richard Le Gallienne, *The Lonely Dancer and Other Poems*
       Alice Meynell, *The Shepherdess and Other Verses*
       Henry Newbolt, *Drake's Drum and Other Songs of the Sea*
       Katharine Tynan, *Irish Poems*
       Katharine Tynan, *The Power of Peace: A Collection of Devotional Poetry
         of Katharine Tynan*
       W. B. Yeats, *Responsibilities: Poems and a Play*

INTRODUCTION

Joseph Bristow

How exactly might we characterize the fin-de-siècle poem? In the present volume, eleven scholars formulate fresh answers to a question that most introductions to the literary history of this time would suggest had been resolved many years ago. In the chapters that follow, the contributors provide detailed studies of men and women writers who established their careers in the 1880s and 1890s: a literary period whose supposed affectations and mannerisms have been subject to considerable misrepresentation. Such misrepresentation occurs especially in commentaries that trace the affective, formal, and stylistic shifts from what is sometimes styled the High Victorian rhetorical grandeur of Alfred Tennyson and Robert Browning to the modernist poetics of T. S. Eliot and Ezra Pound. On occasion, critics have viewed the poetic fin de siècle as a somewhat effete transitional era located between two altogether more momentous epochs.

As a result, the poetry that historians have classified under this rubric tends to be valued not so much for its artistic eminence or technical prowess as for the liminal position in which it bears witness to the attenuation of what had been one monumental age (the Victorian) and the consequent need for cultural revitalization by another (modernism). More particularly, commentators have identified the nature of fin-de-siècle poetry's intermediary uncertainty by drawing attention to a limited repertoire of features that seem more often than not to be connected with patterns of disillusioned self-destruction, purposeless immorality, stylized indolence, and sensual indulgence. Moreover, the implicitly marginal status of these writers would appear to be evident in the fact that, more often than not, they issued their works in precious editions whose print runs rarely ran to more than five hundred copies. Such characteristic qualities purportedly manifest late nineteenth-century poets' unwilling acknowledgment that their impotent art hardly mattered to anyone but themselves.

In the main, the alleged inadequacies of the poetry of this period are frequently linked with the largely negative associations that the somewhat exotic term "fin-de-siècle" quickly acquired when it began to circulate in 1890. From the outset the French epithet was never the neutral designation of an age. In a sense, it entered British literary culture as a morally dangerous French trend. In 1916 Elizabeth Robins Pennell recalled that in the 1890s "everything suddenly became *fin-de-siècle* in the passing catchword of the day borrowed from Paris."[1] Rather like racy novels and titillating comedies associated with stereotypical French permissiveness, the term suggested depraved attitudes, especially in ever-sprawling London: the largest capital city in the world, where toffs and lowlifes appeared to intermingle as never before. Not surprisingly, then, *fin-de-siècle* promptly became a slogan for any artistic fashion favored by the cultural elite that might raise eyebrows. As Holbrook Jackson observes in his 1913 classic study of the era, "Anything strange or uncanny, anything which savoured of freak or perversity was swiftly labelled *fin de siècle*."[2] But the French expression's capacity to startle related to something more serious than naughtiness. In particular, critics attached this tag, whether as adjective or noun, to anything peculiar that could be explained by the growing trend of identifying the end of the century with an overwhelming sense that cherished moral conventions and traditional artistic protocols were hastening toward their doom.

Some of the most perverse products of these ostensibly deteriorating times were the male poets whose manifest belief that their culture was suffering a fall became the subject of censure among reviewers. According to the common wisdom of the day, to be a fin-de-siècle poet was to be the kind of man who explored of the seedier side of the imperial metropolis rather than championing the upstanding spirit of empire. On this view, a typical example would be Arthur Symons whose third collection, *London Nights* (1895), proved too undignified even for avant-garde publisher John Lane to add to his prestigious list. In the volume's prologue, Symons's poetic voice declares in emphatic tetrameter: "My life is like a music-hall."[3] To bear out this simile, he hallucinates his "very self" on a stage that "turns and trips" like the "pathetically gay" women dancers (3). In these brash surroundings he gazes through veils of cigarette smoke, and the house "light flares" garishly; this delirious nighttime poet eventually wearies of the "loud" and "riotous" entertainment that has dislocated his senses (3).

Countless poems in *London Nights* deepen the impression that every aspect of the poet's life, especially his art, has been adulterated through contact with boisterous popular culture. In "To a Dancer," it seems as if the very "rhythms" of the woman performer's "poising feet," as well as her "body's melody," are not so much the object of poetic contemplation as the entrancing cadence of Symons's poetry (6). As he senses that her compelling rhythmical movement possesses his art, Symons's overwrought speaker imagines that the female dancer wishes to seduce him, since he fantasizes that her "eyes," "feet," and "body" perform for him and him alone. Such musing affects him, in a telltale adverb, "intoxicatingly," as if he recognizes that this exhilarating fantasy serves to counter his feelings of impotence. Elsewhere in the same volume, the poet's fear of sexual powerlessness noticeably intensifies. In another poem, he shows that in the nocturnal music-hall world romantic fulfillment might be impossible. As he waits outside the stage-door, he watches "the curls, / And thin bright faces of girls" emerge from amid "the crowd, the blent noises, blurred lights of street" ("At the Stage-Door," 16)—indistinct phenomena that Symons's readers would know characterized the urban settings of many impressionist paintings dating from the 1870s. While trying to catch sight of his "sweet," the poet notices the cheeks of the various attractive *danseuses,* who still have "the blush of the paint yet lingering" and "the circle of black around their eyes" (16). These women dancers, such details suggest, resemble the painted ladies who paraded along the streets to rendezvous with their clients. In the end, the poet is left "expectant," hoping not to miss his beloved's "[r]ose-leaf cheeks, and flower-soft lips" (16). But there is no sign yet that the two of them will embrace, suggesting perhaps that the anticipated "smile in her heart" will not respond to his yearnings (16).

This brief cento of quotations from *London Nights* certainly supplies the kinds of images that strengthen the still widespread view that the 1890s poet was a dissolute artist who shamelessly recorded his fleeting encounters with demimondaines. And when this type of writer broadened his vision beyond the half-world of London, he could see only the bleakest of prospects in the countryside. In his poem on Dieppe, a favorite seaside haunt among the fin-de-siècle elite, Symons extends his impressionist method to describe not a rapturous landscape but "[a] sea of lead, a sky of slate" (32). This French resort, which attracted a well-heeled crowd, presents to Symons's disenchanted eyes a "grey-green stretch of sandy grass," which appears "[i]nfinitely desolate" (32). Thus, an initial reading of Symons's volume may well conclude that his insidious desolation, ennui, and frustration testified to his perverse interest in vaunting his poetry's inability to idealize nature and splendor in romantic passion. But to make such an inference a reader would need to ignore the cultural forces and aesthetic preoccupations that informed Symons's finely crafted lines. Why, we might want to ask instead, should this quintessentially fin-de-siècle poet find himself in such a dispiriting condition?

In this introduction, I begin by showing why this type of question has often proved somewhat difficult to answer: the male poets who established their reputations during the 1880s and 1890s, and whose names have traditionally been closely linked with this period, are seldom well served by the critical terms—such as "fin-de-siècle," "aesthetic," and "Decadent"—that have come to define their art. I also draw attention to the persistent tendency within the most widely touted myths of aestheticism and Decadence to occlude, almost to the point of invisibility, the remarkably strong presence of women writers in the thriving literary culture of the time. Even if literary historians have for years rightly recognized Symons as one of the most distinctive late-century voices of a decidedly innovative city-based poetics, they have until recently been far less attentive to the comparable urban aesthetics of a writer such as his accomplished contemporary Amy Levy. By November 1887, when Symons published one of his earliest poems about intoxication, "The Opium-Smoker," in the *Academy*, Levy's adroit lyric "London in July" had been known to the readership of this well-respected periodical for some four months.[4] Her early death, which took place not long before her second major collection, *A London Plane-Tree, and Other Verse*, appeared in late 1889, to a limited degree accounts for her almost immediate exclusion from even the most comprehensive literary-historical accounts of the age.[5] But as for Levy's gifted women peers who consolidated their reputations during the 1890s—one thinks of Mary Coleridge, Olive Custance, Michael Field (Katherine Bradley and Edith Cooper), Alice Meynell, E. Nesbit, Dollie Radford, and Graham R. Tomson (known by 1895 as Rosamund Marriott Watson)—their sidelining in most of the twentieth-century retrospectives on the period raises more complicated questions about why for the best part of a hundred years commentators typically identified the temper of fin-de-siècle poetry among an exclusive band of seemingly dissolute males.[6]

It therefore almost goes without saying that the prevailing critical perspective on 1890s poetry has largely been a selective, if not distorted, one. Only by clearing our minds of the frameworks that make the fin-de-siècle poem appear a willfully freakish or perverse phenomenon can we begin to understand why Symons's estimation that his life was "like a music-hall" related to a desire—evident among his contemporaries—not to titillate his audience but to redefine the locations, the forms, and the language in which his art might make sense of modern culture at the century's end. At the same time, in the process of understanding why many twentieth-century writers, especially the leading lights of modernism, proved hostile to their late-century precursors, we can begin to see why it proved convenient to characterize the poets of the 1890s as uniformly male, generally immoral, and artistically questionable figures whose eccentricities have livened up many a memoir.

In large part, it is because of these influential attacks that modern scholarship has found it hard to grasp that the poetry of a fine writer like Symons deliberately aimed at shifting the register in which traditional aesthetic precepts of truth and beauty were based. Correspondingly, the long-standing critical inclination to devalue the avant-garde male writers of the period too often has made it difficult for modern scholars to witness the equally strong achievements of a diverse group of distinguished women contemporaries who joined the lists of pioneering publishers, such as John Lane, who issued volumes by Symons and his colleagues. Moreover, there has been a tendency in literary history to dissociate the connotations of perversity and freakishness traditionally attached to the term "fin de siècle" from a number of highly praised male poets whose work gained authority in the 1890s because it embodied patriotic and imperial sentiment. In this regard, the writings of the immensely prolific Tory nationalist Alfred Austin, who succeeded Tennyson as poet laureate in 1896, make a stark contrast with *London Nights*. But it would be mistaken to suggest that all of the 1890s poets who championed empire and nation were decidedly separate from the sexually subversive worlds that Symons characteristically inhabited. To be sure, the fine lyrics that A. E. Housman published anonymously in his 1896 collection *A Shropshire Lad* would be absorbed into cultural history because they betoken an elegiac nostalgia for the English countryside; it was for this reason that copies of his much-reprinted collection were issued to British soldiers during World War I. Housman's work and the bold, triumphal, and patriotic heroism of W. E. Henley's *The Song of the Sword* (1892) might appear remote from Symons's unapologetic celebration of the seamier side of London's night-life. But, on reflection, Housman's fascination with the youthful male body in his 1896 volume is not entirely distant from the subject matter of those contemporaries—such as Horatio Brown, Alfred Douglas, John Gray, John Gambril Nicholson, Marc-André Raffalovich, and Oscar Wilde—who wrote altogether more explicitly about male homosexual desire.[7]

Likewise, as Linda K. Hughes has shown, during his editorship of the *Scots Observer* and the *National Observer* in the late 1880s and early 1890s, Henley may have been surrounded by a nicknamed "Regatta" of enthusiastic male supporters, and he was one of the earliest sponsors of the imperial-minded Rudyard Kipling's outspoken poems on the life of the everyday soldier Tommy Atkins.[8] Yet Henley's poetry, like that of the Decadent Symons, would also celebrate the sexual energy generated by the urban scene, although he places greater emphasis on the daytime rather than nighttime metropolis. His short sequence titled "London Voluntaries" sounds the note of spontaneous musical performance in order to animate the "freshet of desire" aroused by the "spring clouds trooping slow," which, in an audacious (if ill-advised) simile, move "[l]ike matrons heavy-bosomed and aglow."[9] This quirky performance becomes somewhat embarrassing when Henley's male speaker eroticizes Mother Nature's fertility. As he watches the clouds gather like "[m]ilk from the wild breasts of the willful day" and then witnesses the "buxom leafage of the Park" (20), it is little wonder that the excited poetic voice claims that any man must "feel . . . the primal blessing in his blood," since "the sacred impulse of the May / Brighten[s] like sex made sunshine through her veins" (21). That said, even if Henley shares aspects of Symons's fascination with the city's overwhelming *eros,* his avowedly imperialist journals were on occasion hostile to aesthetes and Decadents. Then again, he gave space in his weekly paper that enabled women writers such as the feminist Tomson to print not only poems but also commentaries on fashion that reflected their aesthetic interests. (Henley died in 1903. Rosamund Marriott Watson, as Tomson was then known, wrote a poem cherishing his memory.[10])

It is with these kinds of points in mind that the present collection builds on established, if at times underrated, research that has countered the conventionally negative and remarkably incomplete approach to the fin de siècle by producing searching insights into the innovations (rather than enervations) of a divergent body of poetic writings that emerged during this comparatively brief period of time. In what follows, I explain how and why literary history has frequently connected the leading ideas associated with this decade with largely disapproved-of qualities. I show, too, why unconstructive critical attitudes toward some of the apparent excesses of the period have frequently foreclosed scholarly appreciation of not only the poetic inventiveness of the era but also noteworthy developments in the production of the poetic book. In their challenge to received wisdom about the period, the studies that follow reconsider the fin-de-siècle poem in relation to a much broader ensemble of aesthetic principles, styles of versification, representational strategies, and cultural rhythms than conventional literary history has for the most part been prepared to recognize in connection to the era.

Defining Terms: "Fin-de-siècle," "Aestheticism," "Decadence"

As Holbrook Jackson reminds us, the negative connotations of "fin-de-siècle" would escalate in the "Jeremiah of the period"—namely, *Degeneration,* the rambling tome by European doctor Max Nordau.[11] In his 1893 volume Nordau turns to the already degraded catchword "fin-de-siècle" in order to make the staggering assertion that modern artists shared the same degenerate mentality as criminals and neuropaths. Moreover, Nordau maintains that members of the artistic avant-garde, like these other reprehensible types, had the ability to contaminate everyone who came within their reach. "Under the influence of an obsession," Nordau writes forbiddingly, "a degenerate mind promulgates some doctrine or other—realism, pornography, mysticism, symbolism, a diabolism," ensuring that "other neuraesthetical minds" absorb the vile creed and then unthinkingly propagate it.[12] While numerous commentators in England concluded that Nordau was perhaps as fanatical as the "aesthetic schools" he impugned, the polemic contained in his unwieldy book proved immensely attractive to many of his English readers.

In any case, long before Nordau's rant went on sale the charges against fin-de-siècle writers rested on their commitment to two frequently misconstrued developments. First, these unsavory individuals were supposed to be upholders of *l'art pour l'art,* the doctrine whose earliest manifestations have been traced to early nineteenth-century French culture. In 1804 Benjamin Constant used the phrase in his summary of a lecture he had heard by Immanuel Kant.[13] After that time, the idea that art should aim at aesthetic rather than moral ends would circulate in polemical, widely read works, such as Théophile Gautier's 1835 preface to his sexually experimental novel *Mademoiselle de Maupin.* A small but influential number of British authors proved highly responsive to this widespread, though never fully elaborated, French trend. During the 1860s and 1870s Algernon Charles Swinburne and Walter Pater were frequently attacked for their celebration of sensuous and sensual pleasure at the expense of making conclusive moral judgments. By the 1890s it was possible for critics to see how Pater's and Swinburne's writings left their stamp on a rather loosely defined movement that had become known as "aestheticism." At no point, however, was there a particular grouping or coterie on either side of the English Channel that issued a manifesto that laid out, once and for all, what advocates of either French *l'art pour l'art* or British aestheticism could or should believe. Likewise, even late nineteenth-century writers who were thought to be advocates of aestheticism remained skeptical of its vague premise.

Secondly, we need to consider the frustration, world-weariness, and dissipation that many literary historians assume vitiate the work not only of Symons but also his poetic friends in London, including (to give the most prominent names) Ernest Dowson, John Gray, and Lionel Johnson. In their own time, these writers—who hailed from a variety of backgrounds—would be labeled, in convenient but mostly uncomplimentary ways, "Decadent": the English appropriation of another French term, *décadent,* which most critics agree was coined by Maurice Barrès in 1884 in order to define a school of French poetry whose interest in sexuality and pessimism descended from the late Charles Baudelaire. (The most controversial figure among the newly named *Décadents* was Paul Verlaine, the bisexual writer who had fired a shot at and slightly wounded his male lover, the experimental poet Arthur Rimbaud, in 1873. This crime led to eighteen months of imprisonment, during which time Verlaine experienced a severe spiritual crisis, which resulted in his conversion to Catholicism.) Unlike aestheticism, which (as Ruth Z. Temple observes) never had an official or self-appointed spokesperson,[14] during the fin de siècle the phenomenon of Decadence became the object of considerable explanation in both England and France.

Even then, as Asti Hustvedt has pointed out, the contributions to the literary journal *Le Décadent,* which Anatole Baju edited in the late 1880s, "never articulated a coherent position."[15] Certainly, Baju claimed that "decadism," in Hustvedt's words, marked "an age in which civilization was 'deliquescent' (with its connotations of liquification and dissolution) and modern man neurotic." But even before the word had crossed the English Channel Baju had lost faith in it. Elsewhere in Europe at this time Friedrich Nietzsche (whose works would not be authoritatively translated into English until the late 1890s), in *The Case of Wagner* (1888), would elaborate his thoughts on the French term *décadence* in relation to necessary bodily processes of eliminating waste. Yet, as Charles Bernheimer observes, "Nietzsche has very little to say concerning French decadence, about which he is not particularly well informed."[16] Taken together, these examples from Baju's and Nietzsche's work suggest that the term *décadence* provided a platform on which divergent thinkers could contemplate different models of cultural and physical decline. It would, however, be left to the populist Nordau to attach the greatest stigma to its name.

London literary culture engaged seriously with Decadence somewhat belatedly. It was in 1891—a threshold moment after Baju abandoned Decadence and before Nordau railed against it—that Lionel Johnson attempted to make one of the first, necessarily inchoate assessments of this novel French import.[17] In an issue of the *Century Guild Hobby Horse* (a leading art journal that featured impressive poems by Ernest Dowson, Michael Field, and Herbert P. Horne), he tried to create a clear distinction between Decadence and its near-twin *Symbolisme*—a term that Jean Moréas in 1886 devised to classify a tradition of modern French poetry that also traced its roots back to Baudelaire. Johnson writes, "In English, *décadence* and the literature thereof, is this: the period, at which passion, or romance, or tragedy, or sorrow, or any other form of activity or of emotion, must be refined upon, and curiously constructed, for literary treatment: an age of afterthought, of reflection."[18] As Johnson saw it, such reflexivity resulted in "one great virtue, and one great vice." There was "the virtue of much and careful meditation upon life, its emotions and its incidents," and there was "the vice of over subtilty [*sic*] and of affectation, when thought thinks upon itself, and when emotions become entangled with a consciousness of them." By comparison, *Symbolisme*—which was seldom explicitly linked in the 1890s with British poetry[19]—referred to a complementary, but in Johnson's view more affirmative, tendency within aesthetics. *Symbolisme* involved

> a recognition, in things, of a double existence: their existence in nature, and their existence in mind. The sun sets: what is the impression of that upon your mind, as you say the words? Clearly, that is the "true truth" of the thing; its real and eternal significance: not the mere natural fact, but the thing, as it is in thought. So, literature is the evocation of truth from the passing show of things: a view, curiously like many philosophical views, from the days of Heraclitus to the days of Kant.

On this basis, Decadence and *Symbolisme* point to fin-de-siècle writers' preoccupation with the distinction between what they perceived and the medium through which they represented that perception.

Two years later Symons would enlarge on Johnson's basic definitions by suggesting that Decadence could embrace not only *Symbolisme* but also impressionism—a term whose familiar usage had been extended to describe the recent work of novelist Joris-Karl Huysmans. Symons made a brave attempt to lend dignity to what he called "The Decadent Movement in Literature" in *Harper's New Monthly Magazine*, a widely circulated transatlantic journal that had recently given pride of place to a number of English poets, including Graham R. Tomson. In his essay, which juxtaposes recent works by French and British writers, Symons drew, as unapologetically as he could, on a vocabulary that specified the aesthetic qualities of perversity, disease, and decay:

The most representative literature of the day—the writing which appeals to, which has done so much to form, the younger generation—is certainly not classic, nor has it any relation with the old antithesis of the Classic, the Romantic. After a fashion it is no doubt a decadence; it has all the qualities that mark the end of great periods, the qualities that we find in the Greek, the Latin, decadence: an intense self-consciousness, a restless curiosity in research, an over-subtilizing refinement upon refinement, a spiritual and moral perversity. If what we call the classic is indeed the supreme art—those qualities of perfect simplicity, perfect sanity, perfect proportion, the supreme qualities—then this representative of literature of to-day, interesting, beautiful, novel as it is, is really a new and beautiful and interesting disease.[20]

In other words, Decadence was thought to express an intense dissatisfaction with the idealism of inherited cultural forms. By finding beauty in disease, truth in insanity, and pleasure in perversity, Decadence for Symons defined the shared project of a group of mostly French writers who sought to bring traditional aesthetics to a decisive *fin*.

Symons's essay remains of interest because it engages with a skeptical discussion by one of his peers, the poet and essayist Richard Le Gallienne, who remarked the previous year: "In all great vital literature, the theme, great or small, is always considered in all its relations near and far and above all in relation to the sum total of things, to the infinite, as we phrase it; in decadent literature the relations, the due proportions, are ignored."[21] On this basis, Le Gallienne concluded that Decadence displayed "limited thinking" that amounted to the "euphuistic expression of isolated observations." Le Gallienne's passing allusion to euphuism registers what he believed to be the unwelcome impact that Walter Pater's thought had on fin-de-siècle writers. In the finest exposition of Pater's legacy to literary Decadence, Linda C. Dowling observes that the preoccupation with euphuism had come to serious attention in both his novel *Marius the Epicurean* (1885) and his famous essay on "Style" (1889). In Pater's view, the classical euphuists of second-century Rome, Apuleius and Cornelius Fronto, believed their writing in the Latin vernacular had to be conducted with respect for the protocols of the ancient Greek rhetorical tradition.

As Dowling sees it, Pater's thinking implied that his contemporaries should pay "assiduous attention to the complex linguistic textures of old and new, archaism and neology."[22] In some respects, it is this interest in integrating antiquated modes with modern idioms that explains Symons's reference to fin-de-siècle writers' "restless curiosity in research." Much of the poetry from this period reveals a fascination with fixed forms—like the ballade, which derived from fourteenth-century Old French. These forms were updated in order to represent a bustling urban center whose energies could produce states of exhilaration as well as exhaustion. Dowling's argument thus helps to shift the scholarly understanding of literary "Decadence" in Britain from a term that indicates a superficial "cult of artifice" to a word that signals urgent intellectual debates about the aesthetic autonomy of "language and style." Dowling traces these debates to the new comparative philology, taught at Pater's Oxford, in which the linguistic medium was a "system blindly obeying impersonal phonological rules in isolation from any world of human values and experience" (xi–xii).

But despite attempts by Johnson and Symons to give critical legitimacy to the subtlety, refinement, and research that motivated Decadence, it proved practically impossible in England to establish the case that this literary mode might be understood as an intellectual project that owed much to Pater's sophisticated thought. In Britain, Decadence met with abundant criticism, not least because these movements insinuated that their proponents either had lost all grip on the redemptive purpose of art or aimed simply at undermining moral principle. In every sphere of artistic production the term "Decadence," like "fin de siècle," became disreputable. In 1892 the positivist philosopher Frederic Harrison voiced a typical complaint about Decadence in modern painting: "A dirty old woman vacantly staring at a heap of stones, a pig wallowing in fetid mud, a dusty high road between two blank walls, a sand-bank under a leaden sky—such are the chosen spectacles of genius."[23] And when it came to works of literature the fulmination proved unstoppable. In a famously overstated example, Hugh M. Stutfield, who applauds Nordau's diatribe, condemns what he sees as the unhealthiness of fin-de-siècle poetry and prose: "To the aesthete and decadent, who worship inaction, all strenuousness is naturally repugnant."[24] "It is time," he adds, "that a stand were made by sane and healthy-minded people against the 'gilded and perfumed putrescence' which is creeping over every branch of art" (843).

Stutfield's excesses aside, it is true that both aestheticism and Decadence proved so unpalatable to the larger proportion of the reading public that the term "Decadence" had to be done away with altogether, even by its advocates. By the late 1890s, when Symons was developing his essay into a full-length book, now focusing solely on French writers, he decided to call his study *The Symbolist Movement in Literature* (1899).

The Fin-de-Siècle Poetic Book: Wilde, Ricketts, Gray

Perhaps the strongest evidence for detractors of the literary fin de siècle in England lies not only in the vitiating qualities associated with aestheticism and its successor, Decadence. The stylized indulgence of the period is also visible in the excessively ornate designs that some publishers devised for the slender volumes of verse that they issued in limited editions. In this respect, the most lambasted figure to iconize the transmogrification of "art for art's sake" into Decadence was Oscar Wilde, who took steps to establish a poetic identity that would enshrine the widely disparaged spirit of the era.

By the 1890s Wilde had been in the public eye for more than ten years, during which time he had gained much celebrity as a "professor of aesthetics" before turning to the writing of fiction, critical essays, and a great deal of journalism as a means of earning a living. Among Wilde's most significant contributions to the development of literary aestheticism was his editing of the *Woman's World* between 1887 and 1889. In this remarkable magazine, which addressed an educated, politically aware female readership, he made a point of publishing new work by emergent women poets such as Elizabeth Rachel Chapman, Violet Fane, Amy Levy, E. Nesbit, and A. Mary F. Robinson. Whether in his editing, his lectures, his plays, his reviews, or his stories, Wilde made a calculated point of ignoring philistine moralizing about art, and his irreverent wit ensured that he proved a particularly challenging butt for the satirist's pen. In 1894, when the editor of a conservative journal asked him to write a piece that would "slash" the term *fin-de-siècle*, he made a sharp reply: "All that is known by that term," he observed, "I particularly admire and love." "It is," he added, "the fine flower of our civilisation: the only thing that keeps the world from the commonplace, the coarse, the barbarous."[25] He reminded the editor that "slashing" was fit only for crude journalists, not for accomplished artists. But it was not just his refusal to capitulate to this type of moral censoriousness that singled out Wilde as the most notorious representative of all that fin-de-siècle culture had come to connote. His volatile career—which witnessed his rise to fame as a popular playwright in early 1892 and his rapid descent as a man guilty of committing acts of "gross indecency" with other males in May 1895—ensured that he ultimately represented to an unsympathetic public all that was most artificial, bohemian, and stylized during an era whose artistic elite was thought to celebrate a sickening delight in cultural and moral decline.

In keeping with his professional and personal upheavals, Wilde's contribution to fin-de-siècle poetry was marked by ups and downs. At first glance, his lyrics and narrative poems may well appear to exemplify the weakness that has long been linked with the period's avowed decay. When his uneven volume *Poems* appeared in 1881, *Punch* memorably dismissed it as "Swinburne and Water."[26] The *Athenæum*, somewhat more temperately, observed that even if the collection was supposed to be "the evangel of a new creed," it happened to "com[e] after, instead of before, the cult it seeks to establish."[27] But such reproofs hardly deterred Wilde from bringing these poorly received works before a new generation. Wilde, eager to capitalize on his growing fame in the early 1890s, seized on the opportunity to reprint his 1881 *Poems* in a mode that marked one of the most significant innovations in modern publishing. In May 1892 Elkin Mathews and John Lane, who had been issuing beautifully printed volumes under the Bodley Head imprint since 1889, removed the old binding from 220 remaindered copies of the eleven-year-old volume, inserted new endpapers, and interleaved an arresting decorated title page (fig. 1). The extraordinary insertions and binding were by Charles Ricketts, a young illustrator whose contribution to book design during this period was matched only by that of the even younger Aubrey Beardsley, who consolidated his controversial reputation through his highly erotic drawings in the English edition of Wilde's *Salome* (1894).

In its depiction of various shoots of an unidentifiable plant bursting forth from the earth, Ricketts's striking design defamiliarizes the various botanical drawings and sentimental depictions of flower lore that had won favor with preceding generations. As the largest frond curls sinuously upward, looking as though it will enwreathe the oversized letter *P,* the plant

FIGURE I. Charles Ricketts, title page, *Poems,* by Oscar Wilde (London: Elkin Mathews and John Lane, The Bodley Head, 1892). Courtesy of the William Andrews Clark Memorial Library, UCLA

takes on a puzzling aspect; it is not at all clear whether this prolific out-growth is carrying seed toward its leaf tips or if the leaf is in fact a flower filled with anthers. (In another respect, the illustration bears a passing re-semblance to a flamboyant peacock's tail.) Distorting figurative represen-tation, this boldly flourishing image makes natural growth look, in a word, unnatural. The evident perversity of Ricketts's design has the power to prompt readers to rethink age-old conceptions about harmony between poetry and nature—such as the famous Keatsian idea that if po-etry should come, then it must arise as naturally as leaves to a tree.[28] Rick-etts's image suggests quite the contrary: the plant is about to entwine its tendrils, almost parasitically, around poetry. Put another way, no matter how many shoots sprout from the soil, the result will not necessarily be pretty, delicate, or regenerative.

The same point emerges when we consider the imposing design that Ricketts prepared for the pale-violet binding (fig. 2). As Nicholas Frankel observes, the Bodley Head's publicity for the volume drew attention to the fact that Ricketts's design had a name of its own: *The Seven Trees*. By stat-ing that Ricketts's work possessed a title (one wholly independent from any of Wilde's poems), the publishers were breaking "with the Victorians' assumption, widespread until the end of the 1880s, that bookbinding was merely a 'decorative' art, as distinct from an 'expressive' (or what we would call *representational*) art."[29] Thus, when viewed as an artwork in its own right, the dazzling device—which involves almost unrivaled amounts of gilt—ensures that *Poems* does not appear simply as an exquisitely bound luxury item that sold at the costly price of 15 shillings. Instead, Ricketts's bold group of identical trees, which depart from naturalistic representation, thrust themselves upward like a defiant set of spears on the boards of a decidedly new kind of object for aesthetic contempla-tion—one that suggests that the reader, as Frankel remarks, should real-ize "that *what* the binding represents is perhaps a less interesting question than *how* it represents."[30]

Like many of the volumes issued by the Bodley Head until the middle of 1894 (when the partnership between Lane and Mathews broke up), Wilde's 1892 *Poems* circulated among a restricted market of bibliophiles, connoisseurs, and literary enthusiasts, many of whom were well ac-quainted with one another in the fin-de-siècle metropolis. To such a co-terie considerable value was attached to the limited distribution of such

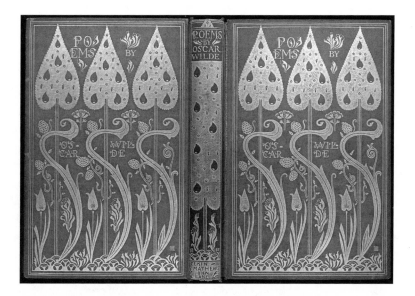

FIGURE 2. Charles Ricketts, decorated boards and spine, *Poems*, by Oscar Wilde (1892). Courtesy of the William Andrews Clark Memorial Library, UCLA

tasteful artifacts, and not just for their collectible rarity. In late 1893 Le Gallienne produced a short polemic on limited editions for exclusive distribution among Mathews, Lane, and their intimates. "Why do the heathen," he inquired, "so furiously rage against limited editions, large-papers, first editions, and the rest? For there is certainly more to be said for than against them. Broadly speaking, all such 'fads' are worthy of being encouraged, because they, in some measure, maintain the expiring dignity of letters, the mystery of books."[31] Such sentiments plainly show that limited print runs aimed to repudiate a mass-market publishing trade whose increasing desire to profit from newly coined "best-sellers" could only, as far as Le Gallienne could tell, vulgarize the literary profession. Moreover, such exclusivity maintained the belief that the literary world was the preserve of the cognoscenti, whose rites and rituals were shared only with the initiated. While Mathews and Lane were hardly averse to reaping handsome profits from commercially successful works (the sales of George Egerton's first collection of controversial short stories, *Keynotes* [1893], had topped four thousand by 1894[32]), they proved especially receptive to the publication of volumes, like Wilde's 1892 *Poems*, of which the typeface, binding, and title page enjoyed an artistic eminence equivalent to—if not greater than—the poetry printed inside. In any case, such finely produced works, as Josephine Guy and Ian Small observe, were certainly priced to sell at a profit; *Poems,* notably, "sold out within days."[33]

The extremes to which Mathews and Lane were prepared to take this unique variety of publication come into sharp focus in Wilde's *The Sphinx* (1894), which appeared, as did so many volumes at the Bodley Head, in small- and large-paper editions of two hundred copies and twenty-five copies, respectively. (The latter, aimed at the collector's market, were printed on unbleached Arnold handmade paper, and consequently priced at £5 5s.[34]) Wilde started making arrangements for this volume not long after his 1892 *Poems* went out of print. Here, too, he recycled an earlier work, which he had drawn to completion, though not published, in 1883. In his design for the volume, Ricketts's talents reached unforeseen heights, which would be sustained in later years with the outstanding editions he created for Michael Field's works.[35] As Ricketts recalled in 1899, *The Sphinx* was "the first book of the modern revival printed in three colours, red, black, and green."[36] Moreover, in this volume Ricketts's skills extended well beyond designing the binding and making yet further innovations in the use of typeface (in this instance "the small bulk of the text and unusual length of the lines necessitated quite a peculiar arrangement of the text"). Ricketts devised "pictures" that strove "to combine, consciously or unconsciously, those affinities in line work broadcast in all epochs." Thus he attempted "to evolve what one might imagine as possible in one charmed moment or place, just as some great Italian masters painted as they thought in the antique manner, studying like Piero della Francesca, for instance, to fulfil the conditions laid down by Apelles, whom he had of course never seen, but had taken on trust."[37] Between gracefully decorated ivory boards Ricketts's illustrations overshadowed Wilde's extravagant octameter: "Come forth my lovely languorous Sphinx! and put your head upon my knee!" Wilde's speaker declares, "[a]nd let me stroke your throat and see your body spotted like the lynx!"[38] Little wonder that *The Sphinx* would go down in the annals of literary history as a work famed far more for its gorgeous binding than for the eighty-seven lengthy couplets to be found within.

On the evidence of such volumes it would be easy to assume that Mathews and Lane remained more interested in the market for uncon-

ventional high-quality printing than in the caliber of the poetry they published, whose florid Decadence, in this case, is evident in each and every
line. It was for this reason that critics generally mistook *Silverpoints*
(1893), the debut collection of twenty-nine short poems by John Gray, as
the type of affected volume whose graceful binding and layout, again by
Ricketts, excelled an untalented poet's mistaken wish to emulate the
leading *Symbolistes* (fig. 3). Gray was a largely self-educated writer who
maintained a humble day job as a foreign office clerk. In all probability,
he came into contact with Wilde in 1889, an event that helped to broaden
his contacts in literary London. (Many readers, rightly or wrongly, have
concluded that the young working-class poet must have been the beautiful prototype for Wilde's ageless Dorian Gray.) And it was Wilde, initially
at least, who agreed to underwrite the costs of Gray's striking-looking first
book. It is impossible not to be taken aback by the panache with which
Ricketts devised its vivid green boards and spine, enhanced by an un-
dulating gilt-stamped design of willow leaves, and the care he took in
fashioning the peculiar dimensions of this collection (it measures 8 9/16
by 4 1/8 inches) based on those of the Persian "saddle-book," which had
found favor with the fine printers of the Italian Renaissance.[39] The same
is true of the pioneering manner in which Ricketts modeled the layout
of each tall, thin page—typed in a minute, elegant Caslon font—on one
of "those rare Aldus italic volumes" from sixteenth-century Venice "with
its margins uncut."[40] The tiny italic typeface meant that Gray's lyrics
were overwhelmed by exorbitant amounts of margin on each page. Such
features memorably prompted the satirist Ada Leverson to jest with
Wilde that he should follow Gray's example and "publish a book *all*
margin: full of beautiful unwritten thoughts."[41] Without question, hardly
any other collection of poetry from the fin de siècle rivals the preciosity
of *Silverpoints*.

Yet while it is evidently the case that Ricketts's growing reputation as
a designer made *Silverpoints* a notable event, the volume occasioned an
unambiguously 1890s approach to the poetic book in ways that are
equally, if not more, instructive. This stylishly produced collection, as the
contents acknowledge, reveals the very close connections between members of a London avant-garde that never strayed far from controversy
during this era. Moreover, *Silverpoints* has been the subject of a thoughtful line of recent scholarship that has begun to take the typographical

FIGURE 3. Charles Ricketts, front board and print layout of opening page, *Silverpoints*, by John Gray (London: Elkin Mathews and John Lane, The Bodley Head, 1893). Courtesy of the William Andrews Clark Memorial Library, UCLA

eccentricity of its finely bound poems with increasing measures of seriousness. Undoubtedly, the reappraisal of Gray's role in the making of this extraordinary book for some time proved difficult. The fact that in the late 1890s Gray chose to reject his earliest poetry suggests that even he realized that it would be inadvisable to attribute value to the intensely mannered style in which he fashioned his twenty-eight precious lyrics. In later years, Gray's embarrassment was such that he sought to buy up, in order to dispose of, any remaining copies he could find.

On the face of it, Gray's *Silverpoints* appears a brazen attempt to curry favor with the cultural and literary elite of the time. The dedications to his lyrics display his connections with other poets (some of them Bodley Head authors), his intimacy with fashionable figures (such as actress Ellen Terry), his friendship with a well-known translator (Henri Teixeira de Mattos), and his affiliation with French writers (Charles Baudelaire, Arthur Rimbaud, and Paul Verlaine). More to the point, the larger proportion of Gray's dedicatees belonged to Wilde's far-reaching circle. There was Pierre Louÿs (who assisted Wilde with the French composition of *Salomé* [published in 1893]), Robert Harborough Sherard (who, in 1902, would write the first sustained memoir of Wilde's life), and Charles Shannon (who, together with his life-partner Ricketts, furnished the design and decoration for Wilde's *A House of Pomegranates* [1891]). Wilde, who introduced Gray to many of the figures in this cenacle, unsurprisingly numbered among the various dignitaries whom Gray honored. One might reasonably infer that the patently fin-de-siècle project of *Silverpoints* owed as much to Wilde's considerable benevolence, artistic contacts, and cultural tastes as it did to any poetic talent that Gray might have had.

But such allegiances hardly worked to Gray's advantage. Even if Wilde pledged his faith in Gray's poetic gifts, and even if copies were as a matter of course mailed to reviewers, as well as to some of the dedicatees, comparatively few notices appeared in the major periodicals. And where the volume received attention it was mostly of the kind that no one would want. The widely circulated *Saturday Review* was unexpectedly scathing, not least because the notice was by the very person, Frank Harris, to whom Gray had dedicated "Charleville." (Harris had advised Gray on this imitation of Rimbaud's "A la Musique.") Observing the "singularly beautiful design by Mr. C. Reckitts [*sic*]," Harris—one of Wilde's closest acquaintances—declares it is impossible not to feel that in poems like Gray's (which are "as modern and decadent as they can be") the poet's desire to "shock" the reader has "come a little late."[42] From Harris's jaded perspective, there is only one poem in the book ("The Barber") that comes "up to the level of the binding." Elsewhere, it seems, Gray's efforts to pay homage to Baudelaire's "Femmes damnées" (one of the poems whose lesbian subject matter ensured the censure of *Les Fleurs du mal* by the French state in 1857) result in a "mangled" adaptation. In the end, Harris contends that even though *Silverpoints* at times proves that Gray ranked as a poet, it remained the pitiful case that the young author was "anxious to be mistaken for a *poseur*." For decades *Silverpoints* would be remembered more for the witticisms it inspired than the value of what Leverson styled its "tiniest rivulet of text." These merciless assessments would suggest that whatever worth *Silverpoints* might have resides in its status as a landmark aesthetic artifact within the history of late nineteenth-century literary publishing.

Yet, as subsequent research has disclosed, Ricketts's design for *Silverpoints*—whose contents displayed Gray's aesthetic pretensions, *Symboliste* affiliations, and opulent Decadence—should not be understood as enhancing what was in fact the empty-headed work of an attractive young man after whom Wilde lusted. In 1977 Dowling began the recovery of this volume by showing that the opening poem, "Les Demoiselles de Sauve," comprises a thoughtful critique of the kinds of female icons that an earlier aestheticism had sought to uphold. Fourteen years later, when Jerusha McCormack published her definitive biography of Gray, she showed how the "construction of a *Silverpoints* poem is almost always a fabrication."[43] Thus in a lyric such as "Complaint" (dedicated to the French critic of *Symbolisme* Félix Fénéon) the "I" appears only too aware that the poetic register in which it seeks to give shape to heart-rending emotion remains an ensemble of gestures, or tokens, whose value has been diminished through overuse.

> Men, women, call thee so or so,
>   I do not know.
>   Thou has no name
> For me, but in my heart a flame
> Burns tireless, neath a silver vine.
>   And round entwine
>   Its purple girth
> All things of fragrance and of worth.
> Thou shout! thou burst of light! thou throb
>   Of pain! thou sob!
>   Thou like a bar
> Of some sonata, heard from far
> Through blue-hue'd veils! When in these wise,
>   To my soul's eyes,
>   Thy shape appears,
> My aching hands are full of tears.[44]

Even while rebutting the belief that certain names cannot adequately express the anguish of this "complaint," the poetic voice discovers—through an irruption of apostrophes in the third stanza—that it remains impossible to find representational alternatives to the routine words that men and women "call thee." To be sure, the speaking "I" would like to think that the eternal "flame" that "[b]urns tireless" in the heart (the emotional center of a human subject) has great value. But no sooner has the lyric voice assumed that elaborate synesthesia (initiated in Baudelaire's poetry), which combines vision and olfaction, should lend "worth" to such intense emotion than the mood shifts abruptly. The heart emits only an anticlimactic "shout," followed by a "burst of light," a "throb of pain," and—most disappointingly—a "sob." By the time we reach the fourth stanza, the very idea that in this "wise" the "shape" of such a feeling should result in "aching hands . . . full of tears" sounds absurd. It scarcely looks as if the lyricist weeps in despair because the sorrowful emotion has been experienced sincerely. Instead, the speaker hints that the tears have emerged from the failure of poetic language to authenticate the rending of the heart. As McCormack sees it, "Complaint" is a highly reflexive lyric in which Gray "project[s] an apprehension of his own consciousness."[45] In other words, rather than express heartfelt emotion, the lyric "tries to catch the *effect* of emotion"—in a manner that can only remain distrustful of the very form and language in which such poetic self-consciousness has made itself known.

Some readers might contend that this style of interpretation would be far more appropriately applied to the work of the *Symbolistes* than to a book of verses that feebly tries to imitate them. Even Ruth Z. Temple, who acknowledges Gray's talents, singles out "Complaint" as an "exceedingly inept poem, full of padding (one of Gray's common faults) and nonsense."[46] But, as later critics have shown, Gray—despite whatever "padding" we might find—is best regarded, in Ellis Hanson's words, as an "aesthetic *bricoleur*"; that is to say, in his imitations of Baudelaire, Mallarmé, Rimbaud, and Verlaine, the young English poet judiciously "refigure[ed] . . . beautiful fragments" from these French writers' works, "reassembling them in a new context, a new configuration, that reflected his own sensibility."[47] In 1893, however, the influential *Pall Mall Gazette* chose to dismiss Gray as "Le Plus Decadent des Decadents," at the expense of exploring the critical dialogue that he staged with the *Symbolistes*.[48]

Remembering Fin-de-Siècle Poets: Beerbohm, Pound, Yeats

Gray may have been lampooned in the press, but it remained his good fortune to escape the attention of some of the sharper parodists who recorded the evident excesses of the fin de siècle. (In many ways, Gray luckily made a discreet exit from the era. Before *Silverpoints* appeared, he turned his back on Wilde, and by 1898 he had settled in Rome in order to train for the priesthood.) Gray eluded the piercing scrutiny of Max Beerbohm, who, at an early age, moved within Wilde's circle. Born in 1872, Beerbohm became closely acquainted with the leading figures associated with Decadence while he was still at Oxford, and by the mid-1890s he had managed to provoke a little controversy with a playful essay in the *Yellow Book* (1894–97): the remarkable literary periodical launched by the Bodley Head, whose first issue tends to be remembered for Beardsley's cover image of a devilish male leering at a buxom woman who takes glee in what appears to be a licentious *bal masqué*. In "A Defence of Cosmetics," Beerbohm puckishly declared that "of all the good things that will happen with the full renascence of cosmetics, one of the best is that surface will finally be severed from soul."[49] Beerbohm learned that some readers thought he was preaching a doctrine of superficiality; he published a letter to the editor stating that maybe his "essay, so grotesque in subject, in opinion so flippant, in style so wildly affected" should have been signed "D. Cadent or Parrar Docks."[50] By entering such frays Beerbohm made sure that he ranked among the literati whose distinctive mannerisms, physical characteristics, and styles of dress he never ceased to mock.

In countless illustrations and prose writings, Beerbohm continued well beyond the fin de siècle to create enduring images of a bygone era marked by pretentious eccentricities. But even if Beerbohm possessed privileged knowledge of the circle he caricatured, he still bears some responsibility for the manner in which modern scholarship would for years underestimate 1890s poetry. In this respect, one of Beerbohm's most striking caricatures, dating from 1925, is "Some Persons of 'the Nineties,'" which exaggerates the gestures and demeanors of eleven figures—all of them male. In the foreground, we see Symons, with his droopy moustache, engaging in what looks like dreary chitchat with long-haired Henry Harland, editor of the ill-famed *Yellow Book*. To their right stands the diminutive portraitist Will Rothenstein, who peers upward at the tall,

painfully thin illustrator Aubrey Beardsley. Between these two dispropor-
tionate individuals, Beerbohm depicts a young dandy with a heart-shaped
face, large eyes, and a very small mouth. It is, self-mockingly, himself.
Meanwhile, in the background a portly Wilde, sporting a fancy waistcoat
and florid boutonnière, stands alone smoking a cigarette, as if expecting
an audience. Various others, including a conspicuously frizzy-haired Le
Gallienne, who would write the important memoir *The Romantic '90s*
(1925), form the rest of the company. Yet there is one personage who almost slips out of sight. Just behind W. B. Yeats, who would also live to tell
many tales about members of this group, is the especially obscure poet
whom Beerbohm named "Enoch Soames": the protagonist of a hilarious
fictional account of a fin-de-siècle author who took Decadence to excru-
ciating extremes.

In 1919 Beerbohm's short story "Enoch Soames" presented an
image of the zany poetic 1890s that said much about how superannuated
the once avant-garde male Decadents had become in the interwar period.
Set in 1893, the story, which draws on some factual information, records
the young Beerbohm's first meeting at Oxford with the twenty-one-year-
old Will Rothenstein, who has been commissioned to produce portraits
of twenty-four members from different sections of the university; the
Bodley Head is to print it in lithograph. (This handsome volume happens
to be real. It came out in 1896.) In Rothenstein's company the under-
graduate Beerbohm visits the Café Royal—that "haunt of intellect and
daring," which, though the narrator does not mention it, was frequented
by Wilde.[51] In the domino room of the café Beerbohm encounters the
absinthe-drinking Enoch Soames, who declares, affectedly, in French:
"Je me tiens toujours fidèle . . . à la sorcière glauque" (7). As Beerbohm
watches the young man sip his blue-green potion, he learns that Soames's
obscure first volume is called *Negations*. Later, Beerbohm unearths it,
only to be baffled by what he finds. *Negations* comprises a preface, which
provides "no clue to the exiguous labyrinth of contents"; a story "about a
midinette who . . . murdered, or was about to murder, a mannequin"; "a
dialogue between Pan and St. Ursula"; and some aphorisms (presumably of the kind Wilde published) (10). Unable to extract much meaning
from the book, Beerbohm remains intrigued to discover what Soames's
second volume, a collection of poems fatefully named *Fungoids*, might
yield.

But before he reads Soames's new volume Beerbohm learns a little more about this fin-de-siècle poet's peculiar interests. Soames confides to Beerbohm that after studying the works of Milton he was, of all things, converted to "Diabolism" (13). So perverse is Soames in his interpretation of *Paradise Lost* (which of course sought to teach the ways of God to humanity) that his Devil worship has merged with his Catholicism. "Yes," Soames proclaims, reveling in his unorthodoxy, "I'm a Catholic Diabolist" (13). "Je l'étais à cette époque," Soames portentously informs Beerbohm (13). Assuming that Soames must have some affiliation with the soi-disant *Décadents*, Beerbohm asks the poet for his opinion of Baudelaire. This acknowledged grandfather of the avant-garde, Soames scoffs, "was a *bourgeois malgré lui*" (13). As if such disrespect were not enough, the obscure poet claims that the still-living Verlaine, who was toasted by London's so-called Decadents at this time, was nothing more than "an *épicier malgré lui*" (14). After Beerbohm learns that Soames "owe[s] nothing to France," he reads the poems in *Fungoids*, finding them just as arcane as the bizarre contents of *Negations*. Beerbohm recalls looking at a lyric titled "To a Young Woman," which opens with this outburst: "*Thou art, who has not been!*" (14). Soames's poetic voice proceeds to describe "[p]ale tunes irresolute," together with other clashing sounds, before remarking, incoherently, by way of double negative: "Nor not strange forms and epicene / Lie bleeding in the dust, / Being wounded with wounds" (14). In their reference to "epicene" (a word that of course signifies sexual ambiguity), these frightful lines share an end rhyme with "Faustine," one of the poems that created the greatest shock when Swinburne's *Poems and Ballads* (1866) appeared. This allusion shows that Beerbohm viewed the most pretentious of London's Decadents as the shabby heirs to an earlier generation of aesthetes.

A similar point arises in Beerbohm's puzzled response to another poem by Soames. Titled "Nocturne," the lyric promises to evoke the kind of dreamy nighttime scene made famous in James Whistler's 1870s impressionist paintings, which Wilde echoes in his own "Nocturne" ("The moon hath spread a pavilion / Of silver and of amethyst," Wilde writes rather flatly ["Nocturne," 68]). But instead of describing the "fleecy cloud" and "veil of seagreen mist" that Wilde drapes around the moon, the speaker of Soames's poem celebrates drinking "black wine" with the Devil before challenging his idol to a race (15). Understandably, Beerbohm remains bemused by the "joyous and rollicking note of comradeship" in the first stanza, the "slightly hysterical tone" of the second, and the "bracingly orthodox" manner of the third (16).

It comes as no surprise when Soames's publisher tells him that the inept *Fungoids* has sold only three copies. When, with the Devil's assistance, Soames travels through time to the British Museum reading room of the 1990s, he learns—much to his horror—that he has gone down in cultural memory as a truly diabolical poet. He orders from the stacks a recent literary history that is written in a madcap type of phonetic spelling, which Beerbohm feared would become common practice in years to come. The 1992 volume declares that none other than Max Beerbohm is responsible for preserving Soames's negligible reputation. In a "somwat labud satire," as the absurd future document puts it, Beerbohm discusses Soames as a third-rate poet who mistakenly believed himself a great genius (36). Beerbohm's self-conscious narrative, which is well aware of its legacy to posterity, reveals that Soames serves as an example of "how seriusli the yung men ov the aiteen-ninetiz took themselz" (36).

A year after Beerbohm's "Enoch Soames" sought to disparage the posturing of fin-de-siècle poetry, Ezra Pound produced an illustrious collection of eighteen short poems titled *Hugh Selwyn Mauberley*, which reflects more critically on the selective manner in which memories about the 1890s were passed down to the next generation. In this great work, which has long been regarded as a momentous contribution to literary modernism, Pound considers why, after the devastation of World War I, the time had come for him to make a decisive break with the kinds of poetry he had developed after his entry into London's literary circles in 1908. No sooner had Pound stepped off the train from Europe, where he had sought to begin his career as a writer, than he made his way to the bookshop of Elkin Mathews. Pound approached Mathews because the publisher had long maintained an excellent list that contained one of Yeats's finest early volumes, *The Wind among the Reeds* (1899). Pound offered Mathews a copy of his first book, *A Lume Spento*, which the poet had printed privately earlier that year; it was his hope that Mathews would stock copies on his shelves. Mathews obliged him, as did Mathews's former partner, John Lane, who occupied premises on the opposite side of the street, where he, too, ran a bookstore and publishing firm.

It was through Mathews that Pound met a number of artistic and literary figures who were central to developments in what had become the receding memory of the fin de siècle. The older men whom Pound met included Selwyn Image, Ernest Rhys, and Victor Plarr. Each of them had some connection with the distinguished Rhymers' Club, whose thirteen male members included Yeats, and which published two collections of their poetry, the first in 1892 with Mathews, and the second in 1894 with Mathews and Lane.[52] They held many of their gatherings at the Cheshire Cheese public house off Fleet Street. Among Pound's new acquaintances from this era, Rhys proved very hospitable, entertaining at his home some of the Rhymers who had survived into the twentieth century, while at the same time welcoming emergent writers such as D. H. Lawrence. But it was Plarr (more than twenty years Pound's senior) who spent his Sunday dinners weaving compelling tales of how some of his onetime contemporaries had met their untimely ends.

Pound devoted two densely allusive poems in *Mauberley* to both Plarr's unsettling recollections of the Decadent fin de siècle and the supposed emergence of Decadence from a disreputable aestheticism, one whose origins lay in the Pre-Raphaelite art and poetry of the 1860s and 1870s. He named one of these lyrics after a famous line from Dante's *Purgatorio,* "Siena mi fè, disfecemi Maremma" (Siena made me, Maremma undid me), which the Pre-Raphaelite painter and poet Dante Gabriel Rossetti had used in *La Pia de' Tolomei* (1868–80). This famous oil painting features Rossetti's mistress, Jane Morris, posing as Dante's isolated La Pia. In the *Purgatorio* La Pia's husband has cruelly exiled her to a fortress by the poisonous swamps of the Maremma, where she will of course die.

Pound's reference to Rossetti's glorious painting of a tragic scene from Dante's works creates a subtle link with the preceding poem in *Mauberley.* In the earlier poem in the sequence, called "Yeux Glauques" (a title probably derived from Gautier's *Mademoiselle de Maupin*), Pound's lyric voice mentions the time when "Swinburne / And Rossetti [were] still abused."[53] Plarr's circle presumably passed on tales to Pound's generation about the bitter controversies that surrounded the two Pre-Raphaelites' avant-garde, frequently sensual writings. Swinburne's publisher withdrew *Poems and Ballads* from sale when it was charged with immorality in the press, and Rossetti's *Poems* (1871) was met with an incoherent attack on its so-called "fleshly" indulgence. In the latter case, the culprit, as Pound observes, was "Fœtid Buchanan" (552)—namely, the minor poet Robert Buchanan, who leveled spurious charges at Rossetti's poetry.[54]

Meanwhile, the title "Yeux Glauques" alludes to another aspect of Pre-Raphaelite aestheticism that also had the capacity to shock the more moralistic members of late-Victorian society. The alluring eyes belonged to Maria Zambaco, who became artist Edward Burne-Jones's mistress from 1867 to 1869.[55] Burne-Jones, whom Rossetti had known since the mid-1850s and whose Pre-Raphaelite techniques in drawing and use of color owed much to Rossetti, remained haunted by Zambaco's face, which he continued to represent in celebrated paintings that would be reproduced in art magazines throughout the fin de siècle. Pound here is recalling Zambaco's "vacant gaze" (552), which looks out "[b]ewildered" (553) in Burne-Jones's famous *King Cophetua and the Beggar-Maid*. The painting was first exhibited, to great acclaim, at the fashionable Grosvenor Gallery in 1884. Pound's speaker observes that it is painfully ironic that the

> world
> Shows no surprise
> At her last maquero's
> Adulteries.

(553)

As we trace the intricate cultural history that lies beneath these two poems in Pound's sequence, we can infer that it is as if the public had always taken Rossetti's, Swinburne's, and Burne-Jones's sexual indiscretions as the basis on which they built their aestheticism.

At first glance, in these two poems from *Mauberley* it appears that the immoral dissipation that the public attributed to Swinburne, Rossetti, and Burne-Jones became the hallmark of the later, even more degenerate Decadents. In "Siena mi fè, disfecemi Maremma" Pound records how Plarr, who had for many years served as librarian to the Royal College of Surgeons, moves among the grotesque "pickled fœtuses and bottled bones" of his workplace, recalling the dissipation that afflicted Johnson and Dowson, both of whom were dependent on alcohol. Under the guise of "Monsieur Verog," Plarr stands as a sterile figure whose once-distinguished lineage is in obvious decline. Associated with the preservation of dead body parts, this "last scion of the / Senatorial families of Strasbourg" (Plarr was born in Alsace) reminisces that "Johnson (Lionel) died / By falling from a high stool in a pub" (553). (In fact, Johnson died from a series of strokes after collapsing from a seizure in Fleet Street. But his peers continued to tout the tall story.[56]) Since, as Plarr (contradictorily) reports, the autopsy showed there was "no trace of alcohol" in Johnson's blood, it remains possible to think of Johnson as having had a "pure mind," one that turned to thoughts of John Henry Newman, even "as the whiskey" ironically "warmed" (553). In this reference to Newman, which relates to Johnson's conversion to Catholicism in 1891, together with the rather wry allusion to alcohol, M. Verog's anecdote conjures an irreverent, if not incoherent, image that appears not so very distant from the absinthe-sipping Soames's "Catholic diabolism."

In "Siena mi fè, disfecemi Maremma," Pound's speaker also mentions Dowson. Dowson, too, converted to Rome, soon after Johnson. But in Pound's poetic meditation on Plarr's sensational accounts it appears that religious faith could bring about no redemption for either of these fin-de-siècle poets. Dowson, we learn from M. Verog, "found harlots cheaper than hotels" (553). But such information distorts the truth. Destitute, impoverished, malnourished, Dowson died of tuberculosis at the age of thirty-two. As Plarr himself was willing to concede, Dowson's brief life of cruelly curtailed genius readily lent itself to legend making. In *Ernest Dowson, 1888–1897: Reminiscences, Unpublished Letters, and Marginalia* (1914), Plarr records that to Ezra Pound Dowson the man had become "a kind of classical myth."[57] Yet he acknowledges that "[p]oor Ernest Dowson through his sufferings is becoming almost as famous as that earlier poet [Thomas Chatterton] who by self-destruction set apart his life-story in the sorrowful annals of literature" (9). Indeed, Plarr's volume ostensibly seeks to shift away from the "legend of an inebriate Ernest Dowson" (14). To prove his point, he observes that in the thirty letters he has edited there is no "ugly slur of passion" or "ill savours." But Plarr, we can only infer from *Mauberley,* enjoyed elaborating in private those fanciful stories that he sought publicly to dispel. Pound thus had good reason to show that the not entirely honest "M. Verog" was "out of step with the decade" (the 1910s, which included the bomb-blasted war years) because of the nostalgic introspection of such misleading "reveries" (553).

Elsewhere Pound expressed some respect for the contributions that members of the Rhymers' Club had made to literary history, even if their diction, their choice of form, and their syntax were by the 1910s conspicuously outmoded. In 1915 he edited Johnson's poetry for Elkin Mathews, furnishing a preface that draws attention to Johnson's "hatred of amateurishness" and his commitment to "the art of good writing" rather than the presumed misery of the Decadent poet's life.[58] Certainly, in this document Pound caused some offense by declaring that the "'nineties' have chiefly gone out because of their muzziness" (viii). "They riot," he adds, "with half decayed fruit" (viii). And to prove his point he quotes extensively from the critical notes that Johnson compiled on 1890s poets, including Richard Le Gallienne ("Should take a long course of Arnold and Dr. Johnson" [xi]), Arthur Symons (a "singular power of technique . . . mostly wasted upon obscenities" [xi]), and Michael Field ("The earlier work is the best: becoming too subtle and eccentric" [xii]). With Pound stating that Johnson's judgments are "true in kind" (xiv), the incisive tone of the preface proved so upsetting to some readers that Mathews withdrew the volume from sale.[59] Yet when we compare Pound's prefatory remarks with those attributed to M. Verog in *Mauberley,* we can reasonably conclude that self-appointed chroniclers like Plarr had a conceited interest in preserving—if not pickling—Johnson's and Dowson's biographical decay instead of providing fair assessments of their fine, if by this time noticeably dated, poetry.

Plarr's dubious disclosures, however, pale in comparison to the memories of the same era written by another Rhymer, one whose survival after the fin de siècle went hand in hand with a desire not only to divulge intriguing stories about the era but also to maintain a deliberate distance from it. To be sure, in "The Grey Rock," the poem that opens *Responsibilities* (1914), Yeats honors his fellow Rhymers: "Poets with whom I learned my trade, / Companions of the Cheshire Cheese, / Here's an old story I've re-made."[60] Yeats proceeds to eulogize "those who had to face" their "ends when young" (150). "Dowson and Johnson," Yeats adds, "most I praise."

But as time went by Yeats would remake his story of the legacy of those erstwhile "tavern comrades" who had died (150). In 1936, when Yeats commanded a poetic reputation that was second to none, he looked back on the Rhymers who did not share his longevity by styling them, after a term coined by his father, the "Hamlets of our age."[61] The phrase originated when Yeats *père* heard his son talking at dinner about the immensely eccentric Count Stenbock—"scholar, connoisseur, drunkard, poet, pervert" (x). Stenbock, whose career displayed a number of Soames-like eccentricities, certainly gained notoriety for Catholic ritualism, dandyism, drug addiction, and homosexuality. (Symons described him as "a degenerate, who had I know not how many vices."[62]) Stenbock's poetry was blatantly suicidal: "Shall I not lay me down and be at peace," he wrote in 1893, "[w]hen the leaves are all laid low. . . . / Shall not then sorrow cease?"[63] Based on such lines, the *Pall Mall Gazette* assumed that Stenbock's volume "must be a parody—an elaborate and screaming parody of that latter literary abortion, the youthful *décadent*."[64]

With some license, Yeats took Stenbock, who had died of cirrhosis of the liver in 1895, as the model for the other—far more notable—poets whose personal decline happened to coincide with the fin de siècle. "Some of these Hamlets," Yeats wrote in 1936, "went mad, some drank, drinking not as happy men drink but in solitude, all had courage, all suffered public opprobrium—generally for their virtues or for sins they did not commit" (x). And, just to show that these saddening behaviors were specific to the miserable world of the fin-de-siècle poet, Yeats remarked that after 1900 "everybody got down off his stilts; henceforth nobody drank absinthe with his black coffee; nobody went mad; nobody committed suicide; nobody joined the Catholic Church; or if they did"—he added mordantly—"I have forgotten" (xi–xii). Even if Yeats recognized that his hyperbole was a mite strenuous, it remains significant that he resorted to it in the name of making the 1890s appear wretched.

Yeats's withering remarks endorse sentiments that he had already elaborated, in a classic piece of myth making titled "The Tragic Generation" (1922): the influential memoir in which he shows how the untimely deaths of the tubercular Dowson (in 1900) and the alcoholic Johnson (in 1902) bear a similarity to the suicide (in 1909) of Scottish writer John Davidson. By 1908, it is worth remembering, Symons had suffered a severe mental breakdown, from which it took two years to make what appears to have been only a partial recovery. In "The Tragic Generation," Yeats extends a profound belief in the hopeless destiny of a tightly knit band of writers to include the demise (in 1900) of Wilde, who, if not a Rhymer, enjoyed close association with the club. By the time Yeats spun his dubious tale for readers of the *Oxford Book of Modern Verse,* his audience had for twenty years been told—by another literary teller of tall tales, Frank Harris—that Wilde's early passing at the age of forty-six was the result of syphilis. (Wilde died, as later research would confirm, from meningitis.) It is perhaps too convenient to single out Yeats as the figure who should bear the greatest burden of blame for this doom-laden account of fin-de-siècle poetry. Wyndham Lewis, after all, virulently disparaged the ways in which "the 'Nineties' movement in England . . . was the Seventies in France, reproduced upon our miniature island stage," noting that Wilde's career largely recapitulated that of Verlaine, since both men went to jail for a "particular vice."[65] Yet, even if Yeats did not sink to the depths of Lewis's contempt, it remains impossible to overstate the deleterious influence his pronouncements would have on critics' apprehension of a talented company of writers who were committed to perfecting their art.

Some detractors might contend that the Rhymers' productions make it hard to deny that their members at times display a self-mortifying sadness. But, then again, it is worth reflecting on how some of their more seemingly dejected poems defy literal-minded interpretations. In, for example, John Todhunter's "Euthanasia," tellingly subtitled "Fin de Siècle," the speaker aches with an erotic yearning for life to end:

> Yes, this rich death were best:
> Lay poison on thy lip, kiss me to sleep,
> Or on the siren billow of thy breast
> Bring some voluptuous Lethe for life's pain.[66]

Yet it would be erroneous to infer that such writing thoughtlessly celebrates cultural malaise. These lines, among other things, ironize the tropes of the lovelorn suitor common to many of the seventeenth-century lyrics that were a source of excited rediscovery in the 1880s. The lines also evoke—to the point of lightly joking about—both Keats's "Ode on Melancholy" (1819) and the sensuality of Tannhäuser's death-driven desires in Swinburne's "Laus Veneris" (1866) (a poem, like "Faustine," that caused ructions in the press). Put another way, Todhunter's lyric voice points to the uncanny manner in which the gestures common to earlier styles of English poetry might be reworked in order to summon the *maladie* that characterized the century's end.

In any case, the self-consciousness of "Euthanasia" becomes evident in the poem that opens the first collection of the Rhymers' Club. In "The

Toast," Ernest Rhys makes it clear that the club wishes to take its example in part from Robert Herrick and Ben Jonson. Moreover, Rhys's poem makes it plain that the Rhymers' sense of affiliation with these poetic forbears derives not from self-destruction but from "laughter that was lyric, / And roystering rhymes and glad."[67] Such sentiments acknowledge that the Rhymers felt obliged to work within, rather than militate against, inherited lyric forms. Thus the speaker raises a glass, by way of a rousing tribute (rather than some inebriated sputtering), to his colleagues' spirit of "defiance / . . . to all but Rhyme." Even if the lyricist recognizes that his pluckiness is indebted to the rhymes of yore, he nonetheless knows full well that he and his fellows are participating in a poetic tradition that has no reason to apologize for its endeavors.

There was, however, a rather different—and telling—note of apology in one of the Rhymers' lyrics that appeared two years after their second collection went into circulation. In 1896 Ernest Radford reflected on the sexual exclusivity of the poets who met at the Cheshire Cheese. In his poem, "The Book of the Rhymers' Club, Vol. II," he implicitly addresses a woman poet:

> Had you increased our number,
> What sweetness might have been
> Uprising as from slumber
> We bards, in all thirteen,
> Amassed this muck and lumber—
> Sad work without a Queen!
> Had you increased our number,
> What sweetness might have been![68]

Radford's "Queen," as his fellow Rhymers would have known, was his spouse, Dollie Radford, a writer of well-crafted, witty, and at times outspoken poems that enjoyed greater acclaim than his. She was acutely aware that the woman poet, even in an era increasingly emancipated by the feminist causes that she championed, had to work hard to articulate her most intimate emotions in verse. In an ingenious eight-line lyric, she reflects, in a quietly controlled manner, on the difficulty of trying to compose lines that will adequately represent her love:

The little songs that come and go,
In tender measures, to and fro,
Whene'er the day brings you to me,
Keep my heart full of melody.

But on my lute I strive in vain
To play the music o'er again,
And you, dear love, will never know
The little songs which come and go.[69]

The intelligence of this lyric lies in the manner in which its careful "measures" counterpoint the sentiment, expressed in the second stanza, that it always proves hard to "play the music" of the inspiring "melody" that arises when the woman speaker is in the presence of her lover. In other words, although the poetic voice claims that it is impossible for her to reproduce the "little songs" that love inspires, she has expressed that modest thought in two highly polished quatrains.

The juxtaposition of Ernest Radford's and Dollie Radford's lyrics reminds us that while the Rhymers adopted a somewhat ironic posture toward their hearty "roistering rhymes," their female contemporaries produced impressive works whose reflective confrontations with the difficulty of writing good poetry were equally sophisticated. And when we study her career we learn that Dollie Radford was hardly isolated from other writers simply because she could not join the male poetic club in which Dowson, Johnson, Symons, and Yeats enjoyed lively exchanges. She counts among the many women poets who, though excluded from the Rhymers, played a central role in the intellectual cenacles and literary salons that flourished in fin-de-siècle London.

The opening page of the absorbing diary that Dollie Radford began in 1891, for example, gives an immediate sense of the lively sociability enjoyed by literary men and women based in the metropolis. Dollie Radford records a tea party that she and her husband arranged with Arthur Symons at his rooms in Fountain Court, The Temple (the district where two of London's Inns of Court are based).[70] The list of "very nice people" (as she enthusiastically calls them) is striking, since it includes poets such as Mathilde Blind, Michael Field, and Graham R. Tomson; painter Arthur

Tomson; publisher John Lane; novelist George Moore; and freethinkers Havelock Ellis and Edith Lees. Later, in June 1894, she recalls attending a Women Writers dinner, where she was pleased to have a seat near to the well-regarded Irish author Katharine Tynan. Such information throws light on the fact that fin-de-siècle poets, including the Decadent Symons, frequently engaged in a hectic social life that involved rounds of parties, visits to the theater, and attendance at gallery openings. In addition, as we discover more and more about the literary networks of London in the 1890s, we learn that women with contacts similar to Dollie Radford's ran significant literary salons. Both the acclaimed English poet A. Mary F. Robinson and the well-established American author Louise Chandler Moulton (who helped to strengthen transatlantic literary relations) opened their homes to a broad range of literary men and women at this time.

But it remains difficult for anyone who seeks to find out more about the poets of the 1890s to grasp the liveliness of the bustling cultural activities that brought them together in the metropolis. The skewed picture of the era, which owes much to such figures as Beerbohm, Plarr, and Yeats, is only too visible in the seventh edition of the *Norton Anthology of English Literature,* one of the most widely used volumes of its kind on college campuses in the United States. The anthology's editors word their unflattering summary of the 1890s as follows: "Melancholy, not gaiety, is characteristic of its spirit. Artists of the nineties, representing the Aesthetic movement, were very much aware of living at the end of a great century and often cultivated a deliberately fin de siècle ('end-of-century') pose. A studied languor, a weary sophistication, a search for new ways of titillating jaded palates can be found in both the poetry and the prose of the period."[71]

It is almost as if the stereotypically languid 1890s author were committed to self-annihilation, if only he (and, in this context, it is usually he) had the energy or willpower to end such melancholy. Admittedly, it is in the nature of college textbooks to issue blanket statements in support of condensed histories that aim to lend some semblance of intelligibility to literary periods. And it is of course scarcely the case that all preceding scholarship has promulgated this largely downbeat literary-historical tale suggesting that the fin-de-siècle generation of poets was for the most part a male group of debauchees suffering from *Weltschmerz.* But in the case of fin-de-siècle poetry the unenthusiastic picture that the *Norton Anthology* paints is arguably more distorted than what one would find anywhere else in its synoptic accounts of specific eras. This is hardly to say that it is impossible to detect "sensationalism," in all its seemingly repetitive manifestations, in the work of poets who came to prominence in the two decades leading up to 1900 (there is, unquestionably, much of it). And it would be unfair to ignore the editors' concession that Decadence, with all of the depreciatory associations that they attach to it, was barely the only poetic development during a time when "more various" types of poetry—especially by women—appeared (1,741). Then again, it is perhaps symptomatic of the *Norton Anthology*'s view of what is representative of the age that the only women writers it mentions are Michael Field and Mary Coleridge (who published as "Anodos"), as if these truly talented poets, who never entered the precincts of the Cheshire Cheese, adequately supplemented the altogether better known, if pervasively melancholic, male "sensationalists" of the 1890s.

If we look elsewhere, at more detailed literary-historical accounts of fin-de-siècle poetry, we find that scholars who survey the field tend to treat the supposedly characteristic poetry of this era as merely symptomatic of a pessimistic impulse to deny the high-minded positivism of the preceding Victorian age. Thus David Perkins, in what still counts as the most comprehensive overview of late nineteenth-century and early twentieth-century poetry in English, contends that the London avant-garde—the metropolitan coterie of poets whose work for him absorbs the ether of the 1890s—"derived much of its identity from a negation: it was not so much *post* as *anti*-Victorian" (31). But no sooner has Perkins made this claim than he portrays this assembly of poets—even if "diverse in personality, in literary and cultural background, in opinions and beliefs" (32)—as having reacted against their predecessors in a manner motivated more by sickly surrender than spirited rebellion.

In this regard, Dowson—who "fits almost too well our stereotype of the fin-de-siècle poet" (37)—may well have pursued noble themes gleaned from Horace, Catullus, and Propertius. But whether writing about "the frustration or transitoriness of love, the vanity of life, the allure of the grave," he did so in a style that lacks the "concrete imagery" associated with "the Spenser-Keats tradition" and the "compression and wit of English neoclassicism" (38–39). To be sure, Perkins admits that Dowson's work may evince (as does the work of many of his contemporaries) "intricacy and subtlety of versification" (39). Yet this poet's representative fascination with fixed forms, such as the villanelle and rondeau, results depressingly in the "cataloguing" of "love and laughter in the same tone as weeping and hate" (39). These uncomplimentary qualities are most evident to Perkins in Dowson's "Non sum qualis era bonae sub regno Cynarae": a poem that takes its title from Horace's ode 4.1 and whose content is modeled on Propertius's elegies to Cynthia. Here the male speaker, in a state of postcoital *tristesse,* recalls a night of lustful abandonment with a prostitute to whom he would like to believe he has been honorably "faithful" in his own "fashion."[72] To Perkins, "Non sum qualis . . ." amounts to "the most complete expression of the fin de siècle in England" because it manifests a characteristic, if depleted, impulse to "defy middle-class morality," while displaying its "plush and gaslit classicism, its elaborate and musical artifice, its nostalgia of the libertine for lost innocence, its desperation and hopelessness" (40). Certainly, Perkins points out the well-known fact that T. S. Eliot's admiration for this poem resulted in its echo in "The Hollow Men" (1925). And he comments on the equally important fact that "Non sum qualis . . ." shows Dowson's expert handling of the alexandrine, which displays the poet's adroit translation of the meter from French to English verse. But in Perkins's account such an achievement seems subordinate to the observation that "Non sum qualis . . ." was "written in a bar" (40).

At the same time as the *Norton Anthology* and David Perkins have circulated received wisdom about the lassitude of the literary 1890s, a number of researchers have made crucial contributions to an otherwise neglected critical tradition that acknowledges the richness, diversity, and achievements of fin-de-siècle poets. Even early in the twentieth century— when Beerbohm, Plarr, and Yeats looked back somewhat wryly at the 1890s—there were one or two affirmative accounts of fin-de-siècle poetry, as Holbrook Jackson's enduringly valuable study shows. In many ways, it is Linda Dowling's indispensable *Aestheticism and Decadence: A Selective Annotated Bibliography* (1977), together with her important *Language and Decadence in the Victorian Fin de Siècle* (1985), that provides the most comprehensive lists of materials for scholars who wish to gain a detailed knowledge of what has long stood as a marginalized, all too easily dismissed area of literary inquiry. Moreover, since the 1970s, developments in feminist and lesbian and gay approaches to literature have created a hospitable climate in which the wealth of accomplished poetry by women and homophile authors of the period can be given serious attention.[73] It is now possible, thanks to advances in electronic technology, together with welcome reprints of previously scarce editions, for readers to gain access to an archive of poetry that for many years remained the preserve of special collections held in rare book libraries.[74] Further, the increasing responsiveness of literary studies to interdisciplinary analysis has made the fin-de-siècle poem, which frequently celebrates the unity of the arts, a particularly fertile area of scholarship. The chapters in the present volume have benefited from all of these initiatives.

Readers of the present volume will certainly encounter the styles of intoxicated headiness that have become all too proverbially associated with the poetry of the 1890s. But the range of works explored in these eleven studies discloses that this much-misrecognized literary decade was not entirely a doom-laden affair that hurtled the Victorian age toward its terminal point. Instead, it was a time whose apparent freakishness and faddishness, naughtiness and neurosis, pretensions and perversions are better understood as signs of its authors' well-considered interest in devising fresh poetic models that could engage with the modern before further shifts in poetics became identifiably modernist.

Notes

1. Elizabeth Robins Pennell, *Nights: Rome, Venice in the Aesthetic Eighties—London, Paris in the Fighting Nineties* (London: William Heinemann, 1916), 119–20.

2. Holbrook Jackson, *The Eighteen Nineties: A Review of Art and Ideas at the Close of the Nineteenth Century* (New York: Alfred A. Knopf, 1913), 20.

3. Arthur Symons, prologue to *London Nights,* second edition (London: Leonard Smithers, 1896), 3; further page references appear in parentheses.

4. Symons's "The Opium-Smoker" appeared in the *Academy,* 19 November 1887, 336, and Levy's "London in July" appeared there on 30 July 1887, 70. Symons had already made his mark in this influential review earlier in the year with "The Nun," 29 January 1887, 76.

5. A number of appreciative articles about Levy's work appeared in the 1890s, including Ada Wallas, "The Poetry of Amy Levy," *Academy,* 12 August 1899, 162–63. Since

the 1990s a great deal of significant research—by, in particular, Linda Hunt Beckman, Cynthia Scheinberg, and Ana Parejo Vadillo—has appeared. Her achievements, however, are not recognized in what remains the most detailed survey of the poetry of this era: David Perkins, *A History of Modern Poetry: From the 1890s to the High Modernist Mode* (Cambridge, MA: Harvard University Press, 1976); further references appear in parentheses. Perkins's discussion alludes to a limited number of fin-de-siècle woman poets: Mary E. Coleridge, Michael Field (i.e., the coauthors Katharine Bradley and Edith Cooper), Laurence Hope (Adela Florence Cory Nicolson), and Alice Meynell. Perkins's comments on these writers are not inspiring; for example, he refers to Meynell's work, which commanded high respect during the 1890s, as "distinguished minor poetry, thoughtful, high-minded, disciplined, but without freshness or power of language, and without sufficient exploration of self or the world to go widely or deeply into human experience" (21). Cf., in the present volume, Yopie Prins's discussion of Meynell's writing (chapter 9).

6. The volume that has drawn the greatest attention to the breadth and scope of women's participation in aestheticism is Talia Schaffer and Kathy Alexis Psomiades, eds., *Women and British Aestheticism* (Charlottesville: University Press of Virginia, 1999).

7. There have been a number of studies about Housman's homoerotic poetics; the most sustained discussion is Carol Efrati, *The Road of Danger, Guilt, and Shame: The Lonely Way of A. E. Housman* (Madison, NJ: Fairleigh Dickinson University Press, 2002).

8. Linda K. Hughes, *Strange Bedfellows: W. E. Henley and Feminist Fashion History,* Occasional Series, 3 (n.p.: privately printed for the Eighteen Nineties Society, 1997). Tomson's third life-partner, H. B. Marriott Watson, was a member of "Henley's Regatta." Some of Kipling's most famous early poems, later collected in *Departmental Ditties, Barrack-Room Ballads, and Other Verses* (1890, reprinted as *Barrack-Room Ballads and Other Verses,* 1892), first appeared in the *Scots Observer.*

9. W. E. Henley, "London Voluntaries," in *London Voluntaries, The Song of the Sword, and Other Verses,* revised edition (London: David Nutt, 1983), 20; further page references appear in parentheses.

10. Rosamund Marriott Watson, "The Lost Leader (I.M. W.E.H)," in *The Poems of Rosamund Marriott Watson* (London: John Lane, 1912), 331.

11. Jackson, *Eighteen Nineties,* 18.

12. Max Nordau, *Degeneration* (Lincoln: University of Nebraska Press, 1993), 51.

13. John Wilcox, "The Beginnings of l'Art pour l'Art," *Journal of Aesthetics and Art Criticism* 11 (1953): 360.

14. Ruth Z. Temple, "Truth in Labelling: Pre-Raphaelitism, Aestheticism, Decadence, Fin-de-Siècle," *English Literature in Transition (1880–1920)* 17 (1964): 201–22.

15. Asti Hustvedt, "The Art of Death: French Ficiton at the Fin de Siècle," in *The Decadent Reader: Fiction, Fantasy, and Perversion from Fin-de-Siècle France,* ed. Hustvedt (New York: Zone Books, 1998), 13; further quotation is taken from page 13.

16. Charles Bernheimer, *Decadent Subjects: The Idea of Decadence in Art, Literature, Philosophy, and Culture of* Fin de Siècle *Europe,* ed. T. Jefferson Kline and Naomi Schor (Baltimore: Johns Hopkins University Press, 2002), 8.

17. There has been some debate about the earliest moment when British writers began to discuss *décadence.* R.K.R. Thornton suggests that the freethinker Havelock Ellis's "A Note on Paul Bourget," which reviews two of the French writer's recent books in the *Pioneer* for 1889, is perhaps the first piece of journalism to characterize the French term (*The Decadent Dilemma* [London: Edward Arnold, 1983], 38–39. Kirsten MacLeod suggests that the earliest source is George Moore, "Les Décadents," *Court and Society Review,* 19 January 1887, 57–58; see *Fictions of British Decadence* (Basingstoke: Palgrave Macmillan, forthcoming). The point is that the term was not familiar in British culture until the early 1890s.

18. Lionel Johnson, "A Note upon the Practice and Theory of Verse at the Present Time Obtaining in France." *Century Guild Hobby Horse* 6 (1891): 64; further quotations are taken from page 64.

19. In the 1890s discussions of *le Symbolisme* focused on French poetry. But that is not to say that British poets remained unresponsive to *Symboliste* poetics, as my discussion of John Gray's poetry makes clear below (19–23). Symons, clearly, took many of his poetic leads from *les Symbolistes.* In the present volume, the chapters by Linda Hunt Beckman (chapter 7) and Ana Parejo Vadillo (chapter 8), in particular, identify the extent to which *Symboliste* modes inspired the avant-garde work of Amy Levy and A. Mary F. Robinson, respectively.

20. Arthur Symons, "The Decadent Movement in Literature, *Harper's New Monthly Magazine* 87 (1893): 858–59. It is noticeable that this important essay appeared in a transatlantic monthly edited in New York City; it may well have been that *Harper's,* always eager to provide its large readership with up-to-date information about the European literary scene, proved altogether more hospitable to his defense of Decadence than any British monthly or quarterly would have been. The only British poet whose works Symons discusses in this essay is W. E. Henley. Henley's *A Book of Verses* (London: David Nutt, 1888) reprints his 1875 sequence of experimental lyrics, "In Hospital" (which contains a fine poem titled "Suicide"); his volume also contains a section devoted to the fixed French forms—"Ballades, Rondels, Sonnets and Quartozains, Rondeaus"—that

gained popularity in the mid-1870s. The trend of writing in these fixed forms, which was fostered by Austin Dobson and Andrew Lang, persisted until the end of the century, most notably in Ernest Dowson's work.

21. Richard Le Gallienne, "Considerations Suggested by Mr. Churton Collins' 'Illustrations of Tennyson,'" *Century Guild Hobby Horse* 7 (1892): 81; further quotation is taken from page 81.

22. Linda C. Dowling, *Language and Decadence in the Victorian Fin de Siècle* (Princeton, NJ: Princeton University Press, 1985, 123); further page references appear in parentheses.

23. Frederic Harrison, "Decadence in Modern Art," *Forum* 15 (1892): 430.

24. Hugh M. Stutfield, "Tommyrotics," *Blackwood's Edinburgh Magazine* 157 (1895): 842; further page references appear in parentheses.

25. Oscar Wilde to Leo Maxse, c. 1894, in *The Complete Letters of Oscar Wilde*, ed. Merlin Holland and Rupert Hart-Davis (London: Fourth Estate, 2000), 580.

26. [Anonymous], "Swinburne and Water," *Punch*, 23 July 1881, 26.

27. [Anonymous], review of *Poems*, by Oscar Wilde, *Athenæum* 23 July 1881, 103.

28. Keats's famous comment appears in his letter to John Taylor, 27 February 1818, in *Selected Letters of John Keats*, rev. ed., ed. Grant Scott (Cambridge, MA: Harvard University Press, 2002), 97.

29. Nicholas Frankel, *Oscar Wilde's Decorated Books* (Ann Arbor: University of Michigan Press, 2000), 114.

30. Frankel, *Oscar Wilde's Decorated Books*, 118.

31. Richard Le Gallienne, *Limited Editions: A Prose Fancy, Together with Confession Amantis, a Sonnet* (London: privately printed for Richard Le Gallienne, Elkin Mathews, John Lane, and their friends, 1893), reprinted in Le Gallienne, *Prose Fancies* (London: Elkin Mathews and John Lane, 1894), 119.

32. James G. Nelson, *A Checklist of Early Bodley Head Books: 1889–1894* (Oxford: Rivendale Press, 1999), 52. Nelson notes that over six thousand copies were printed in the four issues dating from 1893 to 1894. The first issue cost 3s 6d, while the second was priced at 5s.

33. Josephine M. Guy and Ian Small, *Oscar Wilde's Profession: Writing and the Culture Industry in the Late Nineteenth Century* (Oxford: Oxford University Press, 2000), 151. The contrast with the poor sales of Wilde's 1881 *Poems* is striking.

34. Nelson, *Checklist*, 59.

35. Some of Ricketts's most impressive designs appear in the volumes he prepared for the Vale Press, the imprint that he ran with his life-partner Charles Shannon. Vale Press books were frequently printed at the Ballantyne Press and distributed by Hacon

and Ricketts. Katharine Bradley and Edith Cooper, who became extremely close friends with Ricketts and Shannon, issued several of their volumes through the Vale Press, including *The World at Auction* (1898), *The Race of Leaves* (1901), and *Julia Domna* (1903). Together with Aubrey Beardsley, Ricketts and Shannon were arguably the most impressive designers of finely printed books during the fin de siècle; see Paul van Capelleveen, *A New Checklist of Books Designed by Charles Ricketts and Charles Shannon* (The Hague: Museum van het Boek/Museum Meermanno-Westreenianum, 1996).

36. Charles Ricketts, *A Defence of the Revival of Printing* (London: Vale Press, 1899), 25.

37. Ricketts, *Defence*, 25.

38. Wilde, *The Sphinx*, in *The Complete Works of Oscar Wilde*, vol. 1, ed. Bobby Fong and Karl Beckson (Oxford: Oxford University Press, 2000), 181.

39. Ricketts, *Defence*, 21. Ricketts's friend Gleeson White emphasized that the artist's skill lay in "evolv[ing] new triumphs, austere yet seductive" from "the best founders" of printing ("The Work of Charles Ricketts," *Pageant* 1 [1896]: 84).

40. Ricketts, *Defence*, 20–21.

41. Ada Leverson, preface to *Letters to the Sphinx from Oscar Wilde* (London: Duckworth, 1930), 19; further quotation is taken from page 19. Leverson, with some exaggeration, observes that at the time, Gray was regarded as "the incomparable poet of the age" (19).

42. [Frank Harris], review of *Silverpoints*, by John Gray, *Saturday Review* 75 (1893): 493; further quotations are taken from page 493. The attribution of this review to Harris is made in Linda C. Dowling, "Nature and Decadence: John Gray's *Silverpoints*," *Victorian Poetry* 15, no. 2 (1977): 160.

43. Jerusha Hull McCormack, *John Gray: Poet, Dandy, and Priest* (Hanover, NH: University Press of New England, 1991), 117.

44. Gray, *Silverpoints*, 9, reprinted in *The Poems of John Gray*, ed. Ian Fletcher (Greensboro: ELT Press, 1988), 23.

45. McCormack, *John Gray*, 118; further quotation is taken from page 118.

46. Ruth Z. Temple, "The Other Choice: The Worlds of John Gray, Poet and Priest," *Bulletin of Research in the Humanities* 84 (1981): 53. Cf. Matthew Sturgis's remark on the "sterile verses" of John Gray (*Passionate Attitudes: The English Decadence of the 1890s* [London: Macmillan, 1995], 139).

47. Ellis Hanson, *Decadence and Catholicism* (Cambridge, MA: Harvard University Press, 1997), 312.

48. [Anonymous], "Le Plus Decadent des Decadents" [review of *Silverpoints*, by Gray], *Pall Mall Gazette*, 4 May 1893, 3.

49. Max Beerbohm, "A Defence of Cosmetics," *Yellow Book* 1 (1894): 71.

50. Max Beerbohm, "A Letter to the Editor," *Yellow Book* 2 (1894): 282.

51. Max Beerbohm, "Enoch Soames," in *Seven Men and Two Others* (Oxford: Oxford University Press, 1980), 5; further page references appear in parentheses.

52. In their second book, dating from 1894, the Rhymers presented work by thirteen male poets: Ernest Dowson, Edwin J. Ellis, G. A. Greene, Arthur Cecil Hillier, Lionel Johnson, Richard Le Gallienne, Victor Plarr, Ernest Radford, Ernest Rhys, T. J. Rolleston, Arthur Symons, John Todhunter, and W. B. Yeats. I discuss the sexual exclusivity of the Rhymers' Club below (34–35).

53. Ezra Pound, "Yeux Glauques," in *Poems and Translations,* ed. Richard Sieburth (New York: Library of America, 2003), 552; further page references appear in parentheses.

54. Buchanan's notorious attack on Dante Gabriel Rossetti's poetry appeared under a pseudonym in a journal that prided itself on signed reviews: Thomas Maitland, "The Fleshly School of Poetry," *Contemporary Review* 17 (1871): 334–50. Buchanan's onslaught sparked a literary row that lasted another five years.

55. Some of the scholarship on this poem suggests that Pound thought that the model in Burne-Jones's painting was Rossetti's spouse, Elizabeth Siddall, who died of an overdose of laudanum in 1861; see, for example, John J. Espey, *Ezra Pound's Mauberley: A Study in Composition* (Berkeley and Los Angeles: University of California Press, 1955), 91.

56. "Lionel Johnson fell backward from a stool in a tavern and was carried off to hospital insensible" (Ernest Rhys, *Everyman Remembers* [New York: Cosmopolitan, 1931], 227). In the present volume, Holly Laird discusses these reports of Johnson's death (see chapter 2).

57. Victor Plarr, *Ernest Dowson, 1888–1897: Reminiscences, Unpublished Letters, and Marginalia* (New York: Lawrence J. Gomme, 1914), 28; further page references appear in parentheses.

58. Ezra Pound, preface to *Poetical Works of Lionel Johnson* (London: Elkin Mathews, 1915), ix; further page references appear in parentheses.

59. On the controversy aroused by Pound's preface, see James G. Nelson, *Elkin Mathews: Publisher to Yeats, Joyce, Pound* (Madison: University of Wisconsin Press, 1989), 98–99. Nelson's book counts among a small number of studies that identify the continuities, as well as breaks, between fin-de-siècle and modernist writing.

60. W. B. Yeats, "The Grey Rock," in *The Poems,* ed. Daniel Albright (London: J. M. Dent, 1990), 149; further page references appear in parentheses.

61. W. B. Yeats, introduction to *The Oxford Book of Modern Verse, 1893–1935* (Oxford: Oxford University Press, 1936), x; further page references appear in parentheses.

62. Arthur Symons, quoted in John Adlard, *Stenbock, Yeats and the Nineties* (London: Cecil and Amelia Woolf, 1969), 91.

63. Count Stanislaus Eric Stenbock, *The Shadow of Death* (London: Leadenhall Press, 1983), 6.

64. [Anonymous], review of *The Shadow of Death*, by Stenbock, *Pall Mall Gazette*, 1 March 1894, 4.

65. Wyndham Lewis, *Wyndham Lewis the Artist: From "Blast" to Burlington House* (London: Laidlaw and Laidlaw, 1939), 70. Lesley Higgins discusses why Lewis wrote with such concentrated antipathy toward leading aesthetes, such as Pater and Wilde; see *The Modernist Cult of Ugliness: Aesthetic and Gender Politics* (New York: Palgrave Macmillan, 2002), 79–119.

66. John Todhunter, "Euthanasia (Fin de Siècle)," in *The Second Book of the Rhymers' Club* (London: Elkin Mathews and John Lane, 1894), 62. Nicholas Frankel looks in more detail at Todhunter's poem in the present volume (chapter 4).

67. Ernest Rhys, "The Toast," in *The Book of the Rhymers' Club* (London: Elkin Mathews, 1892), 1.

68. Ernest Radford, "The Book of the Rhymers' Club, Vol. II," in *Old and New: A Collection of Poems* (London: T. Fisher Unwin, 1895), 62.

69. Dollie Radford, "The Little Songs that Come and Go," in Dollie Radford, *Songs and Other Verses* (London: John Lane, 1895), 20; further quotations are taken from page 20.

70. Dollie Radford's diary, which covers the years 1891–1900, is called "The Tragic Diary," since it records Ernest Radford's mental breakdown in 1892. This document is held at the William Andrews Clark Memorial Library, UCLA.

71. "The Nineties," in *The Norton Anthology of English Literature*, 7th ed. (New York: W. W. Norton, 2000), 1,054; further page references appear in parentheses.

72. Ernest Dowson, "Non sum qualis era bonae sub regno Cynarae," in *Second Book*, 60–61. Nicholas Frankel discusses Dowson's poem from a perspective that differs from Perkins's viewpoint in the present volume (chapter 4).

73. Among the most significant studies and anthologies that have drawn attention to the wealth of homoerotic poetry that appeared during the fin de siècle are Timothy d'Arch Smith, *Love in Earnest: Some Notes on the Lives and Writings of English "Uranian" Poets from 1889 to 1930* (London: Routledge and Kegan Paul, 1970); and Chris White, ed., *Nineteenth-Century Writings on Homosexuality: A Sourcebook* (London: Routledge, 1999).

74. While many volumes of fin-de-siècle poetry have long remained out of print, a number of electronic databases have recently made a large range of poetic works from the 1890s accessible to readers; in this regard, two electronic resources have proved

particularly useful: the Literature Online website, Chadwyck-Healey (http://lion
.chadwyck.com) and the Victorian Women Writers Project, Indiana University (http:
//www.indiana.edu/~letrs/vwwp/). In addition, the Victorian Web (http://victorianweb
.org) provides a gateway to a large number of databases whose contents include primary
and secondary sources relating to fin-de-siècle writing.

ENGENDERING TRAGEDY

Toward a Definition of 1890s Poetry

Jerusha McCormack

As everyone knows, the 1890s poet is not just someone who wrote poetry during the 1890s. In the minds of most readers, the 1890s poet would not have been a woman; he would have been a man, neither middle-aged nor prosperous; and he certainly would have been neither happy nor successful. But how has this drastic narrowing of the definition of the 1890s poet come about? Is it enough to point simply to the typecasting of the "tragic generation" by such poets as W. B. Yeats, whose elegy for the artist who lived hard and died young appears to be permanently inscribed as the myth of the decade? Or are other forces at work, with which the critics have, wittingly or unwittingly, colluded?

Just as the decade of the 1890s is regarded as special, its poetry is often made a case for special pleading. Critics would be among the first to concede that, as a rule, the 1890s poem is slight and its merits uncertain; its appearance in print these days is usually regarded as a triumph of scholarly research and resuscitation. Thus the stereotype of the 1890s poem has tended to mimic the status of the 1890s poet—that of a shadowy man who hovered for a few crucial years on the edge of literary notice before sinking into a fog of despair, drink, dissipation, and death. Typically, the life was as brief as the fleeting lyric cries that accompanied its descent into obscurity.

The significant exception to this stereotype is Oscar Wilde—who escaped from obscurity into notoriety. And yet that very notoriety has itself provided the agency by which his poems are preserved. In other words, Wilde is the most explicit example of the rule: the 1890s poem survives because of whom it was written by, and not necessarily because of how well it stands on its own as a literary artifact.

As a result of this collapse of art into biography, the decade (as the 1890s scholar knows too well) has become virtually synonymous with the phenomenon of "Decadence." According to Arthur Symons in his groundbreaking essay, "The Decadent Movement in Literature" (1893), Decadence "is really a new and interesting disease . . . typical of a civiliza-tion grown over-luxurious, over-inquiring, too languid for the relief of action, too uncertain for any emphasis in opinion or conduct." Having identified Decadence with contemporary avant-garde literature in France, Symons compounds the confusion by ending his essay with the assertion that, essentially, the achievement of Decadence is "to be a disembodied voice, and yet the voice of a human soul."[1] No amount of backtracking in subsequent years could undo Symons's fatal association of Decadence with poetry that was profoundly morbid, male, and morally perverse, even though a number of scholars have done their best to resist the stereotype. In recent years, for example, students of this period have turned their attention toward the 1890s poet who happened to be a woman (or women, in the case of Michael Field, i.e., coauthors Katharine Bradley and Edith Cooper)—as well as to other minor poets such as Herbert Horne, who by any account lived an accomplished and success-ful life.[2]

Further, revisionist accounts of the decade are now quick to point out that the prevailing stereotype of the 1890s poet has been heavily gen-dered. Such critics as Talia Schaffer have argued that "Decadence was actually a brief defensive reaction of embattled elite male writers who per-ceived themselves to be losing status to popular women writers and con-sequently fetishized their own decay."[3] And yet, I believe, this rearguard attack will only strengthen the male hold on the imaginative appeal of Decadence. It is not only a case of history forgetting, as history is wont to do, the contributions of women. It is also a case of the 1890s poem itself generating a seminal (i.e., indisputably male) mythos, which operates as crucially for the definition of "Decadence" as for evaluations of the art of the twentieth century; in both cases the lifestyle of the artist is often ren-dered as inseparable from his art.

It is significant that women poets of the 1890s themselves often courted obscurity, either by being self-consciously private or (worse still) by playing to the conventions of their time. Women writers of the 1890s were not then conceded much of a public presence; some, like the aesthetic novelist Ouida (the pen name of Marie Louise de la Ramée [1839–1908]), reacted like prima donnas, parading themselves in a performative revenge. (Recounting one of many such incidents which marked her appearances, Marc-André Raffalovich recalled that Ouida, vexed because she had been invited into the company of writers rather than of politicians, made a scene by loudly refusing to retire upstairs with the ladies after dinner,[4] a convention observed at all Victorian dinner parties, regardless of the identity of the ladies in question.) Other women writers, such as Alice Meynell, simply erased themselves into the conventional role of "The Angel of the House"—that mid-Victorian icon of womanhood immortalized in the poem of the same name, first published in 1854 by Coventry Patmore. In fact, it has been said that Alice Meynell's "most successful act of literary creation was her own angelic reputation."[5] Men, however, conducted their lives in public; and many—like Oscar Wilde—behaved badly. The phenomenon of men behaving badly is nothing new, even on the English literary scene (consider Lord Byron, who made an art form of bad behavior). But for the 1890s poet, the poetry had become part of that behavior; indeed, in many ways, the poetry can be said to have prescribed it.

How did this happen? By the 1890s the ability to turn out a competent poem had become a sign of a cultured man. Indeed the whole Decadent movement, as Schaffer points out, has been defined as a commemoration of "a dying literary culture held by privileged men" that mimed its performance of "esoteric scholarship, aristocratic affiliation, rarefied taste."[6] In this new aristocracy of culture, such outsiders as Raffalovich, John Gray, and Wilde could gain admittance by means of their poetry. Raffalovich was a rank outsider, having in 1881 arrived in London from Paris, to which city his parents had been exiled from Odessa for refusing to convert from their native Judaism. Wealthy and talented, Raffalovich was one of the first to write a cleverly disguised homoerotic poetry that gained him admittance to such circles as that of Robert Browning and George Meredith. Gray, who would become Raffalovich's life-long companion, was born into a working-class family, but was taken in hand by the artists Charles

Ricketts and Charles Shannon, and later by Wilde himself. Gray's name was made by a slender book of poetry, *Silverpoints* (1893), about half of which provided translations from the French of poets whom Symons was to identify firmly with Decadence.

Finally, Wilde himself was an outsider by virtue of being Irish. Determined to force open the closed ranks of English high society, he first sought to make his literary career as a poet and not as a dramatist. (In assessing his priorities, it is helpful to note the earmarked recipients of his first book of poetry: Robert Browning, Matthew Arnold, William Gladstone, and Algernon Charles Swinburne.[7]) For the poet using his art as a means of social entrée, amateur status could be regarded almost as a mark of authenticity: poems were the inevitable issue of a certain temperament (which contemporaries identified as "aesthetic"). Indeed, in the popular press, the amateur poet—inevitably "minor"—was regarded by some as one of the major nuisances of the decade. (The other major nuisance, by the way, also regarded as a sign of Decadence, was the smoking of cigarettes—once again, a male prerogative.)

Such poetry—that is, male poetry of the 1890s—was often performed publicly. Memoirs of the period describe how poetry was often recited as a party piece after formal dinners or at other informal gatherings of the great and the good. Gray is remembered as having recited his verses to Walter Pater as well as at a dinner for that esteemed patroness of the arts Princess Alice of Monaco.[8] The poets of the Rhymers' Club all (in a memorable phrase by Lionel Johnson) "inflicted" their latest compositions on one another.[9] Among them, Yeats is eloquent about the impact of such a recitation, writing years later: "I shall . . . remember all my life that evening when Lionel Johnson read or spoke aloud in his musical monotone, where meaning and cadence found the most precise elocution, his poem suggested 'by the Statue of King Charles at Charing Cross.' It was as though I listened to a great speech."[10] "It was," Yeats recalls, "perhaps our delight in poetry that was, before all else, speech or song, and could hold the attention of a fitting audience like a good play or good conversation" that made the Rhymers the poets of their age.[11]

These are only some of the signs that poetry in the 1890s was still part of that public as well as oral culture on which Charles Dickens would capitalize in his reading tours across England and America. In our contemporary print age, when words first come to us almost invariably as script, we tend to forget how important the performance of a poem was to its late nineteenth-century audience and how such a theatrical context served to confirm the equation of the poet and the poem.[12]

The 1890s poets themselves consciously drew on this theatrical analogy. Ernest Dowson, as well as Yeats and Michael Field, wrote poetic dramas. Wilde's poems, initially published in 1881, became successful only in their second incarnation, in 1892, when they could be marketed as the work of an emerging young playwright.[13] Many of the 1890s poets were also connoisseurs of drama. They attended the opening nights of controversial new plays produced by such experimental enterprises as the Independent Theatre.[14] They may claim responsibility as well for extending the definition of drama itself to the music halls, which had particular resonance for Symons: "My life," his poetic persona declaims, "is like a music-hall."[15] Gray was even more emphatic: in his version of a cultural manifesto, he declared that the true modern actor was nothing less than the music-hall singer—a bohemian, an outcast, and a poet.[16]

It is not surprising, then, that the 1890s poet often looked to the dramatic monologue as a model, particularly as refined in the work of Robert Browning. Thus stereotypically, but not inevitably, the male 1890s poem was conceived of as a dramatic performance, by means of which the poet fashioned his public persona.

Just as 1890s poetry was often perceived as male, public, and performative, so in the popular mind did the actual performance become part of the poetry. Long before public relations people and spin doctors, the poets of the 1890s understood the importance of manipulating appearances, or at least playing up to their image. Oscar Wilde was an impeccable dandy, as was his disciple, John Gray. Wilde understood the inherently theatrical potential of the closed London society of the 1890s; the heroines of his early plays are eloquent tribute to the power of society to make or break a reputation. It strikes me that one of the factors we underestimate in analyzing Decadence is the power of gossip—the way the oral tradition worked to fashion the literary reputations of Dowson, Gray, Johnson, Symons, and Wilde, as well as the Scottish writer John Davidson. It can be reasonably argued that Wilde's career was made, and broken, by gossip. The printed gossip columns of papers such as the *Star,* for instance, played a crucial role in making the reputation of John Gray—a more minor figure—by naming him as "the original" of Dorian

Gray, the eternally beautiful young hero of Wilde's homoerotically inflected story, which caused a furor in the British press when it appeared in 1890. Gray threatened to sue; the potential libel was withdrawn; but in virtually every memoir Gray is still remembered as "the original of Dorian."[17]

Dowson is often regarded as the purest representative of Decadence. His life was tragic and short; he drank and whored while writing the exquisite lines that appeared as *Verses* (1896) and *Decorations in Verse and Prose* (1899). His works are now among the most quoted in English—phrases such as "gone with the wind" and "days of wine and roses," as well as the refrain "I have been faithful to thee, Cynara, in my fashion," remain resonant in cultural memory.[18] A convert to Catholicism, Dowson understood sin as a mode of expanding his experience. He was as much at home on the Left Bank of Paris as on the Embankment in London. Dowson was not living to stereotype: it could be said that he was creating it. But, in fact, it was being created for him.

How did that happen? Dowson complained that in London he moved within a cloud of whispered asides about his personal life, to which he vehemently objected. Yeats speaks of Dowson writing "in protest against some friend's too vivid essay upon the disorder of his life."[19] Thus Dowson had begun to dispute his own legend even before it took form in an essay by Symons for the *Savoy* of August 1896. Writing of Dowson "with some of that frankness which we reserve usually for the dead," Symons reported that "his favourite form of intoxication had been haschich" at Oxford (even though Symons did not know Dowson until three years after he left Oxford) and that later Dowson habitually drank "the poisonous liquors of those pot-houses which swarm about the docks."[20] Rumor—and Yeats—did the rest to establish Dowson's legend. Although Yeats insisted in his *Memoirs* that he had "no intimate knowledge of Dowson" except through Symons,[21] Yeats's portrayal of Dowson as drug addict, drinker, and womanizer became definitive. It is not that Yeats set out to distort ("I have changed nothing to my knowledge; and yet it must be that I have changed many things without my knowledge," he writes in his preface to *Reveries over Childhood and Youth*[22]). It is simply that Yeats was a mythologizer who knew that myth was always more powerful than actuality, and that his lurid portrait of Dowson as a dissolute John Keats would survive all the gray complexities of fact.

And so today, even after generations of protest from friends and scholars about the persistence of the "Dowson myth," evidence continues to
emerge that the "myth" is still more powerful—and arguably, in some
cases more true—than the colorless biographical accounts that seek to set
the record straight.[23]

Perhaps, in the light of this analysis, we as critics should concede that
Decadent culture has become one of the first great urban myths. The
myth was generated by a poetry consciously aware of itself as a city poetry,
which addressed itself not to a coterie but to the larger world of London
society and even to readers of the popular press. Can we not go further,
and say that in some sense the Decadents were the first modern artists to
understand how art could be used to invent their lives, even to dictate
their own destiny? How else (for instance) is one to read Oscar Wilde's
early sonnet "Helas!" (1881)?

> To drift with every passion till my soul
> Is a stringed lute on which all winds can play,
> Is it for this that I have given away
> Mine ancient wisdom, and austere control?
> Methinks my life is a twice-written scroll
> Scrawled over on some boyish holiday
> With idle songs for pipe and virelay,
> Which do but mar the secret of the whole.
> Surely there was a time I might have trod
> The sunlit heights, and from life's dissonance
> Struck one clear chord to reach the ears of God:
> Is that time dead? lo! with a little rod
> I did but touch the honey of romance—
> And must I lose a soul's inheritance?[24]

This is a stagy poem. It is public, hyperbolic, and self-consciously grand,
if not a bit grandiose. It is written as if it were intended to be publicly de-
claimed. In this sonnet, the poetic voice performs, or seems to perform,
a choice: between austere control and passionate collapse. But of course
the decision has already been taken, reducing the poem to a complaint as
to what fate (not personal choice) has dictated: the loss of a "soul's inheri-
tance." In reading the poem one becomes aware that the emotions that it

enacts are not in themselves noble. Instead, they fabricate a pose of no-bility—the unworthy choice, after all, has already been made. In fact, it is this sense of patent inauthenticity—of a kind of fake theatricality—that gives the piece its true Wildean tone, one that derives from what Yeats would identify in Wilde as "an attempt to escape from an emotion by its exaggeration."[25] Finally, one might note how, in the course of its closing lines, the poetic voice begins to teeter on the verge of self-pity.

Wilde's greatest biographer, Richard Ellmann, cites this poem as the one that speaks most eloquently of the divisions within Wilde's personal-ity: between the "drift" of the modern, passionate, Catholic soul, on the one hand, and the rebuke of the ancestral, austere Protestant conscience, on the other hand.[26] In the poem's last lines Wilde alludes to the appeal of Jonathan to Saul ("I did but taste a little honey with the end of the rod that was in mine hand, and lo! I must die" [1 Samuel 14:43]) as para-phrased in the penultimate essay of what Wilde called his "golden book," Pater's *Studies in the History of the Renaissance* (1873).[27] In analyzing the use of these lines from Pater's essay on the great eighteenth-century clas-sical scholar Johann Joachim Winckelmann, Ellmann suggests, although he does not name, another division: namely, that between the incipiently homoerotic Wilde and the conventional heterosexual Wilde—who within the next few years was to become both husband and father.[28]

If one actually reads "Helas!" aloud, then what one hears might sug-gest another line of interpretation. As it is spoken, the title sounds un-nervingly close in pronunciation to the Greek word for the Greek nation: Hellas (Ellas). And with that insight the auditor is thrown into the divi-sions of Wilde's soul, as expressed through contemporary interpretations of Hellenism itself: on the one hand, that brand of Hellenism identified as a philosophy of "austere control" of the baser passions; on the other hand, that Hellenism identified with homoeroticism, known to contem-poraries under the rubric of "Dorian boy-love."[29]

Most startling, however, in the poem's performance is the overwhelm-ing sense that the poem is somehow fatal—in that it appears to predict an outcome to Wilde's life as a fait accompli. More and more, as one studies the life of Wilde, one has the sense that Wilde himself deliberately sought to "drift" into a homoerotic affair with Robert Ross (1869–1918), a young Canadian attending Oxford who seemed set on seducing him,[30] at pre-cisely the time when such an action might be deemed most provocative—

that is, during the months following the Criminal Law Amendment Act of 1885, which infamously proscribed acts of "gross indecency" between men, even in private.[31] (It was under this law that Wilde endured a two-year prison sentence.) Does this poem have to do with Wilde's insight into events to come? (The fact that he used "Helas!" as the introductory sonnet to the 1881 edition of his *Poems* suggests that it had the significance of a credo.) Or did the poem help to generate Wilde's own tragedy, by writing his unconscious so exactly that it virtually conscripted the poet into performing it?

The poet notes that he feels as if his life has already been scripted by the "twice-written" scroll over which he now scrawls his own lines. Certainly the poem conscripts the reader as well. An 1880s audience would have been lulled into thinking that the choice made by the poet was inevitable—in the sense that what happened was not, in fact, a matter of choice at all. From our own perspective, it is safe to say that no reader after the spring of 1895 would be able to separate out his or her knowledge of Wilde's biography from a reading of this poem as literally "fatal."

What would happen, for instance, if we did not recognize this poem as one by Wilde? Does the reader think that, if he or she came upon this piece without knowing the author's identity or anything about his life, its value would be greater than that of a competent, if somewhat skewed, late-Romantic poem? I am conscious that many scholars who research the 1890s have welcomed the definitive edition of Wilde's poetry, which comprises volume 1 in the Oxford English Texts *Complete Works of Oscar Wilde*. The way the general editor, Ian Small, addresses the problem of the value of Wilde's poetry is fascinating. Small conducts his defense in several stages. First of all, Small observes that Wilde's contemporaries frequently criticized his poetry as derivative and thin. Having noted many instances in which Wilde draws on other sources—including his own work—Small concludes that in Wilde's writing the very "reworking of existing material . . . constituted real originality."[32] Despite the obvious technical skill of Wilde's work, Small's ultimate justification for it is not its inherent value as poetry, but the author's status as a cultural icon of the emerging consumer age, in which critics have noted Wilde's importance "as a prototypical product of the media . . . admired for the way he and his publishers market or 'package' his works, as much as for the works themselves."[33]

And yet, if we are to be responsible critics, it is necessary for us to ask: How many of these poems of Wilde's would still be read, much less edited with such care and published to such fanfare, if they were (for instance) by Alfred Austin—an appalling, if respectable, verse maker who succeeded Alfred Tennyson as poet laureate in 1896? What role, in other words, does the life myth play in enabling minor poetry of these decades to survive? And how many of these and other 1890s poems would still be published—never mind read—if they were the private compositions of, say, obscure civil servants?

To push this line of questioning further: Is it indeed possible to read any 1890s poem without the context of its life myth? Or, to phrase the question in another way: Is it not true that the stereotypical 1890s poem works by actually generating the life myth by which it is to be read? Consider this poem by Ernest Dowson:

A Last Word

Let us go hence: the night is now at hand;
The day is overworn, the birds all flown;
And we have reaped the crops the gods have sown;
Despair and death; deep darkness o'er the land,
Broods like an owl; we cannot understand
Laughter or tears, for we have only known
Surpassing vanity: vain things alone
Have driven our perverse and aimless band.
Let us go hence, somewhither strange and cold,
To Hollow Lands where just men and unjust
Find end of labour, where's rest for the old,
Freedom to all from love and fear and lust.
Twine our torn hands! O pray the earth enfold
Our life-sick hearts and turn them into dust.[34]

This is a poem designed to bring down the curtain. Its purpose is acknowledged in its placement at the end of the poetry section of Dowson's last published book, *Decorations: In Verse and Prose* (1899). The poem is a final address to an audience, and its cadences convince through an exquisite music—rarely audible except when read aloud. (One should recall that Dowson's recitations amazed Yeats, who later remarked that the poems were "not speech but perfect song, though song for the speaking voice."[35]) A theatrical poem, "A Last Word" plays out desire to its logical conclusion, which is the extinction of all desire. But even while its rhetoric mimes a series of stern injunctions, the voice seems to lapse from line to line, finally praying to be returned to "dust" in music of the most exquisite despair. Certainly the poem's genius is of precisely such music. Reading this poetry a generation later, Rupert Brooke (1887–1915) would comment that Dowson's cadences had created for all subsequent poetry the equivalent of "a new sigh."[36]

But the rhetoric of Dowson's poem is perhaps even more powerful than its music. From the first line the poem commandeers its audience by means of the imperative: "Let us go hence: the night is now at hand." Here Dowson is, in effect, inscribing a kind of life manifesto for all who know themselves to be of "our perverse and aimless band." Who would have belonged to this "us" if not the other male poets of the so-called Decadence? Certainly this is another aspect of Decadence that critics often overlook. This was the first group of English writers since the Romantics who self-consciously thought of themselves as a "band" or a generation distinct unto themselves. To think of themselves in this way implies several things. First of all, these artists aimed consciously to break with the poetry that preceded them. Secondly, these writers considered themselves to be performing a limited, self-defining task, one that would be played out during their lifetimes (in fact, it was more brief than this, as Decadence effectively ended with the sentencing of Wilde on 25 May 1895). Finally, these artists believed that in carrying out this work, they embodied the life stance of a whole generation, in a way that was to become definitive for other such movements: one thinks of the self-conscious attitudes of the "Lost Generation," the "Beat Generation," or even "Generation X."

Of course it was one of the band—Yeats, who later escaped—who gave the movement its name. In doing so, Yeats dictated that the mythos of this group—which in part he forged (in collaboration with Symons)— would effectively determine any future discussion of the poetry of the 1890s. The chapter of Yeats's *Autobiographies* entitled "The Tragic Generation" is a confused and confusing exploration of the dynamics of what Symons in 1893 named "Decadence." The confusion is best expressed by the rhetorical questions that dominate the chapter's discourse. But rather than invoke its confusions, it would be simpler to note how Yeats's stubborn return to anecdote and episode throughout these memoirs makes them a paradigm of the complicity of life and art—a complicity crucial in generating the drama of Decadence.

Such complicity of life and art in fact defines what we think of as the standard 1890s life and poem. The word for such complicity in the 1890s was "fatal." The poem was fatal because it not only dictated the poet's fate but also dictated that his actual experience must be secondary to the script of the poem. "As for living, our servants will do it for us": this was the motto that Yeats appended to his generation.[37] Yeats noted that Lionel Johnson—one of the finest poets and critics of the new literary movement, who was to meet his end in a fall from a bar-stool—had lost "the faculty of experience"; in fact, Johnson avoided experience altogether by sleeping during the day and working at night.[38] For poets such as Johnson, to live the literary life meant, in effect, not to live at all, except within the imaginative world created from the theater, the music hall, their reading, and their self-appointed literary gatherings. Even Dowson's excursions into the underworld of London and Paris became performances of his imaginative transformation of them: as Yeats remembers, Dowson remarked upon passing one "particularly common harlot": "She writes poetry—it is like Browning and Mrs. Browning."[39] Of such implicitly theatrical habits of the poets of the Rhymers' Club, Yeats wrote to his father: "The doctrine of the group, or rather of the majority of it, was that lyric poetry should be personal. That a man should express his life and do this without shame or fear. Ernest Dowson did this and became a most extraordinary poet, one feels the pressure of his life behind every line as if he were a character in a play of Shakespeare's."[40] To this idea of theater Yeats returns obsessively, remarking that by the middle of the 1890s the "Rhymers had begun to break up in tragedy, though we did not know that till the play had finished."[41] In such passages, Yeats articulates the submerged metaphor for the careers of these poets, who thought of their lives as drama and their characteristic drama as a tragedy. Wilde echoed the metaphor in responding to the news of Dowson's death: "Poor wounded wonderful fellow that he was, a tragic reproduction of all tragic poetry, like a symbol, or a scene."[42] Could one any more eloquently describe the collapse of a life into icon?

Thus Dowson and Wilde demonstrate that to turn one's life into a scene, and the scene into tragedy, was a fate inscribed in male Decadent poetry—which was then deemed "fatal." But for us today there are other consequences of this syndrome, ones that (in terms of reputations) also prove to be fatal. First of all, this stereotype of the 1890s poet has doomed to obscurity the work of other poets, who were private and even reticent about their personal lives. These poets are mainly, although not exclusively, women. Ironically, the women who are now being recognized as among the true artists of this generation are those who can be written into this tragic script because they were outside strict heterosexual norms and/or because they died by their own hand. Here I speak specifically of Michael Field, Charlotte Mew, and Amy Levy. Those women who do not fit the tragic stereotype, such as Meynell, are still ruthlessly excluded from the select ranks of the 1890s poet.

Meynell did not live a tragic life. She was a loving wife and a somewhat distracted mother of eight children, seven of whom survived. She had a public presence as well, both as a suffragist and as a prose writer of some significance. Her books (of prose and poetry) were published during her lifetime to critical acclaim. Her poems are still deemed to be among the finest of the decade. And yet they are stubbornly overlooked. Why? First of all (and obviously), she was a woman, and thus did not fit the male stereotype. Secondly, she was regarded as conventional. In fact, Meynell played up to the womanly conventions of her time. The third factor relates to the second: she was intensely, almost notoriously, private. It has been said (by her granddaughter, for instance) that, during her entire lifetime, Meynell was never seen by any of her children to enter, or leave, a bathroom.[43] Such a record speaks of a determined, sustained, and even exhausting effort to maintain a reserve that was almost pathological.

Meynell's determination to lead a hidden, if privately vivid, life prejudices the readings of her poetry. The poems themselves are reticent and often take reticence as their subject. An example is one of the early works, "Renouncement":

> I must not think of thee; and, tired yet strong,
>> I shun the thought that lurks in all delight—
>> The thought of thee—and in the blue Heaven's height,
> And in the sweetest passage of a song.

O just beyond the fairest thoughts that throng
This breast, the thought of thee waits, hidden yet bright;
But it must never, never come in sight;
I must stop short of thee the whole day long.

But when sleep comes to close each difficult day,
When night gives pause to the long watch I keep,
And all my bonds I needs must loose apart,
Must doff my will as raiment laid away,—
With the first dream that comes with the first sleep
I run, I run, I am gathered to thy heart.[44]

Among modern poets, George MacBeth is not alone in praising Meynell's "nearly perfect lyrics."[45] "Her ear," he writes, "is as fine as Dowson's,"[46] although the intensity of feeling is often concealed by an austere control of verse forms and a severe reticence of diction. This is not a histrionic poem; it is in fact about the avoidance of drama and a repression so strict that true release of feeling is permitted only during sleep, in dreams.

That the poem is about the renouncement of a love affair is certain. Of this affair we have only a hint, in a memoir stating that, while still beginning to write poems, Meynell was encouraged by a priest. A recent convert to Catholicism, Meynell—as Vita Sackville-West observed—found his intelligent perception of her gift "so close a bond between them that [in the words of someone who knew Meynell] 'in keeping with the strict precautionary rules of his priesthood it was considered best that this friendship should end and that they should see each other no more.'"[47] It is significant that Meynell chose not to include the poem, written some years previously, in her first volume of poetry, *Preludes*, published in 1875.[48] For, in her work as a whole, it seems clear that when Meynell expresses her hidden life it is in a series of quick, guarded exposures— which often speak precisely of the dangers of such exposure. In many ways, her writing resembles an intricate game of hide-and-seek, which either charms or tires the reader. (It is a matter of temperament.)

Throughout her career, Meynell's poetry adhered to a prosody of passionate restraint, to such an extent that John Drinkwater notes that "of the work after 1875 there is little essential to be said that might not well have been suggested by the first volume."[49] Thus, as several of her recent critics have noted, although Meynell did move ahead technically as her mode of expression matured, her poetics of reserve, intellection, and detachment remained intact, preventing her from accepting, or being accepted by, the modernists.[50] Meynell's poetry, then, is of that school of English poetry that developed not from the stage but from more classical models: the school of Ben Jonson and George Herbert rather than that of John Donne and Andrew Marvell. This school of poetry eschews the theatrical for the chaste bonds of a quieter, more restrained, more intimate art. The renouncement, in effect, is of the whole ethos by which the 1890s poem, as we know it, was in her time being generated.

I am writing not to make a case for Meynell per se, but to point out that the literary reputations of 1890s poets have been made and unmade by the stereotyping of the decade's poetry as male, public, performative, and prescriptive. It is also important to understand that the male poets of the 1890s, by self-consciously identifying with this mythos and with one another, to a large extent colluded in constructing this stereotype. I am, however, much heartened by recent contributions to 1890s scholarship that focus on women poets who are outside this construction—although it might be argued that their histories again point to the ways in which these women have been hampered in gaining the recognition they deserve as genuine poets.

As a case in point, I wish to instance the work of Rosamund Marriott Watson. That she was an accomplished poet there is little doubt. That her work was prolific, that she was not shy in promoting it, and that she gained some measure of public acclaim are evident from her biography.[51] Unlike most other women poets of the decade, Rosamund Marriott Watson was a member of a Ladies Literary Club—and perhaps participated in one of the many salons at which women recited their poems to one another. Thus these women imitated the successful tactics of such poetry circles as the Rhymers' Club in banding together to help forge a new poetics for the decade.[52] Most important, for the 1890s aesthetic, in her own life Watson generated the material for a scandal and/or a tragedy (depending on how you read it) by divorcing two husbands and living "in sin" with a third male companion. A male poet might have written about these marital breakups, might have made a scene, literally, through his poems—might, in short, have capitalized on the gossip that swirled around Rosamond Armytage (as she then wished to be known),[53] particularly at

the time of her first divorce. For a man, in fact, the gossip might have become a kind of glamour, as it did for Wilde and Dowson. Indeed, there
are indications that Rosamund Marriott Watson sought to inscribe her
fate in such poems as "'Mariage de Convenance—After!' (*Orchardson*)"
(1886) or even "Vespertilia" (1895), although her muffled outbursts were
sporadic and often heavily masked. More significantly, since she was a
woman, Watson took decisive action in her personal life to defend her privacy: she changed what had become her well-established nom de plume
of "Graham R. Tomson" (at a crucial period in her career), and in so
doing losing all the symbolic capital she had invested in it. In 1895, retir-
ing into the obscurity of a third name ("Rosamund Marriott Watson") and
a new life, she disrupted what a modern public relations person might
designate her "brand identification." By these tactics she also managed to
avoid a feeding frenzy in the press, and she eluded the notoriety that
would, in fact, probably have increased her name recognition in the literary marketplace.

There is a famous moment in George Eliot's *Middlemarch* (1871) when
Will Ladislaw describes to Dorothea his idea of a poet as having "a soul in
which knowledge passes instantaneously into feeling, and feeling flashes
back as a new organ of knowledge." "But you leave out the poems,"
Dorothea objects. "I think they are wanted to complete the poet. . . . But
I am sure I could never produce a poem." To which Will replies: "You *are*
a poem."[54] In such an exchange, one sees exactly the dangers for woman
poets, particularly within the 1890s ethos. It is striking, for instance, that
Meynell, Marriott Watson, and A. Mary F. Robinson are all recorded as
having been stunning presences, of great personal beauty and charm. Is
this not a danger that particularly haunts women writers? It is frequently
the case that critics assume that a woman's poetry, rather than representing an artistic performance of femininity, represents her very person. As
a consequence, readers tend to conflate women poets' work with their
presentation of themselves as women, including how they look and where
they are seen. (The personal appearance culture of our publications marketplace today works in a similar way.)

Addressing this question in a discussion of Robinson's poetry, Lynda
Ely speculates that implicit in Will Ladislaw's statement is an understanding of the common practice of focusing attention on the biographies of
women writers in such a way that their art is eclipsed or dismissed as

charming and ancillary—in fact, as little more than a social ornament.[55] Several crucial questions should be raised here. Was there a distinction in the performance/practices of women poets as against men poets during this period? How varied were the contexts in which men and women poets presented their work (with men meeting in pubs, say, and women in salons)? Was there, in fact, a striking gender distinction in the way poets of the 1890s generated their own mythos through the modalities of their poetry? How crucial is public knowledge of private lives in the reception of this poetry? And, finally, how does this material enter critical assessment? Does it do so in perceptibly differentiated and gendered modes? These are the kinds of questions one must ask in examining the construction of literary reputations during this period.

This chapter originated as a provocative piece encouraging 1890s scholars to think about how literary reputations are made and sustained. When this issue is examined, it becomes clear that the performance/practices of poetry in the 1890s comprise a key to understanding the way that the poems were, and are, received—particularly as such performance/practices tend to privilege a male performative ethos, in which the life myth is incorporated into readings of the work, both by the poet and by his audience.

In this context, it may be instructive to devise a hypothetical anthology of women poets of the 1890s—for no such comprehensive collection as yet exists.[56] If one were to undertake such an enterprise, how, as editor, would one set its parameters? Obviously the collection would be produced with the explicit purpose of recovering the work of women poets of the 1890s whose writing remains difficult to access. But how would one decide which of these women poets to select? What about those who, fashionable in their own day, now exemplify only different values in poetic taste? And what about women poets not fashionable in their day, such as those from the working class or from the colonies, or those who wrote in a style that did not appeal to a late-Victorian audience?

In making such choices the editor would also have to ask several leading questions about the role of context in providing, literally, life support for these texts. First of all, would biographical material be included? And what role and what weight would such material be ceded? Secondly, would the editor provide a short primary bibliography, which would establish the poet as a serious or professional writer, on the same level as her male peers? Finally, perhaps most crucially, would portraits or photographs of the women poets be provided? In chapter 8 of the present volume, Ana Parejo Vadillo writes persuasively on the role of A. Mary F. Robinson's photographic presence in projecting "a haunting, ghostly, disembodied, and unreal quality" onto her poetry as well as her poetic reputation. But, in an anthology such as the one contemplated, should portraits be included at all? Would not visual representations prove dangerous, as they implicitly subject women writers to all sorts of judgments concerning gender stereotypes (since women tend to be reduced to their appearance)?

Certainly the time is now ripe for an anthology that includes all the 1890s women poets of considered value who have been excluded from the male preserve of the "Decadent." But in pursuing such a venture, how could one begin to counter the powerful mythos inscribed by the generation of male Decadent poets? Is there a countering female life myth (or myths) that enabled these women to produce their own distinctive poetry? And—if it exists—how would such a life myth enable us to understand better their poetry? On the negative side, surely, every precaution must be taken to avoid compromising or otherwise diminishing the work of these formidable women, whose own engagement with the stereotypes of their age is ambiguous—and highly ambivalent.

What I have tried to demonstrate here is that there is no poet during this decade whose poetry survives without the gloss granted by a compelling life myth. And it is such a gloss, I suggest, that will dictate whether the poetry of these women will be acknowledged, in the final analysis, to have composed lives as passionate and resonant as those of the men who historically gave the decade its reputation.

Notes

1. Arthur Symons, "The Decadent Movement in Literature," *Harper's New Monthly Magazine* 87 (1893): 858–67; reprinted in Karl Beckson, ed., *Aesthetes and Decadents of the 1890s: An Anthology of British Poetry and Prose* (Chicago: Academy, 1981), 136, 151.

2. On Herbert Horne's poetry, see Jerome McGann, "Herbert Horne's *Diversi Colores* (1891): Incarnating the Religion of Beauty," in the present volume, chapter 5.

3. Talia Schaffer, *The Forgotten Female Aesthetes: Literary Culture in Late-Victorian England* (Charlottesville: University Press of Virginia, 2000), 6.

4. Alexander Michaelson [Marc-André Raffalovich], "Giles and Miles and Isabeau," *Blackfriars* 9 (1928): 26–27.

5. Schaffer, *Forgotten Female Aesthetes*, 62.

6. Schaffer, *Forgotten Female Aesthetes*, 6.

7. *The Complete Letters of Oscar Wilde*, ed. Merlin Holland and Rupert Hart-Davis (London: Fourth Estate, 2000), 111, 112, 113, and 114.

8. Jerusha Hull McCormack, *John Gray: Poet, Dandy, and Priest* (Hanover, NH: University Press of New England, 1991), 62, 70.

9. Raymond Roseliep, "Some Letters of Lionel Johnson" (PhD diss., University of Notre Dame, 1954), 109. Nicholas Frankel discusses the poetry of the Rhymers' Club in "'A Wreath for the Brows of Time': The Books of the Rhymers' Club as Material Texts," in the present volume, chapter 4.

10. W. B. Yeats, *Autobiographies*, in *The Collected Works of W. B. Yeats*, vol. 3, ed. William H. O'Donnell and Douglas N. Archibald (New York: Scribner, 1989), 234.

11. Yeats, *Autobiographies*, 234.

12. For an elaboration of this point, see Garrett Stewart, *Reading Voices: Literature and the Phonotext* (Berkeley and Los Angeles: University of California Press, 1990), in particular chapters 4 and 5. See also Eric Griffiths, *The Printed Voice of Victorian Poetry* (Oxford: Oxford University Press, 1989).

13. For information on the publication history of Wilde's *Poems*, see Ian Small, introduction to *The Complete Works of Oscar Wilde*, vol. 1, *Poems and Poems in Prose*, ed. Bobby Fong and Karl Beckson (Oxford: Oxford University Press, 2000), xx.

14. For a history of the early years of the Independent Theatre and the plays it produced cf. N. H. G. Schoonderwoerd, *J. T. Grein, Ambassador of the Theatre, 1862–1935* (Assen, Netherlands: Van Gorcum, 1963), 60–130; and Anna Irene Miller, *The Independent Theatre in Europe, 1887 to the Present* (New York: Ray Long and Richard R. Smith, 1931), 169–71. For an account of Michael Field's 1893 play, *A Question of Memory*, see John Stokes, "A Literary Theatre: The Lessons of the Independent Theatre," in *Resistible Theatres: Enterprise and Experiment in the Late Nineteenth Century* (London: Paul Elek, 1972), 148.

15. Arthur Symons, "Prologue: In the Stalls," in Beckson, *Aesthetes and Decadents*, 154. Symons's poem first appeared in 1895.

16. John Gray, "The Modern Actor" (1892), in *Selected Prose of John Gray*, ed. Jerusha Hull McCormack (Greensboro, NC: ELT Press, 1992), 30–37.

17. For the history of this episode, see McCormack, *John Gray*, 82–87.

18. Ernest Dowson, "Vitae summa brevis spem nos vetat incohare longam" and "Non sum qualis eram bonae sub regno Cynarae," in *The Poems of Ernest Dowson*, ed. Mark Longaker (Philadelphia: University of Pennsylvania Press, 1962), 58, 38.

19. In a personal letter to Sam Smith written in 1895, Dowson is on record as declaring: "But I *do not* go about in Paris with a halo of ghosts and tears, having been gifted by God with a sense . . . of humour!" *The Letters of Ernest Dowson*, ed. Desmond Flower and Henry Maas (London: Cassell, 1967), 320.

20. Arthur Symons, "A Literary Causerie: On a Book of Verses," *Savoy* 1, no. 4 (1896): 91, 92; Symons, "Ernest Dowson," *The Poems of Ernest Dowson* (London: The Bodley Head, 1919), xvi.

21. W. B. Yeats, *Memoirs*, ed. Denis Donoghue (London: Macmillan, 1972), 93.

22. Yeats, *Autobiographies*, 39.

23. For an extensive and detailed account of the fabrication of the "Dowson legend," see R. K. R. Thornton, *The Decadent Dilemma* (London: Edward Arnold, 1983), 75–85.

24. Wilde, "Helas!" in *Complete Works*, 1:156–57; cf. 1:292–93n90.

Strictly speaking, Wilde's "Helas!" is not a Decadent poem, since it is probably a production of the late 1870s; it appeared in *Poems* (1881), and is thus of the aesthetic movement. "Helas!" was, however, reprinted by John Lane in the 1892 edition of Wilde's *Poems*, and it has since been regarded as a kind of prediction of Wilde's later life. Wilde himself gave it pride of place, positioning it as the epigraph for his entire collection.

25. Yeats, *Autobiographies*, 224.

26. Richard Ellmann, *Oscar Wilde* (New York: Knopf, 1988), 139.

27. Wilde's description of Pater's *Studies in the History of the Renaissance* as a "golden book" appears in Yeats's *Autobiographies*, 124.

28. Ellmann, *Oscar Wilde*, 138–40.

29. Cf. Linda Dowling's examination of the Greek practice of *paiderastia* in the chapter on "The Socratic Eros" in *Hellenism and Homosexuality in Victorian Oxford* (Ithaca, NY: Cornell University Press, 1994), 67–103.

30. Ellmann, *Oscar Wilde*, 475ff. Ross was later to become one of Wilde's most devoted and loyal friends and, after Wilde's death, the executor of his literary estate.

31. This is the most accurate estimate for the beginning of Wilde's affair with Robert Ross; see Ellmann, *Oscar Wilde*, 275–77.

32. Small, introduction to *Complete Works of Oscar Wilde*, 1:xxiii.

33. Small, introduction to *Complete Works of Oscar Wilde*, 1:xxi.

34. Dowson, *Poems*, 138. The predictive power of this poem can be judged by the fact that it is deemed to have been written as early as 1886 (cf. 249–50n30).

35. Yeats, *Autobiographies*, 234.

36. Rupert Brooke, preface to *The Prose of Rupert Brooke*, ed. Christopher Hassall (London: Sidgwick and Jackson, 1956), xv.

37. Yeats, *Autobiographies*, 236.

38. Yeats, *Autobiographies*, 246, 236.

39. Yeats, *Autobiographies*, 327.

40. William Butler Yeats, *The Letters of W. B. Yeats*, ed. Allan Wade (London: Rupert Hart-Davis, 1954), 548.

41. Yeats, *Autobiographies*, 233.

42. Wilde to Leonard Smithers, c. 24 February 1900, in *Complete Letters*, 1173.

43. Gabriella Bergonzi, personal communication, May 1974.

44. Alice Meynell, "Renouncement," in *The Poems of Alice Meynell* (London: Oxford University Press, 1940), 69.

45. George MacBeth, ed., *The Penguin Book of Victorian Verse* (Harmondsworth, UK: Penguin Books, 1969), 322.

46. MacBeth, *Penguin Book of Victorian Verse*, 322.

47. V[ita] Sackville-West, introduction to *Alice Meynell: Prose and Poetry*, by Alice Meynell (London: Jonathan Cape, 1947), 13.

48. See *The Poems of Alice Meynell*, ed. Frederick Page (London: Oxford University Press, 1940), 211n69. This early poem was first published in Hall Caine's *Sonnets of Three Centuries* (1882).

49. John Drinkwater, quoted in Vanessa Furse Jackson, "'Tides of the Mind': Restraint and Renunciation in the Poetry of Alice Meynell," *Victorian Poetry* 36 (1998): 460.

50. Jackson, "'Tides of the Mind,'" 460. This is also the conclusion of Maria Frawley in "'The Tides of the Mind': Alice Meynell's Poetry of Perception," *Victorian Poetry* 38 (2000): 62–76.

51. Linda K. Hughes, "Rosamund Marriott Watson," in *Dictionary of Literary Biography*, vol. 240, *Late Nineteenth- and Early Twentieth-Century British Women Poets*, ed. William B. Thesing (Detroit, MI: Gale Group, 2001), 308–20. The following passage is derived from this source. Cf. Hughes's discussion of Rosamund Marriott Watson's poetry, "A Woman on the Wilde Side: Masks, Perversity, and Print Culture's Role in Poems by 'Graham R. Tomson'/Rosamund Marriott Watson," in the present volume, chapter 3; and Hughes, *Graham R.: Rosamund Marriott Watson, Woman of Letters* (Athens: Ohio University Press, 2005).

52. Ana I. Parejo Vadillo, "New Woman Poets and the Culture of the *Salon* at the *Fin-de-Siècle*," *Women: A Cultural Review* 10 (1999): 22–34.

53. The poet changed the spelling of her first name from "Rosamond" to "Rosamund" when she became partnered with H. B. Marriott Watson in 1895.

54. George Eliot, *Middlemarch* (Boston: Houghton Mifflin, 1956), 166.

55. M. Lynda Ely, "'Not a Song to Sell': Re-Presenting A. Mary F. Robinson," *Victorian Poetry* 38 (2000): 94–108.

56. At present, the closest thing to a complete anthology of fin-de-siècle women poets is a volume by Linda K. Hughes, who selects important poems by women engaged with the political issues of their day; see Hughes, *New Women Poets,* Lost Chords no. 1 (London: The Eighteen Nineties Society, 2001).

THE DEATH OF THE AUTHOR BY SUICIDE

Fin-de-Siècle Poets and the Construction of Identity

Holly Laird

The birth of the reader must be at the cost of the death of the Author.
—ROLAND BARTHES, "THE DEATH OF THE AUTHOR" (1968)

I

In "The Death of the Author"—an essay that, along with the writings of Jacques Derrida and Michel Foucault, had a profound impact on the development of Anglo-American theory and criticism in the late twentieth century—the French theorist Roland Barthes promulgates the notion that written texts supersede whatever their origins might be, thus suicidally "killing off" their "authors."[1] Although many critics think that Barthes pushed this manifesto-like formulation too far, this celebrated idea, now a critical commonplace, remains alluring for its implicit reminder that we rely on literary storytelling as well as documentary records for the reconstruction of not only texts' informing intellectual contexts but also their authors' lives and deaths. The notion of "the death of the author" becomes further complicated and rendered richly ironic, however, when applied to the question of suicide in the lives and works of a set of writers long associated with their deaths—the English fin-de-siècle poets. As a result of critical mythologization of these poets' deaths, together with these writers' frequent preoccupation with self-murder, scholarship has shown

a marked tendency to construct poetic identity at the end of the nineteenth century as specifically suicidal.

Yet, as suicidologists have continually demonstrated, suicide is itself
among the most elusive of human constructions.[2] Moreover, particularly
in the case of the best-known male poets of the fin de siècle, suicide has
largely been the production of legend or outright fiction rather than the
recording of autopsical fact. Thanks in no small part to W. B. Yeats's famous 1922 memoir, "The Tragic Generation"—an essay that succeeded
in formalizing prior mythologizing gestures,[3] especially by the broadly
influential critic-poet Arthur Symons—these poets have been allotted a
problematic yet fascinating niche of their own in the English canon. In
this chapter, then, I devote less space to what the poets wrote about self-
murder than to the ways in which critics have memorialized these writers not only as personal suicides but also as identity constructions of the
author as a suicide. Even while suicide provides these studies with an
absolute identity for a suicidal poet, in biographical and critical analysis
self-murder becomes a crux that cannot easily be logically explained, rationally adjusted, or tamed.

When we look at male poets of the 1890s, notably Ernest Dowson, Lionel Johnson, John Davidson, and James Thomson ("B.V."), it becomes
clear that the small mark their signatures left in the literary canon has
long been associated with such epithets as "tragic," "weak," "minor,"
"failed," "melancholic," "self-destructive," and "feminine." Although all
but one died from multiple causes with only underlying suicidal tendencies, these poets have been repeatedly represented as (mostly lovelorn)
suicides. With the women poets of the fin de siècle, a different yet cognate
story emerges. The best known of the suicidal women of the fin de siècle—Amy Levy, Adela Cory Nicolson ("Laurence Hope"), and Charlotte
Mew—killed themselves quite deliberately. Yet these women's histories
are also unlike the men's in having disappeared almost entirely from the
public sphere after some early responses to their deaths. No women poets
appear in Yeats's account of the "tragic generation." Doubly produced as
absent—through their displacement as poets by their male contemporaries and through the displacement of their literal suicides by their male
compeers' figurative ones—these women poets are extra casualties of the
legendary death of the author associated with the end of the nineteenth
century. These days Levy, Nicolson, and Mew are receiving critical atten-

tion that for the most part pivots around their identities as women who were, variously, Jewish, Anglo-Indian, and/or lesbian or queer. Suicide, when prominently featured in the criticism, is piggybacked on those ethnic and sexual identities.

I begin here with the ample historical reception of the male poets, before turning to recent scholarly attempts to recover the work of the critically neglected women poets. In the process of exposing some of the taller tales about self-murder in critical writing about these poets' lives and works, I argue for a loosening and refinement of the "suicide"-as-identity construct. I hardly wish to dismiss any consideration of suicide in the contextualizing of fin-de-siècle poetry. On the contrary, the discourse of suicide, when suicide is analyzed as a topic that preoccupies all of these writers, makes possible a compelling rereading of a divergent body of lyrics, monologues, and narrative poems. These poets' work calls out for critical discussion that can help generate conceptual frameworks for considering any poetry about self-murder, whether by suicidal poets or not. Thus in my concluding section, I turn to some suggestions for how, once the legends have been debunked and the notion of "suicide" as absolute identity has been exposed and complicated, we may begin to read this poetry anew.

II

Among all of the men and women poets I have mentioned, Ernest Dowson is the one most often discussed and, not coincidentally, the source of the most famous legend in the construction of the fin-de-siècle generation as suicidal. Even before Dowson died, Arthur Symons propounded what John Gawsworth famously termed (and sought to demythologize as), forty-two years later, "the Dowson legend."[4] In a purportedly favorable review of Dowson's book *Verses* (1896), Symons layers adjectival layer on layer to develop an impressionist caricature that no one would be likely to forget. Dowson, he writes, is "delicate, mournful, almost colourless, but very fragrant," "so essentially poetic, and at the same time so fragile," that he appears "a very ghostly lover . . . wandering in a land of perpetual twilight, holding a whispered 'colloque sentimental' with the ghost of an old love."[5]

Gender noticeably seeps into Symons's portrait, such that if the "delicate" adjectives had not already feminized Dowson, then the following association of Dowson with lilies (albeit weedy) would. It was, Symons argues, a young girl with whom Dowson was infatuated who "had the gift of evoking and, in its way, of retaining all that was most delicate, sensitive, shy, typically poetic, in a nature which I can only compare to a weedy garden, its grass trodden down by many feet, but with one small, carefully-tended flower-bed, luminous with lilies."[6] Dowson is less a Lewis Carroll figure in this account, obsessed with the "most exquisite and appropriate impossibility" of a preteen girl, than a young girl himself, with "virginal devotion."[7] But despite the "disappointment" (an idea repeated thrice in relatively close succession in this short piece) that Dowson must feel, he must also not, "for the good fortune of poets," come to a happy end, nor does he: "So the wilder wanderings began, and a gradual slipping into deeper and steadier waters of oblivion."[8]

Symons shows his artifice and canon-making impulse more blatantly when he duplicates what were already at that time standard clichés drawn from Walter Pater's (1839–94) famous conclusion to *Studies in the History of the Renaissance* (1873). Dowson, Symons says, is "in search of new sensations" and prey to "passionate and tender adoration of the most escaping of all ideals, the ideal of youth."[9] Moreover, Dowson is a "demoralized Keats," both more "exquisitely refined" than his precursor and "dilapidated."[10] Here Symons is not merely producing Dowson as a descendant of Pater or Keats. While superficially structuring this portrait as an ironic contrast between the "delicate" art of the poet and the Decadent life, Symons collapses one into the other until, at the end, he can claim to have discovered the "secret" of Dowson's self-destruction within the very contours of his "delicate," unrevealing verse: "[I]n these few, evasive, immaterial snatches of song, I find, implied for the most part, hidden away like a secret, all the fever and turmoil and the unattained dreams of a life which has itself had much of the swift, disastrous, and suicidal energy of genius."[11] It is difficult to read this review and recall that Dowson was at the time still living, if—as Symons puts it—"indifferent, to most things, in the shipwrecked quietude of a sort of self-exile."[12]

It would be an error, however, to credit Symons with originating the legend of the death of the fin-de-siècle poet, since it would have developed with or without the existence of Symons and Dowson. In the 1890s there were plenty of other poets pursuing the rhetoric of melancholy—now at least half a century old—to its logical end. Almost a decade prior to Dowson's demise, another poet had declined into alcoholism, illness, and death, and he was enshrined in a nearly identical legend, nicknamed "the Matilda Weller legend": the poet was reputed to have been so enamored of a thirteen-year-old girl (dead by the time she was fourteen) that he spent the rest of his short life secretly mourning her and driving himself to death with drink. This legend substituted nicely for the nearly nonexistent facts recorded of James Thomson's love life and death.

The myth of the lovelorn Thomson was not debunked until the midtwentieth century, late in the anti-intentionalist era of the American New Criticism; debunking this legend became a means also to discard the unappealing bathwater of literary biography. In his strongly worded 1965 study, William Schaefer indicts scholars for falling into "the biographical trap, a seemingly unavoidable propensity on the part of [Thomson's] critics to intermingle, and thus thoroughly confuse, his personal unhappiness with his intellectual position as an atheist and a pessimist."[13] Schaefer went so far in disassociating the poetry and the philosophy of pessimism from the narrative of the life that he came closer to eradicating Thomson from critical consideration than had the poet's prior biographical tragedians.[14] Unsurprisingly, the pendulum has swung back. In a recent book, Richard Pawley pursues the specter of a lovelorn Thomson and tracks a classically Freudian version of the suicidal poet. Inevitably, as in practically all accounts of allegedly suicidal poets, Thomson, with the "wild, weird air of one who has done with the world," reaches the end that he himself—and at least one friend—"predicted."[15]

Meanwhile, biographical critics have advanced convoluted apologetics for their subjects' depression, depicting it as intermittent, periodic, amply motivated from outside, and/or as an illness outside the poets' control. In addition, whether defending their subjects against literal selfmurder or resigning themselves to the verdict of suicide, biographical critics almost invariably feel compelled to single out one ultimate (forensic) cause of death, usually a cause that is physiological and, if possible, one for which the subject cannot be held responsible. Commentators prefer to avoid dwelling in uncertainty about their subjects' final ends, despite how much or, for that matter, how little contradictory information is available.

If, for example, we look closely at Schaefer's study, we discover that even he is not immune from the urge to explain what precisely in the life led to Thomson's early death. After sharply denouncing Thomson's biographers, Schaefer turns around and concludes that the poet "suffered" not from "constitutional melancholia" but "from chronic alcoholism," "today properly classified as an illness."[16] "Unhappiness was not the cause but the result of his alcoholism," and alcohol, "in medical terms," oppressed Thomson until he "'either consciously or subconsciously toy[ed] with the thought of self-destruction.'"[17] Still not finished, Schaefer turns to another explanation—lack of religious belief—for Thomson's pessimism: "Thomson awoke one morning to discover that he was alone in the universe without a god, flung through meaningless space on what he became convinced was a meaningless journey to death. . . . [He was] forced to disown his former views on God, on society, and on his own role in society."[18] This undocumented narrative moment is the basis on which Schaefer argues contradictorily that Thomson was (1) not pessimistic because he was unhappy and (2) not unhappy because he was pessimistic. Surely such a moment, if it occurred, could be more easily narrated as support for the reverse of both of these conclusions.

"Grave," "gray," "impersonal," and "cold" (even "frigid"), in addition to "delicate," "frail," and "weak," are the adjectives that inhabit stories of Lionel Johnson. Caught in a game of tag with Dowson in the annals of a twentieth-century who's who, Johnson is usually perceived either as comrade and shadow figure to Dowson (i.e., lesser than Dowson) or as comrade and precursor of Yeats (i.e., greater than Dowson). In either case, critics erect a morbid monument for him. Although no one has been able to come up with a Missie (Dowson's "young girl") or a Matilda Weller (Thomson's love object) for this poet, scholars have been no less prone to subjecting this seemingly suicidal writer to multiple reconstructions: "Johnson's rejection of life," as Murray Pittock explains, "has been ascribed to many causes, from his father's death to his alcoholism."[19] Still, almost all of the early legends in Johnson's case have been recuperated as facts.

Biographers like to think that Johnson did not die (as rumored), in G. A. Cevasco's words, from "overbalancing on a bar stool in the Green Dragon, nor after falling and fracturing his skull on Fleet Street, nor after being knocked down by a hansom cab while intoxicated; but after a series of strokes" and after drinking heavily.[20] Although Johnson probably did fall from a bar stool in the Green Dragon, "the cause of his death," as Cevasco argues, "was a ruptured blood vessel, not a fractured skull." Johnson had become a virtual "recluse" in the last half decade of his life, prowling the pubs at night and suffering from "what they thought was repeated influenza" as well as uncontrollable alcoholism.[21] Surprisingly few commentators, however, have noted the impact that Oscar Wilde's trials in 1895 would have had on a homosexual man (whether or not, in Cevasco and others' views, an "active" one),[22] or the coincidence of Johnson's increasing reclusiveness and intensifying alcoholism after that time. Earlier in his life, Johnson had fallen in love with men like Wilde (another prominently featured writer in Yeats's "The Tragic Generation"); Johnson introduced his cousin, Lord Alfred Douglas, to Wilde, then one year later wrote the poem "The Destroyer of a Soul" (1892)—based on Wilde's *The Picture of Dorian Gray* (1890, revised 1891)—against Wilde.[23]

Much as Dowson was Symons's supreme fiction for many years, so did Johnson become one of Yeats's mythologized figures. In one critical commentary after another, a central point adduced about this introverted member of the Rhymers' Club—the most feted group of 1890s poets, whose members included Dowson, Johnson, and of course Yeats—is authorized through citation of Yeats's legend-making essay, "The Tragic Generation."[24] Thus Barbara Charlesworth titles an article "The Gray World of Lionel Johnson," and begins it as follows: "William B. Yeats called them 'the Tragic Generation.' . . . Yeats describes [Johnson] as a tiny, frail man who slept through the day-time and spent his nights reading or moving silently among his books in a room almost shrouded in gray— 'grey corduroy over door and window and book-case.'"[25] By means of one memorable essay, Yeats—once a follower, quickly a peer, forevermore a suicide survivor—became, like Symons, more than the author of a legend here or there; he became, as it were, a meta-author, solidifying the canonical niche of the "tragic generation."

Squarely in the center of "The Tragic Generation" there appears an entire section devoted to John Davidson, who represents masculinity and Scottish difference as opposed to effeminate Englishness, with Yeats playing a somewhat clownish yet central antagonistic role as protector and preserver of the Rhymers' Club against Davidson's assault. This part of Yeats's essay is often quoted in defense of Yeats's involvement with the Rhymers'

Club. But if we look at what Yeats actually wrote, we uncover a thoroughly strategic decanonizing postmortem portrait of Davidson. The piece begins with Yeats's blunt judgment of a Davidson "hidden behind failure"; Yeats then recalls Davidson, in the British Museum reading room, describing himself as a "loafer" who worked only an hour a day due to "exhaustion."[26]

Yeats further describes Davidson as looking "older than his years," "older by ten years than his fellow Rhymers," wearing a wig to disguise his receding hairline, and suffering "a life of tragic penury, which was made much harder by the conviction that the world was against him. . . . [H]is Scots jealousy kept him provincial and but half articulate."[27] Davidson—doddering and faking it—is in poor form to make the attack, next in Yeats's account, that has become Davidson's chief claim to notoriety: Davidson "saw in delicate, laborious, discriminating taste an effeminate pedantry, and would, when the mood was on him, delight in all that seemed healthy, popular, and bustling. . . . 'If a man must be a connoisseur [says the Yeats-inflected Davidson], let him be a connoisseur in women.'"[28] Yeats himself, we later learn, is the sole Rhymer considered by Davidson to possess "blood and guts."[29] With an eloquence pitched at the peak of his rhetorical range and with a good dollop of false modesty, Yeats seizes this moment to moralize:

> I think he might have grown to be a successful man had he been enthusiastic instead about Dowson or Johnson, or [Herbert] Horne or Symons, for they had what I still lacked, conscious deliberate craft, and what I must lack always, scholarship. They had taught me that violent energy, which is like a fire of straw, consumes in a few minutes the nervous vitality, and is useless in the arts. . . . A few months after our meeting in the Museum, Davidson had spent his inspiration. "The fires are out," he said, "and I must hammer the cold iron."[30]

Here Yeats hammers out his own post-Paterian creed, explaining for posterity's benefit how and why he survived and succeeded while Davidson (and the others) failed and died before their time.

Yeats concludes with retrospective prophecy: "When I heard a few years ago that he had drowned himself, I knew that I had always expected some such end. . . . [A]nd now no verse of his clings to my memory."[31]

That Davidson's verse clung lingeringly to the memory of T. S. Eliot is something few scholars know, probably because Eliot did not do Davidson (or any of his fellows) the favor of writing a major memoir about them.[32] The deaths of these writers, burdened from the start with the various stigmata of alcoholism, pedophilic fixation, and homosexuality, as well as self-murder, turned in the hands of their commentators into self-willed inevitabilities: conveniently symbolic "suicides" of failed writers of a conveniently long-gone, implicitly failed century.

III

In the late 1970s and 1980s, paradoxically, tragedy, melancholy, reticence, "dis-ease," renunciation—self-destructiveness of various kinds— pervaded critical recuperation of nineteenth-century women writers: "failure" received reconsideration from newly arrived feminist critics, and the successful expression of despair could at last be viewed as success of a distinctive kind.[33] The woman poet most often viewed as the founding "mother" of Western traditions of women's writing was Sappho, the non-Homeric, non-Virgilian suicidal poet of Lesbos. In the nineteenth century itself, successive generations of women poets looked back to the powerful precedent of Letitia Landon (known by initials "L.E.L."; 1802–38), the immensely popular poet who died from an overdose of prussic acid in mysterious circumstances at Cape Coast Castle, Ghana. They also looked to the memorable pathos of Elizabeth Siddall (1829–62), the Pre-Raphaelite artist and model, and later spouse of Dante Gabriel Rossetti, who died of an overdose of laudanum. There were of course longer-lived poets also who served as models, from Felicia Hemans (1793–1835) to Elizabeth Barrett Browning (1806–61), both of whom were fascinated by legends of suicidal and self-destructive women.[34]

With so prominent a suicidal lineage, one might have expected to find more suicidal women poets at the fin de siècle. Women, after all, were thought at special risk of suicide (despite all evidence to the contrary), particularly suicide caused by failure in love, as Barbara T. Gates has pointed out.[35] Yet none of the three women poets discussed here killed herself in the notorious decade of the 1890s: Levy died in 1889, Hope in 1904, and Mew in 1928. Then again, precisely because suicide had been dramatically available to women and to their poetry for centuries, self-murder would not have constituted the next logical step for women, as it arguably did for men. (Mew's death arrived so late that her inclusion in this group might seem odd, but born in 1869 and having come of age in the 1890s, when she published in John Lane's *Yellow Book*, Mew attracts current feminist scholars of Victorian literature as much as she does those of literary modernism.)

In spite of sparse attention to Mew, Levy, and Hope, the focus of the few critics writing on these women is telling. Identity or the elusion of identity—that is, the articulation of identity's differentiating cultural forms or resistance to singular, socially constrained identity norms—remains the issue around which most biographical and critical interest in these women writers circles. Even when strenuously questioning the imposition of a particular identity on a particular woman writer, a critic will base her or his analysis on unquestioned "facts" about that writer—that, for example, the writer in question is lesbian. Those facts usually, though interestingly not always, include the woman's suicide.

Thus Karen Weisman rightly notes that, while most critical attention to Levy's work has focused on the poet's Jewishness and on the controversy surrounding her treatment of Anglo-Jewish culture in her fiction, especially *Reuben Sachs* (1888), this scholarship has failed to register the complexity of (anti-)self-representation in Levy's poems. (Weisman does not mention, however, the comparative paucity of attention to Levy's lesbian desires, though they pose less of a mystery than the desires of Charlotte Mew, whose sexuality has attracted extensive speculation and analysis—here again, the criticism generally shortchanges the multiplicitousness of identity structures.)[36] Weisman proposes that a closer reading of Levy's poetry reveals a pervasive, riddling anxiety about Jewish identity (including anxiety about the anxious Jew as a stereotype). In Weisman's often acute reading, Levy develops a contradictory poetics that is "self-canceling," such that Weisman unwittingly returns Levy to a second identity category. With unintended irony, Weisman writes: "The suicide, in this reading, has triumphed." "Amy Levy," she adds, "died by her own hand, and her death necessarily inscribes itself into the lens of our reading, even as she challenges our modes of cultural refraction."[37]

But the writer's suicide may indeed be overlooked—proving anything but critically "necessary"—especially in contexts in which a scholar chooses to celebrate a feminist feature of the writer's life, as if suicide and feminist positive action could not or should not cohabit within the same essay. Elaine Showalter utters no word of Levy's death when she introduces this poet briefly in her study of fin-de-siècle "sexual anarchy," possibly because such an observation might have confused or undercut her argument about Levy's feminist contribution: "Amy Levy predicted a future [in "A Ballad of Religion and Marriage"] in which the concept of universal marriage and domestic drudgery would decline along with religious faith."[38] More recently, again without reference to Levy's suicide, Ana Parejo Vadillo writes of "Ballade of an Omnibus" as "epitomiz[ing] Levy's greatest achievement: her figuration of the female mass-transportation facilities in general, and the omnibus in particular, as vehicles which enabled late-Victorian middle-class women to defy patriarchal gender and aesthetic ideology."[39] In this reading, "the woman poet's experience of modernity is intrinsically linked to a new rendering of urban life and culture"—that is to say, to a feminist reexperiencing and reconstruction of modernity and of the city.

It is not surprising that Showalter or Vadillo would wish to avoid the determinist stranglehold and interminable indeterminacy that suicide has proved even for the most sympathetic critics trying to capture the complexity of their subjects' lives and writings. Before Vadillo, Deborah Epstein Nord brought Levy into the urban context by affiliating her with independent single women—Margaret Harkness (1861–1921), Eleanor Marx (1855–98), Olive Schreiner (1855–1920), Beatrice Webb (1858–1943)—who tried to live alone in London. Forming a community of women, these five friends dedicated themselves neither to feminism nor to socialism, but to sustaining careers and not husbands. Levy, however, ultimately becomes identified with failure, since Nord frames her argument thus: "Levy published two novels, a novella, three volumes of poetry, and numerous essays and short stories before she took her life in 1889 at the age of twenty-seven. Her suicide, and later Eleanor Marx's, remind us of the tenuousness of the late Victorian independent woman's life."[40] In contrast, Vadillo treats Levy as one would treat a nonsuicidal poet—as someone upheld for a distinctive achievement, accomplished at a time when neither she nor anyone else knew she would one day take her life.

Still, is Levy's "greatest achievement" the representation of mass transportation? A reader who had not encountered Levy's work would never guess there are other reasons to take an interest in her achievements, among which one must count her representations of suicide. Linda Hunt Beckman's biography of Levy partly corrects this tendency by devoting considerable attention both to the complexity of Levy's suicide and to the many ways in which Levy works with suicide alongside other major topics in her poetry. Even though Beckman presents an identity-based reading of Levy, this time as "depressive," she arrives at the rare understanding that Levy's death lacks a "definitive answer . . . not only because the record is forever incomplete . . . [but also because] the fatal act was overdetermined, resulting from the interplay between historical and cultural forces as well as from biology and happenstance."[41]

Charlotte Mew's poetry is similarly caught in the dichotomy between reformist identity reconstruction and poststructuralist anti-identity accounts. It is read by feminist scholars in relation to an additional dichotomy between Victorian and modernist literature—on the one hand, as part of a Victorian tradition of melancholy and, on the other hand, as the work of an impassioned, modernist, anti-Victorian radical. Thus Angela Leighton, in her foundational outline for a Victorian tradition of women poets, places Mew as its terminus: "Out of the essentially Victorian conditions of her life, with its moats and towers of enforced self-repression, Mew develops an aesthetic of poetry bleaker even than the mid-winter secrecy of her great predecessor [Christina Rossetti (1830–94)]."[42] In contrast, not mentioning Mew's suicide, Celeste Schenck—in the influential first edition of the anthology *The Gender of Modernism* (1990)— emphasizes Mew's "lesbian" passion and "sexual frankness overlooked by feminists, her radical politics and erotic choice."[43] It is difficult to square Schenck's portrait with Leighton's depiction of "absoluteness of self-denial and desolation of spirit." By comparison, some critical responses to Mew's poetry return us to an earlier feminist stance, reminding us that one need not dissociate suffering from feminist rebelliousness. In Eavan Boland's view, the "hidden story" of Mew is that of a woman so eccentric and estranged that she broke out of the "poetess" role of Victorian tradition: "[B]etween [the] rosy, tattered dustjacket and sturdy covers [of Mew's *Collected Poems*] burns and screams the music of a true dissident."[44]

Not only has Mew's poetry attracted more critical attention than that of the two other women writers discussed here, but also her death has been more prominently represented as a marker of her struggle with sexual identity, which Suzanne Raitt labels "queer": "[Mew] found it hard to say 'I.' . . . 'I am sorry to say I am.' . . . [Yet] she said 'I' to mortality with an act that can only be performed in the first person. Her death then seems to bring together three issues that have recently been explored in the writings of queer theorists: the question of sibling-loves [named "queer" by Eve Kosofsky Sedgwick], the tragedy of lesbian and gay suicides, and the negotiation of locutionary positions."[45] Raitt subsequently reads this death in the poetry. Indeed, by the end of the essay she nearly reverses her emphasis by suggesting that the poetry manifests "perhaps . . . Charlotte Mew's real 'queer death,' not the tragic suicide with which I opened" (though half of the essay involves analysis of the actual death): in the poetry, "sexual encounters take place on the borders between life and death, confusing the two states in a quasi-necrophiliac mode"—such encounters are "queer"; "[i]n Mew's work, queer desire is also a way of thinking about queer dying."[46] Despite the predictability with which Raitt and other scholars link the "mystery" of Mew's identity, on the one hand, with "lesbian" or "queer" identity (and only that identity) and, on the other hand, with the elusion of identity, this discussion (and Weisman's as well) opens some of the questions posed by "suicide," prodding readers toward more complex consideration of both the poets who killed themselves and the poems on suicide that they wrote.

If an interest in ethnic and sexual identity has provided the occasion for modern critics to reclaim Mew as a queer woman writer and Levy as Jewish writer critical of Anglo-Jewish culture, then the identification of Laurence Hope as transnational Anglo-Indian "translator" will probably help her work wriggle into public view. (Born in England, Hope lived much of her life in India, and she presented her poems as "translations" of Indian love lyrics.) And if Levy's suicide can be attributed to her marginality as a Jewish woman intellectual, and Mew's inscribed as queer, Hope's demise—because she killed herself shortly after her husband's passing—is linked, on the one hand (the Indian), with suttee and, on the other hand (the Western), with Sappho's legendary plunge to death. Travel writer Lesley Blanch begins her narration of this suicide with a caveat: "[T]here were none of the legendary trappings of death in the orient—of some carved jade poison phial, the thrust of a curved dagger, or the ceremonial of Suttee, the widow's immolation on her husband's funeral pyre." Nonetheless, Blanch invites us to imagine just such a scene:

"Once, Hindu widows on their last journey to the funeral pyre, flower-hung and adorned as brides, dipped their hand in a jar of red pigment and on leaving their house, imprinted their mark on the lintel of the door. . . . Laurence Hope, so steeped in Indian tradition, left no such mark. Only her poems. . . ."[47]

When Blanch first mentions Hope's suicide, she is at a loss for an explanation, and so she turns to astrology, for which Blanch claims the authority of Indian tradition:

> Sometimes, puzzled by the inconsistencies of a character, or by conjecture, convictions, even, which do not seem to tally with facts, I have turned to astrology for clarification. The East has always regarded the casting of horoscopes as an exact science. In the India of tradition, and even today, few marriages are considered suitable unless the horoscope of bride and bridegroom, and the chosen day are all propitious. In the case of Laurence Hope, being unable to obtain the precise hour of birth, only a Speculative Chart could be made. Having insufficient data the astrologer assumed the birth-hour to be after sunset, since this fitted the known facts of the life. Marriage, writing success, elements of secrecy, violent emotions and suicide were all indicated on a chart thus timed. . . . The urge for unconventionality in many forms is shown by Uranus, placed so that the emphasis is especially connected with the sex life.[48]

While Blanch provides a more detailed account of Hope's life even than this, these sentences alone dramatize the processes of speculation and mythologization that characterize much of the writing on suicidal writers. No matter how speculative, such mythologization is also always grounded in, and thus fixes, these poets' culturally designated identities.

Less sentimental observers, like Thomas Hardy (1840–1928)—who refrained from linking her death and her Indian "translations" to Hindu tradition—hardly refrained from identifying Hope's death with the "passion" of her poetry, its "Sapphic fervour." In Hardy's words, "[T]he tragic circumstances of her death seem but the impassioned closing notes of her impassioned effusions."[49] Similarly, in 1918 Harold Herbert Williams remarked: "The capacity for intense passion and regret, reflected in her writings, was illustrated in her last act, suicide."[50] Contradictions emerge in Williams's more detailed discussion, but he proceeds as if unconcerned, perhaps because "intensity" (or "youth" or "eagerness") explains it all for him: "The passion and fire of Laurence Hope's lyric inspiration is astonishing," alongside the "melancholy and eager pessimism underl[ying] all her work"; "her temper . . . [is] often melancholy, grave, severe," and her "youth and its passionate joy in loving [are] the chief themes of her song."[51]

The manner in which Levy, Mew, and Hope killed themselves is not a matter of extensive speculation. But the urge to explain why both the men and women poets killed themselves tends to be wild, even while a countervailing urge presses commentators to end the questions by establishing a single primary motive, by making the death consistent with the life, and by finding a genetic linkage with the writer's cultural and gendered position. Even the most sophisticated critics generally find themselves explaining the poet's death in terms provided by what appears to them most marked about the poet's identity; moreover, they describe the poetry in terms provided by the death, without pausing to question the assumptions they possess about suicide. Once the legend making is set aside, it remains to be seen how the poetry might profitably be read, yet the question of suicide stands, potentially, as among the most socially engaged and intriguing themes worth tracing, a theme that yields many more insights when critics approach it as a question than when they take it simply as another identity tag.

IV

While I am hardly the first critic to contest the biographical mythologization of the men poets or the only scholar to warn against a facile imposition of singular identity on the women poets, no one to my knowledge has focused on what these writers have contributed to a discourse on suicide. A number of their poems dwell on the emotional and philosophic, rhetorical and social, as well as ethical and physical, processes and dilemmas posed by self-destructive acts or by the actualities of suicide itself. This is not to claim that any of these poets wrote exclusively either about self-destruction or in a self-destructive mood. This is far from the case;

what they wrote tells us about much more than biographical doom. It is necessary to take emotion and mood (or what critics have begun to theorize as "affect") seriously, to see how these poets grapple with the emotions associated with "pessimism" as a matter of intellectual interest, not solely as defeatism or transparently as expressivism.[52]

Thus I would not be the only person to defend Ernest Dowson against the importation of Arthur Symons's "delicate" poet directly into the poems. Considerably more criticism has been dedicated to Dowson's work than to that of the other male poets discussed here. Yet as long as some of the anthologies used in colleges remain in circulation, it will be difficult to dislodge the view that Dowson's is merely wispy mood poetry. Take, for example, Walter H. Houghton and G. Robert Stange's account of Dowson's poems: "[T]he best known and most characteristic . . . such as the famous 'Non sum qualis eram' [1891] . . . create a mood of tender disenchantment. . . . [M]uch of the effect is the result of Dowson's use of vague, mood-creating words—lilies, roses, pale, desolate."[53] The task of analyzing Dowson's "moods" entails direct engagement with what Houghton and Stange, more articulately, call the poet's "front[ing] the threat of time and change with sardonic epicureanism"—in other words, the poet's deft conceptualizations, sensual evocation, and ironic reenactments of temporal belatedness and antiworldly worldliness. In a study of literary constructions of suicide, Dowson's verse merits close scrutiny for its intriguingly complex attention to ephemera and, in a poem like "Villanelle of the Poet's Road" (1899), for its canny twists of the carpe diem trope, such that the "now" becomes a matter of an interminably living death: "Wine and woman and song, / Three things garnish our way: / Yet is day over long."[54]

Lionel Johnson is more likely than Ernest Dowson to draw sober criticism of the sort that outlines his impressive affinities with classical, Renaissance, and neoclassical poets. But again critics tend to gloss self-destruction as (predictable) mood: "A sense of pathos," B. Ifor Evans observes, "clings around Lionel Johnson's life, strengthened by the elegiac vein of his poetry and by his own consciousness of fate's irony. The lines which preface his Winchester Prize poem seem to symbolize his life to the end."[55] (Interestingly, the epigraph that Evans refers to as "prefac[ing]" Johnson's poem comes from the American Walt Whitman: a poet renowned for his optimistic vision of a democratic humanity and its future possibilities.) Alternatively, scholars treat Johnson's accomplishment as a "narrow" one that rapidly diminishes when, in Ian Fletcher's words, "his curiously solitary spirit succeeds in recording some few moments of painful insight before the advent once again of 'weeping clouds: / Dimness, and airy shrouds.'"[56] The conventional trope of "dimness," however, unconventionally operates here as a dream threshold (or mediating term) between the chiasmic, transposed, and blended opposites of "weeping clouds" and "airy shrouds." For many critics, such as Barbara Charlesworth, the problem of the poetry amounts to the Eliotic flaw of a Hamlet-like personality, a lack of self-coherence between ("weeping") flesh and ("airy") spirit: "Even when all these things have been considered, however, we can say that Lionel Johnson was, after all, a 'Decadent' in that he suffered a self-division which he could not resolve, a fragmentation of his personality which finally destroyed him."[57] But was it "fragmentation of his personality which finally destroyed him"? Or is it the case that the intimate relations between the forms and thematics of "fragmentation" and those of "destruction" are expressly in need of analysis in Johnson's verse?

Ironically, John Davidson is both the one nearly certain suicide in this group of men and the one poet whose suicidal themes critics have sometimes constructed as "heroic." Although the serious, non-Yeats-inflected criticism on Davidson is sharply divided between those impressed by Davidson's vitalism and those impressed by the misery preceding his suicide, both groups are influenced by his heroic personae. Davidson's often performative ballads and dramatic monologues, his Nietzschean philosophy, and his public demeanor were continually characterized as, if anything, too "vital" and "robust," possessing "a burliness of constitution"; the books were made of "plain, honest, dark blue buckram," the personality in Davidson's letter writing was "abrasive" and "cantankerous."[58] Neither F. G. Atkinson nor Derek Stanford sees Davidson's anti-Decadent persona as essentially suicidal. For such readers, the poet's approach, I would suggest, is too "manly" for the term "suicidal," despite the counter-discourse of suicide as defiant choice that survived even during the Christian nineteenth century. In Davidson's best-known poem, "Thirty Bob a Week" (1894), the working-class urban speaker, who complains of exploitation by the rich, reaches a memorable conclusion: "And we fall, face forward, fighting, on the deck."[59] Yet critics overlook that moment in their attention to the poem's message about class struggle. Their emphasis on manliness is exemplified in the words that conclude T. S. Eliot's 1961 tribute to Davidson: "[I]n everything that Davidson wrote I recognize a real man, to be treated not only with . . . respect but with homage."[60]

Other critics, however, suggest that the self-destructive themes often appearing in Davidson's work anticipated his suicide. So it should come as no surprise to find George MacBeth, in his *Penguin Book of Victorian Verse,* writing about a poem he does not even reprint in his anthology: "Good shorter poems by Davidson . . . include . . . the dreamlike ballad 'A Runnable Stag' [1905], with its curious foreboding of his own suicide by drowning."[61] Davidson's balladic fantasy and colloquial Scots account of a hunting scene reaches the climax of its twenty-mile pursuit with the stag "never caught alive" because at the last moment he was possessed by "a wonderful vision of sleep." The stag foresaw himself, "[a] runnable stag in a jewelled bed, / Under the sheltering ocean dead"; so "a fateful hope lit up his eye," and he ran, followed by three hundred men, until he made his "escape on the evening tide, / Far out till he sank in the Severn Sea." Having escaped the hunters, "[t]he stag, the buoyant stag, the stag . . . slept at last."[62] While an excellent poem, this is not the sort of work one normally looks at for autobiography, and it represents as impetuous a choice to kill oneself (rather than be caught and killed) as one might find. Even so, thanks to Davidson's not infrequent representations of suicide in his plays and in the verse-books he called testaments and the end he gave his life of death at sea (though he also appears, prior to his plunge, to have taken a fatal gunshot to his head), his biographers and critics recur to "A Runnable Stag" for evidence of Davidson's attitude toward self-murder.

This is not to argue that "A Runnable Stag" and other poems by Davidson have nothing to add to discourses of suicide. On the contrary, the strikingly defiant story about this "kingly," virile beast with his threefold antlers indicates a significant shift from the "connoisseurship" (Davidson's term) of death in Decadent poetics to a more modern, spare, and tragicomic shock effect. In his 1972 biography of Davidson, Carroll Peterson titles a section with the paradox "Suicide: The Final Triumph of the Will to Live," and he writes specifically of "A Runnable Stag": "There is something in us, in me at least, which grudgingly admires such courage."[63] If we do admire such courage, it is because Davidson's poem means for us to, not because this is the allowable Anglo-American response to suicide.

David Perkins echoes the popularized understanding of Laurence Hope when he says that she wrote "lyrics of intense erotic passion, set in India . . . exotic, oppressive, and sadistic—recall[ing] the Decadence"; she was like "a decadent, female Kipling," and her work had an extra, "almost pornographic interest" for some readers.[64] As Edward Marx observes, thanks to Amy Woodforde-Finden's "extremely popular musical setting," these poems "for decades entice[d] listeners with their distinctive suggestion of erotic strangulation and exotic scenery."[65] Even independent of these songs, Hope's poems captured some critical acclaim and popularity, though they also received their share of criticism for indelicacy. But, as Williams suggests, Hope's "intensity" mixes fierce appetites and heated energies with "youthfulness" and "joy," "gravity and severity," "pessimism" and "eagerness."

Moreover, as Anindyo Roy warns us, readers need to reflect carefully on the fact that Hope's English audience wished to see her as an exotic Anglo-Indian Dowson-esque Kipling, lusting sadomasochistically—as in her best-known poem, "Kashmiri Song" (1902). Here the poetic voice, longing for "[p]ale hands, pink tipped, like Lotus buds that float," avows, "I would have rather felt you round my throat, / Crushing out life, than waving me farewell!"[66] Roy's point is that the critical absorption of Hope's work into a British tradition ignores the ways Hope's interest in Indian culture resists easy assimilation. In order to resituate the emotional and sexual play within her verse, Roy explicates Hope's multiple Indian personae and signatures, all of which destabilize gender. In particular, Roy identifies the poet's affiliation with the *bhakti* tradition and emotion-rich *viraha* (*viraha* is "longing caused by separation," as opposed to "self-disciplining 'yoga'" in *bhakti* poetry).[67] These Eastern modes have precious little to do with Western views about what constitutes a "tragic," "exotic," or "sadistic" life or death.

Thus a poem like "Memory" (1902) would to a Western reader appear excessively Paterian and self-dramatizing in effect:

> Every curve of that beauty is known to me,
> Every tint of that delicate roseleaf skin,
>   And these are printed on every atom of me,

Burnt in on every fibre until I die.
And for this, my sin,
I doubt if ever, though dust I be,
The dust will lose the desire,
The torment and hidden fire,
Of my passionate love for you.[68]

The Paterian aesthetic seems especially excessive and self-dramatizing in a portrait of an exotic foreign erotics in which "burning" is imagined to be literal as well as figurative. But within a *bhakti* context, "Memory" is more interesting for the lack of specificity (in gender or name) of the poetic "I"—the poem is addressed to a female "Aziza whom I adore"—and for its enactment of feminine *viraha*. To return to Roy's reading, rather than seeking mastery of self through a "masculine" and (in its appropriated forms) "imperialis[tic]" yogic asceticism, the "I" of these poems recognizes separation as "the condition of desire": "[S]eparated from the divine presence, the hearer cannot resist its 'charms.'"[69] Similarly, the Western reader might see in "Stars of the Desert" (1903) the sort of poetic cliché that would be edited out of a freshman poem today: "The hungry soul within me burning, burning, / As the stars burn throughout the Eastern night."[70] Roy explains, however, that "the speaker is the night watchman who watches over the sleeping male Akram, separated from him by 'Only the walls of one thin tent of canvas.'"[71] Thus "Stars of the Desert" is "a poem about unrequited love" that "links the 'I' and 'you' spectrally through the description of the play of shadows in the night."[72]

Yet one also needs to consider the way that such effects oscillate in Hope's poetry. Edward Marx quotes Hope's poem "The Temple Dancing Girl" (1902), which climaxes with these striking lines:

Yet, make it not too long, nor too intense
My thirst; lest I should break beneath the strain,
And the worn nerves, and over-wearied sense,
Enjoy not what they spent themselves to gain.[73]

Responding to these lines the Indian-Anglo poet Sarojini Naidu (1879–1949)—a writer, as Marx observes, who "hop[ed] to be the poet of the mysterious East that [Edmund] Gosse [1849–1928] and Symons wanted her to be"—found the "speaker's [erotic] instructions . . . 'vulgar!'"[74] But Hope's lines hardly seem more vulgar or more instructive than conventional renderings of sensual implosion in fin-de-siècle poetry. Moreover, while oscillating in effect between the scandalous and the conventional, as well as between an untranslatable, transgressive Eastern sensibility and a Western normative sensuality, Hope insinuates some irony into this erotic scene, an irony both decadently affect-laden and dramatically situational. We can look at these lines in the context of the work of Baudelaire, Swinburne, and Dowson, in addition to that possibly of Indian *bhakti*. In the context of Western aesthetic verse, these lines resituate fin-de-siècle angst-ridden world-weariness both as an ingredient of a moment just beyond the point when one can no longer endure sexual frustration and as a threat delivered to a lover likely to overdo lovemaking.

In study after study of Mew's poems, as in discussions of Hope's verse, scholars take notice of the dead, claiming—as Schenck does—that "ecstasy and death" are inextricable.[75] Even in the midst of Schenck's project to reclaim Mew's "surprisingly radical politics" of "female sexuality," the epithet "morbid" slips in.[76] In Mew's "The Forest Road" (1916), Schenck maintains, an "image of double suicide . . . closes the poem [and] marks a mutual female climax as well":[77]

> lie you there
> Dear and wild heart behind this quivering snow
> With two red stains on it: and I will strike and tear
> Mine out, and scatter it to yours.[78]

(Schenck is careful not to make this the climax of her analysis, which ends instead with Mew's "appreciation of female sexuality, in both benign and threatening manifestations, [as] at the heart of her best poetry.")[79] If only because of the enmeshment of life and love with death in this verse, critics like Suzanne Raitt and Dennis Denisoff boldly consider Mew's writing as offering a challenge to the hierarchical privileging of vitality over morbidity and to any absolute separation of the one from the other. Denisoff writes that "Mew herself was a lesbian," whose "unique contribution to the genre of graveyard poetry encourages delegitimized and inchoate identities to push and to prod against the enclosures within which conventional society has attempted to confine them"; thus poems like "In

Nunhead Cemetery" (1916) "empower . . . the grave-site with an almost human agency."[80] Still, Mew's poetry is deeply mixed, as Hope's is, with varied moods, and there is so much loss and death that it defies containment by even such a taboo-breaking coinage as "queer death."

Tempting as it may be to position Mew as the culminating point in a development of suicidal poetry because of her chronological position as the last of these 1890s suicidal poets, she does not reach—as Leighton would suggest—"an absoluteness of self-denial and desolation of spirit which are new" or "develop . . . an aesthetic of a poetry bleaker" than anything preceding it.[81] Even in its sexual ghost stories (as in "A Quoi Bon Dire" [1916]), its riveting retrievals of voices from beyond the grave or at its edge (as in "In Nunhead Cemetery"), its close scrutiny of many dead inhabitants of the earth (whether stillborn or aborted babies in "Saturday Market" [1921] or rats and trees in "The Trees Are Down" [1923]), Mew's poetry is less bleak, less absolute in desolation of spirit than that of other fin-de-siècle poets. Nor does her work epitomize the poetry of self-murder, since most of it is far less direct than that of several of her predecessors in its development of thoughts about suicide, more indirect in its narratives of what Christian tradition calls "the dark night of the soul" preceding the "carrion comforts" of self-immolation. If anyone holds the crown in this history, it is Amy Levy, along with her major precursor James Thomson.

What we might call the "affect" of hopelessness would seem unavoidable in any discussion of Thomson's verse, including the most discussed of his poems, the ambitious long poem *The City of Dreadful Night* (1874). But because his critics have been unable to ascribe value to such affect, they have assiduously avoided it. The focus of David Seed's recent article, for example, is the poem's unsparingly skeptical treatment of Christian symbolism, which enables him to say almost nothing about suicide; and Seed expressly argues that "a label like 'pessimist' . . . tends to hypostatise a general tone without examining the symbolic procedures of the work in question."[82] "*The City*," Seed adds, "is far more complex than an expression of hopelessness. This would reduce it to a Victorian tone-lyric writ large."[83] While Thomson's poem remains demanding in its symbolic and intellectual resources ("pessimism" itself was grounded for Thomson in crucial philosophical precedents, especially Arthur Schopenhauer's *Studies in Pessimism* and its arguments about suicide[84]), critics like Seed imply that an "expression of hopelessness" cannot be intricate, that a "tone-lyric" or representation of affect is necessarily vague and of little interest.

With aims similar to Seed's, in his book-length study of *The City of Dreadful Night* Henry Paolucci writes that Thomson "thanked his earliest critic for treating [the poem] 'simply and fairly on its own literary merits,'" that is, "without obloquy or protesting cant." Paolucci cautions against a reader who is "apt to imagine that he hears in its opening lines—'Lo, thus, as prostrate, "In the dust I write / My heart's deep languor and my soul's sad tears"'—an irrepressible cry wrenched from the poet's own agonized heart, despite the fact that they contain literally quoted the words of Shakespeare's *Titus Andronicus,* begging for the lives of his sons."[85] But Thomson displaced those lines from Shakespeare's tragedy into a context in which any desire to "beg for life" is itself dead. On occasion, Thomson's speaker begs instead for no more pain and for death. Moreover, the poetic voice is explicit about the reader for whom the poem is written: "If any cares for the weak words here written, / It must be some one desolate, Fate-smitten, / Whose faith and hope are dead, and who would die."[86] Because the speaker writes "weak words" for "some one desolate," there also linger throughout the poem important questions about the reader: Can a reader exist for this poem? Or would such a person be dead to its language and the world?

Thus in the lines that follow, the poet is not making the assertion that Paolucci would place in his mouth:

> no secret can be told
> To any who divined it not before:
> None uninitiate by many a presage
> Will comprehend the language of the message.[87]

Paolucci would have the poet say "that full appreciation of his work is possible only for those who know the tradition on which he was nurtured."[88] On the contrary, this poem is just as eloquent about the unspeakability, hence unhearability, of pain ("In helpless impotence to try to fashion / Our woe in living words howe'er uncouth"[89]) as it is about the ways in which pain is produced and sought by suicidal people. Thomson's speaker perforce seeks traces of speech about pain in prior poems, yet continually gives up on that search and resorts to metaphor, allegory, symbol, anecdote, and parable—all of which are versions of the literary, thereby intransigently distant from the literal.

At the end, Thomson's speaker turns his back on the poem's most elaborate (and most frequently analyzed) symbol—a verbal reconstruction of Albrecht Dürer's "Melencolia"—and declares:

> But as if blacker night could dawn on night,
>   With tenfold gloom on moonless night unstarred,
> A sense more tragic than defeat and blight,
>   More desperate than strife with hope debarred,
> More fatal than the adamantine Never
> . . . .
> That all the oracles are dumb or cheat
>   Because they have no secret to express;
> That none can pierce the vast black veil uncertain
> Because there is no light beyond the curtain;
>   That all is vanity and nothingness.[90]

He seeks closure to this poem's impossibilities through signifiers of sheer negation piled on negation. Despite its metaphors, its allegorical landscapes, its anti-Christian parables and sermons, the poem ultimately becomes—as Jerome McGann has suggested—an "anti-myth [that] is self-destructive by its very nature."[91] Even so, in spite of such negation, Thomson's *The City of Dreadful Night* has so much to say about the psychology of depression and such powerful means of conveying it—even if suicide itself cannot be experienced genuinely in the imagination—that suicide's emotional and mental thresholds are exhaustively researched.

Some critics who have found themselves captivated by Thomson's great poem have recognized its obvious emotionalism. Their defenses of it, however, have too often endeavored to retrieve it by elevating the verse out of the realm of feeling and into the realm of thought (or philosophy) and vision (or literary symbolism). But nothing is more complex than emotion or more challenging to analysis; and any reader not tone deaf must find Thomson's poem among the most moving she or he has read on pain. Thomson's most important woman successor, Amy Levy, sharply perceived this poetry's value. One of her own most significant poems was probably written with Thomson's death in mind. Soon after her essay "James Thomson: A Minor Poet" appeared in 1883, Levy published the dramatic monologue "A Minor Poet" (1884). As Linda Hunt Beckman and Cynthia Scheinberg have observed, by using the word "minor" Levy means not only to challenge our modern canonical assumptions about "minor" versus "major" but also to evoke something like our contemporary "minority"; for, as Levy explains in her essay on Thomson, he achieves greatness in his verse, not by seeing things "whole," as Matthew Arnold advises, but by seeing sharply a particular facet of a whole and seeing it intensely.[92] Thomson himself identified with the working class. But I would add that this title also suggests the "minor key" of music, for the poet whom Levy ventriloquizes is as much the melancholic poet as he is a man marginalized by social and economic failure.

"A Minor Poet," Scheinberg points out, is an innovative double dramatic monologue with an "epilogue" in which a second inner speech in the first-person occurs, articulated by a second speaker—a suicide survivor, who finishes the poem.[93] True to the dramatic-monologue form, the second speaker, Tom Leigh, can neither overhear nor speak directly to his fellow monologist—that is, the anonymous "minor poet"; indeed, the "minor poet" is dead before Tom Leigh begins his epilogue. Yet a posthumous figure does direct his speech, as if telepathically, to Tom Leigh; as if in continued dialogue with Tom, he ("the minor poet") recalls what Tom had said about his previous suicide attempts and responds. In the second monologue, Tom Leigh replies, in his mind, to his friend, whom he will never see again. But in fact his friend has not left even a suicide note; so only the writer and reader have access to what "the minor poet" was thinking and intending. Or do we?

This elaborate double monologue calls attention to its fictionality, to the act of imagining what the "minor poet" might have thought and what Tom might have said. Simultaneously, Levy's poem sets itself in dialogue with two poetic precursors. First, it seems unlikely that the choice of the name "Leigh" is a coincidence, as it associates Tom Leigh with the famously humbled poet "Aurora Leigh" and her social worker cousin "Romney Leigh" of Elizabeth Barrett Browning's 1856 epic *Aurora Leigh*. Second, "Tom" echoes "Thomson," offering a working-class nickname in lieu of a more formal signature, such as "James." Tom presents himself (if without direct reference to the mythology) as an Echo to his now-dead friend's

Narcissus (Tom indeed regurgitates one of the most common Victorian judgments of suicides, that they are narcissistic or, in Victorian parlance, "self-centered").[94] Named only as "a minor poet," however, the first speaker cannot rise to the status of a Narcissus, but remains just another "Anon," representative of all those lost poets who never gained an authorial name or reputation of their own. Meanwhile, both the "Leigh" and any echo we might catch of "Thomson" in this "Tom" elicit identification of the poet of the first monologue with the elegist/epilogist of the second, as if they were two sides of the same self. The suicide, "Anon," the poet, and the suicide survivor—which, we may wonder, is which?

Unfortunately, if this poem was intended to recall James Thomson, then its most radical act is to represent him as a deliberate suicide. There is no record, so far as I am aware, that Thomson tried to kill himself: a premise with which the poem begins, as (in its first line) he raises the phial to his lips. Thanks to Levy's growing fame in our own time, the legend of Thomson as a suicide is likely to grow stronger, given a fresh twist by what we know of Levy's self-murder by inhaling charcoal fumes in 1889.

On the heels of Symons's and Yeats's mythologizations of the suicidal fin-de-siècle poet, twentieth-century studies of authors as suicides burgeoned, until they became, as they are today, a staple of the modern understanding of authorial identity, especially in relation to the value and meaning attributed to the works of particular authors—such as Virginia Woolf, John Berryman, Sylvia Plath, and Anne Sexton. What this chapter's survey of suicide in critical commentaries on 1890s poets discloses are some of the critical hazards involved in judging writers' works by their supposed or actual acts of self-murder. A group of authors who were directly engaged with the discourse of suicide has suffered from reductive applications of the suicide as identity tag, from defensive backward glances by the poets who survived them, and from modern hesitation to take the emotion of hopelessness as a topic worthy of analysis in its own right.

Notes

1. Roland Barthes, "The Death of the Author" (1968), in *Image-Music-Text*, ed. and trans. Stephen Heath (New York: Hill and Wang, 1977), 142–48; "What Is an Author?" (1969), trans. Josué Harari in *Textual Strategies: Perspectives in Post-Structuralist Criti-*

cism, ed. Harari (Ithaca, NY: Cornell University Press, 1979), 141–60; Jacques Derrida, *Of Grammatology* (1967), trans. Gayatri Chakravorty Spivak (Baltimore: Johns Hopkins University Press, 1976).

2. Suicidology is now a large field. For a useful introduction to it and to its elusive multiplicities, see Edwin S. Shneidman, *Comprehending Suicide: Landmarks in 20th-Century Suicidology* (Washington, DC: American Psychological Association, 2001). For cultural studies of suicide perceived as an "epidemic" in the late nineteenth century, see Barbara T. Gates, *Victorian Suicide* (Princeton, NJ: Princeton University Press, 1988); and John Stokes, "'Tired of Life': Letters, Literature, and the Suicide Craze," in *In the Nineties* (Chicago, IL: University of Chicago Press, 1989), 115–43. A comprehensive study of the statistics of suicide in the nineteenth century is Olive Anderson's *Suicide in Victorian and Edwardian England* (Oxford: Clarendon Press, 1987). Most widely recognized as the first theoretical work in the field of sociology is Emile Durkheim's *Suicide: A Study in Sociology* [*Le Suicide*, 1897], trans. John A. Spaulding and George Simpson, ed. Simpson (NY: Free Press, 1951). Durkheim's work, however, actually built on prior statistical and social studies of suicide, especially in France and Germany in the nineteenth century. In England, four major works should be noted: the English translation of the Italian scholar Henry Morselli's *Suicide: An Essay on Moral Statistics* (London: C. Kegan Paul, 1881), which includes statistics from England; and three works by English medical men—S.A.K. Strahan, *Suicide and Insanity* (London: Swan Sonnenschein, 1893); W. Wynn Westcott, *Suicide: Its History, Literature, Jurisprudence, Causation, and Prevention* (London: H. K. Lewis, 1885), and Forbes Winslow, *The Anatomy of Suicide* (London: Renshaw, 1840).

3. [For a parallel discussion, see Jerusha McCormack, "Engendering Tragedy: Toward a Definition of 1890s Poetry," in this volume, chapter 1; editor's note.]

4. John Gawsworth, "The Dowson Legend," *The Transactions of the Royal Society of Literature*, n.s., 17 (1938): 93–123.

5. Arthur Symons, "A Literary Causerie: On a Book of Verses," *Savoy* 3–4 (1896): 91.

6. Symons, "Literary Causerie," 92.

7. Symons, "Literary Causerie," 92, 93.

8. Symons, "Literary Causerie," 92, 93.

9. Symons, "Literary Causerie," 92.

10. Symons, "Literary Causerie," 91.

11. Symons, "Literary Causerie," 93.

12. Symons, "Literary Causerie," 93.

13. William David Schaefer, *James Thomson (B.V.): Beyond the City* (Berkeley and Los Angeles: University of California Press, 1965), viii.

14. For influential early biographical studies, see Bertram Dobell, "Memoir," in *A Voice from the Nile and Other Poems,* by James Thomson, ed. Dobell (London: Reeves and Turner, 1884), 1:vii–xlix; Gordon G. Flaws, "James Thomson: A Study," *Secular Review,* 24 June 1882, 40–42, and 1 July 1882, 106–8; Henry S. Salt, *The Life of James Thomson ("B.V."),* 3rd ed. (1889; reprint, London: Watts, 1914).

15. Richard Pawley, *Secret City: The Emotional Life of Victorian Poet James Thomson (B.V.)* (Lanham, MD: University Press of America, 2001), 253.

16. Schaefer, *James Thomson (B.V.),* 6, 32, 34.

17. Schaefer, *James Thomson (B.V.),* 34, 35.

18. Schaefer, *James Thomson (B.V.),* 36.

19. Murray G. Pittock, "The Poetry of Lionel Johnson," *Victorian Poetry* 28, nos. 3–4 (1990): 44.

20. G. A. Cevasco, *Three Decadent Poets: Ernest Dowson, John Gray, and Lionel Johnson: An Annotated Bibliography* (New York: Garland, 1990), 255.

21. Cevasco, *Three Decadent Poets,* 267, 266.

22. On critics' uncertainty about Johnson's homosexual "activity," see for example Cevasco, *Three Decadent Poets,* 261; and Ian Fletcher, preface to *The Collected Poems of Lionel Johnson,* 2nd ed., ed. Fletcher (New York: Garland, 1982), xiii.

23. Richard Ellmann, *Oscar Wilde* (New York: Alfred A. Knopf, 1988), 323–24, 414; Lionel Johnson, "The Destroyer of a Soul," in *Collected Poems,* 74. Johnson had earlier written an enthusiastic poem in Latin celebrating the novel *Dorian Gray,* "In Honorem Doriani Creatorisque Eius" (1891), in *Collected Poems,* 209.

24. [Nicholas Frankel discusses the Rhymers' Club in this volume, chapter 4; editor's note.]

25. Barbara Charlesworth, "The Gray World of Lionel Johnson," *Carrell: Journal of the Friends of the University of Miami Library* 4, no. 2 (1963): 20.

26. W. B. Yeats, "*The Trembling of the Veil.* Book IV. The Tragic Generation" (1922), in *The Collected Works of William Butler Yeats,* vol. 3, ed. William H. O'Donnell and Douglas N. Archibald (New York: Scribner, 1999), 243, 244.

27. Yeats, "The Tragic Generation," 244.

28. Yeats, "The Tragic Generation," 244–45.

29. Yeats, "The Tragic Generation," 245.

30. Yeats, "The Tragic Generation," 245.

31. Yeats, "The Tragic Generation," 245.

32. T. S. Eliot wrote of his "peculiar reverence" for and "particular debt" to Davidson in the preface to *John Davidson: A Selection of His Poems,* ed. Maurice Lindsay (London: Hutchinson, 1961), xi–xii.

33. Most famously, see Sandra Gilbert and Susan Gubar, *The Madwoman in the Attic: The Woman Writer and the Nineteenth-Century Imagination* (New Haven, CT: Yale University Press, 1979), 51 passim; and the "feminine" writers in Elaine Showalter, *A Literature of Their Own: British Novelists from Brontë to Lessing* (Princeton, NJ: Princeton University Press, 1977); for a groundbreaking study of "dissociation" in the poetry of Victorian women writers (from the early 1890s), see Angela Leighton, *Victorian Women Poets: Writing against the Heart* (Charlottesville: University Press of Virginia, 1992), 3 passim.

34. For discussion of nineteenth-century women poets' fascination with Sappho—especially her suicide—see Margaret Reynolds, "'I Lived for Art, I Lived for Love': The Woman Poet Sings Sappho's Last Song," in *Victorian Women Poets: A Critical Reader,* ed. Angela Leighton (Oxford, UK: Blackwell, 1996), 277–306; and Yopie Prins, *Victorian Sappho* (Princeton, NJ: Princeton University Press, 1999).

35. Gates, *Victorian Suicide,* 125–30.

36. But see Lucy Hunt Beckman for a discussion of Levy's "homoerotic desire," in *Amy Levy: Her Life and Letters* (Athens: Ohio University Press, 2000), 7 passim; see also Emma Francis, "Amy Levy: Contradictions?—Feminism and Semiotic Discourse," in *Women's Poetry, Late Romantic to Late Victorian: Gender and Genre, 1830–1900,* ed. Isobel Armstrong and Virginia Blain (Basingstoke: Macmillan, 1999), 183–204.

37. Karen Weisman, "Playing with Figures: Amy Levy and the Forms of Cancellation," *Criticism* 43, no. 1 (2001): 60, 77.

38. Elaine Showalter, *Sexual Anarchy: Gender and Culture at the Fin de Siècle* (New York: Viking, 1990), 26.

39. Ana Parejo Vadillo, "Phenomena in Flux: The Aesthetics and Politics of Traveling in Modernity," in *Women's Experience of Modernity, 1875–1945,* ed. Ann Ardis and Leslie Lewis (Baltimore, MD: Johns Hopkins University Press, 2003), 203.

40. Deborah Epstein Nord, *Walking the Victorian Streets: Women, Representation, and the City* (Ithaca, NY: Cornell University Press, 1995), 185–86.

41. Beckman, *Amy Levy,* 6, 202.

42. Leighton, *Victorian Women Poets,* 267.

43. Celeste M. Schenck, "Charlotte Mew," in *The Gender of Modernism,* ed. Bonnie Kime Scott (Bloomington: Indiana University Press, 1990), 317.

44. Eavan Boland, "Charlotte Mew," *Brick* 67 (2001): 113. Boland refers here to *Collected Poems of Charlotte Mew* (London: Duckworth, 1953).

45. Suzanne Raitt, "Charlotte Mew's Queer Death," *Yearbook of Comparative and General Literature* 47 (1999): 72.

46. Raitt, "Charlotte Mew's Queer Death," 77–78.

47. Lesley Blanch, *Under a Lilac-Bleeding Star: Travels and Travelers* (New York: Athenaeum, 1964), 208.

48. Blanch, *Under*, 202.

49. [Thomas Hardy], "Laurence Hope," *Athenæum*, 29 October 1904, 591.

50. Harold Herbert Williams, *Modern English Writers: Being a Study of Imaginative Literature*, vol. 1 (1918; reprint, Port Washington, NY: Kennikat, 1970), 142.

51. Williams, *Modern English Writers*, 142, 144.

52. Probably the most influential theorist to bring "affect" to the forefront of recent critical discussion is Eve Kosofsky Sedgwick. See her collaboration with Adam Frank on the work of psychologist Silvan Tomkins, Sedgwick and Frank, eds., *Shame and Its Sisters: A Silvan Tomkins Reader* (Durham, NC: Duke University Press, 1995); and Sedgwick, *Touching Feeling: Affect, Pedagogy, Performativity* (Durham, NC: Duke University Press, 2003). A historically contextualized account of affect in early nineteenth-century women's poetry can be found in Isobel Armstrong, "The Gush of the Feminine: How Can We Read Women's Poetry of the Romantic Period?" in *Romantic Women Writers: Voices and Countervoices*, ed. Paula R. Feldman and Theresa M. Kelley (Hanover, NH: University Press of New England, 1995), 13–32.

53. Walter E. Houghton and G. Robert Stange, eds., *Victorian Poetry and Poetics* (Boston: Houghton Mifflin, 1968). Since its first publication in 1959, this anthology has been a standard textbook for Victorian poetry classes and is still available for classroom use today, though the popular second volume of *The Norton Anthology of English Literature* (first published in 1962 and covering nineteenth- and twentieth-century British literature) is now commonly used instead. *Victorian Poetry and Poetics* includes poetry by Wilde, Johnson, and Dowson (and no other poets discussed in this chapter) in a separate section on "The Aesthetic Movement" prefaced by selections from Yeats's autobiographies, while the most recent Norton volume selects poems by Wilde and Dowson and none of the other fin-de-siècle poets discussed here: see *The Norton Anthology of English Literature*, vol. 2, 7th ed., ed. M. H. Abrams et al. (New York: Norton, 2000).

54. Ernest Dowson, *The Poems of Ernest Dowson*, ed. Mark Longaker (Philadelphia: University of Pennsylvania Press, 1968), 110.

55. B. Ifor Evans, *English Poetry in the Later Nineteenth Century*, 2nd ed. (New York: Barnes and Noble, 1966), 409. The first edition of Evans's influential study appeared in 1933.

56. Ian Fletcher, preface to *Collected Poems*, lxxi; Lionel Johnson, "Mystic and Cavalier," in *Collected Poems*, 25.

57. Charlesworth, "Gray World," 21.

58. Richard Le Gallienne quoted in Derek Stanford, ed., *Three Poets of the Rhymers' Club: Ernest Dowson, Lionel Johnson, John Davidson* (Manchester: Carcanet Press, 1974), 27; Stanford, *Three Poets*, 23; and F. G. Atkinson, "John Davidson—Some Contributions to Standard Biography," *Notes and Queries* 22 (1975): 449–50.

59. John Davidson, *The Poems of John Davidson*, ed. Andrew Turnbull (Edinburgh: Scottish Academic Press, 1973), 1:65.

60. Eliot, preface to *John Davidson*, xii.

61. George MacBeth, ed., *The Penguin Book of Victorian Verse* (Harmondsworth, UK: Penguin, 1986), 343. MacBeth's widely circulated anthology first appeared in 1969: it includes the four male poets and none of the women poets discussed in this chapter.

62. Davidson, *Poems of John Davidson*, 1:160–61.

63. Carroll V. Peterson, *John Davidson* (New York: Twayne, 1972), 105.

64. David Perkins, *A History of Modern Poetry: From the 1890s to the High Modernist Mode* (Cambridge, MA: Harvard University Press, 1976), 193–94.

65. Edward Marx, "Decadent Exoticism and the Woman Poet," in *Women and British Aestheticism*, ed. Talia Schaffer and Kathy Alexis Psomiades (Charlottesville: University Press of Virginia, 1999), 147.

66. Laurence Hope, *Complete Love Lyrics* (New York: Dodd, Mead, 1955), 99.

67. Anindyo Roy, "'Gold and Bracelet, Water and Wave': Signature and Translation in the Indian Poetry of Adela Cory Nicolson," *Women: A Cultural Review* 13, no. 2 (2002): 153.

68. Hope, *Complete Love Lyrics*, 63–64.

69. Roy, "'Gold and Bracelet,'" 154–55.

70. Hope, *Complete Love Lyrics*, 239.

71. Roy, "'Gold and Bracelet,'" 158.

72. Roy, "'Gold and Bracelet,'" 158.

73. Hope, *Complete Love Lyrics*, 165.

74. Marx, "Decadent Exoticism," 141; Sarojini Naidu quoted in Marx, "Decadent Exoticism," 153.

75. Schenck, "Charlotte Mew," 317.

76. Schenck, "Charlotte Mew," 317, 318.

77. Schenck, "Charlotte Mew," 318.

78. Charlotte Mew, *Collected Poems and Selected Prose*, ed. Val Warner (New York: Routledge, 2003), 25.

79. Schenck, "Charlotte Mew," 318.

80. Dennis Denisoff, "Grave Passions: Enclosure and Exposure in Charlotte Mew's Graveyard Poetry," *Victorian Poetry* 38, no. 1 (2000): 125, 132.

81. Leighton, *Victorian Women Poets*, 267.

82. David Seed, "Hell Is a City: Symbolic Systems and Epistemological Scepticism in *The City of Dreadful Night*," in *Spectral Readings: Towards a Gothic Geography*, ed. Glennis Byron and David Punter (Basingstoke, UK: Macmillan, 1999), 88.

83. Seed, "Hell Is a City," 88.

84. Arthur Schopenhauer, *Studies in Pessimism*, ed. T. Bailey Saunders (London: Swan Sonnenschein, 1891). For Schopenhauer's influence on English intellectual culture, see Patrick Gardiner, *Schopenhauer* (Harmondsworth, UK: Penguin, 1963).

85. Henry Paolucci, *James Thomson's "The City of Dreadful Night": A Study of the Cultural Resources of Its Author and a Reappraisal of the Poem* (Wilmington, DE: Bagehot Council, 2000), 21, 13–14.

86. James Thomson, *Poems and Some Letters of James Thomson*, ed. Anne Ridler (Carbondale: Southern Illinois University Press, 1963), 177.

87. Thomson, *Poems and Some Letters*, 178.

88. Paolucci, *James Thomson's "The City,"* 154.

89. Thomson, *Poems and Some Letters*, 177.

90. Thomson, *Poems and Some Letters*, 204.

91. Jerome McGann, "James Thomson (B.V.): The Woven Hymns of Night and Day," *Studies in English Literature, 1500–1900* 3, no. 4 (1963): 505.

92. Amy Levy, "James Thomson: A Minor Poet," in *The Complete Novels and Selected Writings of Amy Levy*, ed. Melvyn New (Gainesville: University Press of Florida, 1993), 501; Beckman, *Amy Levy*, 104–5; Cynthia Scheinberg, "Canonizing the Jew: Amy Levy's Challenge to Victorian Poetic Identity," *Victorian Studies* 39, no. 2 (1996): 178–79.

93. Cynthia Scheinberg, "Recasting 'Sympathy and Judgment': Amy Levy, Women Poets, and the Dramatic Monologue," *Victorian Poetry* 35, no. 2 (1997): 183; Levy, "A Minor Poet," in *Complete Novels*, 370–77.

94. See, for example, E. K. Chambers, "Poetry and Pessimism," *Westminster Review* 138 (1892): 369, 373.

A WOMAN ON THE WILDE SIDE

Masks, Perversity, and Print Culture's Role in Poems by
"Graham R. Tomson"/Rosamund Marriott Watson

Linda K. Hughes

One of the many paradoxes of fin-de-siècle poetry is its insistence that aesthetic unity derives from the experience of fragmentariness. In Walter Pater's familiar statement, "To regard all things and principles of things as inconstant modes or fashions has more and more become the tendency of modern thought. . . . [I]n the mind of the observer . . . impressions unstable, flickering, inconsistent, . . . burn, and are extinguished with our consciousness of them."[1] Within Paterian impressionism, which conceives of experience as a series of discontinuous fragments, we can know and function only as masks—momentary formations that fade and shift with the moments that give rise to them. Formally, too, the fragment acquired fresh impetus when fin-de-siècle writers adopted the polished epigram as an end complete unto itself in fiction, drama, and poetry. Later, W. B. Yeats went so far as to claim that the poets associated with the Rhymers' Club, whose two collaborative volumes appeared in 1892 and 1894, attempted "to write like the poets of the Greek Anthology"—a collection of classical epigrams.[2] Less ambitiously, newspaper editors targeted minimally literate products of the 1870 Education Act with "tit-bits," and many poets rounded out their incomes by submitting anonymous (and autonomous) paragraphs to papers. Fragmentariness could also function as a radical ideology, a repudiation of traditional wholeness—which was premised on subjects that lived and moved and had their being in God and God's laws—in favor of masks and the experience of moments, whether epiphanic, hedonistic, mundane, or perverse.

As her shifting nomenclature might suggest, the poet whose career I examine—Graham R. Tomson from 1886 to 1894, Rosamund Marriott Watson from late 1894 until her death at fifty-one in 1911—exemplified such fragmentariness. Rather than declaring allegiance to aestheticism or to Decadence in her poetry, she promiscuously alternated between them—or embraced both at once. Her early villanelles, sonnets, and ballades were elegant executions of demanding verse forms that exemplified aestheticism's commitment to art for art's sake. Pledging oneself to the artifice of form itself implied self-conscious performance that opened a space between lyric utterance and authorial identity—a mask, in short. Her interest in fixing fleeting natural processes in poetic images likewise chimed with Paterian aestheticism and Pater's subjective impressionism. Decadence required that she take art for art's sake a step further, playing highly polished poetic style and form off transgressive content, especially sexually suggestive or blasphemous expression. This Decadent strategy multiplied masks (by providing new, perverse possibilities) and further destabilized poetic reference, since shocking content might signal social rebellion or merely literary performance. Decadence also forestalled readers' assumptions of poetic earnestness or the harmony of form with morally uplifting content; for readers, too, wholeness (and wholesomeness) gave way to fragmentariness, self-conscious performance, intensified artifice, and destabilizing frames of reference. As for the shocking content, it could be imported from France (for example, from Charles Baudelaire's *Les Fleurs du mal* [1857]), but it was more likely to be unsettling when it originated on London streets or in the privacy of English walled gardens.

In addition to adopting a range of poetic modes, Graham R. Tomson published art, literary, and fashion criticism as well as occasional paragraphs in periodicals, and in 1889 edited a selection of translations from the *Greek Anthology*. More radically, she was a heterosexual outlaw who celebrated agnostic hedonism in her poems—the impressionable nervousness of which led Katharine Tynan in 1892 to call Tomson "somewhat unstrung."[3] Her adoption of masks rather than a fixed identity and her exploration of sexual perversity are crucial to the two poems that I discuss in detail. But first an overview of her range of poetic modes and her associations with that theorist of masks, Oscar Wilde, is in order.

Tomson's early (and some later) work owes much to the Pre-Raphaelite poets. The epigraph of her first volume, *Tares*, published anonymously in 1884, was drawn from Dante Gabriel Rossetti's "He and I" in *The House of Life* (1870, revised 1881).[4] Like much of Rossetti's sequence, Tomson's lyrics trace the failure of love. "Hereafter," from Tomson's 1889 volume, recalls Rossetti's "The Blessed Damozel" (1850, revised 1870) but more overtly rejects heaven; her use of the sonnet also harks back to his writing, the sonnet's fixed rules here serving to counterpoint earth's delicious multiplicity and unfinished fragments:

> Shall we not weary in the windless days
> Hereafter, for the murmur of the sea,
> The cool salt air across some grassy lea?
> Shall we not go bewildered through a maze
> Of stately streets with glittering gems ablaze,
> Forlorn amid the pearl and ivory,
> Straining our eyes beyond the bourne to see
> Phantoms from out Life's dear, forsaken ways?
>
> Give us again the crazy clay-built nest,
> Summer, and soft unseasonable spring,
> Our flowers to pluck, our broken songs to sing,
> Our fairy gold of evening in the West;
> Still to the land we love our longings cling,
> The sweet, vain world of turmoil and unrest.[5]

"Hereafter," like "The Blessed Damozel," invokes the sacred spaces of heaven only to render them as drear voids haunted by restless human desire: admission to heaven is not a blessing but a curse of denied sensuous pleasure. Tomson's sonorities, her yoking of general emotions with sharp images ("Forlorn amid the pearl and ivory"), and her fluid movement across the lines and staves of an Italianate sonnet likewise recall Rossetti's achievement in *The House of Life*.

By comparison, the influence of Christina Rossetti emerges in Tomson's "An Enchanted Princess" (1891), which like "The Prince's Progress" (1866) depicts a failed lover's quest, and in the compression of later poems that represent subjectivity within the grave—for example, "Requiescat," first published in John Lane's controversial *Yellow Book* in April 1895. William Morris, too, helped inspire some early socialist lyrics and a feminist-socialist narrative drawn from the Prose Edda, "The Quern of the Giants" (1889, reprinted 1895).[6] Tomson turned to Swinburne, however, for the meter of "The Quern of the Giants," which was taken from his "Song in Time of Revolution, 1860" (1866); and her 1890 "A Ballad of the Were-Wolf," in which the apparently docile farm wife is also the monster who attacks her husband, owes something not only to the violent ferocity of Swinburne's "Dolores" (1866) but also to the carnage recorded in "The Bloody Son" (1866)—a ballad (like the "Were-Wolf") narrated in Scots dialect.

If Tomson proved responsive to Pre-Raphaelite aesthetics and politics, she also participated in the revival of fixed verse forms led by notably conservative poets, including Austin Dobson, Edmund Gosse, and Andrew Lang. She contributed a dozen ballades, triolets, and other forms to Gleeson White's *Ballades and Rondeaus* in 1887 (to which, it should be noted, Swinburne, Wilde, and A. Mary F. Robinson also contributed), and she continued to publish poems in Lang's regular column, "At the Sign of the Ship," in *Longman's Magazine* well into the 1890s. One such poem, "Sunset on Henna Cliff" (November 1892), shares Lang's penchant for nostalgia, although its last line betrays the aesthete's self-conscious artifice:

> Lapped in the low light of the westering sun,
> The wild gulls circle seaward one by one . . .
> And yon gaunt headland's massive masonry,
> Towering on high above the sea-birds' hold,
> Gleams like the Mystic Rose
> With dull rich dyes of amaranth and gold:
> . . . .
> A faint sea-fragrance dwells upon the air;
> Autumn's enchantment layeth hold on me,
> Stirring the sense to vaguest pageantry,
> To fitful memories of days so fair
> As no days ever were.[7]

Tomson first entered London literary networks under Lang's sponsorship (when Lang thought he was championing a new young man on the scene), yet she also quickly became the friend of Wilde. In November 1888 she debuted in the *Woman's World*—the largely feminist magazine that he edited from 1887 to 1889—with a lyric entitled "Birds of Passage." The next month, in the society journal *Queen,* Wilde mentioned Tomson as being among those women poets who had done "really good work in poetry."[8] Around this time Oscar Wilde and Constance Wilde also frequented the Tomsons' weekly gatherings at their home in St. John's Wood, where Graham R., a divorcée, wrote poems, and her second husband Arthur, a member of the New English Art Club, painted in his studio.[9] In the June 1889 number of his magazine, Wilde reviewed Tomson's *The Bird-Bride:* he termed her "one of our most artistic workers in poetry," and compared some of her lyrics to "'little carved ivories of speech.'"[10] The next month she published the first part of a two-part essay, "Beauty, from the Historical Point of View," in the *Woman's World,* discussing in one passage the same legend of a beautiful corpse Wilde had cited in his long critical essay "The Truth of Masks," the earliest version of which— titled "Shakespeare and Stage Costume"—appeared in the *Nineteenth Century* in 1885.[11] In September of that year Wilde allotted the cover of the *Woman's World* to New English Art Club member W. J. Hennessey's illustration of Tomson's poem "In Picardy," which appeared in that number (fig. 4). And when Wilde's novel *The Picture of Dorian Gray* appeared in an expanded single-volume edition in the spring of 1891, he presented a copy, now in the Johns Hopkins University Library, to "Graham Tomson, / from her friend / the author / May. / 91."[12]

Coulson Kernahan, the literary editor who worked closely with Wilde on the 1891 edition of *Dorian Gray,* confirmed the friendship between Wilde and Tomson,[13] although no trace survives in Wilde's *Complete Letters.* Their poems demonstrate a shared interest in impressionism and urban lyrics. Echoing the titles of some of the best-known paintings by James McNeill Whistler, his sometime friend, Wilde's 1881 "Impression du Matin" figures London as a "nocturne" of blue, gold, and gray, in which the dissipating shadows and morning fog disclose a prostitute produced by the city and as hardened as its streets. In 1889, in "A Symphony in Yellow," Wilde limns harmonies in yellow and green while tracing the restless movement of traffic, compared to which the flowing Thames is a static "rod of rippled jade."[14] Tomson's knowledge of impressionism came not only through Pater and Whistler but also through the

FIGURE 4. W. J. Hennessey, illustration of "In Picardy," by Graham R. Tomson, *Woman's World*, September 1889. Courtesy of the Bodleian Library, University of Oxford, shelf mark Walpole c.2, 562

New English Art Club and *Art Weekly*, a short-lived paper that she coedited with Arthur Tomson in 1890. One contributor to that paper explained: "[T]he ever-changing arrangement of light and shade, tone, colour, and amount of detail alternately revealed and obscured, put it wholly beyond the power of the mind to grasp [the sky] except as a whole, so the mind does not demand a completely veracious representation of it. The mind merely asks to be stirred to the act of realizing its truth by a sufficiently accurate impression of it."[15] Imagination and artifice, then, construct out of a surging stream of fragments the illusions of a sensory and aesthetic whole.

For a woman to apply such an impressionist technique to the city involved the risk of aligning herself with the prostitute that so memorably capped Wilde's poem. But like Amy Levy before her, Tomson opted to ignore this danger. She instead claimed the freedoms of Charles Baudelaire's *flâneur*, celebrated in his famous essay "The Painter of Modern Life" (1863), in lyrics that register restless female subjectivity abroad in the modern city. Painting, like Wilde, a color harmony out of the disparate components of the city and the fragmented glimpses it affords, Tomson puts herself in the street at the very outset of "In the Rain," first published in May 1890, and structures the poem according to a succession of fragmentary moments:

> Rain in the glimmering street—
> Murmuring, rhythmical beat;
> Shadows that flicker and fly;
> Blue of wet road, of wet sky,
> (Grey in the depths and the heights);
> Orange of numberless lights,
> Shapes fleeting on, going by.[16]

As the percipient artist of the piece, Tomson treats human beings as aesthetic objects to be arranged at will according to their shapes and sounds rather than as persons to whose emotional or sexual needs she must cater.

Tomson also rejects traditional feminine piety when she defamiliarizes a religious term like "nimbus" and applies it to city lights, a gesture as tainted and "prosaical" as the figures she describes:

Figures, fantastical, grim—
Figures, prosaical, tame,
Each with chameleon-stain,
Dun in the crepuscle dim,
Red in the nimbus of flame—
Glance through the veil of the rain.

Rain in the measureless street—
Vistas of orange and blue;
Music of echoing feet,
Pausing, and pacing anew.

This is, on the one hand, a brilliantly accurate rendition of urban crowds surging through gaslit streets on a rainy night, as precise an image of visual objects under specific conditions of atmosphere and light as those created by impressionist painters.[17] It is also, on the other hand, the height of artifice, each figure masked by the visual impression it creates in the poet's mind; and the poet perceives in the figures' movement an intricate, unpredictable dance to the strange music of pattering rain and sounds careering off pavement and walls. Technological artifice also helps create the scene:

Rain, and the clamour of wheels,
Splendour, and shadow, and sound;
Coloured confusion that reels
Lost in the twilight around.

In a superb analysis that forms part of her study of women poets, speed, and the aesthetics of modern urban transport, Ana Parejo Vadillo demonstrates that what strike the poet's perceiving eye in the poem's first half are precisely those impressions created by machines hurling through space.[18] The poet is not walking amid pedestrians but traveling along man-made streets via the transport networks of the modern city, where the natural phenomenon of rain is absorbed to and transformed by technology into a flickering light show. The poem's own insistent sound effects (its driving trimeter rhythm and alliterative echoes) reinforce the meeting of artifice and nature and their mutual transformation into something else. While the rhythm imitates rainfall, the poem's auditory effects are so insistent that they call attention to themselves *as* poetic artifice and contest the poem's striking visual palette; yet, taken together, the visual and auditory create the poem's panoply of "shadow" and "sound" and "[c]oloured confusion."

A speeding transit through London in the poem's first half ends with the usual disembarkation of passengers onto streets in the second. The poem, too, creates shifts in emphasis and pace. The caesuras after "Stark" and "Still," both of which impede forward movement, occur in lines that acknowledge the power of nature, of mortality, to overtake human technology and permanently end life's transit. But the poet no more touches on the natural than she invokes the supernatural, replacing the hope of heaven with the literary trope of the revenant:

> When I lie hid from the light,
> Stark, with the turf overhead,
> Still, on a rainy Spring night,
> I shall come back from the dead.
>
> Turn then and look for me here
> Stealing the shadows along;
> Look for me—I shall be near,
> Deep in the heart of the throng:
>
> Here, where the current runs rife,
> Careless, and doleful, and gay,
> Moving, and motley, and strong,
> Good in its sport, in its strife.

The Decadent revenant is typically a monstrous female that feeds on the blood of men (and so undoes sexual binaries by penetrating the male body), as in Théophile Gautier's "La Morte amoureuse" (1836), Pater's passage on La Giaconda in *Studies in the History of the Renaissance,* or, most famously, Bram Stoker's *Dracula* (1897). Tomson reworks this trope with considerable wit; her revenant expresses both the Decadent's sense of otherness and a sense of solidarity with the urban crowd's joys, sorrows, and disruptions.[19] The poet's promise to haunt later generations as an imaginative presence is a benign expression of every poet's hope. Yet the lines also introduce the uncanny into the poem, the unsettling thought that in every urban shadow there lurks the poet's voyeuristic ghost. Inviting yet dissonant, benign yet threatening, this specter is an aesthetic link to the transgressive *flâneuse* (or passenger) of the poem's first half, a means by which Tomson can unify the poem despite its disjunct moments.

In the final lines of "In the Rain," the poet's imaginative flight ends in an outburst of frustrated mortality and a paean to life itself: "Ah, might I be—might I stay— / Only for ever and aye, / Living and looking on life!" Unlike the greater Romantic lyric, featuring ascent and return, this fin-de-siècle urban impression travels along earth's surface and burrows beneath. In returning to the opening urban scene, this poet, like Keats in "Ode to a Nightingale," may be forced to confront death's sway, but there is no faulting art's inability to cheat fancy or any regret that transcendence is impossible, only an intensification of unresolved mortal, and specifically female, desire.

The expression of female desire is also central to "Chimaera," a far more transgressive poem. It is set in an urban garden, a liminal space between cloistered privacy and public streets. The speaker, similarly, is alone yet in the presence of a sphinxlike roadway as she awaits her lover in the borderland between night and day:

> The yellow light of an opal
> On the white-walled houses dies
> The roadway beyond my garden
> It glimmers with golden eyes.
>
> Alone in the faint spring twilight,
> The crepuscle vague and blue,
> Every beat of my pulses
> Is quickened by dreams of you.
>
> You whom I know and know not
> You come as you came before
> Here, in the misty quiet,
> I greet you again once more.

Welcome, O best belovèd—
Life of my life—for lo!
All that I ask you promise,
All that I seek you know.

The dim grass stirs with your footstep,
The blue dusk throbs with your smile;
I and the world of glory
Are one for a little while.
* * * * * * * * *
The spring sun shows me your shadow,
The spring wind bears me your breath,
You are mine for a passing moment,
But I am yours to the death.[20]

The sheer sounds of the poem—its liquid and susurrous consonants punctuated by plosives—suggest the murmurs, whispers, and quickened heartbeats of desire, while its languorous, sensual rhythms suggest the body's unfolding and shedding of restraint. In the penultimate stanza both the sky and the poem's rhythms throb in tune to the woman speaker's desire, and a moment of fraught erotic tension (signaled by asterisks) gives way to climax, to *le petit mort* of orgasm ("I am yours to the death").

But the speaker's lover is a chimera, transient, elusive, shape-shifting. This woman poet celebrates desire that precedes, and exceeds, any specific lover or that lover's ability to satisfy, a suggestion of voracious female sexuality. To the degree, moreover, that the lover is a figment of the speaker's imagination (another meaning of "chimera"), the poem's readers are suborned into the role of voyeurs of a woman's autoerotic act. And insofar as the poet's desire is autonomous, it accords with the definition of lesbian imagination given by Marilyn R. Farwell, since the poem refuses reproductive sexuality and "privileges a female sexuality [and creativity] that [do] not need or want male energy."[21]

"Chimaera," even more than "In the Rain," participates in Decadence, not only adopting masks but also courting moments of sexual perversity. Not coincidentally, the poem alludes to French forebears—in the word "crepuscle," in the sphinxlike street that presides over the poem like a pagan god, and above all in the poem's title, which harks back to the chimeras of Gustave Flaubert, Théophile Gautier, and Joris-Karl Huysmans. In letter 11 of Gautier's sexually experimental novel, *Mademoiselle de Maupin* (1835), d'Albert asserts: "The monster Chimera, slain by Bellerophon, the Chimera, with the head of a virgin, the paws of a lion, the body of a goat, and the tail of a dragon, was an animal of simple composition beside me," and then goes on to enumerate his perverse desires.[22] In Flaubert's *Temptation of St. Anthony* (1874), a source that more directly illuminates Tomson's oblique allusion to the sphinx at the beginning of her poem, one of the temptation scenes represents a dialogue between an immobile male sphinx and a "[l]eaping, flying," burning female chimera who seeks "new perfumes, . . . vaster flowers, . . . pleasures never felt before" and compares herself to a "hyena in heat."[23] Significantly, in Huysmans's *A Rebours* (1884), so crucial to Wilde's *The Picture of Dorian Gray,* the protagonist's sexual experiments involve a female ventriloquist who throws her voice into statues of a sphinx and chimera and reproduces Flaubert's dialogue. The protagonist concludes of the chimera, "It was to him that this voice, as mysterious as an incantation, was speaking; it was to him that it was describing its feverish craving after the unknown."[24] In Tomson's poem, the chimera who comes to the female speaker and to whom she belongs "to the death" registers French Decadence and perverse, lesbian desire, since the lover awaited by the female speaker is a monstrous, desiring woman.

This outrageously perverse female sexuality, however, is only one mask worn by the poet in "Chimaera." Talia Schaffer has argued that aestheticism, art for art's sake, allowed women writers to explore in pursuit of beauty material that might otherwise have been too volatile and dangerous.[25] "Chimaera" belongs to both aestheticism and Decadence, for if it celebrates deviant sexuality it is also a poem of and about imagination. The chimera that would have been most familiar to Tomson's British readers—namely, that in William Morris's *The Earthly Paradise* (1868–70)—is both an antagonist of Bellerophon and a residue of human imagination in the form of mythic stories told as part of the frame tale. In Flaubert's *Temptation,* too, the chimera is aligned with imagination; the creature declares, "I offer to the eyes of men dazzling perspectives with Paradise in the clouds above, and unspeakable felicity afar off. . . . I urge men to perilous voyages and great enterprises. I have chiseled with my claws the wonders of architecture."[26] The speaker's unending desire in

Tomson's "Chimaera" is also, then, imaginative desire for mystery and the unknown, here represented as a lover who is at once an intimate, familiar presence and a strange alien who can never be naturalized. This uncanny lover, whose shadow the speaker discerns and whose breath she feels, who utterly possesses her yet eludes all but her momentary embrace, is a means by which Tomson pays tribute to art for its own sake, perpetuates the traditional link between poetic creativity and erotic desire, and aligns herself with the Freudian insight that the highest human faculties are inseparably connected to (and driven by) polymorphously perverse sexuality. Insofar as the chimera is a double for both the sexualized woman speaker and the imaginative woman poet, and insofar as the chimera was notoriously able to shift from shape to shape, the chimera also tropes the very poetics, and masks, of Tomson's lyric.

The material production of Graham R. Tomson's 1891 volume would have deepened her identification with "Chimaera" and its commitments to imagination and perverse sexuality. The volume's frontispiece, by Arthur Tomson, is an impressionist painter's rendition of an impressionist poet, who looks away from spectators not from modesty but from indifference, entranced in the shifting borderland between nature and artifice, garden and city (fig. 5). Her hair is partially unbound, suggesting intimate dishabille and repose, but the small writing desk or table at her back signals a state of alert readiness as well. In other words, the frontispiece positions the poet as does "Chimaera"—alone in an urban garden, looking toward the "golden eyes" of street lamps and unknown possibilities beyond, yet never forsaking the artifice of poetry. As Vadillo remarks, the fact that St. John's Wood was a haunt of roaming artists' models and prostitutes means that the woman poet looking over the wall is also oriented toward the city and its opportunities for transgressive sexuality.[27]

In 1894 Graham R. Tomson overtly engaged sexual deviancy when she left Arthur Tomson to live with H. B. Marriott Watson, an Australian novelist and member of W. E. Henley's "regatta" who had previously befriended both the Tomsons. This elopement was the poet's second and led to a second divorce suit before she turned thirty-five, which shocked and alienated many of her colleagues, from Andrew Lang to Joseph Pennell, who now shunned her.[28] This elopement was also a perverse authorial act. The birth of Rosamund Marriott Watson, as she now renamed herself, not only squandered the symbolic capital Graham R. Tomson had

FIGURE 5. Arthur Tomson, frontispiece, *A Summer Night, and Other Poems*, by Graham R. Tomson (London: Methuen, 1891). Courtesy of the British Library, shelf mark 011653.h.13

so carefully accumulated over several years but also destroyed the poet's opportunity for name recognition and citability. No one could now mention Graham R. Tomson and Rosamund Marriott Watson together without narrating the cause of the change, at best an awkward task and at worst a publishing risk, since the publisher might seem to condone adultery. Literary insiders might know who "Rosamund Marriott Watson" was, but purchasers of poems and readers of periodicals and magazines were left to puzzle out the matter for themselves.

Newspapers rarely reported adulteries unless in connection with scandalous divorce trials. Tomson's sexual transgressions thus remained unpublicized and unmentioned, in contrast to the notorious trials involving Wilde a year later. As Ed Cohen observes, print culture could not name the sexual acts at issue in the accusations concerning Wilde's "sodomitical" behavior, so that newspaper accounts relied on metonymic representations of Wilde's body to signify deviant sexuality (rather than sexual practices).[29] If Wilde's deviant body became a public spectacle in the trial and newspaper illustrations, the deviant body of a Graham R. Tomson who could shape-shift, like a chimera, into Rosamund Marriott Watson was banished into invisibility both by social shunning and the omission of any reference to the change in newspapers and magazines. Her deviant body and act of adultery, however, were recuperated and made legible through book production, which also recorded in the body of her work the contingency of her poetic masks. To illustrate this concluding point, I want to track the production history of both of the poems that I have discussed.

"In the Rain" and "Chimaera" were originally published in Henley's *Scots Observer* and *National Observer* (figs. 6 and 7). Henley had in 1890 authorized his sub-editor, Charles Whibley, to attack *Dorian Gray*, and some of Henley's own best-known verses are imperialist, masculinist poems like "Invictus" (1875). But Henley's alternative identities were those of an avant-garde poet who wrote urban impressionist poems in free verse and an avant-garde editor who promoted candor in sexual matters (publishing, for example, the seduction scene in Thomas Hardy's *Tess of the D'Urbervilles* [1892], refused by *The Graphic*).[30] Henley's publication of poems like Tomson's "In the Rain" and "Chimaera" is thus less surprising than it might at first seem.

The two poems next appeared in Tomson's 1891 volume, *A Summer Night,* which was dedicated to Arthur Tomson, the poet's spouse; I reproduce

This cannot be tolerated ; and it is the contemplation of this fact which has made me say publicly that ' the Government bill must inevitably work to compulsion.' But whilst I say this I also recognise that any measure will require time. Under any conceivable system the last cannot be first. Estates must come in order. What I look forward to is a rapid transfer of the land from owner to occupier under the proposed measure. I look forward not to this alone but to prompt and punctual redemption of the liabilities incurred by the purchasers. And, these two conditions fulfilled, I hold it will be simply impossible to maintain the two systems of occupying ownership and judicial rent alongside of each other. I look forward not to legal compulsion, which I heartily dislike : I rather look forward to landlord and tenant recognising the situation and coming to such terms as will enable the landlord to sell, and which will still confer a great boon on the purchasing tenant.

The second objection is much easier disposed of. Lord Melbourne's famous answer to everything that was troublesome—' Why can't you let it alone ?'—is all very well in its way, but it is totally inapplicable to the agrarian situation in Ireland. No doubt Mr. Balfour has worked wonders : no doubt the Irish tenantry have enormous advantages. But if we really desire the permanent pacification of Ireland, if we desire to make an end of Home Rule and all it involves, the way is plainly marked out. The initial fact is that the English system of land tenure never was acceptable to the Irish people. It was forced upon them, and has been at the bottom of most of our troubles in that country. For twenty years we have been labouring hard to amend it. We have striven to protect the tenant's interest and to safeguard his property. Our success has been considerable, but far from complete. We have tried to fix a fair rent between landlord and tenant, and with only indifferent results. Where we have been completely successful is where we have transformed the occupier into the owner. During the past twenty years, and under various Acts of Parliament, we have transformed twenty thousand occupiers into owners. The conditions have differed : some were favourable, others were unfavourable. During this period we have had all kinds of political and agricultural weather : the storm-winds have blown fiercely from every direction. We have had want bordering upon famine ; we have had a great ' No-rent' conspiracy ; we have had incitements to wrong-doing baited with agrarian Socialism. And what have been the results? Individual landlords have, no doubt, gone down in the storm ; but the State tenants have successfully weathered the gale. Their arrears are nominal. The annual instalments have been punctually paid and without pressure ; and on not one of these properties has the National League an atom of power for mischief. This is the result of a great experiment ; why should it be arrested now ? It is not the policy of one party in the State : every party has approved it. It is fiercely opposed now by the Parnellites because the Parnellites see its results and dread their extension. They know that the ruling passion in an Irish peasant's breast is to own a bit of land. For this he will endure hardship and suffering. The few acres he tills bound his whole horizon. Secure him in the possession of these acres, and the dream of his life, the ambition of his family, is realised. He, in fact, becomes a Conservative in the best sense of that word. Mr. Healy understood the whole problem when he declared that the man who purchased his land under the Ashbourne Act made a treaty of peace on his own account with England. I am for the ratification of this treaty, and hence I support the Land Bill.   T. W. RUSSELL.

IN THE RAIN.

RAIN in the glimmering street—
Murmurous, rhythmical beat ;
Shadows that flicker and fly ;
Blue of wet road, of wet sky
(Grey in the depths and the heights) ;
Orange of numberless lights,
Shapes fleeting on, going by.

Figures, fantastical, grim—
Figures, prosaical, tame,
Each with chameleon-stain,
Dun in the crepuscle dim,
Red in the nimbus of flame—
Glance through the veil of the rain.

Rain in the measureless street—
Vistas of orange and blue ;
Music of echoing feet,
Pausing, and pacing anew.

Rain, and the clamour of wheels,
Splendour, and shadow, and sound ;
Coloured confusion that reels
Lost in the twilight around.

When I lie hid from the light,
Stark, with the turf overhead,
Still, on a rainy Spring night,
I shall come back from the dead.

Turn then and look for me here
Stealing the shadows along ;
Look for me—I shall be near,
Deep in the heart of the throng :

Here, where the current runs rife,
Careless, and doleful, and gay,
Moving, and motley, and strong,
Good in its sport, in its strife.

Ah, might I be—might I stay—
Only for ever and aye,
Living and looking on Life !

GRAHAM R. TOMSON

CORRESPONDENCE

THE FIGURE AT HYDE PARK CORNER.

[To the Editor of *The Scots Observer.*]

SIR,—I am the more pleased with your unfavourable comments upon the figure of the Duke of Wellington which Sir Edgar Boehm and a committee set up at Hyde Park Corner because I am inclined to believe, from various passages which have met my eye in your interesting journal, that you must be an artist. I am not an artist. I do not know whether art really exists or is only a chimera constructed out of nothing by your active brain and those of other persons, such as Andrea del Sarto and Sir Frederick Leighton, for the purpose of having smart things said about it, and of irritating people who paint pictures and do sculpture. Also I do not care. But it is pleasant to find that I am supported by the sympathy of an artist in my hatred of a particular statue. I believe that hatred is shared by the vast majority of people not artists whose avocations induce them, as mine do me, to pass Hyde Park Corner on the average about twice a day throughout the year. I therefore proceed to state my views—which, as you will see, have nothing to do with art—about Sir Edgar Boehm's figure of the Duke.

The Duke of Wellington was a great man. He conducted many campaigns and fought many battles. His remarkable energy and skill caused him to be uniformly successful. He helped largely and conspicuously to make an empire in India, to destroy one in Europe, and to save one at home. Among the men who have served this country well since the Revolution, only Pitt and Nelson stand at all on a level with him. He was of course a Tory, but I only mention that as a pleasing corollary. And it is to his memory that somebody has put up that little rubbishing

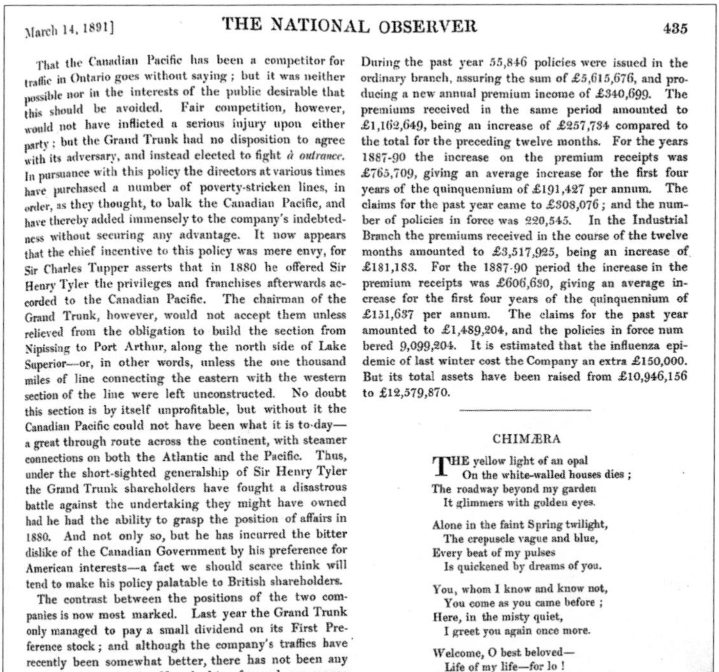

March 14, 1891] THE NATIONAL OBSERVER 435

That the Canadian Pacific has been a competitor for traffic in Ontario goes without saying; but it was neither possible nor in the interests of the public desirable that this should be avoided. Fair competition, however, would not have inflicted a serious injury upon either party; but the Grand Trunk had no disposition to agree with its adversary, and instead elected to fight *à outrance*. In pursuance with this policy the directors at various times have purchased a number of poverty-stricken lines, in order, as they thought, to balk the Canadian Pacific, and have thereby added immensely to the company's indebtedness without securing any advantage. It now appears that the chief incentive to this policy was mere envy, for Sir Charles Tupper asserts that in 1880 he offered Sir Henry Tyler the privileges and franchises afterwards accorded to the Canadian Pacific. The chairman of the Grand Trunk, however, would not accept them unless relieved from the obligation to build the section from Nipissing to Port Arthur, along the north side of Lake Superior—or, in other words, unless the one thousand miles of line connecting the eastern with the western section of the line were left unconstructed. No doubt this section is by itself unprofitable, but without it the Canadian Pacific could not have been what it is to-day—a great through route across the continent, with steamer connections on both the Atlantic and the Pacific. Thus, under the short-sighted generalship of Sir Henry Tyler the Grand Trunk shareholders have fought a disastrous battle against the undertaking they might have owned had he had the ability to grasp the position of affairs in 1880. And not only so, but he has incurred the bitter dislike of the Canadian Government by his preference for American interests—a fact we should scarce think will tend to make his policy palatable to British shareholders.

The contrast between the positions of the two companies is now most marked. Last year the Grand Trunk only managed to pay a small dividend on its First Preference stock; and although the company's traffics have recently been somewhat better, there has not been any marked improvement. Nor, looking forward, can we see any signs of coming change; for it has to divide much business with the Canadian Pacific road, and, moreover, railway rates in the United States seem likely to remain low, and these determine the profits on an important part of the Grand Trunk's traffic. On the other hand, the Canadian Pacific's receipts are steadily increasing; and it is evident that the company will do much better than in 1890. That year was about on a level with 1889, in which the company earned 3½ per cent. upon the shares, apart from the 3 per cent. guaranteed by the Canadian Government. In both years 5 per cent. was paid to the shareholders, and large sums were also carried to a dividend reserve fund, which is being accumulated against the expiration of the guarantee in rather more than two years' time. In these circumstances, and with prospects of great development, it is not surprising Canadian Pacific shares are an attractive investment. On the other hand, Grand Trunk stocks are no better than mere gambling counters in the market; nor are they likely to improve so long as the company is under its present management. Indeed, it is doubtful if much could be achieved even by the most capable directors, for the capital account is out of all proportion to the earning powers of the line. Still, the interests involved are so great that some attempt should be made to get the company into a better position: the first step being the removal of Sir Henry Tyler from his chairmanship.

The forty-second annual report of the Prudential Assurance Company (Limited), which has just been issued, is a record of the continued progress which marks this office. During the past year 55,846 policies were issued in the ordinary branch, assuring the sum of £5,615,676, and producing a new annual premium income of £340,699. The premiums received in the same period amounted to £1,162,649, being an increase of £257,734 compared to the total for the preceding twelve months. For the years 1887-90 the increase on the premium receipts was £765,709, giving an average increase for the first four years of the quinquennium of £191,427 per annum. The claims for the past year came to £308,076; and the number of policies in force was 220,545. In the Industrial Branch the premiums received in the course of the twelve months amounted to £3,517,925, being an increase of £181,183. For the 1887-90 period the increase in the premium receipts was £606,630, giving an average increase for the first four years of the quinquennium of £151,637 per annum. The claims for the past year amounted to £1,489,204, and the policies in force numbered 9,099,204. It is estimated that the influenza epidemic of last winter cost the Company an extra £150,000. But its total assets have been raised from £10,946,156 to £12,579,870.

CHIMÆRA

THE yellow light of an opal
On the white-walled houses dies;
The roadway beyond my garden
It glimmers with golden eyes.

Alone in the faint Spring twilight,
The crepuscle vague and blue,
Every beat of my pulses
Is quickened by dreams of you.

You, whom I know and know not,
You come as you came before;
Here, in the misty quiet,
I greet you again once more.

Welcome, O best beloved—
Life of my life—for lo!
All that I ask you promise,
All that I seek you know.

The dim grass stirs with your footstep,
The blue dusk throbs with your smile;
I and the world of glory
Are one for a little while.

* * * * *

The Spring sun shows me your shadow,
The Spring wind bears me your breath;
You are mine for a passing moment
But I am yours to the death.

GRAHAM R. TOMSON.

LIFE'S INVENTORY

MARTIAL, x. 47

Vitam quae faciant beatiorem,
Iucundissime Martialis, haec sunt:
Res non parta labore, sed relicta;
Non ingratus ager, focus perennis;
Lis nunquam, toga rara, mens quieta;
Vires ingenuae, salubre corpus;
Prudens simplicitas, pares amici;
Convictus facilis, sine arte mensa;
Nox non ebria, sed soluta curis;
Non tristis torus, sed pudicus;
Somnus, qui faciat breves tenebras;
Quod sis, esse velis nihilque malis;
Summum nec metuas diem, nec optes.

THE factors of Life's larger ease,
My dearest Blenkinsop, are these:
Wealth not laboriously hiv'd,
But from one's forefathers deriv'd;

FIGURE 7. Graham R. Tomson, "Chimaera," *National Observer,* 14 March 1891, 435. Courtesy of the Trustees of the National Library of Scotland, shelf mark Q.83

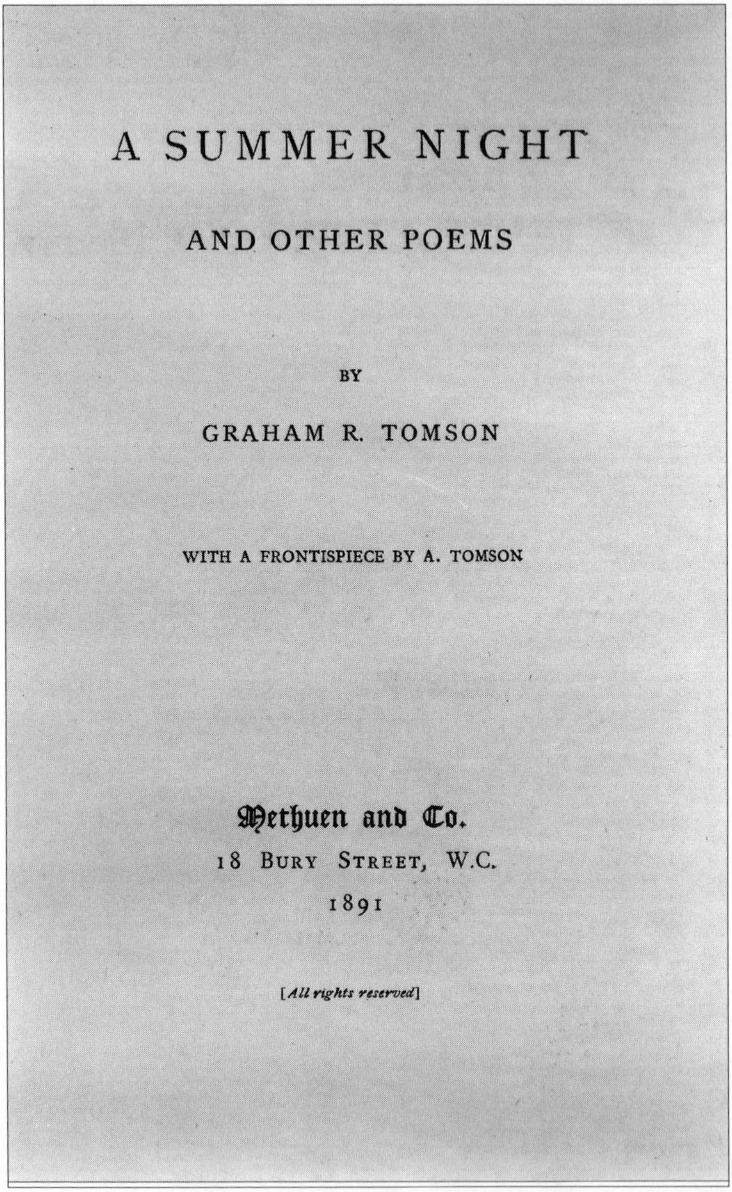

A SUMMER NIGHT

AND OTHER POEMS

BY

GRAHAM R. TOMSON

WITH A FRONTISPIECE BY A. TOMSON

Methuen and Co.
18 Bury Street, W.C.
1891

[*All rights reserved*]

Figure 8. Title page, *A Summer Night,* by Graham R. Tomson (1891). Courtesy of the British Library, shelf mark 011653.h.13

the book's title page here (fig. 8). Four years later, "In the Rain" was reprinted in *A London Garland,* a volume edited by Henley after Joseph Pennell, head of the Society of Illustrators, suggested an anthology of poems and accompanying art.[31] The poems and illustrations were arranged prior to the Tomson-Watson elopement, with the result that her shifting erotic desires were permanently recorded in the anthology's pages. There, "In the Rain" (fig. 9) is attributed to "Rosamond [*sic*] Marriott-Watson," the transitional nature of the signature evident in the spelling of the first name (*o* rather than the *u* in the terminal syllable of "Rosamund" adopted by the poet after her elopement; her legal name remained Rosamond Tomson until her second divorce was final). The poem is illustrated in *A*

A LONDON GARLAND

Turn then and look for me here
Stealing the shadows along ;
Look for me—I shall be near,
Deep in the heart of the throng :

Here, where the current runs rife,
Careless, and doleful, and gay,
Moving, and motley, and strong,
Good in its sport, in its strife.

.   .   .   .   .   .

Ah, might I be—might I stay—
Only for ever and aye,
Living and looking on life !

ROSAMOND MARRIOTT-WATSON.

Figure 9. Rosamond [sic] Marriott-Watson, conclusion of "In the Rain," in *A London Garland: Selected from Five Centuries of English Verse,* ed. William Ernest Henley (London: Macmillan, 1895). Courtesy of the Harry Ransom Humanities Research Center, University of Texas, Austin

FIGURE 10. Chadwell Smith, illustration of "In the Rain," by Rosamond [sic] Marriott-Watson, in *A London Garland* (1895). Courtesy of the Harry Ransom Humanities Research Center, University of Texas, Austin

London Garland by Chadwell Smith, who depicts a woman in a tailored suit carrying an umbrella and slightly exposing the petticoat she holds up to keep it from getting bedraggled (fig. 10). Although the woman's face is crudely drawn, the illustration captures the multifarious urban scene and rainy night celebrated in the poem, as well as its hint of female sexual impropriety. Most likely, however, "In the Rain" was originally intended to be illustrated by a painting favorably noticed in reviews after its inclusion in the New English Art Club spring show of 1891—Arthur Tomson's *Regent's Canal*, which subtly delineates an unusual subject through a veil of evening mist (fig. 11).[32] Arthur Tomson's place next to his spouse, so to speak, was usurped in a book as well as in life, here by a very minor artist indeed; and his own painting was forced into subordinate status following a reproduction of Whistler's *Nocturne: Blue and Silver—Chelsea* (1871) as an illustration of Henley's poem "Nocturn" (1888). Both in the contents of *A London Garland* and in its list of artists and authors, Arthur Tomson and his still-legal spouse were alienated from each other (fig. 12).

"In the Rain" and "Chimaera" also appeared in another volume in 1895. When John Lane, the leading Decadent publisher, published Marriott Watson's *Vespertilia, and Other Verses* that year, he simultaneously purchased and reissued remaining copies of *A Summer Night:* he ripped

FIGURE 11. Arthur Tomson, *Regent's Canal,* in *A London Garland* (1895). Courtesy of the Harry Ransom Humanities Research Center, University of Texas, Austin

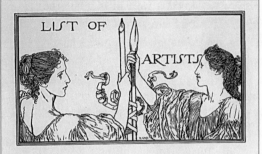

E. A. Abbey, R.W.S.
Cecil Aldin
W. D. Almond
W. Bayes
Aubrey Beardsley
R. A. Bell
A. S. Boyd
R. Burns
R. Vicat Cole
A. H. Collings
Walter Crane, A.R.W.S.
F. H. Crawford
J. S. Crompton
T. S. C. Crowther
Frank Dad, R.I.
J. Barnard Davis
Oscar Eckhardt
G. H. Edwards
Frank L. Emanuel
A. J. Finberg
J. Finnemore
A. Hugh Fisher
J. Fulleylove, R.I.
Ronald Gray
Sir Francis Seymour Haden, P.R.P.E.
G. C. Haité
Chris Hammond

G. D. Hammond
A. S. Hartrick
W. Hatherell, R.I.
E. G. Hill
L. Raven Hill
W. E. Home
Everard Hopkins
Hal Hurst
Fred T. Jane
H. Johnson
F. W. Lawson
Sir J. D. Linton, P.R.I.
W. Luker
Robert W. Macbeth, A.R.A., R.W.S.
Archie Macgregor
D. Macpherson
C. E. Mallows
G. Grenville Manton
J. W. T. Manuel
Phil May
H. R. Millar
E. H. New
Alfred Parsons, R.I.
J. Bernard Partridge
A. Pearse
Fred Pegram
Joseph Pennell

A. R. Quinton
A. R. Rackham
W. Rainey, R.I.
S. Reid
Paul Renouard
W. W. Russell
Frederick Sandys
Claude A. Shepperson
Chadwell Smith
W. Thomas Smith
W. S. Stacey
R. Strudwick
E. J. Sullivan

J. F. Sullivan
Arthur Tomson
H. Tonks
F. H. Townsend
Enoch Ward
J. R. Way
J. McNeil Whistler
W. Gleeson White
Edgar Wilson
W. B. Wollen, R.I.
Alice B. Woodward
W. L. Wyllie, A.R.A.
Jack B. Yeats

LIST OF AUTHORS

Matthew Arnold
William Pulteney, Earl of Bath
Francis Beaumont
W. L. Binyon
William Blake
Wilfrid Scawen Blunt
Robert Bridges
Alexander Brome
George Gordon Byron, Lord Byron
Henry Carey
Geoffrey Chaucer
Sir William Davenant
John Davidson
Charles Dibdin
Austin Dobson
Michael Drayton
William Dunbar
Henry Fielding
John Fletcher
John Gay
Oliver Goldsmith
Thomas Gray
Joseph Hall
W. E. Henley
Robert Herrick
Thomas Hood
Thomas Hudson
Ben Jonson
John Keats

Rudyard Kipling
Andrew Lang
Henry S. Leigh
Amy Levy
Frederick Locker-Lampson
Justin Huntly McCarthy
Rosamond Marriott-Watson
John Milton
Captain Charles Morris
William Morris
Thomas Nashe
Alexander Pope
Winthrop Mackworth Praed
John Hamilton Reynolds
John Wilmot, Earl of Rochester
Dante Gabriel Rossetti
William Shenstone
Edmund Spenser
J. Ashby-Sterry
Sir John Suckling
Henry Howard, Earl of Surrey
Jonathan Swift
Arthur Symons
Alfred Tennyson
James Thomson
Thomas Tickell
William Watson
William Wordsworth

FIGURE 12. List of artists and list of authors, *A London Garland* (1895). Courtesy of the Harry Ransom Humanities Research Center, University of Texas, Austin

out the old frontispiece painted by Arthur Tomson, the title page attributing authorship to Graham R. Tomson, and the dedication page addressed to "A.G.T."; and he substituted a new title page that identified Marriott Watson as the author of this volume, of *Vespertilia,* and of *The Bird-Bride,* the 1889 title authored by Graham R. Tomson (fig. 13). The title page of

FIGURE 13. Title page, *A Summer Night, and Other Poems,* by Rosamund Marriott Watson (London: John Lane, The Bodley Head, 1895). Courtesy of the collection of Linda K. Hughes

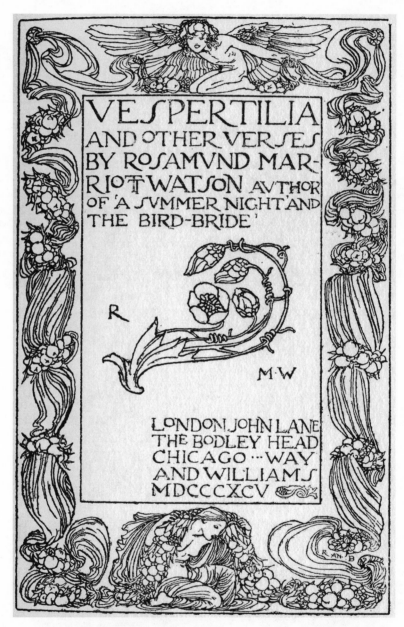

FIGURE 14. Title page, *Vespertilia, and Other Verses*, by Rosamund Marriott Watson (London: John Lane, The Bodley Head, 1895). Courtesy of the collection of Linda K. Hughes

Vespertilia inscribed the transformation of Graham R. Tomson into Rosamund Marriott Watson by once again linking three volumes published under a mutating authorial signature (fig. 14). In part, of course, this linking of *Vespertilia* to *A Summer Night* and *The Bird-Bride* was a necessary advertising strategy, an attempt to capitalize on the poet's prior reputation despite the rift in her identity. The device at the center of *Vespertilia*'s title page and on the front cover, however, was discretionary, and may have been designed by Marriott Watson herself, given the initials placed next to it. (The surrounding border of the title page was designed by Robert Anning Bell, whose initials appear in the lower right-hand corner.) Whether or not Marriott Watson herself executed the design, and whether or not the resemblance was intentional, the curving buds of Marriott Watson's personal insignia recall similar shapes on the title page of Oscar Wilde's *Poems,* which Elkin Mathews and John Lane published at the Bodley Head in 1892 (fig. 15; cf. fig. 1).[33] Fittingly, the title page of Marriott Watson's *Vespertilia* connects the female outlaw who authored its poems with the more notorious sexual outlaw who was incarcerated in Wandsworth Prison when *Vespertilia* appeared.

FIGURE 15. Detail, title page, *Vespertilia,* by Rosamund Marriott Watson (1895). Courtesy of the collection of Linda K. Hughes

Marriott Watson's two 1895 volumes also functioned to disclose authorial identity as nothing more than a mask to be discarded and replaced at will. Neither of the writer's two masks was more authentic than the other, since Rosamund Marriott Watson remained unmarried to her erotic partner until her death. Adopting a name that allowed her to be called "Mrs. Marriott Watson" in reviews or other mentions in the press, the poet remained a transgressive sexual agent operating outside the law—just as "Graham R. Tomson," an equally authentic and inauthentic authorial name, contested and continues to contest the sway of bibliographic law that insists on a unitary, authoritative name for historical records.

Both Tomson and Marriott Watson would lose their place in literary history and nearly disappear forever. However, not only the poet but also her fragmentary identities and impressionist poems like "In the Rain" and "Chimaera" merit remembrance for their connection to major figures such as Wilde, and, more important, for their role in illuminating the adoption of masks and sexual perversity by a highly accomplished woman poet of the 1890s.

Notes

1. Walter Pater, "Poems by William Morris (1868)," in *Westminster Review*, n.s., 90, no. 34 (1868): 300–312, reprinted in James Sambrook, ed., *Pre-Raphaelitism: A Collection of Critical Essays* (Chicago: University of Chicago Press, 1974), 114. First articulated in his 1868 review of volume 1 of William Morris's *The Earthly Paradise* (1868–70), Pater's statement was selectively adapted for the conclusion to his *Studies in the History of the Renaissance* (1873).

2. Yeats's comment is quoted in Norman Alford, *The Rhymers' Club: Poets of the Tragic Generation* (London: Macmillan, 1994), 51. For another detailed account of the Rhymers' Club, see Nicholas Frankel, "'A Wreath for the Brows of Time': The Books of the Rhymers' Club as Material Texts," in the present volume, chapter 4.

3. K[atharine] T[ynan], "A Literary Causerie," *Speaker*, 29 October 1892, 535.

4. Whence came his feet into my field, and why?
    How is it that he finds it all so drear?
    How do I see his seeing, and how hear
    The name his bitter silence knows it by?

Dante Gabriel Rossetti, "He and I," in *Dante Gabriel Rossetti: Collected Writings*, ed. Jan Marsh (London: J. M. Dent, 1999), 324. Many of the poems in *Tares* adopt a male persona that traces the downward spiral of a relationship. A second epigraph was drawn from the work of fifteenth-century French poet François Villon, to whose work Algernon Charles Swinburne had called attention in such poems as "A Ballad of François Villon" in *Poems and Ballads: Second Series* (1878).

5. Graham R. Tomson, "Hereafter," in *The Bird-Bride: A Volume of Ballads and Sonnets* (London: Longmans Green, 1889), 55.

6. The Prose Edda, by medieval Icelandic poet Snorri Sturlson, included extensive material drawn from Norse mythology.

7. Graham R. Tomson, "Sunset on Henna Cliff," *Longman's Magazine* 21 (1892): 108.

8. Oscar Wilde, "English Poetesses," *Queen*, 8 December 1888, reprinted in *The Collected Works of Oscar Wilde*, ed. Robert Ross (London: Methuen, 1908), 14:115.

9. This information appears in John Lawrence Waltman, "The Early London Journals of Elizabeth Robins Pennell" (PhD diss., University of Texas, Austin, 1976), 391.

10. Wilde, "Some Literary Notes," *Woman's World* 2 (1889): 447–48, reprinted in *The Collected Works*, 13:509; this last phrase, which Wilde states was taken from Pater's writings, modifies a line from chapter 20 of Pater's *Marius the Epicurean* in which the narrator mentions "elaborate, carved ivories of speech" (1885; reprint, Harmondsworth, UK: Penguin, 1985), 222.

11. Wilde's "The Truth of Masks" was first published under that title in *Intentions* (London: James R. Osgood / McIlvaine, 1891), 217–58.

12. I wish to thank Mark Samuels Lasner for informing me of the existence of the presentation copy. Tomson used her own journalism covertly to support Wilde at a key point, after Wilde's earliest version of *The Picture of Dorian Gray* (*Lippincott's Monthly Magazine* 46 [1890]: 3–100) had been savagely attacked for homoeroticism in W. E. Henley's *Scots Observer* (5 July 1890, 181, reprinted in Karl Beckson, ed., *Oscar Wilde: The Critical Heritage* [London: Routledge and Kegan Paul, 1970], 75). Tomson contributed an anonymous fashion column to Henley's journal; in it, she deliberately compares two gowns to the jewel-encrusted binding that Dorian selects for his edition of Théophile Gautier's *Émaux et camées* (1852) and that Wilde alludes to in his critical essay "Pen, Pencil, and Poison" (1889, revised 1891). Tomson uses the comparison to suggest the possibilities of beauty and innocent pleasure, as well as fatality, in Wilde's writings. The gold brocaded yoke of one gown, she avers, "lends countenance to gold embroidery thick-sown with jewels as the page of Mr. Oscar Wilde's original. Also in green—(a good colour sometimes, but capable of being as fatal as Original Sin)—is a

quaint yet pleasing morning-gown." "Between the Seasons," *Scots Observer,* 20 September 1890, 455.

13. E. H. Mikhail, ed., *Oscar Wilde: Interviews and Recollections* (Basingstoke, UK: Macmillan, 1979), 2:302.

14. Wilde, "Impression du Matin" and "Symphony in Yellow," in *The Complete Works of Oscar Wilde,* vol. 1, *Poems and Poems in Prose,* ed. Bobby Fong and Karl Beckson (Oxford: Oxford University Press, 2000), 153, 168.

15. W. W. Fenn, "Sky Sketching," *Art Weekly,* 21 June 1890, 137.

16. Graham R. Tomson, "In the Rain," in *A Summer Night, and Other Poems* (London: Methuen, 1891), 10–12.

17. In her unsigned art column of 10 September 1892 in the *Morning Leader,* for which she served as art critic, Tomson identifies the crucial components of landscape painting, including light, a sense of open air, weather, and time of day (3). For evidence of her staff position at the *Morning Leader,* see "Journals and Journalists of To-Day. XVI. Ernest Parker and the 'Star' and 'Morning Leader,'" *Sketch,* 25 April 1894, 685. This published interview with the paper's editor includes the assertion "I fancy I know your *Leader* staff: . . . art, Mrs. Graham R. Tomson."

18. Ana Parejo Vadillo, *Women Poets and Urban Aestheticism: Passengers of Modernity* (Basingstoke, UK: Palgrave Macmillan, 2005), 148–50.

19. Tomson customarily tempered Decadence. She remarked in an 1892 essay, "Yet is the meadow as real as the midden, and those aspects of life with which we are happily most familiar, are none the less actualities for being wholesomely sorrowful or sanely gay" ("Mrs. Alexander," *Independent,* 9 June 1892, 1). Similarly, her 1892 review of Arthur Symons's *Silhouettes* in the *Illustrated London News,* mostly a laudatory notice of Symons's urban impressionism, chided his poem "Maquillage" for appearing "rather to strain after raffishness"—most likely a hit at what she considered male posturing as well as at the commodification of female sexuality on which the poem turns (*Illustrated London News,* 10 December 1892, 747). For a further account of Tomson's responses to literary decadence, see Linda K. Hughes, "Feminizing Decadence: Poems by Graham R. Tomson," in Talia Schaffer and Kathy Alexis Psomiades, eds., *Women and British Aestheticism* (Charlottesville: University Press of Virginia, 1999), 119–38.

20. Graham R. Tomson, "Chimaera," in *Summer Night,* 4–5.

21. Marilyn R. Farwell, "Toward a Definition of the Lesbian Literary Imagination," *Sexual Practice/Textual Theory: Lesbian Cultural Criticism,* ed. Susan J. Wolfe and Julia Penelope (Oxford: Basil Blackwell, 1993), 73. I wish to thank Marion Thain for calling my attention to Farwell's essay.

22. Théophile Gautier, *Mademoiselle de Maupin*, trans. Joanna Richardson (Harmondsworth, UK: Penguin, 1981), 231.

23. Gustave Flaubert, *The Temptation of St. Anthony*, trans. Lafcadio Hearn (New York: Modern Library, 2000), 179.

24. Joris-Karl Huysmans, *Against Nature [A Rebours]*, trans. Maureen Mauldon, ed. Nicholas White (Oxford: Oxford University Press, 1998), 88–89.

25. Talia Schaffer, *The Forgotten Female Aesthetes: Literary Culture in Late-Victorian England* (Charlottesville: University Press of Virginia, 2000), 3–6.

26. Flaubert, *Temptation*, 181.

27. Vadillo, *Women Poets*, 144.

28. Henley's circle maintained loyalty to the Marriott Watsons; Elizabeth Robins Pennell, forced by Joseph Pennell's objections and fondness for Arthur Tomson to give up her friendship with the errant poet, referred to the elopement as a "tragedy" (Elizabeth Robins Pennell, *The Life and Letters of Joseph Pennell* [Boston: Little, Brown, 1929], 1:280). For further details, see Linda K. Hughes, *Graham R.: Rosamund Marriott Watson, Woman of Letters* (Athens: Ohio University Press, 2005), chapter 8.

29. Ed Cohen, *Talk on the Wilde Side: Toward a Genealogy of a Discourse on Male Sexualities* (New York: Routledge, 1993), 101–2, 119–72. As Merlin Holland notes, "[T]he words 'sodomy' and 'sodomitical' are seen to have been used in court, rather than the Millard/Hyde circumulocutions of 'unnatural practices.'" See *The Real Trial of Oscar Wilde: The First Uncensored Transcript of the Trial of Oscar Wilde vs. John Douglas (Marquess of Queensberry), 1895*, ed. Merlin Holland (New York: Fourth Estate, 2003), xli. "Millard/Hyde" refers to Stuart Mason [Christopher Sclater Millard], ed., *Oscar Wilde: Three Times Tried* (London: Ferrestone Press, 1912); and to H. Montgomery Hyde's *The Trials of Oscar Wilde*, Notable British Trials Series (London: William Hodge, 1948).

30. On the difficulties that Hardy encountered in trying to include this famous scene in the version of the novel accepted for serialization by the *Graphic*, see Michael Millgate, *Thomas Hardy: A Biography* (New York: Random House, 1982), 307.

31. Pennell, *Life and Letters*, 1:296–98.

32. The notice of the April 1891 New English Art Club show in the *Star* included this sentence:

> Mr. Arthur Tomson also, has been painting in London, and he makes one wonder why no one has heretofore seen the picturesqueness of 'The Regent's Canal' . . . in the evening, with the lights of the houses on its banks throwing golden reflections into the dark waters, and the white horse at

the end of the towing rope, and the boy leading him, looming out of the shadows; the deep blue of the London evening sky and misty distances is admirably suggested. (*Star*, 13 April 1891, 4)

33. The reformatted *Summer Night* also recalled Bodley Head practices in publishing Wilde's 1892 *Poems;* the binding of the 1881 edition of Wilde's *Poems,* published by David Bogue, had been removed and replaced by a new binding with a cover and title page designed by Charles Ricketts. See Josephine M. Guy and Ian Small, *Oscar Wilde's Profession: Writing and the Culture Industry in the Late Nineteenth Century* (Oxford: Oxford University Press, 2000), 89.

"A WREATH FOR THE BROWS OF TIME"

The Books of the Rhymers' Club as Material Texts

Nicholas Frankel

A book is a Book when it does not reflect someone who might have made it and when it is as unsullied by his name and as detached from his existence as it is from the reader's.
—MAURICE BLANCHOT, *THE BOOK TO COME* (1959)

The book is indeed the subject of the poet, the speaking and knowing being who *in* the book writes *on* the book.
—JACQUES DERRIDA, "EDMOND JABÉS AND THE QUESTION OF THE BOOK" (1978)

In the early 1890s, the publishers Elkin Mathews and John Lane published two books of poetry—*The Book of the Rhymers' Club* (1892) and its sequel, *The Second Book of the Rhymers' Club* (1894)—collectively authored by the "Rhymers' Club," a loose association of male poets who met periodically, at London's Cheshire Cheese pub and elsewhere, in order to provide a forum for one another's poetry.[1] Few members of this club had published much poetry prior to the appearance of these books, and the club seems to have had modest expectations as a result. But the two volumes, which sold out quickly and were widely noticed in their day, are now regarded as epitomizing the aesthetic or "Decadent" spirit of the 1890s while at the same time containing some of the finest poetry written in that decade.[2] Just as important, these two volumes helped launch a number of distinguished, if short-lived, literary careers (notably those of

Ernest Dowson and Lionel Johnson) while consolidating the reputations of other writers (in particular, William Butler Yeats and Arthur Symons) now regarded as bastions of early modernism.

For much of the twentieth century, critical discussion of these books was dominated by this last-mentioned feature: Rhymers' poetry was seen primarily as a transitional phenomenon in the history of British poetry, reflecting a period between a dying Victorianism and an emerging modernism, when Yeats, in particular, schooled himself in the technical discipline necessary to his subsequent career as a modernist poet. R.K.R. Thornton and Marion Thain, for instance, write, "Yeats was indisputably one of the great poets of the twentieth-century: the significance of the 1890s in his development is that it was a period of searching for a stance, a style, a mask, a period of forming his ideas, and of course a time when he was learning his trade."[3] This view owes much to Yeats himself, who, like many poets active in the first decades of the twentieth century, felt it necessary to discard the aesthetic mantle of 1890s poetry in order to identify himself with a vigorous modernism untainted by the "effeminacy" or "sterility" with which the 1890s had become associated. Yeats's elegiac account of the Rhymers in his 1922 autobiography *The Trembling of the Veil* describes Rhymers' poetry as something of a blind alley—as exhibiting a touching faith in the speaking voice, as misguided and traditional in its pursuit of literary ideals—but, more important, it describes the Rhymers themselves as "overwrought, unstable men," the children of a tragic generation, doomed to poetic failure as a consequence of their dissipated, self-destructive personal lives.[4] As Holly Laird and Jerusha McCormack observe elsewhere in this volume, Yeats's comments, at once sentimentalizing and disparaging, created a mythology about the Rhymers that has proved hard to dislodge, in part because Yeats was one of the latest-surviving Rhymers and his characterizations could not, in 1922, be effectively challenged.[5] As a consequence, criticism of the Rhymers' poetry has been haunted ever since by the specter of the Rhymers themselves. In spite of Michel Foucault's well-known deconstruction of the "author-function," modern criticism of the Rhymers' poetry still generally operates according to a biographical imperative, viewing it as the expression of a Decadent, "tragic generation," fatally enslaved to an intoxicated eroticism at odds with the bourgeois morality of Victorian England.[6]

This biocritical approach has, at its best, enlivened us to the alienation, sensuousness, and philosophic pessimism embodied in Rhymers'
verse.[7] But in general this approach concerns itself with poetry at the
level of the signified, with speculations on the author's mode of living
or the poem's decadent subject matter, and as a result it constrains our
understanding of what is programmatic and distinctive about the
Rhymers' project *as poetry*.[8] (As biographers of Dowson have argued, this
biocritical tendency has also led to gross misrepresentations of the
Rhymers' lives.[9]) The contours of the Rhymers' project, as it cohered at
the group's gatherings in 1890 and 1891, are implicit in the matter-of-
fact title of their first published collection: the achievement of a poetry
at once concrete, material ("The Book") and collective or anonymous ("of
the Rhymers' Club"), free from what Foucault has called "the dimension
of expression."[10] Publishing their poetry under the sign of the book, the
Rhymers announce a poetry, to adopt Maurice Blanchot's words, that
"does not reflect someone who might have made it"[11] but that aspires instead to a purely textual or authorless condition. Speculations about the
life and experience of the author, the collection's title suggests, should
not be allowed to impede one's experience of the poetry (or "Rhyme") in
its own right: such poetry—as Foucault's reflections on authorship remind us—is "an interplay of signs arranged less according to its
signified content than according to the very nature of the signifier."[12]
Programmatic and deliberate, the titles that the Rhymers chose for their
collections announce a poetry that refers only to itself, identified not
with its interior confines or subject matter but rather with its own concrete, performative instance.

This concern with the performative instance or "exteriority" of the
poetic signifier runs through the two books of the Rhymers' Club at just
about every level. The first and last poems in both collections, for instance, take poetry (or "rhyme") as their subject, announcing the arrival
of a new content-less poetry and swearing "[d]efiance / . . . to all but
Rhyme" (*BRC*, 1). "A Rhyme on Rhyme," which concludes *The Second
Book of the Rhymers' Club*, is especially noteworthy in this respect, scorn-
ing a poetry in which one appeals to some higher authority in order to
"measure all the meaning" and promising in its place "sounds so
sweet and few / That make metre all one vessel and her singers all one
crew":

Who made first our words resemble
With division and with tremble,
Saving them from song's perdition
The abyss of repetition,
And gave the flower of rhyme from earth to air for air's fruition?

Did he measure all the meaning
Of the rhymes he left for gleaning
In the dancing hand and hand?
Did he know the joyous band?
Did he see the singing sisters, did he love and understand?

There was no such old Magician.
The blind murmurs of Tradition
Dimly shaped and never knew
Of those sounds so sweet and few
That make metre all one vessel and her singers all one crew.

Music pouring from the boundless
Sheds her life upon the soundless.
Pretty rhyme, while doves are cooing,
Looking down on lovers wooing,
Adds the sisterhood of saying to the brotherhood of doing.

(EDWIN J. ELLIS, "A RHYME ON RHYME," *SBRC*, 135–36)

With its insistent true rhymes and with its regular trochaic meter, "A Rhyme on Rhyme" itself flirts with "the abyss of repetition" ("song's perdition") and has fared poorly with serious-minded critics as a result.[13] Yet the poem is fiercely self-reflexive in its comments on "pretty rhyme"; and to dismiss the poem as insubstantial is to miss its "aesthetic" note of defiant purposelessness as well as certain echoes of William Blake's *Songs* (with which its author, as a coeditor of Blake's works, was intimately familiar).[14] Like Blake's *Songs of Innocence* (1789), the poem embraces an artful and innocent language that contains a revolutionary charge: the poem refuses to produce meaning (here associated with "the brotherhood of doing") independent from the act of its own "saying." Its true rhymes and rhythmic regularity are deliberate signs of this refusal, marks of the Rhymers' determination to foreground the poem's performativity in the face of a world that "measures meaning" only at the expense of the poetic signifier.

This determination marks other poems that frame the two collections. G. A. Greene's "Song of the Songsmiths," for instance, which concludes *The Book of the Rhymers' Club,* articulates a vision of poetry that aspires to the condition of pure, unalloyed sound:[15]

> Ours are the echoes at least
> > That fell from the golden prime;
> Ours are the echoes at least,
> Ours are the crumbs from the feast
> > At the feet of the queenly rhyme:
> Ours be the task to prolong
> The joy and sorrow of song
> > In the midst of years that begrime;
> In the clinging mist of the years,
> With reverent toil and with tears,
> > To hammer the golden rhyme,
> > Hammer the ringing rhyme
> > > Till the mad world hears.
>
> (GREENE, "SONG OF THE SONGSMITHS," *BRC,* 93–94)

As with Ellis's "Rhyme on Rhyme," Greene's poem is notable for its self-conscious embrace of true rhyme, to the extent that the very word "rhyme" is rhymed with itself three times. Easily mistaken for creative weakness or "anxiety," such truer-than-true rhymes ringingly enact the poem's determination—which is also conspicuous in the typographical arrangement of closely identical lines—to prolong "the joy and sorrow of song" in the face of a "mad world" dead to sensation. Poetry's mission, Greene suggests, is to renew the realm of experience through a kind of sonic activism or self-consciously forged materialism. In this respect, Greene's poem is a forerunner of an idea that, according to the contemporary poet Charles Bernstein, dominates the modern "sound poem": "[P]oetry readings . . . are a performance of the carnality of language—its material, sensuous embodiment."[16]

The concern with poetry as concrete and performative that runs through these framing poems is implied by other features of the Rhymers' two books. Both of these volumes possess an almost architectural integrity, linking poem to poem—by means of thematic, formal, and typographical continuities—in a way that makes it hard to extract particular poems without damaging the whole. Ernest Dowson's "Non sum qualis eram bonae sub regno Cynarae," for instance, is preceded by the poem "Deer in Greenwich Park" by Victor Plarr (with whom Dowson separately planned to collaborate on a joint collection of poems). In Plarr's poem "the exile's doom" is discovered in the "beautiful clear eyes" of "lordlier brutes . . . / Pant[ing] for the hours of dark"; and "some dim instinct from primaeval years / Thrills, on a sudden, through each dappled breast" (*SBRC*, 57–59). Plarr's poem rehearses a process of temporal and physical dislocation that will be encountered again in Dowson's poem, whose speaker likewise remains trapped within a past that deadens him to any active, engaged experience of the present. Perhaps even more tellingly, "Non sum qualis eram bonae sub regno Cynarae" is followed by John Todhunter's "Euthanasia" (subtitled "Fin de Siècle"), whose opening, "Yes, this rich death were best," makes explicit a suicidal self-contempt always latent within Dowson's lines:

> Yes, this rich death were best:
> Lay poison on thy lips, kiss me to sleep,
> Or on the siren billow of thy breast
> Bring some voluptuous Lethe for life's pain,
> Some langorous nepenthe that will creep
> Drowsily from vein to vein;
> That slowly, drowsily, will steep
> Sense after sense, till, down long gulfs of rest
> Whirled like a leaf, I sink to the lone deep.
>
> (TODHUNTER, "EUTHANASIA," *SBRC*, 62)

The fatal kiss and the "siren billow of thy breast" with which Todhunter's poem begins clearly echo the ghostly kiss and the lovers' embrace with which Dowson's poem opens. These continuities carry over into subsequent stanzas, too, notably in the symbolism of the rose (in both poems, this is a symbol of beauty scorned), in the atmosphere of almost claustrophobic sensuality, and in a determination—discernible in both poems—to "measure the soft pulsations" of some other life or body from which its anemic speaker remains fatally shut out.[17]

Such pairings or groupings of individual poems are a conspicuous feature of both Rhymers' volumes, and they lend to the two collections a symphonic quality that disappears when any one poem or grouping is taken in isolation. This quality is reinforced typographically by what Jerome J. McGann would term the "bibliographic codes" of the Rhymers' collections.[18] The books' page openings, for instance, are dominated by the running header "The Rhymers' Club" in a fashion that eclipses individual poems' titles and to some extent counteracts the efforts of individual Rhymers to sign their poems (see fig. 16). This subordination of poem to book is reinforced by the self-conscious attention given to the book's pagination in the printing: many of its page numbers are bracketed, while others occupy a bibliographical position usually assigned to a poem's title or an author's name (see fig. 17). But the indivisibility of the Rhymers' collections is even more a result of the typographic uniformity with which poems of sometimes vastly different character and quality are printed. Where previous collaborative ventures by multiple authors can be faulted for certain inconsistencies of visual design, reflecting conflicting intentionalities on the parts of their contributors and editors, the books of the Rhymers' Club achieve a remarkable uniformity by virtue of their printing alone, so much so that one comes away hardly aware that one has been reading an anthology or an "edited" volume.

This uniformity, whose hermeneutic implications for our understanding of any one poem are profound, is especially remarkable given that in the early 1890s textual decoration and typographic experimentation flourished in both trade and private press publications. At the time of its production in late 1891, the producers of *The Book of the Rhymers' Club* might easily have chosen the well-worn path that descends from the Pre-Raphaelites to the private presses of the Arts and Crafts Movement, in which poetry was printed artistically, often in the company of illustrations or decorative devices, with an air of self-conscious experimentation. Indeed, the producers of such artistic productions as the *Century Guild Hobby Horse* and the *Dial*—two major serial vehicles for the dissemination of fin-de-siècle literature and art—were following in precisely this path at the time *The Book of the Rhymers' Club* was produced.[19] But some

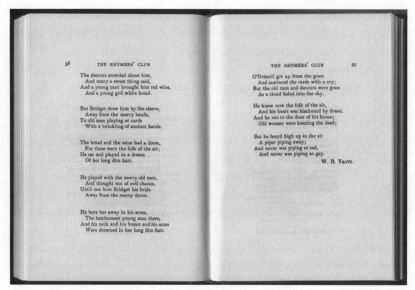

FIGURE 16. Page opening, *The Second Book of the Rhymers' Club* (London: Elkin Mathews and John Lane, 1894). Courtesy of the collection of Nicholas Frankel

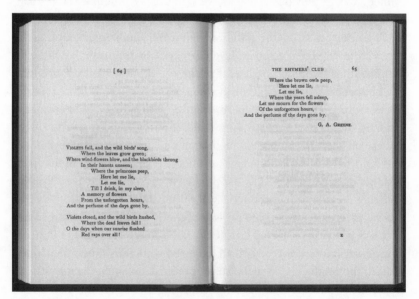

FIGURE 17. Page opening, *The Second Book of the Rhymers' Club* (1894). Courtesy of the collection of Nicholas Frankel

Rhymers, such as Ernest Rhys, found there to be a "preciosity" about the pages of the *Hobby Horse* and implied that in such artistic productions the print medium eclipsed or overshadowed a full engagement with the text.[20] By contrast, as McGann has written, the typographic style of the Rhymers' books represents a conscious decision, on the part of their producers, to achieve a "crisp aura of contemporaneity" while eschewing the air of studied exclusivity that hangs over the artistic page.[21]

This point becomes clear if we contrast the early appearance of Dowson's "Non sum qualis . . ." in the *Century Guild Hobby Horse*, where it first appeared in April 1891 (see fig. 18), with its later appearance in *The Second Book of the Rhymers' Club* (see fig. 19). In the *Hobby Horse*, Dowson's poem appears incommensurate with the texts surrounding it, subsumed within a heterogeneous visual style that reflects the diverse artistic interests of that magazine's editors.[22] (The poem is printed discontinuously with the texts that precede it, some of which are nonliterary in character, others of which are punctuated by "drawn" and engraved decorative devices.) By contrast, the typographic style of *The Second Book of the Rhymers' Club* lends Dowson's poem a continuity or collective integrity with the book as a whole. By gathering individual poems so completely into the collection by virtue of a crisp, uniform typographic style, the Rhymers' books constitute important precedents for titles issued by twentieth-century publishers such as Faber and Faber (in Britain), and Grove and New Directions (in the United States). The modernism of these later publishers was flagged in part by a collective house style that eschewed the deliberate ornamentalism that characterized the printing of so much late-Victorian poetry.

But the integrity of Rhymers' poems with one another in a multi-authored collection is by no means simply a function of their shared bibliographic coding. Noting that "placement of a poem within a collection occupies a middle ground between its linguistic and bibliographical codes," the textual theorist George Bornstein has proposed the term "contextual code" to describe the effects on interpretation of a poem's physical position in relation to other poems in a collection.[23] Bornstein's term nicely captures the continuities, at once bibliographic, thematic, and linguistic, between "Non sum qualis . . ." and "Euthanasia," and it is of particular relevance to poems in the Rhymers' books by Yeats, Dowson, and a handful of others who have since achieved canonical status in their own

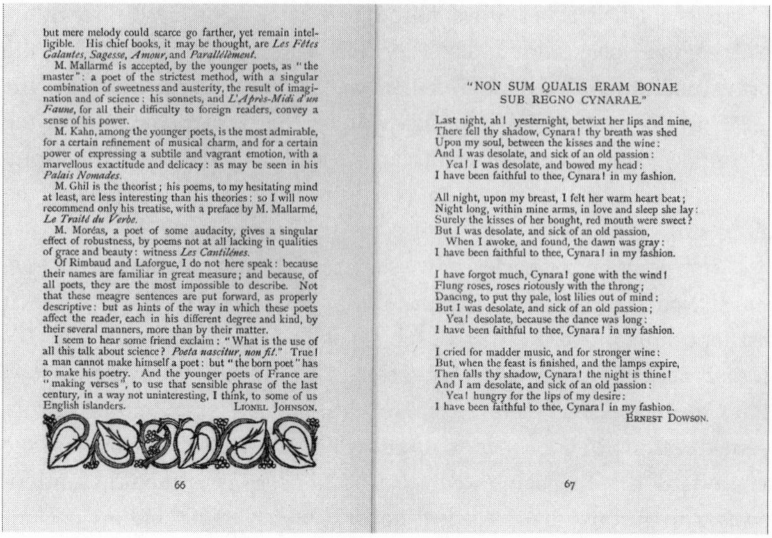

FIGURE 18. Conclusion of essay by Lionel Johnson, facing Ernest Dowson, "Non sum qualis eram bonae sub regno Cynarae," *Century Guild Hobby Horse* 6 (1891). Courtesy of the William Andrews Clark Memorial Library, UCLA

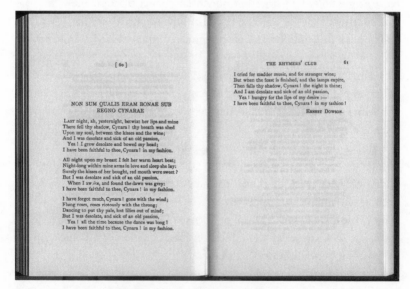

FIGURE 19. Ernest Dowson, "Non sum qualis eram bonae sub regno Cynarae," in *The Second Book of the Rhymers' Club* (1894). Courtesy of the collection of Nicholas Frankel

right or who are now customarily read in the context of their individual poetic careers. Yeats's "The Lake Isle of Innisfree," for instance, acquires an aura of mortality and a sense of unconscious vanity by virtue of appearing in *The Book of the Rhymers' Club* on the page opposite Ernest Radford's "A Sundial—Flowers of Time." This pairing is itself lent further resonance by virtue of the fact that it is surrounded by a number of poems that represent sunset, exhaustion, and the passage of time. Radford's poem is dedicated to the memory of "R. A. L., Sculptor," and it concerns the mortality of the imaginative artist who "even whilst he wrought did he / Close a great bargain with the years" (*BRC*, 85). Radford's poem operates as a kind of rejoinder to Yeats's poem, throwing into relief the vanity ruling Yeats's speaker and ultimately casting a deathly pall over his apparently unselfconscious Romanticism. The appearance of Dowson's "Villanelle of Sunset" just before Yeats's poem adds further layers of irony: "Sleep rounds with equal zest / Man's toil and children's play," Dowson's villanelle declares (*BRC*, 83). Yeats's speaker imagines that constructing a "small cabin . . . of clay and wattles made," and erecting "nine bean rows" and a "hive for the honey bee" (*BRC*, 84), will satisfy the longing of the "deep heart's core." But this Thoreauvian idyll is merely a prefiguring of "sleep," Dowson's poem states, like "flowers confest / Of slumber" (*BRC*, 83). The figure of a final "sunset" haunts "The Lake Isle of Innisfree" on either side; and by explicitly associating that sunset with a "weary West," at once home and final resting place, Dowson lends an undercurrent of bitter irony to the westward turn ("to Innisfree") so temptingly rehearsed in Yeats's poem.

No doubt some might argue that this reading of "The Lake Isle of Innisfree" is largely the result of an accident of printing, reflecting the taste and intentions of some unspecified editor or, still worse, of the volume's printer, J. Miller and Sons of Edinburgh. After all, individual poems in both *The Book of the Rhymers' Club* and *The Second Book of the Rhymers' Club* are signed, enabling modern critics to single out the contributions of Yeats, Dowson, and Johnson in particular as masterly expressions of a lyrical late Romanticism. From our current standpoint, it may appear sacrilegious to read a long-canonized poem interdependently with poems that wear their influences more anxiously. But such singling out misses the central impulse behind these volumes—to merge the individual voice with that of the collective or club—and comes in for explicit critique in the already-quoted "Rhyme on Rhyme," in which the effort to make "our words resemble / With division and tremble" is described as inflicting a confused violence on "music pouring from the boundless." The poet's effort to sign his poem notwithstanding, as Maurice Blanchot has written, it remains the case that "the poet has no direct relation to, and still less ownership of, the poem." "He cannot lay claim to what he has written," Blanchot adds, "and what he has written remains anonymous, even under his name."[24] Paradoxically, the Rhymers' efforts to authenticate their poems on an individual basis only underscore more forcibly their absorption into the collective whole of the book. In this respect, the Rhymers' books embody a drive—to supplant what might be termed the "authorly" text—that is as characteristic of 1890s writing as it is a prefiguring of the "edited" or "little" magazines that would play such an important role in the formation of poetic modernism.

If the graphic appearance of the Rhymers' books represents the Rhymers' drive to collective utterance, then the subsequent critical isolation (and consequent canonization) of some poems over others represents an immaterializing process that paradoxically flies in the face of the Rhymers' books while remaining partly a function of the Rhymers' poems themselves. In the Rhymers' collections the urge to abstract oneself from life's material conditions, manifested in the self-conscious failure to "forget" or in a perverse attachment to a persistent "remembering," is shown to be problematic in poem after poem:

> Here let me lie,
> Let me lie,
> Till I drink in my sleep,
> A memory of flowers
> From the unforgotten hours,
> And the perfume of the days gone by.
>
> (G. A. GREENE, "VIOLETS FULL AND
> THE WILD BIRDS' SONG," SBRC, 64)

> I have forgot much, Cynara! Gone with the wind;
> Flung roses riotously with the throng;
> Dancing to put thy pale, lost lilies out of mind;
> But I was desolate, and sick of an old passion,

Yea! all the time because the dance was long!
I have been faithful to thee, Cynara, in my fashion.

(Dowson, "Non sum qualis . . . ," SBRC, 60)

He stood among a crowd at Drumahair,
His heart hung all upon a silken dress,
And he had known at last some tenderness
Before earth made of him her sleepy care;
But when a man poured fish into a pile,
It seemed they raised their little silver heads
And sang how day a Druid twilight sheds
Upon a dim, green, well-beloved isle,
Where people love beside star-laden seas;
How Time may never mar their fairy vows
Under the woven roofs of quicken boughs;—
The singing shook him out of his ease.

(Yeats, "A Man Who Dreamed of Fairyland," BRC, 7)

Acts of imagination and remembering meet their equivalents here in the persistent failure to forget, and in each case this results in a kind of "disease" or nostalgia that is deliberately shown to be morbid, even fatal: in these poems, the Rhymers do not invite us to take refuge from present contingencies so much as warn us, as it were belatedly, of the dangers of doing so. And yet this flight from material contingency is precisely what has been accomplished by those editors who, seeking to canonize certain poems over others, have placed them in anthologies, where Yeats's poems in particular appear far less anxious about their own Romantic impulses than in their original context.[25]

If it is prefigured as problematic in Rhymers' poetry itself, however, this willful surrendering to the aestheticizing impulse was by no means such an easy option for the Rhymers' contemporaries. For the earliest readers of these books, such a term as "lyrical late-Romanticism" would have been relatively meaningless, and the fluidity and integrity of the Rhymers' collections would have been correspondingly more apparent. Early reviews of *The Book of the Rhymers' Club* emphasized the Rhymers' collectivity and made little of any individual "genius" on display.[26] In reviewing *The Book of the Rhymers' Club*, for instance, the *Daily Chronicle* called the Rhymers "a poet with twelve heads" and "a round table of rhymers," commending them for approaching their work "with no airs of genius—no red-hot artistic propaganda."[27] Admittedly, the *Chronicle* singled out Johnson's poems as "quite among the best in the book," perhaps giving undue weight to Johnson's emerging reputation as a man of letters ("we know well of him as a critic").[28] But behind most of the reviewers' judgments ("They are in no hurry to be heard; they are not overconfident that they are worth hearing" or "The Rhymers' Club do not *hammer* their rhyme, nor is their muse as degraded, changed and faded as Mr. Rhys pretends") one can sense an emphatic determination, even eagerness, to judge the book as a collective whole.[29]

Certainly there is some truth to the argument that reading the individual poem as interdependent with the collective whole cuts against the intentions of certain individual Rhymers, as is perhaps demonstrated by the later efforts of Yeats and Symons (in particular) to assert ownership over poems they had once freely surrendered for collective publication. Yet Yeats appears to have been happy in the early 1890s to be bound up with the Rhymers' Club, which he seems to have construed initially as a predominantly Celtic grouping. In 1892 he introduced the Rhymers to readers of the *Boston Pilot* as a "little body" into which "have gathered well nigh all the poets of the new generation"; and, while he recognized that the Rhymers were "not . . . a school of poets in the French sense," he clearly rejoiced in the publication of *The Book of the Rhymers' Club* as the "manifesto" of a "circle."[30] Just as important, the Rhymers were collectively responsible for the sequencing or arrangement of the overall volume, which was decided by a committee including Greene, Johnson, Richard Le Gallienne, Todhunter, and Dowson.[31] As the tables of contents in both of the volumes announce, multiple poems by any individual are not grouped together under the name of the "author"—as they are in Elkin Mathews's 1899 anthology *The Garland of New Poetry by Various Writers* and in such important twentieth-century anthologies as *An Anthology of "Nineties" Verse* and *Aesthetes and Decadents of the 1890s*—but rather interwoven with those of other Rhymers into a single, many-stranded, textual web.[32] The Rhymers themselves, it seems fair to conclude, were determined at the time of publication that the collections should constitute a collective utterance, exceeding and to a certain extent overwhelming the individual intentions of any one member of the gathering.

In these respects, the books of the Rhymers' Club perfectly exemplify what Gilles Deleuze and Felix Guattari memorably term the "third characteristic of minor literature," in that everything in them takes on a collective value.[33] Posterity may have insisted on dividing the Rhymers' Club into its constituent individuals or "poets" (to the eternal detriment of the contributions made by such figures as Plarr, Todhunter, Rhys, and Ellis), but the *Books of the Rhymers' Club* are predicated on the idea that, as Deleuze and Guattari put it, "talent isn't abundant" and "there are no possibilities for an individuated enunciation that would belong to this or that 'master' and that could be separated from a collective enunciation." Indeed, scarcity of talent "is in fact beneficial," suggest Deleuze and Guattari, since it "allows the conception of something other than a literature of 'masters.'"[34] In the Rhymers' books, *poetry* (in the senses of the word meant by mid-Victorian critics such as John Stuart Mill and Matthew Arnold[35]) is eschewed in favor of the rhetoric of *rhyme;* and a poem like Radford's "A Sundial: Flowers of Time" is given equal weight with "The Lake Isle of Innisfree." As a result, the Rhymers actively invite the question posed directly by one of their number, written into *The Book of the Rhymers' Club* roughly midway through the collection: "Bethink ye, Rhymers, what your claim may be, / Who in smug suburbs put the Muse to nurse?" (*BRC,* 44). By refusing to distinguish poem from poem, or poet from poet, the Rhymers challenged the very idea of the poet laureate, determined that their poetry should acquire the force of a collective action.

This collective determination gives a particular resonance to the coincidence of the publication of *The Book of the Rhymers' Club* with the year of Alfred Tennyson's death, as is registered in John Todhunter's poem "The Rhymers' Club: In Westminster Abbey, October 12, 1892," which opens *The Second Book of the Rhymers' Club*.[36] The Rhymers' challenge to Arnoldian and liberal notions of poetry is registered too in contemporary reviews, which frequently express discomfort in the face of a book with no pretensions to genius or individual authorship. "We cannot profess to be in love with the tendency towards co-operative production," remarks the *Athenæum*, which also notices a similarity between the Rhymers and the New English Art Club: "[T]he strongest work is always done by those who stand apart from all such coteries."[37] By comparison, when reviewing *The Book of the Rhymers' Club* anonymously for the *Star,* Richard Le Gallienne—whose own poetry features in the book—remarks on the self-consciously modest "spirit" with which "these rhymers . . . sit in the seat of their dead masters." He further comments: "It might seem likely that a book into which eleven had put their best would be a better book than any one of them could do single-voiced."[38] But Le Gallienne implies that this cannot be said of the Rhymers' collection: in his view *The Book of the Rhymers' Club* aimed at something less than the sum of its "single-voiced" parts, whereas "mathematically it should be eleven times as good."[39] The problem that the collection posed, however, was not simply its producers' refusal to distinguish individual authors but rather their evident determination to eschew those criteria by which poetry and poets had conventionally been judged as great: "[T]here is nothing in the volume which contains any definite promise, or more than the mere possibility, of great poetic achievement in the future. . . . The note of distinction, of originality, is wanting. The scale, moreover, is very small."[40]

Such early reviews reflect squarely on the collective, anticanonical spirit that informs the production of the Rhymers' books *as* books. But the Rhymers' collective spirit does not reside solely in the bibliographic and visual features of their books. Their embrace of the books' material features is matched by a determination to foreground language itself, at the most primitive level, as something material and concrete. Perhaps this determination is implied in their books' titles, as I suggested earlier. It is implied too in the Rhymers' self-conscious attention to the sound or action of the poem in its recitation—as if the poem's printed text somehow couldn't leave behind the spoken condition in which it originated. Surviving accounts of Rhymers' Club's meetings are dominated by descriptions of the Rhymers' curiously weightless recitations of their own poems; and residues of those recitations, which seem to have taken on something of the character of the modern "poetry reading" as Charles Bernstein articulates it, can be traced in the Rhymers' acute attention to marks of silence, pause, and interruption.[41] For instance, by far the most important emendations Ernest Dowson introduced into the text of "Non sum qualis . . . ," as it appeared in *The Book of the Rhymers' Club,* were the deletion or addition of some three dozen commas and other marks of punctuation, indicating his acute hypersensitivity to the periodic inflections of the speaking voice.[42] Dowson's exquisite poem "O Mors" meditates on precisely this "spoken" condition and stands in stark, ironic contradiction to the *will to silence* paradoxically embodied in the poem's speech:

Be no word spoken,
Weep nothing; let a pale
Silence, unbroken
Silence, prevail:
Prithee! be no word spoken,
Lest I fail.

(DOWSON, "O MORS!" *BRC*, 30)

Even as it exists typographically in the form of a printed text, Dowson's poem stands self-consciously as the echo of "an embodied acoustic performance."[43] Indeed it announces itself *as* an acoustic performance at the same time as it speaks of its attempt to transcend or nullify this condition in its search for a "[s]ilence, unbroken."

This lingering attachment to the poem as speech acquires an interesting resonance when viewed in the light of Deleuze and Guattari's theory of minor literature. Deleuze and Guattari write that, for the majority of speakers, language usually compensates for the "deterritorializing" action of the mouth and teeth by "a reterritorialization of sense. Ceasing to be an organ of the senses, language becomes an instrument of Sense."[44] But in the mouths of minorities, sound itself remains deterritorialized irrevocably, unable or unwilling to be subordinated to a language of sense. If these comments on the economy of speech imply a political dimension to the self-conscious spokenness of much of Dowson's poetry, they also lend a special relevance to the fact that the Rhymers' Club was composed almost entirely of Irish, Scottish, Welsh, or provincial poets. As Lionel Johnson's important poem "Celtic Speech" makes clear ("Never forgetful silence fall on thee, / Nor young voices overtake thee, / Nor echoes from thine ancient hills forsake thee"), speech from "the far, fair Gaelic places" or from the "desolate Land's End" is forced to occupy cramped metropolitan spaces, obliged to articulate itself in a fashion at once alienated and subversive even as it acquires the force of a collective enunciation (*SBRC*, 123). Celtic speech, in Johnson's vision of it, is minor speech, unable or unwilling to become subordinate to a hegemonic signified. The poetry produced by minor speech, for all its material intensity, possesses a certain emptiness as a result, perhaps coming far closer to verse (or rhyme) than to Wordsworth's "breath and finer spirit of knowledge." Or, as Deleuze and Guattari put it, the "organized music" of minorities is "traversed by a line of abolition—just as a language of sense is traversed by a line of escape—in order to liberate a living and expressive material that speaks for itself and has no need of being put into a form."[45]

This drive to "liberate a living and expressive material" can be seen in the Rhymers' acute sensitivity to matters of prosody, rhyme, and punctuation—a sensitivity that is announced in the very titles of some of their poems (e.g., "The Sonnet," "Quatrain," "Ballad of the 'Cheshire Cheese,'" "Villanelle of Sunset," "The Song of the Songsmiths," and "A Rhyme on Rhyme"). But it is a mistake to view the Rhymers' technical self-consciousness as a purist's cultivation of literary form for its own sake. One can detect beneath this parade of technical virtuosity a refusal to make the primary elements of signification (tongue, mouth, teeth, book) serve the public ends of the referent, as well as a profound interest in returning "literary" form to the aurality that precedes it: as Ellis puts it,

> The blind murmurs of Tradition
> Dimly shaped and never knew
> Of those sounds so sweet and few
> That make metre all one vessel and her singers all one crew.
>
> (*SBRC*, 135)

If the Rhymers' technical self-consciousness is a reflection of their "minor" concern with language as material intensity, so too is the negative capability that motivates many of the Rhymers' poems. At the same time as it foregrounds the individual poem's acoustic and textual performance, Rhymers' verse conspicuously strives to "obliterate all consideration," in John Keats's immortal phrase,[46] defying what the first volume's opening poem ("At the Rhymers Club") terms "[s]cience / And all such skins of lions / That hide the ass of time" in favor of a poetry of "folly" and "pure wit" (*BRC*, 1). Many poems in the two collections meditate explicitly on the conditions of absence and nothingness, inhabiting what Ernest Dowson calls "a garden of shadow"; and the best of them strive to provide a concrete form for nothing by cultivating effects of echo, circularity, repetition, and finality.

A VOICE on the winds,
A voice by the waters,
    Wanders and cries:

Oh! What are the winds?
And what are the waters?
    Mine are your eyes.

Western the winds are,
And western the waters,
    Where the light lies:

Oh! What are the winds?
And what are the waters?
    Mine are your eyes!

                  (Johnson, "To Morfydd," *SBRC*, 55)

Come hither, child! and rest:
    This is the end of day,
Behold the weary West!
Sleep rounds with equal zest
    Man's toil and children's play:
Come hither, child! And rest.
My white bird, seek thy nest,
    Thy drooping head down lay:
Behold the weary West!
Now are the flowers confest
    Of slumber: sleep, as they!
Come hither, child! and rest.
Now eve is manifest,
    And homeward lies our way:
Behold the weary West!
Tired flower! upon thy breast,
    I would wear thee, always:
Come hither, child! and rest;
Behold, the weary West!

              (Dowson, "Villanelle of Sunset," *BRC*, 83)

At first glance, such poetry appears to embody a narrow aestheticism, driven by the determination to ignore or nullify the complex social fabric in which poet and poem are inextricably involved. But on closer inspection—or, more accurately, on closer audition—it becomes apparent that the Rhymers' interest in seemingly closed linguistic structures masks a deep, collective concern with shifting poetry away from the persona of the author and a corresponding insistence on the textual event of the poem in performance.

In the end, criticism that views Rhymers' verse as the expression of a perverse Decadence or a narrow aestheticism is as misguided as that which insists on sifting it for signs of individual "mastery." The books of the Rhymers' Club constitute a de facto attack on the ideology of authorship and the notion of literature it entails, shifting attention away from the subject (or author) presumed to inhabit poetry and heralding a poetics that has started to challenge the critical hegemony of authorship and form. Far from constituting a Decadent pursuit of lyrical form for its own sake, the collections articulate a notion of poetry as at once concrete, social, and performative. Like many other poetic works of the 1890s, the books of the Rhymers' Club emphasize the active role played by the reader's senses in the production of poetic meaning, calling attention to the composite medium of the book even as they embrace the event of the text's publication.

By activating their books' graphical and lexical resources at just about every level, the Rhymers underscored poetry's collective ambitions. And by calling attention to their poetry's performance, in both recitation and print, the Rhymers strove to liberate speech from any narrow enslavement to the referent. In both these respects, the collections advance a sustained critique of certain Romantic ideas about authorship that had, by the year of Tennyson's death, become dominant in English poetry and that were to be temporarily reinvigorated in the early twentieth-century reaction to fin-de-siècle aestheticism (a reaction of which Yeats's *The Trembling of the Veil* formed a part). Rhymers' poetry shares a number of affinities with certain materialist tendencies in late twentieth-century poetry as well as with that broader late-Victorian inquiry into the ontology of the artwork, whose implications for poetic practice remain poorly understood more than a century later.

Notes

I am grateful to Susan Barstow, Jerome McGann, and David Latané for help with this essay.

1. For ease of reference, I have used the abbreviations *BRC* and *SBRC* to denote *The Book of the Rhymers' Club* (London: Elkin Mathews, 1892) and *The Second Book of the Rhymers' Club* (London: Elkin Mathews and John Lane, 1894), respectively. Technically speaking, John Lane was a sleeping partner in the publication of *The Book of the Rhymers' Club* (which bears only Elkin Mathews's imprint). For details of Lane's and Mathews's publishing arrangements at the time of the first volume's publication, see James G. Nelson, *The Early Nineties: A View from the Bodley Head* (Cambridge, MA: Harvard University Press, 1970), 1–35.

2. See Karl Beckson, "The Rhymers' Club" (PhD diss., Columbia University, 1959); Joanne Gardner, *Yeats and the Rhymers' Club: A Nineties Perspective* (New York: Peter Lang, 1989); Norman Alford, *The Rhymers' Club: Poets of the Tragic Generation* (1994; reprint, New York: Macmillan, 1997); and Nelson, *Early Nineties*, 150–83. For contemporary reviews of *The Book of the Rhymers' Club*, see Gardner, *Yeats*, 216–19. *The Book of the Rhymers' Club*, consisting of 350 copies for sale in Britain (a further 100 copies were held back for private or review purposes), sold out within one month of publication (see Ernest Dowson to Victor Plarr, 3 March 1892, *The Letters of Ernest Dowson*, ed. D. Flower and H. Maas [Rutherford, NJ: Fairleigh Dickinson University Press, 1968], 228). *The Second Book of the Rhymers' Club* was slower to sell out (50 large paper and 650 standard copies printed; of the 650 standard copies, 400 were for sale in Britain and 150 for sale in the United States).

3. R. K. R. Thornton and Marion Thain, eds., *Poetry of the 1890s* (Harmondsworth, UK: Penguin, 1997), 310.

4. William Butler Yeats, *The Trembling of the Veil*, book 4 ("The Tragic Generation"), in *Autobiographies*, ed. William H. O'Donnell and Douglas N. Archibald (New York: Scribner, 1999), 233.

5. See especially the comment with which Yeats dismissed Ernest Rhys's reminder that some of the original Rhymers were still alive and kicking in 1922: "One begins to think of the 'Rhymers' as those who sang of wine and women—I no more than you are typical" (quoted in Karl Beckson and George Mills Harper, "Victor Plarr on 'The Rhymers' Club': An Unpublished Lecture," *English Literature in Transition, 1880–1920* 45 [2002]: 381).

6. This biocritical view of Rhymers' poetry, in which the poem becomes indistinguishable from the psychic drives of its author, was initiated in 1896 by Arthur Symons's homage to Dowson: "A Literary Causerie: On a Book of Verses," *Savoy*, August 1896, reprinted in Alford, *Rhymers' Club*, 152–54. This view is forcefully rearticulated in Karen Alkalay-Gut's "Aesthetic and Decadent Poetry," in *Cambridge Companion to Victorian Poetry*, ed. Joseph Bristow (Cambridge: Cambridge University Press, 2000), 228–54. Alkalay-Gut writes, for example, that the "fundamental substance" of Dowson's poetry is "an intoxicated eroticism" or "sensuous pleasure in the name of art"; "each poem . . . shows both the growing needs for fulfillment through various types of sensuousness and sensuality and the increasing impossibility of such fulfillment" (230). Michel Foucault's famous critique of modern assumptions about authorship appears in "What Is an Author?" (1969), trans. Josué Harari, in *The Critical Tradition*, 2nd ed., ed. David H. Richter (New York: Bedford St. Martin's, 1998), 890.

7. See, for example, Chris Snodgrass, "Aesthetic Memory's Cul-de-Sac: The Art of Ernest Dowson," *English Literature in Transition, 1880–1920* 35 (1992): 26–53; Houston Baker, "A Decadent's Nature: The Poetry of Ernest Dowson," *Victorian Poetry* 6 (1968): 21–28; John R. Reed, "Bedlamite and Pierrot: Ernest Dowson's Aesthetic of Futility," *English Literary History* 35 (1968): 94–133.

8. In some recent critical discussions, poems that either took shape in, or helped define, the Rhymers' collective project have become detached from that project and taken as independent "expressions" of their authors' decadent worldview. Karen Alkalay-Gut, for instance, writes that Ernest Dowson's poem "Non sum qualis eram bonae sub regno Cynarae" "suggests that once sensual pleasures have been experienced, they can be only numbingly repeated," with the result that "the poetic voice [is left] in a state of frustrated weariness" ("Aesthetic and Decadent Poetry," 242). But Alkalay-Gut attends here only to what Pierre Macherey terms the text's "banal surface," on the assumption that literary texts produce meaning transparently, as mere objects for critical consumption. She makes no mention of the fact that Dowson's "most famous" poem seems to have been born in a collective enterprise (prior to the poem's appearance in *The Second Book of the Rhymers' Club*, an early version of it appeared in the *Century Guild Hobby Horse* in April 1891); and she neglects to point out that at the time of the poem's early composition, in February 1891, Dowson was an enthusiastic member of the Rhymers' Club. As we shall see, these facts, which are coded into Dowson's poem in its first two printings, bear directly on how the poem invites interpretation. As Macherey remarks, "A straightforward reading reveals only the banal surface, but behind the scenes is enacted the astonishing and controlled drama of *genesis*" (Pierre Macherey, *A Theory of Literary Production*, trans. Geoffrey Wall [London: Routledge, 1978], 23). Arthur Symons comments that "it is a

matter of . . . legitimate speculation what sort of person is called up before the mind's eye . . . as the author" of poetry at once "so reverent and so disembodied" (Symons, "Literary Causerie," 152). Similarly, Alkalay-Gut's remarks on "Non sum qualis . . ." remain trapped within the poem's own self-representations, willing victims to the ideology of "Decadence" that lays itself open to conscious inspection in the various collaborative projects with which Dowson's poetry was first bound up.

9. See John Gawsworth, "The Dowson Legend," *Transactions of the Royal Society of Literature,* March 1939; and Alford, *Rhymers' Club,* 79–91.

10. Foucault, "What Is an Author?" 890.

11. Maurice Blanchot, "The Book to Come" (1959), trans. S. Rabinovitch, in *A Book of the Book: Some Works and Projections about the Book and Writing,* ed. Jerome Rothenberg and Steven Clay (New York: Granary Books, 2000), 145.

12. Foucault, "What Is an Author?" 890.

13. "The sum total is not materially affected, for better or for worse, by the laborious lispings of Mr. Edwin J. Ellis and Mr. G. A. Greene" (anonymous review of *The Second Book of the Rhymers' Club, Athenæum,* 25 August 1894, quoted in Alford, *Rhymers' Club,* 43).

14. Compare, for instance, Ellis's description of poetry's descent from "the boundless" with Blake's dramatizations of the origins of poetic inspiration in his introduction to *Songs of Innocence and of Experience,* ed. Geoffrey Keynes (1967; reprint, Oxford University Press, 1970), pl. 4. With W. B. Yeats, Edwin J. Ellis coedited *The Works of William Blake* (London: B. Quaritch, 1893).

15. Two features underscore the status of "Song of the Songsmiths" as a collective manifesto. It is subtitled "First Anniversary of the Rhymers' Club," and it is the only poem in either collection, with the conspicuous exception of Ernest Rhys's "At the Rhymers' Club," printed entirely in the declamatory form of roman italics.

The concern with poetry's performativity witnessed in "Song of the Songsmiths" carries over two years later into *The Second Book of the Rhymers' Club,* whose opening poem, John Todhunter's "The Rhymers' Club: In Westminster Abbey, October 12, 1892," reflects on the status of British poetry in the wake of Tennyson's death. Despite its determination to mourn Tennyson in "music serene" and "solemn service of high song," Todhunter's poem registers an impassive awareness that, with Tennyson's passing, "some rich strain superbly rolls away / Like the close of an Olympian day" (*SBRC,* 1–2). But a note of cold finality increasingly characterizes the poem's depictions of Tennyson's life, poetry, and death; and with its emphatic final line, "We leave him to his rest," one can sense the poets of a younger generation rushing to embrace the opportunity offered by the disappearance of the old order. Positioned at the opening of *The Second Book of the Rhymers' Club,* the poem generates a sense of expectancy that is immediately taken up by the following poem, "Beyond?" which implies the coming into being of an as-yet-undefined or emergent language.

16. Charles Bernstein, introduction to *Close Listening: Poetry and the Performed Word*, ed. Bernstein (New York: Oxford University Press, 1998), 22.

17. The anemia underpinning Dowson's "All night upon my breast I felt her warm heart beat" (*SBRC*, 60) is made explicit in these lines by Todhunter:

> So let the clock tick on,
>
> Measuring the soft pulsations of Time's wing,
>
> While to the pulseless ocean, like a swan
>
> Abandoned to an unrelenting stream,
>
> Floating, I hear thee faint and fainter sing.
>
> (*SBRC*, 63)

18. Jerome McGann, *The Textual Condition* (Princeton, NJ: Princeton University Press, 1991), 13. See also McGann's comment in chapter 5 of the present volume: "For printed and scripted work, language and meaning unfold through the reader's transaction with visible phenomena," that is, "in the foul rag and bone shops where type meets ink and kisses paper and where paper gets gathered and bound for glory."

19. On the impact of the *Century Guild Hobby Horse* and the *Dial* during the fin de siècle, see Ian Fletcher, "Decadence and the Little Magazines," in *Decadence and the 1890s*, ed. Fletcher (London: Edward Arnold, 1979), 172–202.

20. Ernest Rhys, *Wales England Wed: An Autobiography* (London: J. M. Dent, 1940), quoted in Alford, *Rhymers' Club*, 7.

21. Jerome McGann, *Black Riders: The Visible Language of Modernism* (Princeton, NJ: Princeton University Press, 1993), 12.

22. The *Hobby Horse*, which ran to seven volumes of approximately 160 pages each, was published from 1886 to 1892. Volume 6 contains eight illustrations by various artists including Charles Shannon and Selwyn Image; thirteen poems (by Selwyn Image, Lionel Johnson, Laurence Binyon, Michael Field, Joseph Skipsey, Gustave Kahn, Ernest Dowson, and Horne); and sixteen essays (four of which are by Horne). Figure 3 features, on the left page, the conclusion of Lionel Johnson's essay "A Note upon the Practice and Theory of Verse at the Present Time Obtaining in France." On the "disciplined eclecticism" of Herbert Horne and Arthur Mackmurdo, joint editors of the *Hobby Horse* in 1891, see Fletcher, "Decadence," 179.

23. George Bornstein, "What Is the Text of a Poem by Yeats?" in *Palimpsest: Editorial Theory in the Humanities*, ed. Bornstein and R. G. Williams (Ann Arbor: University

of Michigan Press, 1993), 179. McGann's chapter in the present volume is a fully materialist elaboration of what Bornstein means by "contextual coding."

24. Blanchot, "The Book to Come," 143.

25. See, for example, the exclusion of Yeats's Rhymers' Club poems from the section devoted to "The Nineties" in *The Norton Anthology of English Literature*, vol. 2, 7th ed. (New York: W. W. Norton, 2000), 1,740–1,896. Yeats's 1890s poems appear in the *Norton Anthology* under the heading "The Twentieth Century" (2,085ff.). See also the remark with which the *Norton Anthology*'s editors (inaccurately) disparage Yeats's early poetry: "He began in the tradition of self-conscious Romanticism, which he learned from the London poets of the 1890s" (2,085).

26. The situation is somewhat different with *The Second Book of the Rhymers' Club*, published in 1894, when the reputations of Yeats, Johnson, Symons, and Dowson went before them.

27. Anonymous, review of *The Book of the Rhymers' Club, Daily Chronicle*, 26 February 1892, quoted in Alford, *Rhymers' Club*, 26–27.

28. Anonymous, review of *The Book of the Rhymers' Club*, 29.

29. Anonymous, review of *The Book of the Rhymers' Club*, 27–28.

30. Yeats, "The Rhymers' Club," 23 April 1892, quoted in Alford, *Rhymers' Club*, 143, 145.

31. *Letters of Ernest Dowson*, 202–3, quoted in Nelson, *Early Nineties*, 162.

32. *The Garland of New Poetry by Various Writers* (London: Elkin Mathews, 1899); A. J. A. Symons, ed., *An Anthology of "Nineties" Verse* (London: Elkin Mathews and Marrot, 1928); and Karl Beckson, ed., *Aesthetes and Decadents of the 1890s*, 2nd ed. (Chicago: Academy, 1981). For the hermeneutic and cultural implications of the production of anthologies, see Anne Ferry, *Tradition and the Individual Poem: An Inquiry into Anthologies* (Stanford, CA: Stanford University Press, 2001); and Leah Price, *The Anthology and the Rise of the Novel* (Cambridge: Cambridge University Press, 2000).

33. Gilles Deleuze and Félix Guattari, *Kafka: Toward a Minor Literature*, trans. Dana Polan (Minneapolis: University of Minnesota Press, 1986), 17.

34. Deleuze and Guattari, *Kafka*, 17.

35. In his 1833 essay "What Is Poetry?" John Stuart Mill remarks, "The truth of poetry is to paint the human soul truly" (*Essays on Poetry by John Stuart Mill*, ed. F. Parvin Sharpless [Columbia: University of South Carolina Press, 1976], 8). Similarly, in reinforcing his call for poetry to take the place of religion in English national life, Matthew Arnold approvingly quotes Wordsworth's definition of poetry as "the breath and finer spirit of knowledge" and comments: "In reading poetry, a sense for the best, the really excellent, and of the strength and joy to be drawn from it, should be present in our

minds and should govern our estimate of what we read" (Matthew Arnold, "The Study of Poetry" [1880], in *Selected Poems and Prose,* ed. Miriam Allott [London: J. M. Dent, 1978], 243).

36. Cf. note 15. This historical coincidence is registered too in Dowson's correspondence, with an explicit reflection on the Rhymers' effort to differentiate a new collectivist, demotic ideal of poetry: "It is settled that we are to hold the Laurelship as a corporate office, and present the butt of Canary to the patron du Cheshire" (*Letters of Ernest Dowson,* ed. Desmond Flower and Henry Maas [London: Cassell, 1967], 243).

37. Anonymous, review of *The Second Book of the Rhymers' Club, Athenæum,* 25 August 1894, reprinted in Alford, *Rhymers' Club,* 42. According to Marysa Demoor (private email to the author, 27 March 2004), who has studied poetry reviewing arrangements at the *Athenæum* in the 1880s and 1890s, this review was written by H. F. Wilson. See her *Their Fair Share: Women, Power and Criticism in* The Athenæum, *from Millicent Garrett Fawcett to Katherine Mansfield, 1870–1920* (Aldershot, UK: Ashgate, 2000), 114.

38. "Logroller" [Richard Le Gallienne], review of *The Book of the Rhymers' Club, Star,* 11 February 1892, quoted in Alford, *Rhymers' Club,* 37. Le Gallienne chose for the purposes of this review to exempt himself from the twelve poets whose work he was reviewing.

39. [Le Gallienne], review of *The Book of the Rhymers' Club,* 37.

40. Anonymous review of *The Book of the Rhymers' Club, Church Quarterly,* October 1892, reprinted in Alford, *Rhymers' Club,* 40–41.

41. Yeats's 1922 account of club meetings is implicitly critical of the Rhymers' collective dedication to oral recitation: "The meetings were always decorous and often dull; some one would read out a poem and we would comment, too politely for the criticism to have great value; and yet that we read our poems, and thought that they could be so tested, was a definition of our aims" (Yeats, *Trembling,* 233). Plarr's account of the Rhymers' meetings concurs with that of Yeats in emphasizing an atmosphere of timidity and "gloom" subtly counteracted by "our individual alacrity to read when duly pressed to do so" (390). But Charles Bernstein argues that this undramatic or "anti-performative" quality goes to the very heart of the modern poetry reading: "[T]he most problematic aspect of the poetry reading may turn out to be its essence: that is, its lack of spectacle, drama and dynamic range, as exemplified in a certain minimal—anti-expressivist— mode of reading" (introduction to *Close Listening,* 10). Rather than "dramatizing" the poem in "a style of acting that frames the performance in terms of character, personality, setting, gesture, development, or drama," the "project" of the poetry reading, Bernstein argues, "is to find the sound in the words, not in any extrinsic scenario or supplemental accompaniment. . . . In short, the significant fact of the poetry reading is

less the presence of the poet than the presence of the poem" (11–13). See also Peter Middleton, "The Contemporary Poetry Reading," in Bernstein, *Close Listening*, 262–99.

42. See *The Poetical Works of Ernest Christopher Dowson*, ed. Desmond Flower (London: Cassell and Co. and John Lane, The Bodley Head, 1934), 253–54.

43. Bernstein, introduction to *Close Listening*, 14.

44. Deleuze and Guattari, *Kafka*, 20.

45. Deleuze and Guattari, *Kafka*, 21.

46. John Keats to George and Thomas Keats, December 1817, in *Selected Letters of John Keats*, rev. ed., ed. G. F. Scott (Cambridge, MA: Harvard University Press, 2002), 61.

HERBERT HORNE'S *DIVERSI COLORES* (1891)

Incarnating the Religion of Beauty

Jerome McGann

Thy soul I know not from thy body, nor
Thee from myself, neither our love from God.
—DANTE GABRIEL ROSSETTI, "HEART'S HOPE" (1881)

The notorious passage from Rossetti standing at the head of this chapter identifies the kind of generic upheavals that mark the whole of the transitional period of the late nineteenth century. The passage records an experience of categorical dissolutions that will play out in various ways in all of Rossetti's work. He writes a story, "Hand and Soul," that is more a revisionary account of art history, an aesthetic manifesto, and a theory of art than an imaginative tale. More than that, its *argument* is an incarnation of the work's stylistic procedures. Forecast in "Hand and Soul" are various works of a similar kind—Oscar Wilde's "The Portrait of Mr. W. H." (1889), obviously, but also Vernon Lee's marvelous story "The Virgin of the Seven Daggers" (1896), which is an account and a theory of baroque art.

A metadistinction between content and form licenses the superstructure of all genre distinctions. When that foundational distinction is regarded as heuristic rather than categorical—a full-blown event in the work of Pater, Whistler, and Wilde—the ground is prepared for James Joyce's *Ulysses* (1922), Laura Riding's *Anarchism Is Not Enough* (1928), all of Marcel Duchamp, and the widespread twentieth-century metastasis of traditional genre epitomized—even incarnated—in Eliot's *The Waste Land* (1922).

We have a clear general sense of these events, of course. What we do not have is a comprehensive methodology for studying and analyzing them. In this chapter I look closely at a single work by a minor, if not insignificant, figure of the English aesthetic movement. I do this because Herbert Horne's little book *Diversi Colores* is a good, clear example of a work that wants to show the kind of knowledge we gain when we decide *not to know* a difference between the soul and the body—which is to say, in this case, between the physical design of a book and its (so-called) conceptual content. This critical undertaking is even more modest, perhaps, than Horne's book. Still, unless we are prepared to execute our dreamed-of "comprehensive methodology" at such a microlevel, the methodology will remain just that—a sublimation, a soul without a body.

I

For printed and scripted work, language and meaning unfold through the reader's transaction with visible phenomena. In recent years, this view has energized a resurgent body of bibliographical scholarship grown increasingly aware of its foundational position in any interpretive act. As a result, the cognitive functions of the material signifier are now regularly taken for granted in literary and cultural studies.

Rarely does this work engage the question of meaning at the most primitive textual levels, however—that is, in the foul rag and bone shops where type meets ink and kisses paper and where paper gets gathered and bound for glory.[1]

The difficulty is not theoretical; it is practical in a very specific sense. Even where a work clearly, and as we might say "deliberately," aims to integrate message and medium, the ideative contribution of the most elementary textual materials usually slips past notice or gets short shrift. The case of Stéphane Mallarmé's *Un coup de dés* (1897) is exemplary: for while the poem has drawn to itself a large body of interpretation, the explications almost always seek to resolve themselves at levels of meaning above the level of the signifiers.[2] Those interpretations implicitly declare that the signifiers are vehicular forms—not incarnations of meaning but hired bearers. In contrast, the case of William Morris shows how the full significance of visible language can get lost at the other end of the interpretive schedule. Commentators on Morris so foreground the artisanal scene of his writing that they turn it into a spectacle of Work and Beauty, as if a record of vital statistics obviated any need for those nuanced critical reflections so characteristic of Mallarméan studies.

We need to *execute* in regular ways our theoretical views about the material and performative character of textual works of imagination. Theory will not take us very far, as the history of scholarship for the past fifty and more years has proved. Roland Barthes's work set forth all the required theoretical lines, and others since have refined and reiterated them. Despite the limitations of theory, and despite much lip service to materialist and phenomenological ideas, interpretive method today remains largely committed, at the practical level, to referential and vehicular— rather than to incarnational and performative—models of meaning.

Real change will come about when we develop a set of regular interpretive procedures that command attention to the textual action that takes place at the signifying system's most primitive levels. We have come pretty far, especially in the past twenty years, in developing explication procedures for a work's production and reception histories. Even the best of these, however, tend to organize their data at so-called higher order frames of reference. While such moves are necessary, even crucial, they compromise their own critical strength when they fail to pursue a fully articulated interpretational representation at the craft level of the signifying process.

No one now knows how to do this, and if history is any guide, as it usually is, we will learn only through the continuous efforts of many persons over some period of time.

So let us take a small step in that direction by looking at a particular book—Herbert Horne's *Diversi Colores*. The book seems to me especially useful, in the interpretational context we are considering, because (a) its principal subject is bookmaking's relation to poetry, and (b) it makes itself the focus—the performative and material focus—of that larger subject. Unlike Mallarmé's *Un coup de dés* or Morris's *The Earthly Paradise* (1868–70), Horne's book tries to regulate its orders of meaning, including its cultural and ideological orders, in bibliographical aesthetics.

Before we look more closely at what Horne does with *Diversi Colores*, let me recall briefly the book's context. First of all, Horne was not primarily a poet, and *Diversi Colores* is the only book of verse he ever published. He wrote more poetry than appears in this book, but his primary interests were in book design, in typography, and later in architecture and art history. He designed three different typefaces and wrote an important work on bookbinding. In the late 1880s and 1890s—which is the immediate context of *Diversi Colores*—Horne's attention was focused on the aesthetics of the book, and he established himself as a major figure in the British "renaissance of printing" movement. He was—in all but name until 1893—the editor of that key arts and crafts periodical the *Century Guild Hobby Horse,* and he seems to have been indispensable in organizing the meetings of the Rhymers' Club. He himself, it appears, never read his own poetry at those famous gatherings, though he was a regular participant.[3]

When we locate *Diversi Colores* in that general context we can see very clearly the contrast Horne's book makes with other books of aesthetic and Decadent poetry. His corpus is not a sequence of volumes of his own verse, as are those of "Michael Field," John Davidson, Ernest Dowson, John Gray, and Lionel Johnson. Horne's corpus is a designer's corpus—a series of books, mostly books of verse, one of which prints his own verse. *Diversi Colores* is the second in a series that climaxes in 1895 in a splendid book of Lionel Johnson's *Poems,* published by Elkin Mathews.

When poets write poems, part of the writing is a quest to explore and develop their own resources. The same is true of all artists, and in this case we trace a clear line of advance in Horne's powers as a book designer. Simply in point of book design, Horne's work in 1895 is more certain and accomplished than in 1891, when he put his own book of poetry together. Because the texts in *Diversi Colores* are Horne's own, however, that book provided him with a unique opportunity. Somewhat like Blake one hundred years before, even more like Rossetti a few decades earlier, Horne took comprehensive control of his book's principal expressive features. In doing this he fashioned an aesthetic manifesto for an art of "the total book" quite as interesting in its way as that pivotal manifesto of the immediately preceding period, Rossetti's "Hand and Soul" (1850). But whereas Rossetti constructs a contemporary historicist argument via his fictional tale, Horne's book proceeds as a demonstration of method. It lays down his aesthetic precepts by setting an example of how to carry them out.

Consequently, in *Diversi Colores* graphic design is not a bearer of other meanings; it is meaning's informing principle. To borrow a figure from the Christian lexicon so central to *Diversi Colores*, the book's "outward and visible signs" incarnate its "inward and spiritual condition." That idea pervades the book in recurrent forms of what Horne calls in one of the book's poems "the secular image."[4]

II

The argument begins on the title page, which is printed entirely from a woodcut (fig. 20). The presence of woodcut textual forms is a notably self-conscious initial move—partly a historicist allusion to pre-fifteenth-century printing, partly a reminder that books and texts can be printed in diverse ways. This title page is also a virtual emblem for aestheticism as the religion of Beauty, although the emblem is by no means transparent. In that respect it signals a procedure of obliquity that runs through the book as a whole.

Several things on the title page are especially significant. The central flower ornament, a woodspurge, deliberately recollects Rossetti's poem "The Woodspurge" (1870), in which the poet makes his remarkable argument for emptying natural forms of their religious symbolism in order to restore their primary value as secular images. Furthermore, heading an 1891 letterpress book with a woodcut makes a clear aesthetic gesture, a move underscored by the reference to Chiswick Press. William Morris had issued his first call for an arts and crafts revival in the 1850s by having his own work printed at Chiswick, which represented an antithesis to the age's commercially driven butcher printing.

These are not transparent signs, though they are perhaps more recondite now than they were in 1891. Most striking of all, however, are the least transparent features of this page: its title and author line. These primary informational elements are, in one case, secretly coded and, in the other, invisible. They are, in short, conventional signifiers that call attention to themselves by *not* functioning in their customary informational way.

I will shortly comment in greater detail on the specific historical character of the book's aestheticism. But first let us consider the way meaning is withheld or obscured on the title page. The page arranges an ensemble

FIGURE 20. Title page, *Diversi Colores*, by Herbert Horne (London: printed by the author at the Chiswick Press, 1891). Courtesy of the University of Virginia

of reading difficulties that command a heightened level of attention to the material signifiers. It thus sends forward, into the body of the book, a signal to the same effect. Unlike Horne's title page, however, where the privacy of the book is emphasized, the typographical main text lays down an inherently more public and accessible set of signifiers: not just the letterpress characters but also a set of well-established presentational conventions for a book of poems. The ideal of a noise-free channel of message delivery controls most printed texts, which have usually turned off their reveal-codes option. Such books do not want to draw attention to their typographical and bibliographical codes lest the vehicular division of signifier and signified collapse into what has been called a "symbol standing for itself." Such books solicit readers who expect a transparency of the signifier.

Horne's book also solicits these kinds of readers, but not in order to satisfy their customary expectations. *Diversi Colores* is organized to short-circuit a vehicular transaction (and theory) of its texts in order to make an argument—it is also a demonstration—of a very different approach to textuality.

What is most notable about Horne's book is the simplicity of the means he chooses to make his argument. The famous displays of complex textuality that lay in the future of *Diversi Colores*—for instance, Mallarmé's *Un coup de dés,* Guillaume Apollinaire's *Caligrammes* (1918), Blaise Cendrars' *La Prose du Transsibérien* (1913), or Ezra Pound's *Cantos* (especially the first two installments [1925–28])—are far too spectacular for Horne. Equally removed are those elaborate private adventures in textuality that preceded Horne's work: Blake's illuminated books, which Horne knew and admired; the Brontës' fantastic worlds of Gondal and Angria; the "sumptuary" textualities spun from Emily Dickinson's scripts.[5] Had Horne possessed Alfred Jarry's ebullience he might have sought a more startling or crazed typographical surface. But Horne's imagination, though acute, ran to spareness and reserve, not to styles of excess, as the book's small and modest format makes very clear (the book measures 6 1/4 by 4 inches). In that miniaturized textual world he is able to foreground the material signifier—or rather, the integrated system of material significations—by playing relatively simple variations with roman and italic type across a book space (as opposed to a page space) carefully organized in three distinct parts. Aside from on the title page, he deploys only one other type of textual manipulation: a special *mise en page* procedure in the first section of the book.

Let us look more closely at how Horne's book design works. Although no table of contents signals individual poems and no sections of the book are separately marked, *Diversi Colores* falls into three distinct parts. Leaving the divisions unmarked puts a special demand on the reader's attention. If these unmarked parts are not observed, one misses a key expressive feature of the book. The first section, running from page 7 to page 16, holds four pastiche works; the second, pages 17–40, shifts to a series of poems that exploit a first-person style. Note that both of these sections end on a verso and face the recto of the section to follow. The third section, pages 41–47, unfolds an integral sequence of six numbered poems presenting themselves as a kind of homage to Robert Herrick.

To appreciate the importance of the sectioning, consider the poem that opens the second part. I offer it here as it appears on the recto side of its bibliographical "opening." Forget about the poem on the left for the moment and read only what New Critical exegetes used to call the "poem itself."[6] This is the poem whose meaning emerges from the book space of a single page (fig. 21).

Despite the lucid syntax and the clear arrangement of images, this text by itself is surely quite enigmatic. The problems begin with the title, which must mean either "By the Watchers" or "To the Watchers"—whoever they are. The difficulty ripples through the second-person pronoun as well as the poem's implied first person. Who are they, and what do they

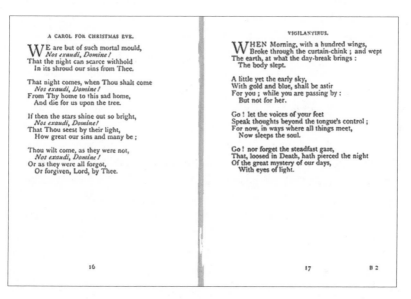

FIGURE 21. Horne, *Diversi Colores* (1891), 16–17. Courtesy of the University of Virginia

have to do with one another? Similar elementary questions proliferate: Is the imperative of the last two quatrains addressed to the "you" named in line 7? How do we read the references to the sleep of the body and the sleep of the soul and the temporal relations between them?

The "poem itself" does not resolve such problems. The difficulty here calls attention to a more general issue of textual interpretation that requires some comment at this point, though it bears only indirectly on the immediate issue. That is to say, the very concept of a "poem itself," or indeed of any kind of self-identity in any textual unit, distorts our apprehension of the signifying mechanism of poetical textualities. Like all critical deformations, the New Critical "poem itself" can serve useful critical purposes so long as, applying it, we bear in mind that the method *is* a simplifying distortion. Forgetting that, we flay the poem alive, stripping it to some thematized death, or what Blake might have called "A Poetic Abstract."

Setting that matter aside for the moment, let us look again at the text—this time by restoring it to its position in the book. For we want to keep in mind that bibliographical position is a key element in any book's three-dimensional coding system. The poem is the first poem of the second section and lies on the recto side of an opening. The verso opposite carries another poem whose four-quatrain text makes a visible rhyme with the four quatrains of "Vigilantibus." The opening thus draws a connection between two parts of Horne's book that are, in other crucial respects—as we shall see—utterly different. The opening, in short, creates a visible *hinge* moment in the book, turning us from one part to the next and signaling the turn not through some conventional section marker (say a half title) but by means of a far simpler, far more discreet gesture. The discretion of the move issues a metadeclaration about the cognitive import of bibliographical position and the special functional opportunities licensed at a page opening for any bibliographical field.

The connection between the first two sections of the book is reinforced in the way Horne deals with the physical presentation of the poem's title. Printed in roman small capitals, it rhymes with the other titles in the book. But the book also locates the title in relation to italic types, for a presentational rule holds that whereas all of the central poetic texts are roman, all paratexts (like marginalia), most of which are Latin texts, are italic. That differential in the typefaces exposes the wit secreted in the title

"Vigilantibus." The title names those vigilant readers who can trace the discourse of typographical signs to locate the reference of the title. The word *vigilantibus* references the *voces vigilantium* of part I of the book, those characters marginally printed—"printed" here means "named"—in the second poem of *Diversi Colores*.

That reference takes us to the center of the book's opening section, where *Diversi Colores*'s second most important nonsemantic semiosis is deployed. The four works printed on pages 7 to 16 all emerge from their textual condition as what we now call shaped poems. All of the texts, but especially the first two, are presented as if they were found texts of the late sixteenth or early seventeenth century here presented in a late nineteenth-century orthography. But whereas Horne appears to have modernized the spelling of the texts, he also appears to have preserved an antique rather than a modernized typographical design. The entire scene is a pastiche exercise that recalls nothing so much as certain of Rossetti's works (like "Ave" [1870]). Rossetti never carried his imitative forms as far as Horne does here, however—that is to say, he never attempted to install pastiche at such an aggressively nonsemantic level.

Horne's shaped poems are nothing like those of Apollinaire or e. e. cummings. But we would be much mistaken if we registered these texts as merely ornamental or antiquarian. At an initial encounter they call attention to themselves precisely because their code of signals is far in excess of the apparent (the transparent) religious meanings borne by the poems. No pastiche is needed to deliver the Christian message of these texts. What then is the function of such textual redundancy? That is the question haunting these four strange poems—the first and the last Christmas songs, the second and third dramatic scenes from the Resurrection.

As with "Vigilantibus," deciphering these poems hangs on our ability to draw bibliographical connections between them and other parts and elements of Horne's book. For *Diversi Colores* is finally not a book containing a set of poems containing their subsets of semantic messages. On the contrary, it is a carefully organized arrangement of differential signifiers of various kinds, some of which we have yet to examine. Horne presses our attention on his book's nonsemantic features precisely to break the spell of the sign's transparency. The arrangement is a demonstration of the communicative power of the material signifier *as such,* and the demonstration requires the reader's active participation. Estranged from the easy semantic transfers of a customary textual economy, the reader is asked to reengage with the text as a whole by a fresh passage through its most primitive elements. The book then marshals that process of reexamination toward a general demonstrative argument about the dynamic structure of textual formations.

III

I am now going to shift this commentary into a different mode, because an explication of nonsemantic signifiers presents peculiar, but very interesting, interpretive problems. Let me explain.

Like the alphabet, graphical and bibliographical codes work by patterns of difference, and the emergence of meaningful formations waits on the appearance of some governing form or dynamical rule. The marks and forms do not "mean" anything by themselves. Furthermore, deciphering these textual elements and their (so to say) molecular arrangements requires a reader, and the reader—whose name is Legion—has to decipher by further encoding. We recognize this as a process of textual supplementations, and traditional hermeneutics has worked out procedures for unfolding them. Because the procedures typically focus on the semantic text, however, the reader engages the text—recodes it—at an equivalent semantic level. We can't easily do the same with nonsemantic elements.

At a certain point in any exegesis of nonsemantic forms, therefore, the reader has to situate them in a general reading program that is coded as an explanation rather than as a demonstration or an execution. This explanatory move must not be taken to imply, however, that the nonsemantic forms are the vehicles for semantic meanings. On the contrary, the semantical recoding that we call interpretation is itself the servomechanism for advancing the reader's engagement with the totality of the text. In the present case, it will help to clarify the presence of a network of graphical elements and their relations.

Look at the first text page of Horne's book (fig. 22). How do we know that we are not to read this as a doctrinal work centered in Christian liturgy? More than that, what makes us realize that the page signals the reader to make secular translations of certain key phrases, like "the Word" and "changed to song"? That is to say, how do we know we are

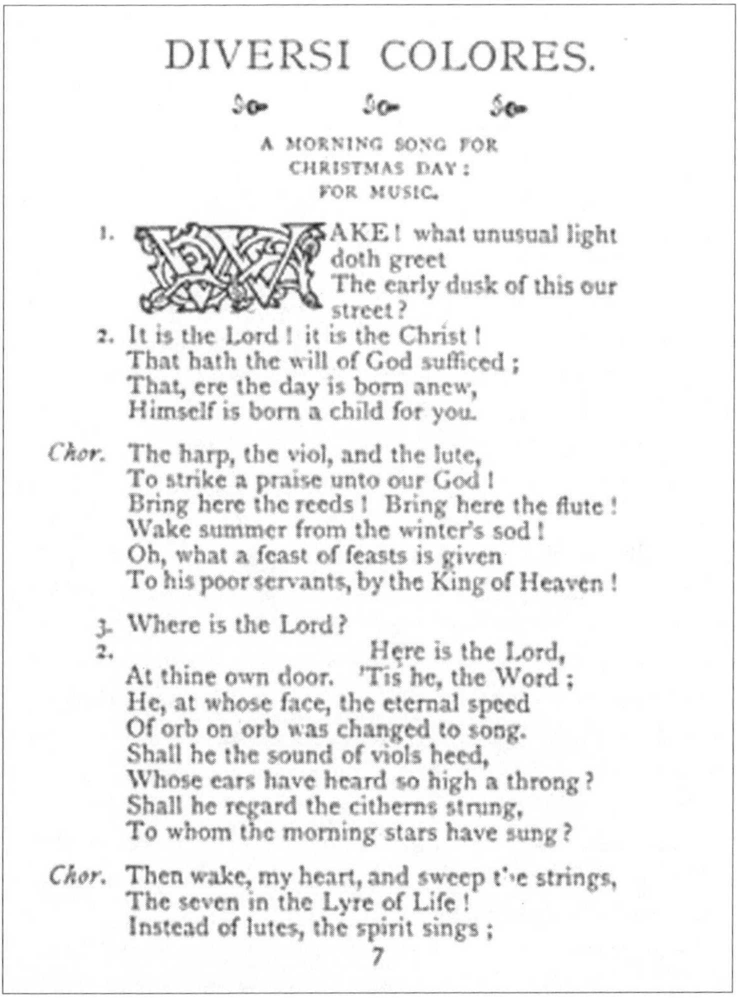

DIVERSI COLORES.

ॐ   ॐ   ॐ

A MORNING SONG FOR
CHRISTMAS DAY:
FOR MUSIC.

1.   ˥AKE! what unusual light
     doth greet
     The early dusk of this our
     street?

2.   It is the Lord! it is the Christ!
     That hath the will of God sufficed;
     That, ere the day is born anew,
     Himself is born a child for you.

Chor.   The harp, the viol, and the lute,
          To strike a praise unto our God!
          Bring here the reeds! Bring here the flute!
          Wake summer from the winter's sod!
          Oh, what a feast of feasts is given
          To his poor servants, by the King of Heaven!

3.   Where is the Lord?
2.   Here is the Lord,
     At thine own door. 'Tis he, the Word;
     He, at whose face, the eternal speed
     Of orb on orb was changed to song.
     Shall he the sound of viols heed,
     Whose ears have heard so high a throng?
     Shall he regard the citherns strung,
     To whom the morning stars have sung?

Chor.   Then wake, my heart, and sweep the strings,
          The seven in the Lyre of Life!
          Instead of lutes, the spirit sings;

7

FIGURE 22. Horne, *Diversi Colores* (1891), 7. Courtesy of the University of Virginia

meant to read both phrases much more literally, as referencing not Christ and the music of the spheres but this text, the "Morning Song" named in the title line?

We know this because the book lays down a diverse pattern of textual phenomena, ranged across its whole length, that (a) trouble or resist the offered transparent meanings, and (b) passively invite such aesthetic transformations as alternative readings. The case here is at bottom no different from the case of "Vigilantibus," or indeed of the recondite title page. Essential to Horne's performative argument is that he does not *declare* these procedures for the reader but leaves their execution to us. Essential to my exegetical argument, on the other hand, is to supply at a certain point a general framework for licensing reading procedures that, if applied anywhere in the book, will find their truth conditions satisfied by a specific interpretive move.

Let me begin to sketch that framework by looking at another resistant text—the title of Horne's book. It hides its reference to a relatively obscure verse in the Vulgate Bible, I Chronicles 29:2. Here is the King James text—though, as we shall see, Horne's Latin title is far from a mere stylistic affectation: "Now I have prepared with all my might for the house of my God the gold for things to be made of gold, and the silver for things of silver, and the brass for things of brass, the iron for things of iron, and wood for things of wood; onyx stones, and stones to be set, glistering stones, and of divers colours, and all manner of precious stones, and marble stones in abundance." The passage makes the book's initial coded announcement of Horne's aestheticist ideas and intentions. Horne's editor's introduction to the January 1889 *Century Guild Hobby Horse* is our common reference point for his beliefs—they can scarcely be called anything less—about visible language and ornamental integrity in writing and bookmaking. These convictions are of course famously executed in the design features of that quintessential aesthetic periodical of the period. The title of *Diversi Colores,* however, indicates the precise devotional character of Horne's position.

I say "precise" and "devotional" because Horne's devotions are, like Rossetti's before him, *precisely* secular. Orthodox commentators, religious or not, too often mistake, or condescend to, the fin de siècle's "religion of Beauty." Certainly many at the time embraced this central period idea in loose, unclear, or even slovenly ways. Horne was not that kind of person, and one of the most important critical features of *Diversi Colores* is the exactitude with which it illustrates this key aestheticist conception.

As the root meaning of the word indicates, religion binds one to a set of practices. These practices will or should mark all aspects of the devotee's life, and when the person is involved in devotional exercises as such, precision is the watchword for behavior. Equally important, a religious practice is directed away from the self. It is a practice aimed toward the praise and glorification of the object of devotion. In this case, Horne devotes himself to glorifying Beauty by making a beautiful thing.

The book's recurrent Latin texts all either quote from the Vulgate Bible or imitate medieval textual usages. This kind of thing is common in Decadent and aesthetic poetry, as we know, but rarely is its programmatic function so clearly exposed. The layout of the poems gives them to us in an ornamental display, as their titles emphasize: "A Morning Song for Christmas Day: For Music"; "Hic incipit resurrectio Domini Nostri Jesu Christi, qui Nos dilexit"; "Ego sum primus et novissimus, et ecce sum vivens in saecula saeculorum, et habeo claves mortis, et inferni"; and "A Carol for Christmas Eve." No style of personal inflection—Horne *in propria persona*—appears in these poems. They are dominated by various impersonal or named voices identified and framed through obsolete bibliographical codes. The first poem has four numbered voices and a chorus; the second has various characters named "Vigilantes," "Maria Magdalene, Joanna, Maria Jacobi et ceterae mulieres"; a prima, secunda, and tertia "Vox"; and an "Angelus." The third poem is spoken by the resurrected Jesus; the fourth is an impersonal carol. The opening four poems thus emphasize their material textuality and subordinate their original Christian semantic meanings to an aesthetic display. As typology yields to typography and the *mise en page,* we find ourselves caught up and even secretly addressed by these dead signs, as if they and we too were coming back to a strange new life: "Wake! What unusual light doth greet / The early dusk of this our street." Like Thoreau in *Walden* (1854)—although here the style is severely impersonal—Horne is moving to wake the neighbors up. Page design works to evacuate the texts of their residual Christian significance and release them to secular construal:

> If ye would be the heirs . . .
> Follow ye Me . . .
> All I have overcome;
> For I have risen
> Out of the jaws of Sin,
> Out of the toils of Sloth,
> Out of the death of Lust,
> Out of the grave of Self:

Therefore now I am made
Even the Son of God;
He that is risen,
He that was dead, and is alive again.

("Ego sum primus et novissimus . . . ," 14)

This is nothing less than the modernist dictum "Make it new" expressed with an aesthetic inflection, as the Latin title of the poem suggests. As a dramatic monologue this poem follows the impersonal rhetoric of the two preceding poems, which have no first person at all. They speak themselves dramatically, through characters (in both senses, we now realize) and the signs of voiced sounds. But since the texts flaunt themselves as pastiche documents, all of these characters collapse into figures of pure textuality, as if the poems were what a later poem in the book describes as "absolute" ("Upon Returning a Silk Handkerchief" [32]). So the passage above translates into an allegorical revelation of a newborn poetry. The poem appears to be speaking itself.

Not without reason, therefore, are Dante Alighieri and Dante Gabriel Rossetti two of the book's key poetic and artistic presences. A heroic model in the pages of the *Century Guild Hobby Horse,* Rossetti is twice explicitly invoked—on the title page, as we've seen, and in "Lines Written in the Glen at Penkill" (28).[7] Both Dante and Rossetti are called to the reader's attention in "Upon Returning a Silk Handkerchief," which invokes Beatrice via a deliberate pastiche of the translational style Rossetti made famous in *The Early Italian Poets* (1861). Rossetti uses that volume to translate Dante's performative argument about a renascence of poetry, *Vita nuova.* That is also to say, Rossetti translates Dante's *Vita nuova* into an argument for a new nineteenth-century life for poetry. Like the *Century Guild Hobby Horse, Diversi Colores* is a conscious move to extend that argument.

This new poetry means to break free of sin, sloth, lust, and self; and the rest of Horne's book will try to show how that escape comes about. Christian sinfulness, especially lust, is abandoned in the pursuit of an erotic ideal that consciously recalls Rossetti's famous declaration "Thy soul I know not from thy body, nor / Thee from myself, neither our love from God."[8] Sloth yields to the book's display of elaborate care in its making, and the ideal of an impersonal address and procedure is realized by this very text and all its companions.

If we return to "Vigilantibus" now, we shall be able to read it in the context that Horne's book has created for itself. The title reaches back to the second poem, "Hic incipit resurrectio Domini Nostri . . . ," which opens with a speech by a group of "vigilantes." After thanking God for the daybreak, they worry that the promise of glory will, as another poet famously lamented, "fade into the light of common day." "Vigilantibus" explicitly reprises that earlier passage in *Diversi Colores,* and in so doing explicates its own strange title. That is to say not that it settles the question of whether the case of the word "Vigilantibus" is dative or ablative, only that both cases function equally well. If the poem is "to" the watchers, then it promises to answer their earlier apprehensions. If it is "by" the watchers, it illustrates that they have overcome those apprehensions.

Who *are* these watchers? The secular allegory established in the four opening pastiche poems settles that question nicely. They are those who watch for the coming of the new day or who, as in the passage from I Chronicles, prepare the house of the coming Lord. They are, in short, artists like Horne and readers like those he solicits. The poems of these vigilant persons are themselves "vigilantes," as we see in lines like the following, which are addressed to the poem itself, quite in a *stil novisti* manner: "Go! Let the voices of your feet / Speak thoughts beyond the tongue's control." That kind of wordplay, recurrent in the book, reminds us of the impersonality of Horne's poetry. "The voices of your feet" are textual voices being addressed by other textual voices.

IV

The fifth poem in *Diversi Colores,* "Vigilantibus," turns the reader over to the book's second section of erotic and secular pieces cast in a first-person address. Some of these are quasi-pastiche poems, like the brilliant *stil novisti* exercise "Upon Returning a Silk Handkerchief." Others adopt a more traditional first-person address. All are focused on the central issue of poiesis, as we see in the recurrent invocation of earlier poets. Catullus, Dante, Blake, Shelley, Keats, Swinburne, and especially Rossetti are all called into presence. They comprise a group of secular saints, revered for their devotion to their craft, on one hand, and for their awareness that a worthy craftsmanship must be measured by an ideal of self-extinction.

The dramatic and presentational poetic method established in the first section of *Diversi Colores* passes its influence over to section 2. Here a romantic first-person style is used in twenty-three poems that appear less as spontaneous overflows or tranquil recollections than as staged examples of those modes of poetic address. As in Pound's *Hugh Selwyn Mauberley* (1920) or Stevens's "Thirteen Ways of Looking at a Blackbird" (1954), each poem takes up the same theme from a slightly different perspective. The poems consider the problematic position, in a purely secular world, of artistic work that aspires to a devotional impersonality.

We see this most clearly, perhaps, in the second section's sonnet "To an Unknown Lady," one of the most brilliant pieces in the book. The sonnet is Italian in form and written after the manner of Rossetti. It represents the thoughts of a first-person speaker—let us say Horne—studying a drawing by Raphael. Horne uses his poem to address the "unknown lady" in the picture. He surmises that her visage was transformed to this "secular image" when Raphael saw the actual woman "face to face" one day "within this very place / This Umbrian valley" now visible to Horne, centuries later and in another country, in Raphael's picture. The locution that climaxes the octave, "face to face," is biblical and suggests a divine or transcendent encounter.

As the sonnet turns to its octave Horne imagines that the lady has forgotten this meeting—perhaps because she is dead, perhaps because she incarnates a being who was rapt away in her own immediate act of living or the ecstasy of living. Horne's Raphael, however, has not forgotten, which is to say that his picture "[h]olds the calm features" of the lady in a daily and ceaseless flowering. Horne reserves for the sonnet's final tercet a startling turn of wit: the revelation that if this (imagined) ordinary woman from Umbria were to look at the portrait Raphael drew, she would behold, not herself, but "[t]he face of Mary, mother of thy [i.e., her] God."

Two things about this poem are particularly important. First, we want to notice the act of imaginative wit that joins this poem to the order of the book conceived as a whole. The connection is made through the secret and devoted artifice of the "secular image"—that is to say, through a linguistic equivalence registered at the level of the signifier. When the pastiche Jesus of "Ego sunt primus et novissimus . . ." declares, "I live for evermore," he is translating part of his own poem's title: "Et ecce sum vivens in saecula saeculorum." Horne's book reconnects that biblical locution for eternal life, *in saecula saeculorum,* to its root mortal meaning, "secular."

Second, we want to see that the sonnet's first person is turned by "his" own poetic action from a living being into an aesthetic character. The "poet" here addresses a frankly imaginary creature and makes no effort to develop a reflective psychomachia. Two alternatives define the limits of an expressivist and romantic style: spontaneity of expression and sincerity of thought. In refusing either alternative the poem reaches an impersonal zenith of subjective expression. Like Swinburne's Sappho in "Anactoria" (1866), the first person here has become "now no more a singer but a song."

The first-person voices in the book's second section thus appear not to see or know themselves as voices. They come before us in diverse emotional states, all of them either troubled or—as in "To an Unknown Lady"—unaware of their aesthetic location. The function of the second part of the book is to stage the romantic program as an aesthetic drama, thereby subsuming it to secular translation and transcendence.

The book's final section completes the process with a marvelous pastiche of Herrick's Cavalier style, as we see so clearly on the section's opening page (fig. 23). As in section 1 of the book, layout here defines the way this corona of poems will be seen and read. We think of shaped poems in relation to concrete poetry, to various works by cummings and Apollinaire, or to famous texts like Herbert's "Easter Wings." But this page is clearly another example of Horne's shaped verse, with page layout raising the ghost of Herrick's Cavalier poetical world. The effect is to translate the text and all its elements into an abstract and aesthetic condition. The "maddening rhyme," "the dancing feet," "this measure done": here these figures become Horne's "absolute images," symbols that stand for themselves and the dance of their purely literal action.

That literality seems to free the poem from the "hastening year" and the "ravening past," which are the enemies this work is proposing to escape. Pastiche cancels the fleeing present and the flown past by collapsing them together. That this action comes simply as an immediate bibliographical apparition only enforces the sense of an escaped temporality. In the spatial form of this page, the antique title ("To His Muse, by Way of Prologue") transforms the first poem into a kind of found object. As in any number of Renaissance poems that follow similar formulae, the

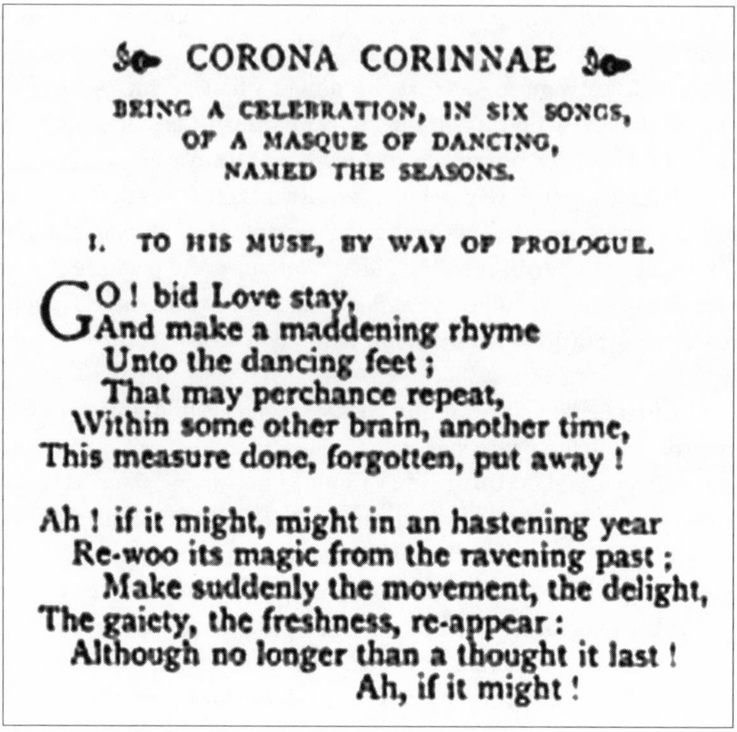

🔊 CORONA CORINNAE 🔊

BEING A CELEBRATION, IN SIX SONGS,
OF A MASQUE OF DANCING,
NAMED THE SEASONS.

I. TO HIS MUSE, BY WAY OF PROLOGUE.

GO! bid Love stay,
And make a maddening rhyme
Unto the dancing feet ;
That may perchance repeat,
Within some other brain, another time,
This measure done, forgotten, put away !

Ah ! if it might, might in an hastening year
Re-woo its magic from the ravening past ;
Make suddenly the movement, the delight,
The gaiety, the freshness, re-appear :
Although no longer than a thought it last !
Ah, if it might !

FIGURE 23. Horne, *Diversi Colores* (1891), 41. Courtesy of the University of Virginia

poem itself appears to issue the imperative of its first stanza and the subjective of its second stanza. In such a case the referent of "His" doubles itself to signal both Herrick and this speaking poem, with both working under a single inspirational form ("His Muse").

Horne's *mise en page* thus supplies the "magic" needed to realize this text's "thought" as a demonstrative and immediate action. The effect makes one think forward to Stevens. If Beauty is fitful and momentary in the mind, "in the flesh it is immortal."[9] Horne's bibliographical codes make his poems' words flesh in a sense very like the one Stevens was pursuing. Alike in the flesh, they differ in the spirit. Horne's neoclassical stance leaves him no room for Stevens's wonderful textual comedies. Nonetheless, both poets were well practiced in the religion of Beauty and its "secular images."

Notes

1. In scholarship devoted to the late nineteenth century, the work of Nicholas Frankel is an especially notable exception; see, for example, his *Oscar Wilde's Decorated Books* (Ann Arbor: University of Michigan Press, 2000). For an incisive recent discussion of the matter in general, see Johanna Drucker, "Graphical Readings and Visual Aesthetics of Textuality," *Text* (forthcoming).

2. The outstanding exception is Ernest Fraenkel's *Les Dessins trans-conscients de Stéphane Mallarmé: A propos de la typographie de Un Coup de dés* (Paris: Nizet, 1960).

3. The main, and nearly the only, published secondary source for information about Horne is Ian Fletcher's *Rediscovering Herbert Horne: Poet, Architect, Typographer, Art Historian* (Greensboro, NC: ELT Press, 1990). A decent facsimile of *Diversi Colores* appears in Woodstock's Decadents, Symbolists, Anti-Decadents: Poetry of the 1890s series; it is printed with a facsimile of Selwyn Image's *Poems and Carols*, edited with an introduction by R.K.R. Thornton and Ian Small (Oxford: Woodstock Books, 1995).

4. Herbert Horne, "To an Unknown Lady," *Diversi Colores* (London: published by the author at the Chiswick Press, 1891), 19; further page references appear in parentheses.

5. I take the word "sumptuary" from Susan Howe's remarkable essay on Dickinson; see *The Birth-Mark: Unsettling the Wilderness in American Literary History* (Hanover, NH: University of New England Press, 1993).

6. "The Poem Itself" is the title of a well-known and entirely exemplary work of New Critical interpretation. Stanley Burnshaw, *The Poem Itself* (New York: Holt, Rinehart, and Winston, 1960). The founding text of this interpretive movement was Cleanth Brooks and Robert Penn Warren's handbook *Understanding Poetry: An Anthology for College Students* (New York: Holt, 1938).

7. The "Glen at Penkill" is a specific reference to a sacred place well known to readers of poetry at the end of the nineteenth century, when Rossetti was such a cultural point of departure. See Rossetti's "The Stream's Secret" and "Farewell to the Glen," in *Dante Gabriel Rossetti: Collected Poetry and Prose*, ed. Jerome McGann (New Haven, CT: Yale University Press, 2003), 54–59, 164.

8. Rossetti, "Heart's Hope," *Dante Gabriel Rossetti*, 129.

9. Wallace Stevens, "Peter Quince at the Clavier," *The Collected Poems of Wallace Stevens* (New York: Vintage, 1990), 91.

THE POETIC IMAGING OF MICHAEL FIELD

Julia F. Saville

In the course of the past twelve years, many valuable studies have recognized the intriguing contribution made by the lesbian aunt-niece duo—Katharine Bradley and Edith Cooper, alias Michael Field—to the development of a nineteenth-century feminist poetics. In this chapter, I want to suggest that while the effect of Michael Field's work might in retrospect be interpretable as breaking new ground in fin-de-siècle women's writing, that was less their driving motivation than was the determination to engage shoulder to shoulder in debate with leading male intellectuals of an avant-garde, fin-de-siècle aesthetic culture. My discussion focuses on the particular aesthetic strategies that Michael Field adopt in their second volume of poetry, *Sight and Song* (1892). I demonstrate the provenance of these strategies in the work of the authors' male contemporaries and consider the implications of their engagement with Walter Pater, Robert Browning, and Bernard Berenson rather than with their female precedents or contemporaries—such as Anna Jameson or Vernon Lee in the field of art criticism, or, among the poets, Elizabeth Barrett Browning or Constance Naden.

In their first volume of poetry, *Long Ago* (1889), Michael Field use the affective style of Sapphic love poetry, with which various female poets of the nineteenth century experimented.[1] However, in their self-reflexive preface to *Sight and Song* Bradley and Cooper distance themselves from this affective style, proposing instead an impersonal, ekphrastic poetics. That is, they claim to write verbal translations of the "poetry" or feeling embodied in paintings, while practicing an authorial self-effacement that belongs to a specifically male Victorian aesthetic genealogy. It is a genealogy traceable in the eighteenth-century aesthetics of Johann Joaquim Winckelmann and returning in the "disinterestedness" of Matthew Arnold, the "impersonality" of Pater, and the "mask" of Oscar Wilde.

By pointing to this shift in style, I do not mean to suggest that in *Sight and Song* Michael Field forfeit the intense affect that is so engaging in *Long Ago*, nor do I wish to suggest that they conform to a narrative of nineteenth-century women's poetry that would read self-effacement as an intellectually progressive movement away from feminine affect or Victorian "slush," toward rigorous Poundian modernism.[2] Rather, I read the austerity of the poetics in *Sight and Song* as Michael Field's experiment in ascetic withholding, learned from Pater. Furthermore, I see this volume not as a moment of progress within a narrative of Bradley and Cooper's intellectual *Bildung*—and certainly not as progress from feminine affect to manly austerity—but rather as another variation of the delectable wit and play evident in a career largely predicated on Michael Field's determination to compete with their male contemporaries and refuse dismissal as two eccentric old biddies. Their experiments in self-effacement demonstrate precisely the aesthetic interaction of affect with reason that an aesthetic theorist such as Isobel Armstrong identifies as catalyzing social change through aesthetics.[3]

Michael Field's preface is the product of an energetic program of art appreciation on which the two women embarked in the early 1890s. A variety of factors conspired to encourage this enterprise, including their friendships with Browning, Pater, and Berenson—all men deeply invested in the study of art—and the death after a protracted illness of Emma Cooper (mother of Edith and older sister of Katharine), which meant that after August 1889, the coauthors could travel more freely. In addition, the accelerated and wide-scale opening of British and European art galleries and museums to the general public in the Victorian period made the discipline of aesthetic interpretation increasingly inviting and available to women. Bradley and Cooper seized every opportunity to visit art galleries at home and abroad and were among the many women who took advantage of extended museum hours that had become the norm at this time.[4] Museums and galleries were still among the few urban havens where unescorted women could pass time unmolested before an evening meeting or theater engagement. On Monday, 24 November 1890, for instance, the poets took the train to London from their home in Reigate to attend the lecture that Walter Pater was giving on Prosper Mérimée at the London Institution. They arrived several hours early, so, in Cooper's words, "Till the appointed hour, we took refuge in the National Gallery."[5] *Sight and Song* emerges out of the copious notes they took during such visits as well as their simultaneous study of the aesthetic theories of Pater and Berenson. The poets' preface engages specifically with the views Pater expressed in his lecture on Mérimée.

Pater gave this lecture initially at Oxford, repeated it in London, and published it a month later, in the *Fortnightly Review* of December 1890. It was thus a text not only available in written form but also very much in the air as Bradley and Cooper embarked on their self-education in the pictorial arts. The essay returns to a dynamic Pater had studied throughout his academic career: the paradoxically seductive power given to both critical and creative work by the authorial practice of self-withholding. According to Pater's interpretation, Mérimée practices another version of the artistic self-discipline referred to in the preface to *The Renaissance:* "the charm of *ascêsis,* of the austere and serious girding of the loins in youth."[6] In its most erotically suggestive form, this self-restraint permits the (implicitly male) viewer to appreciate the beauty of the human body in calm detachment, like the cool "serenity" of Winckelmann, which, in Pater's view, allows the German critic to experience the sensuousness of Greek sculpture dispassionately as "he fingers those pagan marbles with unsinged hands, with no sense of shame or loss."[7] In "Prosper Mérimée," such ascetic practice has become "superb self-effacement," or "impersonality," that withholds "an unsuspected force of affection" in the author.[8] It serves to remind Pater's audience that his seemingly subjective, impressionistic aesthetic theory was always also an ascetic theory; for the sensuousness and affective intensity of his aesthetics arises more from its austerity than from the hedonistic self-indulgence that his critics attributed to it.

As recent scholarship has shown, this Paterian ascesis discreetly signals the male viewer's desire for male beauty within a context of heterodox Oxonian Hellenism.[9] It is this effort to restrain one's own desire, to give oneself over to the artwork, rather than making the artwork serve one's own aesthetic purpose, that Bradley and Cooper strive for in their ekphrastic poems; and, as we shall see, their aesthetic investment in self-effacement yields a dividend of multiply dissident erotic perspectives.[10] Early in the preface to *Sight and Song*, they advocate the need for self-discipline, declaring they will express

> not so much what these pictures are to the poet, but rather what poetry they objectively incarnate. Such an attempt demands patient, continuous sight as pure as the gazer can refine it of theory, fancies, or his mere subjective enjoyment.
>
> "Il faut, par un effort d'esprit, se transporter dans les personnages et non les attirer à soi." For *personnages* substitute *peintures*, and this sentence from Gustave Flaubert's "Correspondence" resumes the method of art-study from which these poems arose.[11]

If we juxtapose this passage with the following extract from "Prosper Mérimée," Pater's role as the earlier advocate of this Flaubertian self-effacement becomes evident:

> Personality *versus* impersonality in art:—how much or how little of one's self one may put into one's work: whether anything at all of it: whether one *can* put there anything else:—is clearly a far-reaching and complex question. Serviceable as the basis of a precautionary maxim towards the conduct of our work, self-effacement, or impersonality, in literary or artistic creation, is, perhaps, after all, as little possible as a strict realism. "It has always been my rule to put nothing of myself into my works," says another great master of French prose, Gustave Flaubert; but, luckily as we may think, he often failed in thus effacing himself, as he too was aware.[12]

Learning from Pater, Bradley and Cooper turn to Flaubert as the master of impersonality, and like Pater, they accept an inevitable alternation between self-suppression and self-expression, the first being a subjective decentering "effort" ("the effort to see things from their own centre, by suppressing the habitual centralisation of the visible in ourselves" [vi]) and the second the release of individual "play" ("the inevitable force of individuality must still have play and a temperament mould the purified impression" [vi]).[13]

While Pater had been an ongoing influence and mentor to Bradley and Cooper, Berenson was a more recent interlocutor who shared their status as outsiders among London's predominantly male aesthetic intelligentsia. While the poets were determined not to be patronized on the basis of a limited, women's education, Berenson was intent on supplementing his Harvard education with study in the cultural centers of England, France, Germany, and Italy. Of Lithuanian Jewish parentage, he had arrived in Paris from Boston in June 1887, shortly after graduating.[14] He visited London briefly in January 1888 armed with letters of introduction to literary circles in both London and Oxford. Although he met Wilde, he was disappointed in his hope of meeting Pater, whom he grouped (with Arnold and Browning) in his trinity of literary gods.[15] Berenson met Bradley and Cooper only in June 1890, in Paris, when the two poets were on the first of their lengthy summer tours of European galleries.[16] In the meantime he had become thoroughly converted to the theories of Giovanni Morelli (1816–91), the Italian politician, art historian, collector, and dealer, who had earned renown for his invention of a new scientific method of identifying and attributing artworks.

Morelli studied painting with minute attention to material details. He was interested, for instance, in the precise pattern of each painter's signature, and the individual style conveyed through the fine details of figure painting, such as in ears and hands. He urged his readers not to depend on the interpretive authority of handbooks and art histories, but to conduct their own "independent and searching inspection of the actual *works* of the masters."[17] Although Morelli's theories were motivated by very particular cultural preoccupations, such as establishing a national respect for Italian art within a newly independent Italy, they nevertheless intersected uncannily with the British aesthetic theories that Berenson most admired—for instance, Arnold's admiration of European, especially French and German, critical objectivity ("the endeavour . . . to see the object as in itself it really is"[18]); Browning's and Pater's enthusiasm for Italian Renaissance painting; and Pater's aesthetic theories of subjective impressionism, refined by "superb self-effacement."[19]

Morelli was well known in London art circles and respected, in particular by Sir Charles Eastlake, president of the National Gallery from 1850 to 1861, and Sir Austen Henry Layard, an active trustee of the National Gallery and advisor to Sir Henry Cole at the South Kensington

Museum (later the Victoria and Albert Museum).[20] Consequently, Berenson's thorough familiarity with Morelli's work gave him cachet at the National Gallery, where he was appointed to conduct lecture tours in the spring of 1891. He began by giving a series of seven lectures on Italian Renaissance painters to a group of eight women, among whom were Bradley and Cooper.[21] Berenson's shared interest in Browning and Pater made his art history especially attractive to them, and by summer of that year, they were on visiting terms with him and his friend Mary Costelloe (née Pearsall Smith), the former American. When the poets set off on their second tour of art galleries in August, they went armed with a list of paintings to see and a recommendation to buy the recently released, revised edition of Morelli's book *Kunstkritische Studien über Italienische Malerei*.[22]

The carefully phrased opening statement of the preface to *Sight and Song* follows the imperative of Berenson and Morelli to respond to each painting on its own representational terms: "The aim of this little volume is, as far as may be, to translate into verse what the lines and colours of certain chosen pictures sing in themselves; to express not so much what these pictures are to the poet, but rather what poetry they objectively incarnate" (v). Phrases such as "the lines and colours of certain chosen pictures" and "objectively incarnate" imply Bradley and Cooper's urgent wish to privilege the concrete materiality of the pictorial image in a manner quite different from that of their ekphrastic predecessors, such as Dante Gabriel Rossetti and Algernon Charles Swinburne. While the latter felt no compunction about taking liberties with the literal and figurative designs of paintings, Bradley and Cooper insist on wanting their paintings of choice to speak on their own behalf.[23] This restraint, interpretable as a manly austerity, paradoxically introduces multiply dissident erotic affect into the customarily male, magisterial register of ekphrasis. Effectively, Bradley and Cooper appropriate for a female eye the ekphrastic convention whereby the male poet looks on painting (often of the female body) that is coded feminine by its associations with space, silence, passivity, and pastoral beauty.[24] But this is not simply a matter of masking themselves with a male name to write a lesbian poetry under the guise of heterosexual erotics. For, in addition, they provide the heterosexual female viewer with an aesthetic alibi for scrutinizing images of the male nude, even as they speak as the manly poet authorized to gaze on the male nude by virtue of his Berensonian objectivity and austere Paterian self-restraint.

In choosing the paintings they will read in *Sight and Song,* Bradley and Cooper again follow the precedents of Browning, Pater, and Berenson, in focusing almost entirely on art of the Italian Renaissance. Of the eighteen painters whose works they include, three (Sandro Botticelli, Leonardo da Vinci, and Giorgione and his school) are the subjects of essays in Pater's collection *The Renaissance,* while all but four receive mention in Berenson's collected lectures (*The Italian Painters of the Renaissance*).[25] The Renaissance had been Berenson's topic at the National Gallery in the spring of 1891, and in later years he developed the lectures into a four-part series, each published as an essay—on Venetian (1894), Florentine (1896), Central Italian (1897), and North Italian (1907) painters—and all eventually collected in a single volume in 1930. Aside from those about Renaissance painting, three of Michael Field's poems focus on works of the eighteenth-century French painter Jean-Antoine Watteau, a favorite in fin-de-siècle aesthetic circles. Watteau features prominently in Pater's imaginary portrait "A Prince of Court Painters" (1885) and was also popular with Wilde. One might recall, for instance, that in the stage directions to the opening scene of Wilde's *An Ideal Husband* (1895), Mrs. Marchmont and Lady Basildon are referred to as *"types of exquisite fragility"* whose *"affectation of manner has a delicate charm. Watteau would have loved to paint them."*[26]

Watteau's figuration of indifference (*L'Indifférent;* fig. 24) opens the collection, while his memorable painting *L'Embarquement pour Cythère* is the subject of the anthology's elegiac conclusion. Aside from this gesture of framing the Italian Renaissance by the eighteenth century, which echoes Pater's view of the eighteenth-century Winckelmann as "the last fruit of the Renaissance," the poems seem randomly arranged.[27] In some cases it is possible to group them thematically—for instance, two respond to portrayals of the martyrdom of St. Sebastian, while at least six are intensely preoccupied with representations of Venus. The poems on which I have chosen to focus are those in which Bradley and Cooper's use of ekphrasis most effectively unsettles the assumptions about gender and power on which this poetic genre usually operates in the later nineteenth century. By attending closely to the details of each painting, they attribute to it a representative authority to which their words appear to defer. For

FIGURE 24. Jean-Antoine Watteau, *L'Indifférent.* Courtesy of the Louvre, Paris. Photo: J. G. Berizzi. Photo credit: Réunion des Musées Nationaux / Art Resource, NY

instance, they perceive agency in an apparently passive female figure, or attribute erotic pleasure to an image of the body in pain.

In the opening response to Watteau's image *L'Indifférent,* Bradley and Cooper dramatize a flirtatious dialogue in which the enthusiastic speaker-viewer presumes on the painting with a sequence of overtures to which

the image refuses to respond. Repeatedly, the lyric voice attempts to im-
pose verbal imagery on the visual image but is forced back into literal,
rather than figurative, language. The first figures of rhetoric are introduced in the opening lines: "He dances on a toe / As light as Mercury's,"
a comparison that invites the assumption that this herald has a message
to deliver. But the presumption is brought up short by the image's refusal
to answer to interpretation: "No, / He dances on" (1). All that the viewer
can do is describe the image in all its blithe self-absorption:

> . . . the world is his,
> The sunshine and his wingy hat;
> His eyes are round
> Beneath the brim:
> To merely dance where he is found
> Is fate to him
> And he was born for that.
>
> (1)

In the lines that follow, Michael Field dramatize poetic presumption in an
invitation to engage: "*Gay youngster, underneath the oak, / Come, laugh and
love!*" (2) and again the image is cast as refusing to answer to the viewer's
flirtation: "In vain we woo" (2). By these repeated invitations, the speaker
performs the viewer's wish to see in an image the confirmation of the fantasies it evokes beyond its own framing: in this case, the dancer's apparent readiness to conspire with his viewer in celebrating life. Yet, again the
viewer returns to the recognition that the figure "is a boy, / Who dances
and must die" (2). One might read this as recognition of the literal
significance of the painting; for to be translated into an aesthetic object
involves the suspension or endless deferral of one's potential to laugh and
love. Yet the figure's apparent indifference to verbal overtures is not simply the effect of its literal inanimacy, or of its own posture. It is also the
product of the verbal title given to it by its painter. As much as words, especially the words of poetry, draw on figuration to expand their denota-
tive, literal capacity, all these visual images draw on the potential stability
of the literal in the language of their titles to curtail the hemorrhage of
meanings released by their figurative capacity.

Bradley and Cooper, as they explain in their preface, are committed to being faithful to the visual semiotics of their chosen paintings, but they apparently do not feel equivalently loyal to the titles of the paintings. All words appear to be grist to their poetic mill. Often the title they use differs from that which art historians were using and thereby authorizes meanings to emerge from the painted figures that can then become the basis for Michael Field's novel reading of what the painting incarnates. One poem that rewrites the title of a painting to interesting effect is "Correggio's *Saint Sebastian*," the first of the two St. Sebastians they study. Commonly this painting is referred to as *The Madonna of Saint Sebastian* (fig. 25). It is an altarpiece believed to have been commissioned by the confraternity of St. Sebastian in Modena in response to an outbreak of the plague in 1523.[28] In *Legends of the Madonna* (1852), Anna Jameson includes this painting in the genre of "Madonna with Child." In Michael Field's translation, Sebastian is not simply distinguished from his earthly companions, St. Gimignano, protector of Modena, and St. Rocco, one of the plague saints, but elevated to the position of Christ's chosen one—the focal point of the painting.

The opening address to Sebastian establishes the poets' Paterian restraint through the priority they give to the sense of sight: "Bound by thy hands, but with respect unto thine eyes how free—" (32). From the outset, the words of the poem thus express intense respect for the silent communication through visual exchange imaged by the painting, the moment when the Christ Child responds with delight to Sebastian's upturned face. What unfolds could be read as simply an evocation of the long-standing Roman Catholic trope whereby the feminized soul of the devout Christian is united with Christ in death: "Oh, bliss when with mute rites two souls are plighted!" (32). In this context physical suffering takes on its own satisfaction, and even sensual pleasure, since it is endured for the benefit of the soul. The figuration of Christ as a baby, sitting in his mother's lap, lends an aura of familial safety to the poem that might seem to belie the erotic suggestiveness of lines such as "Thy spirit dances, / Caught in the play of Heaven's divine advances" (32) and "The Babe looks . . . far below, on thee with soft desire" (32). We might hesitate to identify this Christ Child as a sexualized, polymorphously perverse little putto, but in the final lines, the lyric speaker, whether male (Michael

FIGURE 25. Correggio, *The Madonna of Saint Sebastian*. Courtesy of Gemälde-galerie Alte Meister, Staatliche Kunstsammlungen, Dresden

Field) or female (Bradley and/or Cooper) interjects in the first person (which, true to the aesthetic principles of their preface, has been suppressed up to this point): "Oh might my eyes, so without measure, / Feed on their treasure, / The world with thong and dart might do its pleasure!" (33). At this moment, the poets waive the painting's framing of the field of desire (with all the punning resonance that Yopie Prins has pointed to in the poets' pseudonym[29]). The possible meanings of "treasure," "thong," and "dart" initially authorized by an altarpiece of Sebastian's martyrdom now proliferate to include any number of alternative martyrdoms possible within nineteenth-century fin-de-siècle culture, including stigmatization for participating in same-sex or incestuous relationships. (This yearning to feed the eyes on forbidden treasure would take on yet another nuance in 1892, after the poem's publication in May, as Cooper fought to resist her growing infatuation with Berenson.[30])

St. Sebastian was a particularly fine subject for dramatizing Pater's theory of ascetic withholding. Not only is he a figure of physical restraint, but his exposure in martyrdom made him a particularly suitable subject for the first Renaissance experiments in painting the male nude. Little wonder he has been identified as the favorite saint of fin-de-siècle male homosexual subcultures.[31] Morelli, discussing the *Saint Sebastian* by Antonello da Messina in Dresden, digresses to fill in the history of the saint's place in Renaissance figure painting:

> The representation of life-sized nude figures in painting was first attempted at Florence soon after 1470 by certain distinguished sculptors who also practised the art of painting, their object being to give proof of their knowledge of the human form and of their capacity in treating it. One of the first examples of this kind was, if I mistake not, Antonio del Pollaiuolo's large "St. Sebastian," which he drew from life for Antonio Pucci. . . . St. Sebastian, the Apollo of Christian legend, was the subject almost exclusively represented, of which we have proof in nearly all the galleries of Europe.[32]

In such passages, Morelli provides the informative, matter-of-fact tone authorizing appreciative discussion of the nude that is at this time a mark of aesthetic education and translates readily into the self-effacement that

Bradley and Cooper again cultivate in their treatment of Antonello da Messina's *Saint Sebastian* (fig. 26).

They open with a brief synopsis of the spatial layout—"Young Sebastian stands beside a lofty tree, / Rigid by the rigid trunk . . ." (69)—followed by a minute account of the pictorial ground in Morelli's style. They attend closely to details of color (the "Hyacinthine hue" of heaven; the "lapis-lazuli" of the horizon; the carpets of "an Eastern, vivid red"; and the pillars or "shafts" of "sandy-coloured tone"); to light effects ("Shadiness and thunder"; "tempestuous, sunken beams" of sunshine); and to groupings of figures ("Idle women," "a brutish churl," "Two hard-hearted comrades," and "a mother with her child"), repeatedly circling back to "Sebastian in his grief" (71) or "He who was a soldier late" (70). In the seventh of fifteen stanzas, they settle on the central figure: "Naked, almost firm as sculpture, is his form" (71). They treat the face and head first, reading there a dispute with the will of God. Then they attend to the feet, "swoln with strain, / For he has been standing long" (72). Finally, four of the last five stanzas are reserved for a description of the body itself. These stanzas are worth citation in full:

> Captive, stricken through by darts, yet armed with power
> That resents the coming on of its last hour,
>> Sound in muscle is the boy,
>> Whom his manhood fills
>>> With an acrid joy,
>> Whom its violent pressure thrills.

> But this force implanted in him must be lost
> And its natural validity be crossed
>> By a chill, disabling fate;
>> He must stand at peace
>>> While his hopes abate,
>> While his youth and vigour cease.

> At his feet a mighty pillar lies reversed;
> So the virtue of his sex is shattered, cursed:
>> Here is martyrdom and not
>> In the arrows' sting;

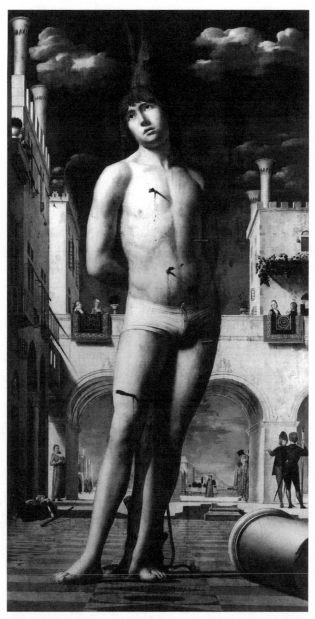

FIGURE 26. Antonello da Messina, *Saint Sebastian*. Courtesy of Gemäldegalerie Alte Meister, Staatliche Kunstsammlungen, Dresden

This the bitter lot
His soul is questioning.

He, with body fresh for use, for pleasure fit,
With its energies and needs together knit
    In an able exigence,
    Must endure the strife,
      Final and intense,
Of necessity with life.

(74)

Like Christ "The Child" or "The Babe" in "Correggio's *Saint Sebastian*," the description of Sebastian here as "the boy" allows a measure of distance to the viewer. Yet boyhood is qualified in overtly sexual terms. It is nascent manhood, experienced physically as a thrillingly "violent pressure," a "force," and "vigour." The ruined pillar next to the boy is read as an analogy for "the virtue of his sex" now "shattered." Even if Michael Field's readers exercise their own interpretive restraint and accept that— in a work written prior to the dissemination of Freud—this detail implies simply the waste of Sebastian's military courage, which might have been used to support the social structure, they must still account for the sexuality implicit in the next stanza's description of his "bitter lot."

Bradley and Cooper's coupling of the body's usefulness with its fitness for pleasure suggests that the reserve they respect and wish to cultivate is more of a kind with the "serenity" of Winckelmann's "unsinged hands" than with the detached indifference of William Rossetti's matron, "to whom naked men were as so many statues."[33] To be sure, their journals suggest that Bradley and Cooper were not themselves familiar with the nude male body in quite the way that their friend Mary Costelloe was. In the summer of 1892, while staying in Paris with Berenson and Costelloe—by then his mistress and estranged from her husband—they were taken by Costelloe to an atelier where a life class was being taught. Cooper records that this was "the first man we have seen in the state of nature at close quarters . . . thin black hair streaks his thighs and back, seat and bosom. I did not know men were such savages—much to Mary's amusement."[34] Nevertheless Michael Field's poetry recognizes the eroticism in Catholic iconography that made it alluring to the likes of Wilde, John

Gray, and Marc-André Raffalovich. The suffering body of Sebastian takes on further erotic affect when read alongside journal entries by both Bradley and Cooper, each identifying the saint's suffering with her own during Cooper's critical illness with scarlet fever in Dresden.[35]

Bradley and Cooper's treatment of the nude female body, combining Pater's impersonality with Berenson's attention to pictorial detail, is even more interesting than their treatment of the male nude, as "*A Portrait* by Bartolommeo [*sic*] Veneto" suggests (fig. 27). They viewed this painting at the Städel'sche Institut at Frankfurt in early October 1891, on their way back to England after Cooper had recovered from her illness. Once again, the change of title is worth attention. All scholarship I have found on this painting refers to it as *Flora,* the Roman goddess of flowers and spring, whose lover was Zephyrus. Michael Field, however, refuse the allegory attributed to the image presumably by its male painter and choose to read it instead as a personal, yet anonymous, portrait, thereby producing an intriguing elaboration on Berenson's discussion of portraiture in Renaissance Venice. According to his account, "Venice was the first state which made a business of preserving the portraits of its chief rulers." Portraits were thus associated with male social power. The likenesses of the Doges were preserved not only in the Ducal Palace, but also in the figures of saints that were the subjects of altarpieces. Berenson also made the special claim for Venetian portraiture that it was expected above all "to give pleasure to the eye, and to stimulate the emotions."[36]

In Bradley and Cooper's poem, Bartolomeo's *Flora* is translated into a courtesan with the agency to determine her own eternal life, and thus, presumably, theirs as well. The male artist, the male patron, and the male viewer who populate Berenson's Renaissance Venice become minor players in this game of wit. By naming the painting simply "*A Portrait* by Bartolommeo [*sic*] Veneto," Bradley and Cooper imply that this is not a passive female model whose identity is effaced when her body is used by the male artist to compose an allegorical image. They refuse the figurative capacity of the title *Flora* and instead describe this female body as autonomous, free terrain, "[w]here neither love nor time has conquered space / On which to live" (27). The trope of withholding, evident in "Watteau's *L'Indifférent,*" is repeated. While the woman's smile is described as illuminating the terrain of the face, the trope of enlightenment does not extend to the viewer: "[H]er leftward smile endows / The gazer with no

FIGURE 27. Bartolomeo Veneto, *Flora*. Courtesy of Städelsches Kunstinstitut, Frankfurt am Main

tidings from the face" (27). According to Michael Field's reading, viewers must admit to their own ignorance before the painting's reserve.

Gradually a song unfolds about woman's recognition of the ephemerality of her beauty and her resolve to prevent the passing of its power. Each feature of the portrait, each color and each texture—the violet larkspur, the columbine of "perfect yellow," the "daisies choicely wide," the coiled box-tree leaf, and the deliberately exposed breast—is transformed into an assertion of female aesthetic agency. The conceit is arranged so that as the poets speak, the woman of the portrait establishes herself as an enigmatic sign, the richness of which lies in its withholding of any specific message. Although she is referred to as a courtesan with no education, no skill, no genius, she gives to art this "vacant eminence," this "fair, blank form" in which her eternity lies. For the image, by virtue of its lack of identity, becomes available to innumerable fantasies and shifting desires.

There are several other poems in which agency is attributed to a female figure customarily associated with passivity; for instance, in "*A Pen-Drawing of Leda* by Sodoma," Leda is described as "[d]rawing her gracious Swan down through the grass" (81). Avoiding representations of Leda as the unsuspecting wife of Tyndareus whose secluded bathing spot is slyly invaded by the disguised Zeus, Bradley and Cooper choose an image of thorough self-possession. In their eyes, Leda takes pleasure in the exposure of her body to light and air: "She joys to bend in the live light / Her glistening body toward her love" (81). In W. B. Yeats's version of 1923, Leda is a "staggering girl," helpless to defend herself against Zeus: "How can those terrified vague fingers push / The feathered glory from her loosening thighs?"[37] In Bradley and Cooper's ekphrasis of Sodoma's postcoital version, such violence is displaced by pastoral pleasure as the healthy body is made accessible to swan, sun, and attentive viewer: "[O]n her breast the sunshine lies / And spreads its affluence on the wide curves of her waist and thighs" (81). As in the previous poem, this attribution of agency and pleasure to Leda mitigates objectification and authorizes the viewer to take pleasure in the spectacle of female nudity.

An even more protracted description of the female nude is given in "Giorgione's *Sleeping Venus*" (fig. 28), which, like the two Sebastians, was on exhibit at the Dresden art gallery, and which Bradley later gave Cooper in photograph form as a birthday present, in January 1892.[38] Morelli was largely responsible for establishing the provenance of the painting, which had initially come to Dresden as a Titian and then been dismissed as a mere copy attributed to Sassoferato. From his readings of Renaissance manuscripts, Morelli recognized it as a Giorgione, with the landscape completed by Titian.[39] In this painting, the challenge of attributing agency to the female figure is compounded by the fact that

FIGURE 28. Giorgione, *Sleeping Venus*. Courtesy of Gemäldegalerie Alte Meister, Staatliche Kunstsammlungen, Dresden

Venus is completely passive in sleep, her body wholly naked and exposed to the viewer's eye.

In the opening stanza of "Giorgione's *Sleeping Venus*," the speaker distinguishes Giorgione's from Botticelli's Venus in "her archèd shell" surrounded by "the barren wave that foams." For Bradley and Cooper, Botticelli's version of the goddess, as they describe her in their ekphrasis of *The Birth of Venus*, is vulnerable and defensive:

> Midmost of the breeze . . .
> Sways a girl who seeks to bind
> New-born beauty with a tress
> Gold about her nakedness.
>
> (13)

She is then variously described as a "[v]irgin stranger" (15) and "[l]ove that hath not loved" (15).[40] Giorgione's Venus (in fact, the first painted depiction of the goddess reclining asleep[41]) has chosen to take up residence within the fecund agricultural hinterland, preferring open ground to the seclusion of a "grot" as her resting place. The poem repeatedly dwells on the correlation between the undulations of Venus's body and those of the landscape, insisting on both as feminine and shameless. The third, fourth, and fifth stanzas all describe some particular aspect of the Venus figure: the positioning of the right arm and breasts, the repose of the legs and feet, and finally the arrangement of the left arm. In each instance, the position of the body is validated as natural on the basis of its supposed harmony with the landscape. This aspect of the poem is particularly intriguing in the fifth stanza, in which the viewer's eye dwells on the left hand. Instead of discreetly passing over this detail—as, for instance, does Berenson's protégé, Kenneth Clark[42]—Michael Field refuse figurative interpretations of the left hand as a signal of modesty, chastity, fecundity, and so on. The lyric speaker reads this gesture as claiming the body's pleasure in itself: as the waters of a river are woven and deflected by the bank's contours, so the body's curves cause the left hand to fall inward in unapologetic onanism:

> Her hand the thigh's tense surface leaves,
>   Falling inward. Not even sleep
>   Dare invalidate the deep,
>   Universal pleasure sex
>   Must unto itself annex—
>   Even the stillest sleep; at peace,
>   More profound with rest's increase,
>   She enjoys the good
>   Of delicious womanhood.
>
> (101)

This attributes to Venus an agency as deliberate as the exposure of the breast in Bartolomeo's *Portrait*. Yet whereas the *Portrait*'s model is represented as exposing herself in a gesture of deliberate composition, communicated to the viewer by her eye contact, Venus by virtue of her closed eyes is presented as absorbed in the pleasure of her own body. Sufficient unto herself, she is indifferent to the presence or absence of any hypothetical viewer's gaze; she apparently needs no Other to constitute her selfhood. This is, of course, an unusual assertion of woman's right not only to enter the realm of aesthetic interpretation, but to use it to articulate the power of female sexuality, which is neither conferred on her by a male authority, nor moralized in association with motherhood. Instead, in this fin-de-siècle poetic imaging of a Renaissance painting, a goddess lies absorbed in the pleasure of her own sexualized womanhood for the observation and admiration of other women as much as men.

Like each of the preceding poems I have considered, "Giorgione's *Sleeping Venus*" becomes the site at which song refuses to take up the obvious figurations of a visual image (Veneto's painting as Flora, goddess of flowers and spring; Correggio's Sebastian as the supplicant of the Madonna and Child). Instead, while adhering meticulously to the literal details of the visual image, song capitalizes on the indeterminacy of sight to construct a fantasy of the freedom of desire in the moment of its articulation. At the same time, what these poems—and, by extension, Bradley and Cooper—resolutely refuse is the stability of any subject position that could be appropriated into what today we might refer to as identity politics. For this reason the poems of *Sight and Song,* unlike the Sapphic poems in *Long Ago,* are difficult to assimilate into the category of fin-de-siècle feminist poetry. If anything, they formalize the slippage and variety of the gender positions with which Bradley and Cooper themselves play in the entries to their joint journal, *Works and Days.*

In the early 1890s, Bradley and Cooper's journal entries are filled with references to eminent male literati such as Browning, George Meredith, Pater, Wilde, Arthur Symons, and Lionel Johnson. Very rarely are women mentioned, and when they are it is usually as hostesses of literary gatherings or social mediators of eminent literary men. For instance, it is the elderly Miss Swanwick, a "dear friend" of Browning, who orchestrates Michael Field's first meeting with the poet, at her home.[43] Marie Meredith invites them on behalf of her father to lunch at Box Hill in spring 1892, and there they meet not only George Meredith himself, but the poet and essayist Richard Le Gallienne as well. In all these accounts women in the party are either relegated to the background as domestic facilitators or more actively dismissed for their conventionality. For instance, at an at-home in July 1890, the hostess Louise Chandler Moulton—herself a popular American writer and socialite who prided herself on her reputation as a facilitator of transatlantic literary exchange—introduced Bradley and Cooper as "a poet, as Michael Field." To Bradley, this was female tea-party affectation from which they had to distance themselves. In her words, "The first moments were misery and humiliation

. . . we stood, our wings vibrating in revolt while hollow fashionable women lisped their enchantment at meeting with us. A moment came when this could be borne no longer. I laid a master-hand on the hostess, and told her to introduce us by our Christian names."[44] At least female first names would not threaten the aesthetic manliness of Michael Field with emasculation. Soon after, the event took on new excitement as they met first Moore and then Wilde.

In some entries, their disdain for decorative and domestic women is overt. For instance, when Bradley and Cooper visited Wilde at his home, they were bored in the presence of Constance Wilde, who is cast as an aesthetically interesting object, but intellectually uninspired. Cooper records their being "received by Mrs. Oscar in turquoise blue, white frills and amber stockings. The afternoon goes on in a dull fashion till Oscar enters. He wears a lilac shirt, a heliotrope tie, a great primrose pink—very Celtic combination, ma foi! His large presence beams with the 'heiterkeit' of a Greek God that has descended on a fat man of literary habits."[45] Bradley, Cooper, and Wilde then engaged in a discussion of their respective works and book illustrations. Similarly, after a visit to Meredith's home, Mrs. Le Gallienne is described as a "boneless heap of green Liberty stuff and smocking" whose "Sphinxian eyes have betrayed Richard into his premature marriage."[46] Of the Pater sisters, Hester and Clara, Cooper writes, "I was never with such slow minds, that creep over a subject as snails over leaves, and yet with a certain comeliness in the unhurried direction they take."[47] What Bradley and Cooper's journals reveal is their delight in the company of literati and aesthetes (most of whom are men), a wish to be respected participants in literary and aesthetic circles, and a resolute refusal of any conventions governing female behavior that might curtail that participation.

From this it follows that, when Bradley and Cooper were snubbed by Wilde at a reception held at the home of R. H. Benson in May 1892 (the very month *Sight and Song* was published), the sting of the snub was located in the exercise of aesthetic rather than gender power. Sensitive to Wilde's reputation not only as an arbiter of women's fashion but also as an advocate of women's literary endeavors, Cooper interpreted his rudeness not as a lack of chivalry or gentlemanliness, but as a grave misjudgment of Michael Field's aesthetic sensibility.[48] As Cooper writes, Wilde "is not of the men who can be rude offensively and yet escape. There is no charm in his elephantine body, tightly stuffed into his clothes—with a grass-gorged effect. . . . When he shows himself a *snob* he is disgustingly repulsive. We were not well dressed, as the day had begun with rain—we do not belong to the fashionable world—so Oscar rolls his shoulders toward us. When next I meet him in my choicest French hat, I will turn my back on him, and that decisively."[49] According to this passage, Wilde's rudeness both misrecognized Michael Field's sense of fashion, which on this occasion was defeated by the weather, and overestimated his own sartorial panache. Cooper's fantasy of revenge was French chic turning its back on elephantine inelegance, although, as Margaret D. Stetz remarks, it is just as likely that Wilde was acting on a whim.[50]

This preoccupation with aesthetic and intellectual recognition from a predominantly male intelligentsia seems the concern common to both *Works and Days* and *Sight and Song*. Recognition as women, or as women-desiring women, seems of less importance to Michael Field than fulfilling the Paterian imperative to expand the short interval of life in art and song. Indeed, in *Sight and Song*, the attempt to get "as many pulsations as possible into the given time"[51] seems to include articulating as many discursive positions as art and song will allow. While in retrospect we may admire Bradley and Cooper as innovative women, we should also recognize that part of their ingenuity came from their capacity to decompose their very gender identity by cultivating a male-dominated aesthetic. Recognition of this capacity is what Michael Field's contemporary reviewers denied them when insisting on the poet's identity as that of two women writing under a male pseudonym. Yeats, for instance, in the opening paragraph of his review published in the *Bookman* in July 1892, announces them as "the two ladies who hide themselves behind the pen-name of Michael Field."[52] With more knowing subtlety, J. M. Gray—the Scots critic and art curator John Miller Gray, to be distinguished from the younger John Gray associated with Wilde's novel—uses the feminine possessive adjective ("In her preface Michael Field informs us that her aim has been . . .").[53] Only an anonymous reviewer writing for the *Glasgow Herald* avoids the question of the poets' identity and gender, simply indicating familiarity with Michael Field's earlier work ("As may be inferred from the author's name, the poems are skilfully shaped and polished").[54]

Thereafter, assumptions about the poets' gender identity shape the critics' various, and often conflicting, evaluations of *Sight and Song*. On the one hand, J. M. Gray's reference to the book as "a dainty little volume" and "eminently a fascinating little volume" has a ring of urbane condescension that continues in his declaration "It was a bold experiment to publish a whole book of poems upon pictures."[55] He identifies "touches of a restraint and purity" in one poem ("Giorgione's *Shepherd Boy*") and remarks of another ("Cosimo Tura's *Saint Jerome in the Desert*") that the painter's "grim austerity . . . finds an echo in the ruggedness of the verse." Yet he qualifies restraint and purity as "Wordsworthian" and interprets the work's "delight in the beauty of human form" as a factor contributing to its Keatsian quality ("[T]he book is one of the most Keats-like things that has been produced since Keats himself went the way of all great poets"). In other words, even as he grants Bradley and Cooper a manly poetics, Gray situates them closer to Romanticism than to fin-de-siècle aestheticism.

Yeats, on the other hand, couches his critique in terms that reject the austerity and impersonality of the verse. In his words, "They [Michael Field] seem to have thought it incumbent upon them to do something serious, something worthy of an age of text-books, something that would have uniformity and deliberate intention, and be in no wise given over to that unprincipled daughter of whim and desire whom we call imagination."[56] Bradley and Cooper's ekphrases do not conform to this poet's expectations of poetics. Yet ironically, while Yeats grants the anthology respect and admiration for its rigor and "intellectual agility,"[57] his feminizing of imagination suggests that it is a quotient of womanliness that is missing from this verse. Slightly earlier, he bemoans precisely the lack of overt affect and subjective emphasis that characterizes the style of nineteenth-century women's poetics I have argued Bradley and Cooper deliberately avoid in *Sight and Song*. As Yeats puts it, "It is impossible not to respect it, impossible not to admire the careful massing of detail, but no man will ever feel his eyes suffuse with tears or his heart leap with joy when he reads it."[58] Whether Pater's lyrical prose would prompt such a response in Yeats remains uncertain, but apparently he finds no playful erotic allusiveness in any of Michael Field's verses. To him, "[t]hey are simply unmitigated guide-book."[59]

Perhaps, in his very bemusement, the reviewer from the *Glasgow Herald* comes closest to registering the suggestiveness of the poems, describing them as "exceedingly curious and worth careful study by our younger versifiers."[60] He himself does not, of course, imply that this curiosity is the effect produced when two lesbian poets, immersing themselves in current male aesthetic theories, graft these onto a traditionally male poetic genre to produce multiply dissident erotic registers. That, however, is what I would argue gives *Sight and Song* its distinction within the genre of the fin-de-siècle poem.

Notes

My warm thanks to Christina M. Walter, fellow Michael Field enthusiast, for her tireless assistance in negotiating permissions for the illustrations in this essay.

1. For an intriguing discussion of various women's treatments of the Sapphic motif, see Yopie Prins, *Victorian Sappho* (Princeton, NJ: Princeton University Press, 1999), 174–245.

2. I allude here to Isobel Armstrong's challenge to Ezra Pound's dismissive treatment of affective Victorian poetry: "Msrepresentation: Codes of Affect and Politics in Nineteenth-Century Women's Poetry," in *Women's Poetry, Late Romantic to Late Victorian: Gender and Genre, 1830–1900,* ed. Armstrong and Virginia Blain (Basingstoke, UK: Macmillan, 1999), 3–32.

3. See Isobel Armstrong, "Thinking Affect," in *The Radical Aesthetic* (Oxford: Blackwell, 2000), 108–48.

4. After the opening of the South Kensington Museum in 1857, it became increasingly common for museums to extend their hours and admissions policies to maximize accessibility to the working classes. Tony Bennett records that between 1857 and 1883, the South Kensington Museum documented over 15 million visits, "over 6.5 million of which were recorded in the evenings": "The Exhibitionary Complex," in *Representing the Nation: A Reader,* ed. David Boswell and Jessica Evans (New York: Routledge, 1999), 343.

5. See the Michael Field journal, British Library (hereafter "BL"), Add. MSS, 46778: 119v (1890). By 1888, the National Gallery was offering free admission on Mondays, Tuesdays, Wednesdays, and Saturdays; staying open as late as 7:00 p.m. in June and July; and staying open until dusk in November and December). See *A Popular Handbook to the National Gallery Including, by Special Permission, Notes Collected from the Works of Mr. Ruskin,* comp. Edward T. Cook (London, 1888).

6. Walter Pater, *The Renaissance: Studies in Art and Poetry; The 1893 Text,* ed. Donald L. Hill (Berkeley and Los Angeles: University of California Press, 1980), xxiii; Hill's

text is based on the fourth and final edition of *The Renaissance* that Pater published in his lifetime.

7. Pater, *Renaissance*, 177.

8. Walter Pater, "Prosper Mérimée," in *Miscellaneous Studies* (London: Macmillan, 1895), 26, 29.

9. Among the most interesting discussions of this topic are James Eli Adams, *Dandies and Desert Saints: Styles of Victorian Masculinity* (Ithaca, NY: Cornell University Press, 1995), 150–51; Richard Dellamora, "Critical Impressionism as Anti-Phallogocentric Strategy," in *Pater in the 1990s*, ed. Laurel Brake and Ian Small (Greensboro, NC: ELT, 1990), 127–42; Richard Dellamora, *Masculine Desire: The Sexual Politics of Victorian Aestheticism* (Chapel Hill: University of North Carolina Press, 1990), 58–68, 102–116; Linda Dowling, *Hellenism and Homosexuality in Victorian Oxford* (Ithaca, NY: Cornell University Press, 1994), 92–99; and Thaïs E. Morgan, "Reimagining Masculinity in Victorian Criticism: Swinburne and Pater," *Victorian Studies* 36 (1992–93): 315–32.

10. As this argument shows, my reading of the aesthetic genealogy behind Bradley and Cooper's ekphrastic approach is based on a very different reading of Pater from that presented by Ana I. Parejo Vadillo in her intriguing essay on *Sight and Song*. While I heartily agree with her fundamental claim that this anthology was a "poetic and aesthetic experiment which aimed at showing the gendered experience of art, both in its production and its perception," I am not convinced by her reading of it as a bold departure from Pater's "subjective vision." To my eye, Bradley and Cooper are Paterian followers and practitioners rather than dissenters. See Ana I. Parejo Vadillo, "*Sight and Song*: Transparent Translations and a Manifesto for the Observer," *Victorian Poetry* 38, no. 1 (2000): 16.

11. Michael Field, *Sight and Song* (London: Elkin Mathews and John Lane, 1892), v; further page references appear in parentheses.

12. Pater, "Prosper Mérimée," 28.

13. Their journal indicates that in the weeks after Pater's lecture, Michael Field studied Flaubert's *Salammbô* (1862) and *Correspondance* intensively. BL, Add. MSS, 46778: 124r, 127r (1890).

14. Ernest Samuels, *Bernard Berenson: The Making of a Connoisseur* (Cambridge, MA: Belknap Press, 1979), 52. Samuels notes that Berenson changed the spelling of his first name, dropping the *h* used by Michael Field, when the United States entered World War I (3).

15. Samuels, *Bernard Berenson*, 61–63, 25.

16. Michael Field journal, BL, Add. MSS, 46778: 134v.

17. Giovanni Morelli, quoted in Samuels, *Bernard Berenson*, 95. Samuels adds that "[s]uch commonsensical advice served as a wholesome counterbalance to the aestheticism

so winningly taught by Walter Pater. It brought art criticism down from the clouds of personal impression to the solid earth of the thing-in-itself" (95). This conclusion reflects a rather limited and dated view of Pater's aesthetics, to which Franklin E. Court draws attention in his essay "The Matter of Pater's 'Influence' on Bernard Berenson: Setting the Record Straight," *English Literature in Transition* 26 (1983): 16–22.

18. Matthew Arnold, "The Function of Criticism at the Present Time" (1864), *Poetry and Criticism of Matthew Arnold,* ed. A. Dwight Culler (Boston: Houghton Mifflin, 1961), 237; here Arnold cites his own earlier use of this phrase in his Oxford lectures of 1860–61. Paul Barolsky argues that Berenson also draws on Arnold's discussion of "Hebraism" and "Hellenism" in *Culture and Anarchy* (1869). Barolsky presents a detailed account of Pater's theory of impersonality and its precedents as ongoing resonances in Berenson's work. He not only draws attention to the numerous citations of English poets in Berenson's work but also hypothesizes that on several occasions Berenson makes allusions to Bradley and Cooper's poetry in *Sight and Song.* See Barolsky, "Walter Pater and Bernard Berenson," *New Criterion* (April 1984): 47–57.

19. Again, I differ from Vadillo in my interpretation of Berenson's understanding of Pater.

20. Jaynie Anderson, *Collecting Connoisseurship and the Art Market in Risorgimento Italy* (Venice: Instituto Veneto di Scienze, Lettere ed Arti, 1999), 24.

21. Michael Field journal, BL, Add. MSS, 46779: 48r, 52r, 53v (1891); Samuels, *Bernard Berenson,* 137–38.

22. Michael Field journal, BL, Add. MSS, 46779: 69r, 69v, 120r, 120v (1891). Morelli preferred German as his language for publication, since he was born of Swiss parentage and educated in German-speaking Switzerland. Early in his writing career, he used the pseudonym "Ivan Lermolieff" (Anderson, *Collecting Connoisseurship,* 3 and 9).

23. For instance, in his ekphrastic sonnet "A Venetian Pastoral by Giorgione," Rossetti represents the female figure on the viewer's left as drawing water rather than pouring it, as the painting would suggest. John Hollander remarks wryly, "Rossetti sees invisible elements of the painting" (*The Gazer's Spirit: Poems Speaking to Silent Works of Art* [Chicago: University of Chicago Press, 1995], 158). Similarly, Kathy Alexis Psomiades points to a variety of ways in which Swinburne's ekphrasis "Before the Mirror" (1866) alters Whistler's painting *Symphony in White, Number 2: The Little White Girl* (1864) (Psomiades, *Body's Beauty: Femininity and Representation in British Aestheticism* [Stanford, CA: Stanford University Press, 1997], 110–13).

24. I draw here on W. J. T. Mitchell's demystification of G. E. Lessing's rules for aesthetic propriety. Mitchell argues that "the decorum of the arts at bottom has to do with proper sex roles" ("Space and Time in Lessing's *Laocoön* and the Politics of

Genre," in *Iconology: Image, Text, Ideology* [Chicago: University of Chicago Press, 1986], 109).

25. Walter Pater's essays "Notes on Leonardo da Vinci" and "A Fragment on Sandro Botticelli" first appeared in the *Fortnightly Review*, n.s., 6 (1869): 494–508, and 8 (1870): 155–60, respectively. Both of these essays were reprinted—as "Leonardo da Vinci" and "Sandro Botticelli"—in Pater's *Studies in the History of the Renaissance* (London: Macmillan, 1873), renamed, in the second edition, *The Renaissance: Studies in Art and Poetry* (London: Macmillan, 1877). Pater's "The School of Giorgione" was first published in the *Fortnightly Review*, n.s., 22 (1877): 526–38, and was reprinted in *The Renaissance*, 3rd ed. (London: Macmillan, 1888).

26. Oscar Wilde, *An Ideal Husband*, in *The Importance of Being Earnest and Other Plays*, ed. Peter Raby (Oxford: Oxford University Press, 1995), 164; this stage direction appears in the first edition of Wilde's play (London: Leonard Smithers, 1899).

27. Pater, *Renaissance*, xxv.

28. David Ekserdjian, *Correggio* (New Haven, CT: Yale University Press, 1997), 178.

29. Prins, *Victorian Sappho*, 94.

30. See, for instance, Michael Field journal, BL, Add. MSS, 46780: 114v, 115r (1892).

31. Richard Ellmann, *Oscar Wilde* (New York: Knopf, 1988), 71n.

32. Giovanni Morelli, *Italian Painters: Critical Studies of Their Works*, trans. Constance Jocelyn Ffoulkes (London: John Murray, 1893), 180–81.

33. W. M. Rossetti, *Swinburne's Poems and Ballads* (1866), reprinted in *Swinburne: The Critical Heritage*, ed. Clyde K. Hyder (New York: Barnes and Noble, 1970), 65. (My thanks to Lauren Goodlad for this reference.)

34. Michael Field journal, BL, Add. MSS, 46780: 129r, 129v (1892).

35. Michael Field journal, BL, Add. MSS, 46779: 99v (1891); and Vadillo, "*Sight and Song*," 29–30.

36. Bernard Berenson, *The Italian Painters of the Renaissance* (Oxford: Clarendon Press, 1930), 28 and 44.

37. Yeats, "Leda and the Swan," in *The Collected Poems of W. B. Yeats* (London: Macmillan, 1967), 241.

38. Michael Field journal, BL, Add. MSS, 46780: 12r (1892).

39. Morelli, *Italian Painters*, 220–24.

40. Barolsky notes that Pater was the first critic to focus on the "ineffable melancholy" of Botticelli's paintings; Barolsky goes on to hypothesize that Berenson's treatment of *The Birth of Venus* is indebted to Michael Field's ekphrastic poem ("Walter Pater," 53).

41. Jaynie Anderson, *Giorgione: The Painter of "Poetic Brevity"* (Paris: Flammarion, 1997), 225.

42. Kenneth Clark, *The Nude: A Study in Ideal Form* (1956; reprint, Princeton, NJ: Bollingen Press, 1990), 115–16.

43. Robert Browning to Edith Cooper, 8 June 1885, in *Works and Days: From the Journal of Michael Field*, ed. T. and D. C. Sturge Moore (London: John Murray, 1933), 9.

44. Michael Field journal, BL, Add. MSS, 46778: 94r (1890).

45. Michael Field journal, BL, Add. MSS, 46779: 54r, 54v (1891).

46. Michael Field journal, BL, Add. MSS, 46780: 82v (1892).

47. Michael Field journal, BL, Add. MSS, 46778: 24r (1890).

48. See Margaret Diane Stetz's discussion of Wilde's significance for later-Victorian women writers: "The Bi-Social Oscar Wilde and 'Modern' Women," *Nineteenth-Century Literature* 55, no. 4 (2001): 515–37.

49. Michael Field journal, BL, Add. MSS, 46780: 97v, 98r.

50. Stetz, "Bi-Social," 534.

51. Pater, *Renaissance*, 190.

52. W. B. Yeats, *Uncollected Prose*, vol. 1, ed. John P. Frayne (New York: Columbia University Press, 1970), 225.

53. J. M. Gray, review of *Sight and Song*, by Michael Field, *Academy*, 18 June 1892, 583.

54. Anonymous, "Poetry and Verse," *Glasgow Herald*, June 1892, n.p.

55. Gray, review of *Sight and Song*, 583–84.

56. Yeats, *Uncollected Prose*, 226.

57. Yeats, *Uncollected Prose*, 227.

58. Yeats, *Uncollected Prose*, 226.

59. Yeats, *Uncollected Prose*, 227.

60. Anonymous, "Poetry and Verse."

AMY LEVY

Urban Poetry, Poetic Innovation, and the Fin-de-Siècle Woman Poet

Linda Hunt Beckman

Cultural historians have called attention to the way London was transformed in the 1880s by the presence of women in the city.[1] Amy Levy, an
Anglo-Jewish woman of letters, was one of the women who moved easily
about London in that decade, and her life as an urban traveler, on foot or
on an omnibus, and her presence in the city's public spaces are recorded
in the correspondence and journals of friends and acquaintances, in her
own letters, and, especially, in her daily calendar for 1889. That calendar
reports visits to the library at the British Museum; to the Philharmonic,
art galleries, and the theater; to the flats of friends or her married sister;
to the University Women's Club, of which she was an active member; to
London's parks, where she sometimes played tennis; and to Industrial
Hall in Bloomsbury, where she often helped in the office of a women's
trade union whose secretary was Clementina Black, Levy's favorite "chum."
Levy also attended private salons, and parties and events sponsored by
London organizations—for example, the first meeting of the Women
Writers Club and the dinner given by the Society of Authors. Fisher
Unwin, who offered to publish her next book of poetry when they ran into
each other at a party in 1886 and who brought out that volume after her
death, knew he spoke for many when he wrote to her father: "Your loss is
one all must feel who had the honour and & pleasure of knowing your
gifted daughter. I . . . like so many others feel I have lost a friend who I
valued & esteemed very highly."[2] Levy's participation in London life was a

professional and personal asset for her and for those who knew her, and the city itself became central to her poetic development.

By calling what turned out to be her final book of poems *A London Plane-Tree and Other Verse,* Levy made central its twelve (out of fifty-one) poems about the city. In order to grasp how unconventional such poems were before the 1890s, we must remember that in England, since the age of sensibility in the latter half of the eighteenth century, poetry had been associated with celebrating the natural world. Levy's decision to focus on the urban scene, then, is as important and daring as the twofold and seemingly contradictory shift in her poetics during 1887 and 1888, when her poetry became symbolist and then, briefly, popular.

Although it has not been recognized, Levy—whose French was fluent enough for her to earn money as a translator—was one of the first British poets to respond to *le Symbolisme,* the aesthetic revolution that had been under way in France for some time.[3] Charles Baudelaire, Paul Verlaine, Arthur Rimbaud, and Stéphane Mallarmé rejected the themes and methods of the Parnassians, who sought to represent mimetically the object world outside of themselves. The symbolists were engaged in a "revolt against exteriority."[4] Levy was part of that revolt. In this chapter, I examine Levy's attempts in her urban poetry to negotiate between the appeal of a wide readership and the lure of symbolism. My chief aim is to show that in the late 1880s Levy was one of England's most innovative poets and a pioneer in writing symbolist poetry in English. Her writings are often approached as if they consisted only of the dramatic monologues and other narrative poems that are the mainstay of her 1884 volume *A Minor Poet and Other Verse.* But Amy Levy's work changed and developed with astonishing velocity in the last three years of her life.

"London in July," published in the *Academy* in 1887, announces her commitment to the city, and is her first symbolist poem; it shows, perhaps, the influence of all four of the founding symbolists, but is especially indebted to the work of Baudelaire and Mallarmé. As Jonathan Culler reminds us, Baudelaire was "the first . . . to create a new situation for poetry by taking as the norm life in large cities and the new human relationships and temporality that urban life creates, as men and women pass among people they do not know."[5] That Levy wrote in this Baudelairian tradition is evident in "London in July," whose speaker wanders about the streets of London scrutinizing strangers. And she does this, as we will see, in order to engage in what Henri Dorra calls "the Baudelairian probing of one's own depths."[6]

The focus of Mallarmé's poems is, of course, inward too; critics often refer to Baudelaire as his mentor. Levy's poetics in her first symbolist poem and elsewhere seem closest to the methods and theorizing of Mallarmé. His work, like that of Baudelaire and all the symbolists who wrote in Baudelaire's wake, was written for a cultural elite—for readers able and willing to make the intellectual effort required. Levy's "London in July," while apparently simple, is difficult to interpret. In this respect it differs from the five urban poems that Levy published next. Appearing in the *Star,* a London daily, in 1888, these poems, as one would expect of verse published in a newspaper, were written to have wide appeal.[7]

In four of the poems in the *Star* Levy's mode of representation is very much at odds with the one that she employs in "London in July." The mode she uses in the *Star* poems, which relies heavily on metonymy rather than metaphor, is related to that of the realist novel, and it reflects her desire to write popular poetry without compromising her artistic principles.[8] While she had in mind the audience that she was targeting, the most accurate way to describe the series is to say that these poems disrupt the traditional distinction between popular and high art. We know from some of the fiction Levy produced in this period—the story "At Prato," for example, and the novel *The Romance of a Shop*—that a goal in 1888 was to write in a manner that would satisfy readers of light literature, yet at the same time offer something of interest to readers of serious literature.[9]

Plane-Tree has six additional urban lyrics that were probably written later in 1888 than the *Star* series and in 1889, Levy's final year; even though we cannot be sure of their dates of composition, it is reasonable to designate them as "late."[10] These late poems show the influence of symbolist aesthetics, but four of them—"A March Day in London," "The Piano-Organ," "London Poets," and "The Village Garden"—lack the ambiguous signification of symbolist poetry. Not particularly difficult, these four works depend on methods that Levy hoped would allow her to marry accessibility and the probing of subjective states—though the idiosyncrasy of Levy's vision and her darkness of mood in these lyrics would have kept them from being entertaining. Two of the six late lyrics, "Out of Town" and "In the Mile End Road," are obscure, enigmatic, and symbolist.

It cannot be established that Levy knew the poems of Mallarmé,[11] except by showing his influence, but there can be no doubt that she knew the work of Charles Baudelaire. Levy refers to Baudelaire (without naming him) in an essay that appeared in January of 1886, the last and by far the best of a series she published in *London Society*, a popular magazine. In this piece, which, like the others, is written as an epistolary travelogue, Levy addresses her letter to "Psyche" and signs it "Melissa."

The essay's title, "Out of the World," is a clear reference to Baudelaire's "N'importe où hors du monde" (1867). Levy reports early in the essay, about her decision to vacation in rural Cornwall, that, although she is a "Genuine Cockney"—in other words, an inveterate urbanite—she began to hate London. She found herself crying out, to express the intensity of her desire to get away from the city, "Anywhere, anywhere out of the world." Her phrasing is a cross between Baudelaire's title and the last words of his prose poem, which, translated literally, are "Anywhere!—Anywhere, provided it is out of this world!" Levy's essay is a repudiation of the stance Baudelaire takes in his poem. He addresses his soul, which is in "a wretched state" because of its apprehension of *néant* (nothingness)—what Baudelaire, elsewhere, and, Mallarmé, eventually, would call the *gouffre* (the abyss). Baudelaire says that "this life of ours is a hospital, in which all patients are obsessed with a desire to change beds" and mocks himself—and others—for thinking that a change of place would alleviate suffering. Convinced that even a radical relocation would make no difference, since suffering is the human lot, Baudelaire has his soul finally cry "out her words of wisdom"—"N'importe où! n'importe où! pourvu que ce soit hors de ce monde!"[12]

In "Out of the World," Levy/Melissa alludes to the French poet's struggle with the void when she says that her sudden loathing of the city was prompted by a spiritual crisis: "[A] great blankness fell upon my soul."[13] Melissa, however, believes that there *is* a way to live in this world, and answers Baudelaire by insisting that location is crucial. She assures her correspondent, "Much as I admire the superior peace, simplicity, and beauty of a country life, I know that my own place is among the struggling crowd of dwellers in cities."[14] By positioning herself as an urbanite, Melissa invents an identity that will provide Levy with a usable self.

The cultural studies theorist Stuart Hall says, "You have to position yourself *somewhere* in order to say anything at all" and "[I]dentities are things we make up, but not just out of any old thing."[15] In 1886, when Levy published "Out of the World," she believed that she could construct a life and find a voice by drawing on her experience as a Londoner. Because Baudelaire's *Fleurs du mal* (1857) represents the urban scene as hell, the "Cockney" position that she chooses is itself a response to the French poet. And, if we read "Out of the World" together with another essay that Levy wrote that same year, 1886, then we see that her urban identity also stemmed from her conviction that there was a strong historical connection between Jews and city life.[16]

The obscurity of Levy's apparently simple poem is a quality that Baudelaire advocated and modeled, and the other symbolists followed his lead. It was Mallarmé who said, "There must always be enigma in poetry";[17] and when Arthur Symons explained *le Symbolisme* to British readers in 1899, he was to write that the poet must "start with an enigma."[18] In this passage Symons is referring specifically to the way Mallarmé structures his poems. Correspondingly, the structure of "London in July" is in part what makes it puzzling. But Levy's poem is enigmatic for several other reasons.

One additional reason is that in "London in July," as well as in her other symbolist poems, Levy relies on an analogy between the mind and the external world. Mallarmé's famous dictum is particularly applicable to Levy's symbolist work—"Peindre, non la chose, mais l'effet qu'elle produit" (Paint not the thing, but the effect that it produces).[19] What he means is clarified by one of his examples: a poem should not include the "dense wood of the trees" in a forest but "the horror of the forest."[20]

Consider Mallarmé's remarks in an interview:

> The Parnassians, who take the object in its entirety and show it, lack mystery; they take away from readers the delicious joy that arises when they believe that their own minds are creating. To *name* an object is to suppress three-quarters of the enjoyment of the poem, which derives from the pleasure of step-by-step discovery; to *suggest*, that is the dream. It is the perfect use of this mystery that constitutes the symbol: to evoke an object little by little, so as to bring to light a state of the soul or, inversely, to choose an object and bring out of it a state of the soul through a series of unravelings.[21]

The word *objet* in this and other statements by Mallarmé is, from what I have seen, always translated into English as "object," but any French-English dictionary reports that among the meanings of *objet* is "subject" "(as in '*être l'objet de la conversation*' 'to be the subject of conversation')." When Mallarmé uses *objet* as he does in the above passage, it would be far better to translate the word as "subject," for by *objet* he means what the poem is ultimately about, which he says should be a "state of the soul" that is never explicitly identified.[22]

Levy's symbols are like Mallarmé's in that they suggest—without actually designating—a complex mental state or spiritual/emotional experience, not a feeling simple enough to be represented allegorically. Her symbolist poems may not at first seem figurative but only mysterious, because their figures provide solely the vehicle or vehicles of private metaphors (symbols). These connote the intensely personal state of mind that is the unnamed tenor; Levy's techniques, like Mallarmé's, go beyond the semantic use of language.

Given that Mallarmé's *Poésies* came out in 1887, Levy—with her interest in Baudelaire—could have read his collection recently and been influenced by it when she wrote "London in July," but it is possible that she already knew his earlier poetry.[23] In her poem she employs both the city and the figure of a missing woman for whom she searches as symbols of the effect that life is having on her, and she structures her poem by replacing logical progression with the interplay of theme and variations, so that its form has the musicality that the symbolists, especially Baudelaire and Mallarmé, sought.[24] The poem reads as follows:

London in July

What ails my senses thus to cheat?
    What is it ails the place,
That all the people in the street
    Should wear one woman's face?

The London trees are dusty-brown
    Beneath the summer sky;
My love, she dwells in London town,
    Nor leaves it in July.

O various and intricate maze,
 Wide waste of square and street;
Where, missing through unnumbered days,
 We twain at last may meet!

And who cries out on crowd and mart?
 Who prates of stream and sea?
The summer in the city's heart—
 That is enough for me.[25]

About inner life, this poem might have had its genesis in an actual relationship, since Levy's desire, from what the surviving evidence suggests, was homoerotic. On the literal level, Levy describes a common experience in the first quatrain. Seeking in vain for a loved one, she thinks she sees that person everywhere, only to be frustrated repeatedly. That the word "ails" appears in *each* of the first two lines, together with the speaker's statement that her senses "cheat" her, indicates that the situation has made her feel quite ill; she projects her sense of being unwell onto her milieu. The final image in this stanza is of a metropolis that is eerily full of people with the same face, and its tone is obsessive, fretful, even paranoid (in the popular, not the psychiatric sense): after all, one should be able to trust one's senses. But if Levy was familiar with Rimbaud's idea that for a poet "[t]he point is to reach the unknown through the unsettling of *all the senses*,"[26] she might be implying that the speaker is at the start of an inner journey that could enable her to arrive at a new understanding of things.

Reading the first two lines of the second quatrain—"The London trees are dusty-brown / Beneath the summer sky"—one feels a lack of connection, a jump, between these lines and the preceding stanza about the missing woman. But there is a link, which is associational rather than logical, for just as the speaker is ailing in the poem's opening lines, in the second stanza London's trees are ailing. The summer has caused them to turn "dusty-brown," presumably from heat and unclean air. The next two lines—"My love, she dwells in London town, / Nor leaves it in July"—are troubling in that nothing good has been said about "London town." Why then should the beloved woman be so inextricable from the city? The speaker's obsession with her appears as unhealthy as in the opening stanza. These lines, about the woman unable to part from London, recall the image of an urban scene peopled by clones of the beloved, and create an equation between the city and the woman. The themes of the first stanza—London as an unsalutary place and London as a place that is almost the personification of the beloved—are repeated with variations in the second.

The opening two lines of the third stanza conjure up a *horror vacui*, or fear of nothingness: "O various and intricate maze, / Wide waste of square and street." The images roused by "maze" and "waste" are reminders that one can get lost in emptiness, and the combination of alliterated *w*'s and long vowels reinforce Levy's meaning. At this point, surely, the reader begins to suspect that the missing woman is an externalization of a dimension of the psyche, because the psychological and philosophical apprehension of the abyss is above all a threat to the self. Levy writes about a state of the soul (*l'état d'âme*) that is almost ineffable.

Levy's sudden evocation of a void is another one of those apparent jumps between stanzas, though the reference to the "squares and streets" of London does connect the third stanza to the first, which speaks of a search. But Levy does what seems to be a 180-degree turn in the middle of the third quatrain, when, in the lines that follow the evocation of nothingness, the speaker declares: "Where, missing through unnumbered days, / We twain at last may meet!" The hypothetical mood in this statement qualifies the speaker's expression of hope, but her surge of optimism certainly comes from the will rather than from a process of reasoning. Because the burst of hope emanates from an inner struggle, a movement of mind whose jumps and connections the careful reader has been following, the speaker's ability to transcend the mental state evoked in the opening stanza is expressed in the very structure of the poem.

And the image of possible reunion in the final line of this stanza is another variation on the opening theme of separation and search. In navigating her way through the horror of nothingness to a state of willed hope in the face of the overwhelming indifference of the universe, Levy would have been influenced most by Baudelaire, who characterizes the *gouffre* as a terrifying pit that could sometimes be a gateway to poetic consciousness, with such consciousness, perhaps, a solution to the chaos and futility of the modern world.[27] Perhaps just as important, as a person who had coped with episodes of depression since childhood, Levy would have understood that, as Andrew Solomon writes in *The Noonday Demon*, "a thing called will" plays a role in "how we put ourselves back together again" after the horrifying emptiness of a depressive state.[28]

Abandoning the abyss and the possibility that she and her counterpart may meet (and the reconnection with a dimension of the psyche connoted by the search), Levy begins the last quatrain of "London in July" with questions that defy the conventional preference for *rus* over *urbs:* "And who cries out on crowd and mart? / Who prates of stream and sea?" These lines suggest that one would do well not to denounce the city and applaud the countryside, because the verb in the second question— "prates" (that is, utters idly or with little purpose)—undermines those people who value "stream and sea" (the natural world). No longer associated with illness, deception, or frustration, the metropolis has been redeemed.

Even so, the depth of satisfaction in the concluding lines of "London in July" astonishes: "The summer in the city's heart— / That is enough for me." (William Blake's famous phrase "the lineaments of gratified desire" comes to mind.[29]) In the first and second stanzas, London is almost synonymous with the sought-after woman, but now that the city is unmistakably personified as a living organism with a heart, it is not necessary to desire the figure (in both senses) of the missing woman, because the speaker can and does will *herself* to become one with the city. Subject and object collapse, and this happy resolution is the final variation on the theme of alienation and longing that runs through the poem until the final quatrain. We should not fail to note the echo of William Wordsworth's "Composed upon Westminster Bridge" (1807), which ends, "And all that mighty heart is lying still."[30]

Levy's "London in July" is taxing in large part because of the way it appears to jump from one subject to another, and commentators on Mallarmé's poetry—those writing both in his time and in ours—have taken note of his discontinuities and gaps.[31] When Symons writes about the French poet's method, he could be describing Levy's. "By the time the poem has reached . . . a flawless unity, the steps of the progress have been . . . effectually effaced; and while the poet, who has seen the thing from the beginning, still sees the relation of point to point, the reader, who comes to it only in its final stage, finds himself in a not unnatural bewilderment."[32]

Another reason that Levy's poem is obscure is that she uses self-reflexive and recondite literary allusions. In the third and final stanzas, the precise answer to "Who cries out on crowd and mart?" is Alfred Lord Tennyson, while the precise answer to "Who prates of stream and sea?" is Robert Browning. In order to hear the echo of Tennyson's *Maud* (1855) in the words "wide waste of square and street" in the third stanza of "London in July," the reader would probably have to remember that Melissa, in "Out of the World," explains her need to leave London temporarily by citing (without attribution) a couplet about how she began to "[l]oathe the squares and streets / And the faces that one meets."[33] This derives from *Maud,* in which the narrator is living wretchedly in a city made hideous by pollution and glare, noisy markets, and indifferent crowds.[34] (Tennyson's attitude toward the metropolis is, of course, the antithesis of Levy's.) One could know Tennyson's long narrative poem well and still not catch the reference.

As for recognizing that the answer to the second question is Browning, near the end of "Out of the World," Levy cites four lines from "Caliban upon Setebos" (1864). These are about an "icy fish" from a stream that tries to live in the lukewarm sea but can only sicken in that milieu.[35] Levy/Melissa's point is that one needs to know what is the right environment for oneself, and the right one for her is London. "London in July" strikes the same note, but the allusion is so condensed that understanding the reference to "stream and sea" goes beyond knowledge of Browning's poem to familiarity with Levy's preoccupation with the particular part of it from which she quotes in "Out of the World" and elsewhere in her writings.[36] A full understanding of the nuances of the final quatrain of Levy's poem is virtually impossible unless the reader is steeped in Levy's work. Yet, if one *is* such a reader, another answer to "who cries out . . . ?" and "Who prates . . ." is "*Poets,* that is who!" Like Baudelaire, but with more hope, Levy posits poetic consciousness as a solution to the abyss, and she playfully encodes her artistic ambitions in the conclusion to "London in July." What she really means by becoming one with the city is that she will become its bard.

It is worth considering the possibility that Levy meant to become for the city what Wordsworth had been for the countryside. That is not the goal of someone who considered herself a minor poet, despite the title of her 1884 dramatic monologue and volume of poetry.[37] The allusions in

"London in July" challenge Tennyson and Browning, just as they bring to mind that Wordsworth's poetic mission was the mirror image of Levy's own: one might even go so far as to say that the reader is asked to put Levy in the company of the major poets of her century.

Levy's adoption of an urban persona and of the city as setting, theme, and symbol certainly released a flood of creative energy, which is manifest in the eleven additional poems that Levy was to write about London. In June of 1887, the month before "London in July" appeared, she wrote in a letter: "I . . . find life opening up, somehow."[38] Her mood suggests that initially her turn toward symbolist methods was an artistic choice, not the result of a psychological crisis. But Levy's history of depression would have made her familiar with the difficulty of maintaining a cohesive self—which, as Solomon explains, often is an aspect of episodes of clinical melancholia[39]—and this would have made the idea of using a beloved as a figure for an aspect of the self readily available to her imagination. That 1887 and the first part of 1888 was a relatively happy and optimistic period for Levy probably explains why the five urban poems that appeared in the *Star* do not employ this trope.

The lyric from which Levy's final book took its title was published in the *Star* on 2 February; its speaker uses her identification with the hardy plane tree to express a preference for urban life that was unusual (at least in poetry at that time). As she looks at the plane tree from her "garret-pane," it is clear that there is a correspondence between the observer and the observed, for both thrive in an urban environment. Their likeness is emphasized by Levy's use of a female pronoun repeatedly in reference to the tree, which functions both as a metonym for London and as the vehicle of the metaphor for which the speaker is the tenor.

Although "A London Plane-Tree" is not symbolist, the analogue between the speaker's consciousness and the tree, which is part of the object world, makes the poem less of a departure from symbolist poetics than those that followed it in the newspaper. There were three more poems in February and another in May of 1888. These provide powerful images of the urban scene rather than evoking individual interiority. Some are lighthearted—for example, a roundel ("Between the Showers"), in which the speaker takes the point of view of a *flâneuse,* and "Ballade of an Omnibus," in which Levy celebrates the new mobility made possible by mass transportation. When the poem is about death ("Straw in the

Streets," another roundel) or sudden calamity ("Ballade of a Special Edition"), the dominant figures are metonyms for emotional experience common to most Londoners rather than expressions of a subjectivity that is highly particular.[40]

"Ballade of a Special Edition" can be used to explain Levy's metonymic system of representation. In this poem, the hawker of tabloid newspapers is not being *compared* with the city. Instead, he is a figure associated with urban life in an age of sensationalistic journalism:

> Of slaughter, theft, and suicide
>> He is the herald and the friend;
> Now he vociferates with pride
>> A double murder in Mile End.[41]

While the hawker's cry seems to have had particular resonance for Levy, she could expect this image to function as an effective signifier for a large and diverse readership.[42] This ballade, like "A London Plane-Tree," is metaphoric as well as metonymic, but, as David Lodge says, the distinction between metonymy and metaphor is not "between two mutually exclusive types of discourse, but a distinction based on dominance."[43] In this ballade, while metaphor is used, metonymy rules. Lodge, expanding on Roman Jakobson's "comment on the metonymic character of realistic fiction,"[44] indicates that metonymy lends itself particularly well to literature that is primarily about the object world; when it is used to represent feelings, I would add, they are ones that are utterable socially. Levy felt, apparently, that a poem that was not about extremely private emotional experience need not place heavy demands on the reader, and "Ballade of a Special Edition" does not.

"The Village Garden," which appeared in the *Spectator* in February 1889, can be viewed as a transition between the poems in the *Star* and the late urban poems. It has the clarity of meaning that characterizes the former, but the focus on private, inner turmoil that marks the latter. For the speaker in "The Village Garden," surely a consciousness close to that of the poet, the city is an actual place, not primarily the vehicle for her state of mind; but what she says about the impact of urban life on her mental health is personal, not communal. She finds city life salutary because it allows her to be less self-conscious. The prepositional phrase that begins the second line of the following quatrain establishes that she is speaking not for all, nor even for most, urban dwellers:

> Of gentler souls this fragrant peace is guerdon;
>> *For me,* the roar and hurry of the town,
> Wherein more lightly seems to press the burden
>> Of individual life that weighs me down.[45]

At the close of "London in July" the speaker is made happy and fulfilled by becoming one with the city, but in "The Village Garden" the benefit derived from subordination of self to the power of the metropolis, rather than being gratifying, is insufficient and merely relative.

Three other late urban poems in *Plane-Tree* show Levy moving further in the direction of symbolist methods, in that London *signifies* her speaker's state of mind, which is increasingly fragmented and distressed. In "The Piano-Organ" the speaker's attempt to study in her garret is interrupted by the sounds of an organ-grinder out in the street. The music "twirls on and on," and its apparent endlessness makes this street scene an externalization of a mental state in which concentration is impossible because of the reiteration of painful thoughts.[46] In "A March Day in London," also about obsessional thinking, the city is described in a manner that leaves no doubt that the speaker's inner world is "all awry": "The wind's in the east, the sun's in the sky / The gas-lamps gleam in a golden line."[47] The reader should remember that in England the east wind is proverbially, as the *OED* describes it, "bleak, unpleasant, and injurious to health." Also, "that the sun should not be shining when the darkness requires gaslights."[48] And "London Poets" empties life of everything but anguish by its chilling assumption that in their obsessive prowling about the city all that poets can desire is death. What these poems and those that follow indicate is that, sadly, "[t]he summer in the city's heart" ultimately was not enough for Levy.

But only two of Levy's late urban poems use private symbols in a manner that places the kind of demands on the reader that are characteristic of symbolist poetry, and both of these once more employ a device by which the self splits and becomes a beloved other. Consider "Out of Town":

> Out of town the sky was bright and blue,
>> Never fog-cloud, lowering, thick, was seen to frown;

Nature dons a garb of gayer hue,
> Out of town.

Spotless lay the snow on field and down,
> Pure and keen the air above it blew;
All wore peace and beauty for a crown.

London sky, marred by smoke, veiled from view,
> London snow, trodden thin, dingy brown,
Whence that strange unrest at thoughts of you
> Out of town?[49]

Identity is probed through what is on the surface the voicing of unreasonable concern for the person who is being addressed, who has left London for the country. For one thing, if we read the poem in the context of "The London Plane-Tree" and "The Village Garden," then we know that it is Levy herself (or her persona) who reverses the conventional attitudes toward city and country. That the speaker in "Out of Town" contrasts the fog, smoke, and dirty snow of London to the pure air and snow out of town makes her disquiet about the "you" who is away strike the reader as perverse. The perverse logic is what creates the puzzle, and it is the puzzle that invites a symbolic interpretation.

Similarly, "In the Mile End Road" can be read as a lyric in which Levy uses a beloved and the city as vehicles for what it feels like to experience a dissociated mental state. Having made that point, I should add that Levy's symbols are multitenored, can be understood in a number of ways.[50] But when I first read and reread "London in July," "Out of Town," and "In the Mile End Road," the intuition that gradually took hold was that these are not so much about a missing, absent, or dead lover as they are about the loss of or fear of losing a crucial dimension of the psyche. At the time that I wrote *Amy Levy: Her Life and Letters*, it had not occurred to me that she was influenced by symbolist poetics, yet the more I read these lyrics, the more convinced I became that Levy was writing about the state of her soul.[51]

Reading about the symbolists, I learned that the process by which I came to apprehend these poems was itself an indication that Levy was indebted to their methods. About Mallarmé's verse, Thomas A. Williams writes: "In the beginning, what one feels far exceeds in meaningfulness what one understands. This initial experience may lead to an effort at exegesis, to a search for total rational comprehension. But such comprehension, even when achieved, seldom . . . heightens . . . the all-important 'suggestion,' which was first called up in the mind by the poem."[52] Since my intuition was that "In the Mile End Road" is about an encounter with a part of the self that is dead, the next step was to comprehend rationally how Levy makes her suggestion felt. This short poem reads as follows:

In the Mile End Road

How like her! But 'tis she herself,
    Comes up the crowded street,
How little did I think, the morn,
    My only love to meet!

Whose else that motion and that mien?
    Whose else that airy tread?
For one strange moment I forgot
    My only love was dead.[53]

Emma Francis notes that "In the Mile End Road" "is haunted by two other poems."[54] One is Tennyson's *Maud* (1855), to which Levy also refers in "London in July."[55] In the second quatrain in "Mile End," the speaker, imagining a reunion with the woman she loves, cries out, "Whose else that motion and that mien? / Whose else that airy tread?" (cf. Tennyson's "She is coming, my own, my sweet; / Were it ever so airy a tread").[56] The narrator in *Maud* fancies that were his beloved to come, he would awaken even if he "had . . . lain for a century dead." By echoing this poem, Levy contrasts her speaker's chilling experience of death-in-life with Tennyson's heated fantasy of life-in-death.

Francis also observes that Levy's poem "replicates the rhythmic structure of Wordsworth's final 'Lucy poem,'" "A Slumber Did My Spirit Seal" (1800).[57] The rhythm that Francis hears is common meter (quatrains of alternating tetrameter and trimeter);[58] four of Wordsworth's five Lucy poems and four of Levy's elusive poems that evoke a missing or dead lover use this meter with an *abcb* or *abab* rhyme scheme—that is, ballad stanza.[59] Francis may be right that Levy had "Slumber" foremost in mind when she wrote "In the Mile End Road," since it, like "Slumber," has only two quatrains, but what matters is that Levy uses the ballad form in four of her lyrics about an absent beloved in order to call the Lucy poems to consciousness. She wants her readers to equate the beloved in her lyrics with Wordsworth's dead or dying maiden because in her poems, as in his, the woman is a figure for a dimension of the poet's identity. The elegiac poems about Lucy are usually, these days, read as utterances about loss of identity. Geoffrey Hartman, for example, writes that Lucy "is an intermediate modality of consciousness rather than an intermediate being. She is seen entirely from within the poet, so that this modality may be the poet's own, and Lucy the 'inner maiden.'"[60]

We have already seen that "London in July" aspires to the condition of music (as Walter Pater would say[61]) in that it is organized by the interplay of theme and variations. But I believe that Levy also found a correlative for musical form by experimenting with the use of the ballad, especially ballad stanza, as a leitmotif in the Wagnerian manner.[62] Just as Richard Wagner uses an associated melodic phrase or figure to accompany the reappearance of a person, situation, or idea, Levy, in "London in July," "In the Mile End Road," and two other poems not about the city, uses the ballad stanza to announce the theme of losing a lover (a ballad convention). She then goes beyond the traditional ballad obsession with lost love to evoke the spiritual crisis of self-estrangement. Two of Levy's four ballads fail to rouse an apprehension of this disturbing psychological state—"Twilight" and "June" are merely sad, even bathetic. Even "London in July," successful in other ways, may not cause the reader to recall the Lucy poems: its elusive beloved is not dead, and so the metrical and thematic parallel with the Lucy poems is far more submerged than in "In the Mile End Road."

In the latter, what works is that Levy uses a number of features associated with the ballad form and/or with the Lucy poems. That the poem culminates with the surprising revelation that the beloved woman is dead is one of these features; others are the quaint diction ("'tis," "morn"), the tone of simple candor, the syntax (mannered in the style of many English ballads, whether song or poem, folk or literary), and, of course, the requisite rhyme scheme, meter, and theme. Together, these aspects of "In the Mile End Road" suggest Wordsworth's lost maiden, and the uncanniness of Levy's little drama pushes the reader to recognize that the dead woman in her poem, like the ones in Wordsworth's poems, can be understood as a symbol.[63]

Wordsworth's ballads, set in nature, and Levy's two short ballads, set in the streets of London, are alike, so that once one has recognized the parallels, Levy's protest in "Out of the World"—"I am *not* playing at Wordsworth"—begins to have a provocative overtone.[64] The Mile End Road—not the poem but the place—is, of course, a major street in the East End of London. In Levy's time the East End was where the new Jewish immigrants lived, the "children of the ghetto" that Israel Zangwill writes about in his novel with that title. The dead self that Levy's speaker encounters on that road may be Levy's Jewish self, the part of her identity that she was afraid of losing as she struggled to find her place in English society.

Levy has another poem, not symbolist and not about the city, that is linked to the lyrics under discussion, and it contributes to my argument about them. Sportive even when writing about anguish, she crafted the epigraph to "The Lost Friend," probably another late poem, so that, although not elusive in meaning, it is strikingly similar in other ways to her symbolist ballads, and in its meaning recalls the theorizing of Mallarmé. The epigraph's metrical form, ballad stanza, is, of course, her signifier of a dissociated mental state; it is explicit about the strangeness of that state; and its tone is simple and sincere. The epigraph reads:

> The people take the thing of course,
> > They marvel not to see
> This strange, unnatural divorce
> > Betwixt delight and me.[65]

The word "thing" calls to mind Mallarmé's repeated use of *chose* (thing) in his remarks about poetry (among them, for example, "Paint not the thing"). In the first line of this epigraph, the "thing" that people "take" is that aspect of the speaker that can be apprehended externally (what Mallarmé says he does not want to represent), and she marvels that what others perceive as part of the object world is so opposed to the inner state, which feels so bizarre.

Symons explains that the symbolist poet "start[s] with an enigma" and "then withdraw[s] the key to the enigma."[66] Levy's "The Lost Friend" is another lament for a side of her personality that is gone and can be thought of as a recovered key. In the sonnet that follows the epigraph, neither difficult to interpret nor multitenored, Levy personifies sorrow and joy, with the speaker insisting, "Joy is my friend, not sorrow," and, "In some far land we wandered long ago"; then her feelings well up, and she invokes "Joy" as the "Beloved—to whose memory I cling."[67] The lover whose loss the speaker mourns is clearly the vehicle of Levy's metaphor, and the joyful component of her psyche is the tenor. That "The Lost Friend" identifies the tenor so unequivocally is further support for my readings of Levy's symbolist poems about an absent beloved, in which what the beloved might signify is not designated but conjured up in a variety of subtle ways.[68]

Levy was one of the poets who pioneered symbolist methods in England, and she seems to have turned to symbolism's poetics with increasing frequency toward the end of her life. This later work includes poems that are not about the city and not ballads, such as "On the Threshold," "In the Night," and "Impotens." Yet, almost every literary history or handbook says that the French symbolists began to influence English poets only in the 1890s, with the poems of Arthur Symons, Ernest Dowson, and W. B. Yeats; with *The Picture of Dorian Gray* (1890, revised 1891) by Oscar Wilde; and with Symons's explanations of symbolist poetry. There are probably other writers besides Levy who used symbolist techniques earlier than is usually supposed, and some of these would have been women, whose innovations often go unrecognized. The poems of A. Mary F. Robinson, written in the 1880s, may show the influence of symbolist ideas, according to Ana Parejo Vadillo, and Graham R. Tomson (Rosamund Marriott Watson) is also a likely candidate.[69]

We need to scrutinize more of Levy's late lyrics to find out if a symbolist reading is fruitful, and we ought to examine the work of other fin-de-siècle female poets to see if they were responding to the pull of what was going on in France. To gaze across the English Channel was to look toward the future, because *le Symbolisme*, as David Lodge, Hugh Kenner, and more recent critics remind us, became a main portal to modernism in poetry and in fiction.[70] It is probably no coincidence that if Levy, Robinson, and Tomson were among the first to clear a path toward the poetics of modernism, they also have in common that they—like T. S. Eliot, James Joyce, Ezra Pound, Virginia Woolf, and other modernists—wrote about the city.

Notes

1. See, for example, Judith R. Walkowitz, *City of Dreadful Delight: Narratives of Sexual Danger in Late-Victorian London* (Chicago: University of Chicago Press, 1992); and Erika Diane Rappaport, *Shopping for Pleasure: Women in the Making of London's West End* (Princeton, NJ: Princeton University Press, 2000). Rappaport even discusses Levy's life as a Londoner and some of the depictions of London in her writing, particularly her fiction.

2. Fisher Unwin to Lewis Levy, 14 September 1889, William Andrews Clark Library, University of California, Los Angeles, MS Wilde U621L, L6681 September 14.

3. Levy translated J. B. Peres's satire of the higher criticism. Her title for his book is *Historic and Other Doubts; or, The Non-Existence of Napoleon Proved* (London: E. W. Allen, 1885).

4. Arthur Symons, *The Symbolist Movement in Literature* (1899), in *Broadview Anthology of Victorian Poetry and Poetic Theory*, ed. Thomas J. Collins and Vivienne J. Rundle (Peterborough, ON: Broadview Press, 1999), 1415.

5. Jonathan Culler, introduction to *Les Fleurs du mal,* by Charles Baudelaire (Oxford: Oxford University Press, 1993), xxvi.

6. Henri Dorra, ed., *Symbolist Art Theories: A Critical Anthology* (Berkeley and Los Angeles: University of California Press, 1994), 137.

7. The poems in the *Star,* in the order that they appeared, are "Between the Showers," "Straw in the Streets" (both called "Roundel"), "Ballade of an Omnibus," "A London Plane-Tree," and "Ballade of a Special Edition."

8. David Lodge talks about metonymy as crucial to the mode of representation we call realism in *The Modes of Modern Writing: Metaphor, Metonymy, and the Typology of Modern Literature* (Ithaca, NY: Cornell University Press, 1977).

9. Levy of course also wrote numerous potboilers—romance fiction—but I am not referring to these.

10. The late urban poems are "Out of Town," "The Piano-Organ," "A March Day in London," "London Poets," "The Village Garden," and "In the Mile End Road." "In the Mile End Road" is not in the "Plane-Tree" section of Levy's last volume, where the other urban poems appear, but it belongs in that category nonetheless.

11. I think that Levy not only knew the work of Mallarmé but also was likely to have been acquainted with the poems of Paul Verlaine and Arthur Rimbaud, whose work was published in her time. Rimbaud's belief in the poet's need to experience *dédoublement*— by which he meant that the poet should have a double nature, that he should be at once participant and observer—has relevance for poems by Levy, which, as I will argue, are

about a split within the self. But since so much of late-Victorian literature in English plays with the idea of a divided self and uses the device of a doppelgänger, Levy need not have been influenced by Rimbaud when she wrote poems in which, to use Rimbaud's phrase, "Je est un autre." (Rimbaud's phrase comes from his letter to his former high school teacher, George Izambard, quoted in Dorra, *Symbolist Art Theories*, 136.)

12. Charles Baudelaire, *The Parisian Prowler (Le Spleen de Paris, Petits poèmes en prose),* trans. Edward W. Kaplan (Athens: University of Georgia Press, 1989), 119–20; Mallarmé too would seem to have known about nothingness, since he read Baudelaire so avidly and wrote so much about ennui. The poem of his that truly probes the *gouffre* was published in 1895, long after Levy's death: "Un coup de dés n'abolira jamais le hasard" offers the individual slight hope, but only if he grasps, accepts, and then defies the futility of life. For a discussion of Mallarmé, Baudelaire, and the *gouffre*, see Anna Balakian, *The Symbolist Movement: A Critical Appraisal* (New York: Random House, 1967), 78.

13. Amy Levy, "Out of the World," *London Society,* January 1886, 53. Some of Levy's readers would have heard in Levy's phrasing an echo of Thomas Hood's poem, "The Bridge of Sighs" (184), which features these well-known lines: "Any where, any where / Out of the world" (see *Selected Poems of Thomas Hood,* ed. John Clubbe [Cambridge: Harvard University Press, 1970], 319). But, as I have said, she is echoing Baudelaire here.

14. Levy, "Out of the World," 56.

15. Stuart Hall, "Ethnicity, Identity, and Difference," *Radical America* 23 (October–December 1989): 18; and Hall, quoted in Henry Louis Gates, "Black London," *New Yorker,* 18 September 1998, 203.

16. In "Jewish Humour," Levy says, "[T]he Jew . . . hardly has left, when all is said, a drop of bucolic blood in his veins. He has been huddled in crowded quarters of towns, forced into close and continual contact with his fellow-creatures" (*The Complete Novels and Selected Writings of Amy Levy, 1861–1889,* ed. Melvyn New [Gainesville: University Press of Florida, 1993], 523). I discuss Levy's essay in *Amy Levy: Her Life and Letters* (Athens: Ohio University Press, 2000), 124–26.

17. Mallarmé, from an interview by the journalist Jules Huret, 1891, in Dorra, *Symbolist Art Theories,* 141.

18. Symons, *Symbolist Movement,* 1421.

19. Stéphane Mallarmé to Henri Cazalis, 30 October 1864, in *Correspondance complète, 1862–1871,* ed. Bertrand Marchal (Paris: Editions Gallimard, 1959), 206.

20. Cited in Symons, *Symbolist Movement,* 1421.

21. Mallarmé, interview by Jules Huret, in Dorra, *Symbolist Art Theories,* 141.

22. Similarly, "state of the soul" (*l'état d'âme*) in this passage is sometimes translated (inadequately) as "mood." In the English version of the interview with Huret,

Mallarmé is responding to a question about "content," which further confirms my translation of the word *objet*.

23. Mallarmé's earliest poetry was published in the 1860s, and by 1887, he had published, among many other poems, the long and brilliant "Hérodiade" and "L'Aprèsmidi d'un faune."

24. Symbolist poetry in general included a new emphasis on musicality. Baudelaire wanted poetry to have the impact of music on the imagination—what he called "an ecstasy made up of rapture and knowledge" (quoted in Balakian, *Symbolist Movement*, 85). Balakian discusses Mallarmé's use of theme and variation to structure a poem in the mode of music. Malcolm Bowie says, "Mallarmé himself made it plain that music was valuable to him, in thinking about poetry, not just as *euphony* but as *structure*, as *organised relationship*" (*Mallarmé and the Art of Being Difficult* [Cambridge: Cambridge University Press, 1978], 169n67).

25. Amy Levy, "London in July," in *A London Plane-Tree and Other Verse* (London: T. Fisher Unwin, 1889), 18, reprinted in *Complete Novels*, 386.

26. See Rimbaud's letter to his former high school teacher, reprinted in Dorra, *Symbolist Art Theories*, 138.

27. See Culler, introduction to *Les Fleurs du mal*, xxxi.

28. Andrew Solomon, *The Noonday Demon: An Atlas of Depression* (New York: Scribner, 2001), 432.

29. William Blake, *Poems from the Notebook, c.1790–91*, in *The Poems of William Blake*, ed. W. H. Stevenson (New York: W. W. Norton, 1981), 167.

30. William Wordsworth, "Composed upon Westminster Bridge," in *William Wordsworth*, ed. Stephen Gill (Oxford: Oxford University Press, 1984), 285.

31. See, for example, Bowie, *Mallarmé*, 8–12.

32. Symons, *Symbolist Movement*, 1421.

33. Levy, "Out of the World," 53.

34. Levy is quoting Tennyson, *Maud*, in *The Poems of Tennyson*, ed. Christopher Ricks, 3 vols. (Harlow, UK: Longman, 1987), 2:575.

35. Levy, "Out of the World," 56; Robert Browning, "Caliban upon Setebos" (1864), in *Browning: The Poems*, vol. 1, ed. John Pettigrew with Thomas J. Collins (Harmondsworth, UK: Penguin, 1980), 805.

36. References to this passage from "Caliban upon Setebos" also appear in Levy's "Euphemia: A Sketch," *Victoria Magazine* 36 (1880): 133–203, and "Cohen of Trinity," *Gentleman's Magazine* 266 (1889): 417–24.

37. Even in our time Margaret Reynolds and other critics assume that Levy's "A Minor Poet," the title poem of her second volume of poems, *A Minor Poet and Other*

Verse, is autobiographical. In addition to what I have said to refute this in the text of this chapter, it is worth considering that a poet who is convinced that she is second-rate does not undertake the difficult task of translating an approach to poetry considered daring in its country of origin into her own language and personal idiom to evoke states particular to her own psyche.

38. Amy Levy to Vernon Lee, [June 1887], in Beckman, *Amy Levy*, 267.

39. Solomon, *Noonday Demon*, 81.

40. In "Variations sur un sujet," Mallarmé makes it clear that mental states particular to an individual, not general ones, were what he had in mind; see *Œuvres complètes*, ed. Henry Mondor and G. Jean-Aubry, Bibliothèque de la Pléiade, vol. 65 (Paris: Gallimard, 1945), 368.

41. Levy, "Ballade of a Special Edition," in *London Plane-Tree*, 23–24, reprinted in *Complete Novels*, 387–88.

42. There is a hawker of newspapers who cries out catastrophic news in "Sokratics in the Strand" (published in the *Cambridge Review* in 1884), "Out of the World," and her novel *Reuben Sachs* (1888).

43. Lodge, *Modes*, 111.

44. Lodge, *Modes*, x.

45. Levy, "The Village Garden," *Spectator*, 9 February 1889, 199, reprinted in *London Plane-Tree*, 30–31; my emphasis.

46. Levy, "The Piano-Organ," in *London Plane-Tree*, 28, reprinted in *Complete Novels*, 388–89.

47. Levy, "A March Day in London," in *London Plane-Tree*, 19–20.

48. Here my discussion of "A March Day in London" is almost identical to that in my *Amy Levy: Her Life and Letters*, 191–92.

49. Levy, "Out of Town," in *London Plane-Tree*, 27, reprinted in *Complete Novels*, 388.

50. For another reading of "In the Mile End Road," see Emma Francis, "Amy Levy: Contradictions?—Feminism and Semitic Discourse," in *Women's Poetry, Late Romantic to Late Victorian: Gender and Genre, 1830–1900*, ed. Isobel Armstrong and Virginia Blain (Basingstoke, UK: Macmillan, 1999), 183–204. Francis notes that the Mile End Road was frequented by prostitutes and was the setting for the Jack the Ripper killings of 1888: for Francis the woman whom the speaker encounters connotes, among other things, sexual commerce. If Levy was thinking of prostitution when she wrote "In the Mile End Road," then she would have had in mind Baudelaire's *Fleurs du mal*, whose urban poems focused on the underworld of criminals and prostitutes.

51. See my discussion of "London in July" and other poems that I interpret as being about the fragmentation of self in my *Amy Levy: Her Life and Letters*, 194–96.

52. Thomas A. Williams, *Mallarmé and the Language of Mysticism* (Atlanta: University of Georgia Press, 1970), 38.

53. Levy, "In the Mile End Road," in *London Plane-Tree*, 50, reprinted in *Complete Novels*, 393.

54. Francis, "Amy Levy," 199.

55. It is interesting that Mallarmé too was drawn to *Maud*, although Levy could not have known this. In a piece written in 1892 on the occasion of Tennyson's death, he said, "I prefer *Maude* [*sic*], romantic and modern, all dreams and passion" (*Mallarmé in Prose*, ed. Mary Ann Caws [New York: New Directions, 2001], 71).

56. Tennyson, *Maud*, in *Poems*, 565; further quotation is taken from page 565.

57. Francis also points out that the word "motion" appears in both lyrics at the start of the second quatrain (cf. Wordsworth's "No motion has she now, no force, " "A slumber did my spirit seal," *William Wordsworth*, ed. Gill, 147); "Amy Levy," 200.

58. Francis, "Amy Levy," 199.

59. Wordsworth's Lucy poem "Three Years She Grew" has six stanzas and a rhyme scheme that follows an *aabccb* pattern, which is also balladlike (*William Wordsworth*, ed. Gill, 154–55).

60. Geoffrey H. Hartman, *Wordsworth's Poetry, 1787–1814* (New Haven: Yale University Press, 1964), 158; for another example, see Richard E. Matlak's "Wordsworth's Lucy Poems in Psychobiographical Context," *PMLA* 93 (1978): 46–65.

61. "All art constantly aspires to the condition of music": Walter Pater, "The School of Giorgione," in *The Renaissance: Studies in Art and Poetry; The 1893 Text*, ed. Donald L. Hill (Berkeley and Los Angeles: University of California Press, 1980), 106.

62. When Baudelaire and Mallarmé looked to music to provoke the imagination in their poems, the compositions that they had most in mind were those of Richard Wagner. See Mallarmé's poem "Homage" (to Wagner) and his essay on Wagner, "Reverie d'un poète français" (1885). What surprises is that Mallarmé never saw a Wagnerian performance: he accepted Baudelaire's enthusiasm for the composer. Levy was also an avid fan of Wagner's music dramas. In a letter from Germany, written in 1884, she refers to meeting a "Wagner-schwaermer [Wagner-enthusiast], who "is going to play me bits of *Walkure* tonight" (Beckman, *Amy Levy: Her Life and Letters*, 250). In 1886 she first published her poem "Löhengrin," in the *Academy*.

63. Wordsworth's Lucy poems use the dead or dying maiden as a symbol in a manner that is related to (though also different from) the aesthetics of *le Symbolisme*, and Charlotte Brontë and Charles Dickens, in their fiction, use a method that could be called symbolist. Also, the poems of Heinrich Heine, the great German-Jewish Romantic, beloved by Levy, in some ways foreshadow Symbolist poetry. Hugh Kenner points out

that "Symbolism is scientific Romanticism," by which he means that the French move-
ment theorized about writing poetry "too subtle for the intellect," poems "held together,
as effects are, by the extra-semantic affinities of their words." He goes on to say: "In the
Symbolist poem the Romantic effect has become a structural principle" (Kenner, *The
Pound Era* [Berkeley and Los Angeles: University of California Press, 1971], 130). Thus
Levy, in adopting symbolist poetics, was not drawing exclusively on the movement in
France, although the late poetry that I talk about in this chapter (and other late lyrics)
would have been impossible without Baudelaire and Mallarmé.

64. About her vacation in Cornwall, Levy/Melissa says to her correspondent, "No,
dear, frankly, I am *not* playing at Wordsworth" ("Out of the World," 54).

65. Levy, "The Lost Friend," in *London Plane-Tree*, 71.

66. Symons, *Symbolist Movement*, 1421.

67. Levy, "The Lost Friend," 71.

68. My discussion of "The Lost Friend" in *Amy Levy: Her Life and Letters* (195–96)
overlaps with what I say here, although it is a bit longer.

69. Vadillo discussed A. Mary F. Robinson's poems about London as somewhat
symbolist in technique at the "Fin-de-Siècle Poem" conference at the William Andrews
Clark Library at UCLA in February 2002; see her "Immaterial Poetics: A. Mary F.
Robinson and the Fin-de-Siècle Poem," in this volume, chapter 8. Linda K. Hughes
points out that, at least by 1892, "Tomson knew the work of Baudelaire and Verlaine";
Hughes, "Feminizing Decadence: Poems by Graham R. Tomson," *Women and British
Aestheticism,* ed. Talia Schaffer and Kathy Alexis Psomiades (Charlottesville: University
Press of Virginia, 1999), 121.

70. Two studies written in the 1990s about the influence of Mallarmé on modern
English, Irish, and American writers are Robert Greer Cohn's "Mallarmé's Wake" and
William Carpenter's "'Le Livre' of Mallarmé and James Joyce's *Ulysses,*" both in *Mal-
larmé in the Twentieth Century,* ed. Robert Greer Cohn (London: Associated University
Presses, 1998); another is Anna Balakian, *The Fiction of the Poet: From Mallarmé to the
Post-Symbolist Mode* (Princeton, NJ: Princeton University Press, 1992).

IMMATERIAL POETICS

A. Mary F. Robinson and the Fin-de-Siècle Poem

Ana Parejo Vadillo

A Ballade of Poetesses

To Miss Mary Robinson

No fairer names hath time than those
    Of girls who smote the lyre with skill,
Who dared to climb the cliffs that rose
    Along the steep Parnassian hill,
    Nor paused for rue or daffodil;
Each shall not lose her godlike share
    Of garlands plucked by Delphi's rill,
Thin leaves around her silken hair.
—EDMUND GOSSE (1879)[1]

I

On Saturday, 28 February 1891, Katharine Bradley and Edith Cooper (the aunt and niece who wrote poetry jointly and secretly under the pen name Michael Field) went for a stroll in London, which they record in their journals:

> A fog—a glower of yellow, ignoring roofs, carriages, the op-
> posite side of the streets—everything in the dear city except the
> immediate pavement before one & the sudden passing faces—
> their flesh-tints strangely emphatic for a moment & then dim
> with disappearance.

The National Gallery was closed—when we left it, the "rose-mesh" of Arthur [Symons]'s cheeks and lips, as he met us, enchanting in the dismal space between one's eyes & the fog.

We walked to Fountain Court. . . . At the top of one of the dull red blocks is Arthur's little room. . . . The walls of the room are olive green, the carpet olive yellow—an oak bureau, an oak-table with pear-drop handles, & a painted bookcase of good length stand round. The books are rare, or interesting, or gifts. Above the case the head of Carpaccio's St. Ursula—on it the magnetic *Sarah*—Olive Schreiner & Mary Robinson & three other portraits of lady-friends on the mantelshelf. We saw a wizard portrait of Meredith—a portrait of Coventry Patmore—shrewd limited face: that of a dean turned poet, with a hint about its lines of his disgusting inconstant uxoriousness. George Moore's new vol. was put into our hands—I saw, unseen, the name of Michael Field under *Théatre Libre*.[2]

This colorful and delightful description is worth exploring for a number of reasons that relate to some familiar and less familiar aspects of English fin-de-siècle culture. First, Michael Field provide a distinctly late-Victorian rendering of an aesthetic day in "dear" London: the visual image of the fog and the glower of yellow intermingled with the noise of the carriages, which is reminiscent of James McNeill Whistler's paintings of the city.[3] To intensify the appealing opacity of this cityscape, they allude to Edgar Allan Poe's "The Man of the Crowd" (1840) by way of those "sudden passing faces—their flesh-tints strangely emphatic for a moment & then dim with disappearance." Such an allusion allows Michael Field to produce an impressionistic picture of an urban mass (one notices in particular the use of words such as "tint" and "dim"). Moreover, the writers insert a Baudelairian image of the passerby, who turns out to be the equally impressionistic "rose-mesh" of Decadent poet and critic Arthur Symons. Finally, Field draw our attention to the series of pictures and volumes of poetry and plays displayed on Symons's bookcase, offering a multifaceted visual panorama of 1890s literature. On his bookshelves they discover works by George Moore as well as their own plays. There, too, they glimpse pictures of the French actress Sarah Bernhardt, the South African novelist Olive Schreiner, and the English poets George Meredith and Coventry Patmore;

the latter made his poetic reputation with his paean to domestic woman-hood, *The Angel in the House* (1854–56). Their negative commentary on Patmore's indulgent "uxoriousness" is crucial in understanding their response to femininity. Considering the admiration Field had for the young English poet A. Mary F. Robinson (fig. 29), it comes as no surprise that one of the focal points of their gaze is her photographic portrait.

FIGURE 29. A. Mary F. Robinson, photograph, c. 1880. Courtesy of Colby College, Waterville, Maine

This revealing excerpt from Michael Field's detailed journals succinctly expresses many of the lines of inquiry that modern literary and cultural critics have pursued when researching the fin de siècle. Established accounts of the 1890s have followed Karl Beckson by stressing how London in this decade came to be an emblem of modernity.[4] Scholars have paid close attention to Symons's role as the English theorist of Decadence. They have explored the avant-garde, naturalist fiction of Moore. They have examined the bold experimentalism of Meredith's novels and poetry. And they have discovered much about Bernhardt's sexually transgressive performances on the European stage. More recently, Schreiner's powerful influence on New Woman fiction of the 1890s has generated much debate about feminism within this era. Similarly, Michael Field's attack on Patmore's conservative ideals of femininity has found an echo in recent studies of the late-Victorian dissatisfaction with domesticated womanhood.[5]

But this passage also suggests further areas that need to be addressed in discussions of 1890s culture. Michael Field's impressionistic perception of London as a site of poetic modernity has important bearing on recent accounts of urban modernity.[6] More particularly, what this extract reveals is the active presence of women in the public sphere, as well as an example of their experiences and articulations of urban space at this time. Further, the journal entry shows the ease with which two women poets could move between the sphere of the public (the populous metropolis) and the sphere of the private (a gentleman's drawing room)—making the increasing freedoms of modern intellectual women absolutely clear.

In other words, Michael Field's careful description of Symons's Decadent library indicates that women were more central to fin-de-siècle literary culture than most traditional surveys of the era would suggest. The passage offers a somewhat unfamiliar configuration of the poetic landscape of the late nineteenth century because it draws attention to three women poets—Michael Field and A. Mary F. Robinson—who commanded considerable attention in their own day but whose achievements modern scholarship has been slow to recognize.

There is no doubt that critical interest in Michael Field's large canon of poetry, which extends from the 1880s to the 1910s, has gone through a long overdue revival since the late twentieth century, and the present volume joins with recent inquiries that illuminate the remarkable breadth of Michael Field's responses and contributions to the poetics of the fin de

siècle. Yet, with the exceptions of an essay by M. Lynda Ely and brief discussions in recent anthologies of nineteenth-century women poets,
Robinson's well-received work has remained largely eclipsed in scholarly
accounts of the period.[7] By focusing on Robinson's meteoric success as a
poet, I suggest that her photographic presence in Symons's drawing room
relates to a haunting, ghostly, disembodied, and unreal quality that both
characterizes her poetic reputation and articulates a vital feature of her poetry. To support my claims, I begin by tracing the authority that Robinson
commanded in late-Victorian literary London. The second part of this chapter proposes that Robinson's exploration of what we might define as immaterial poetics performed a crucial role in the development of Decadent
poetry in its two variations, impressionism and symbolism, thus providing
a significant precedent to later, modernist examinations of urban life.

II

When Michael Field saw Robinson's picture in Symons's drawing room in
1891, Robinson no longer lived in London but resided in Paris, where—
subsequent to her marriage to a French scholar some three years earlier—
she was known as Madame Darmesteter. Why, then, was her photograph
given such prominence in Symons's drawing room? What was the
significance of her photographic presence among his books? The plain answer is that despite her dislocation Robinson, who now published as
"Mme. Darmesteter," remained a vital part of Symons's carefully assem-
bled archive. Moreover, the presence of Robinson's image reveals that she
stood as one of the most esteemed poets of the late-Victorian period.
Michael Field's glance at Robinson registers her success. Bradley and
Cooper, like many other poets of their generation, were attracted by Robinson's fame as one of England's newest and finest voices of the fin de siècle. In fact, Robinson was one of the few poets to whom they had disclosed
their dual authorship (interestingly, Symons was another to whom they
confided their secret). As early as 1882, when Robinson had only two volumes of verse in print, her distinction was such that it prompted Amy
Levy—the aspiring Anglo-Jewish poet who would come to attention with
A Minor Poet and Other Verse in 1884—to write the following to her sister:
"Are we going to be in a very bad way financially all this winter? I mean to

get regular work of some sort if I possibly can. O why doesn't Mary Robinson or Algernon Charles [Swinburne] want a secretary?"[8]

The history of Robinson's rapid fame, together with her pivotal role in London's aesthetic circles, occasions a reexamination of fin-de-siècle poetry. As Talia Schaffer notes in her major reassessment of British aestheticism, "[M]en and women who had similar status in the 1890s have wildly divergent images today." Schaffer contends that "[i]n the late-Victorian era, these writers were rivals, equals, and friends," adding that "the gulf between the foremost and the forgotten is our experience, not theirs."[9] Here Schaffer is referring mostly to women writers of prose and fiction. But her statement is also true of women poets in the late-Victorian period, especially Robinson. Take, for example, the account of new English poetry in the early 1880s that the well-known English editor Edmund Gosse presented to the American public: "The younger English poets at this moment best known in America—whether justly or not—are Mr. Philip Bourke Marston, Miss. A. Mary F. Robinson, Mr. Andrew Lang, Mr. Edmund W. Gosse, Mr. Austin Dobson, not to mention Mr. Oscar Wilde and his unfortunate protégé, Mr. Ronald Rodd [sic]."[10] Further, Robinson enjoyed a reputation similar to Swinburne's. Dressed like an "aesthete" (Moore met her clad in medieval costume),[11] Robinson was a professional woman of letters (she appealed to Wilde's *The Woman's World*) and she developed a career as both a poet and a prolific critic (she was as well published as Symons). The art historian and sexual radical John Addington Symonds thought so highly of her poetry that he wanted to send her 1884 collection of poems, *The New Arcadia,* to Walt Whitman.[12]

The photograph of Robinson confirms that she rose quickly as a celebrity among London's poetic circles. She became famous at the age of twenty-one with the publication in 1878 of her first volume, *A Handful of Honeysuckle.* The following year she was writing verse and articles in prose for such distinguished publications as the *Sunday Times, Cornhill, Belgravia,* and the *University Magazine.* Her fame had also extended outside of England, especially to Germany, where she contributed a series of papers on contemporary British poets to the German magazine *Unsere Zeit.*[13] In fact, to German audiences she was *the* English poet of the moment, as she told Symonds.[14] Gosse's "A Ballade of Poetesses," written in 1879 and dedicated to Robinson, went so far as to compare her poetry favorably with that of Sappho and the classical tradition. While earlier

Victorian critics, as Susan Brown has recently observed, traditionally "invoked Sappho as a precedent for the poetess,"[15] Gosse made the comparison with the head of the lyric tradition because Robinson had acquired outstanding knowledge in Greek language and literature. (Robinson studied Greek for five years at University College, London; she was the first woman to study Greek in a coed classroom.[16]) Little wonder that William Sharp described her as "a brilliant young scholar-poet."[17] In light of her unorthodox academic training, her second book was a translation from the Greek of *The Crowned Hippolytus* by Euripides (published in 1881, and dedicated to Symonds).[18]

It was Robinson's phenomenal success as a poet, however, that prompted Eric Robertson to connect her name with the celebrity that Letitia Elizabeth Landon ("L.E.L.") enjoyed for much of the 1820s and 1830s. In 1883, he observed that

> the cultivated section of the reading public, which watches contemporary poetry closely, took second thoughts about Miss Robinson, and the book which had been talked of on its first appearance as "rather good," made its charms so subtly felt that Miss Robinson came to be quite a topic for discussion, somewhat as L.E.L. had been in her young days. It got wind that Tennyson and Browning liked this modest little collection of verses; it was duly appreciated at Oxford; inquiry led to the understanding that the writer of these verses was quite young, was learned in the classic tongue, and contributed essays to German periodicals.[19]

Such commentary helps to explain why Symons styled her the "spoilt child of literature."[20]

At this point, it makes sense to look closely at Robinson's upbringing. She was the elder daughter of George Robinson, a wealthy architect and decorator who—according to Elizabeth Robins Pennell—was in some respects a "rival of William Morris." Among his clients was the painter Ford Madox Brown, who was to become a close friend of the family. Like many middle-class women in the nineteenth century, she began her education at home at the hand of her father, "a lover of old books" who allowed her "the free use of his library & even used to take some trouble to explain away the difficulties of the old spelling." Robinson developed very early on a deep love for literature, reading the "Old Chronicles, and the Elizabethan

Dramatists in turn with Grimm's fairy tales and Hans Andersons [*sic*] stories." At age five, she "considered [herself] quite an old poet though [she]
could not write [her] verses down," and at the age of fourteen, she was
busy "learning Latin and writing a History of Athens."[21] She and her sister, Mabel Frances Robinson—who would also become a writer—were
then sent to Brussels to complete their education.[22] After their education
on the Continent, the sisters returned to live with their parents, who settled
at 84 Gower Street, at the heart of Bloomsbury in London.

Since the 1850s, Bloomsbury had been associated with the Pre-
Raphaelite Brotherhood, which used to meet at 7 Gower Street. During
the 1870s and 1880s the area still maintained vestiges of the Pre-Raphaelite
movement, with the presence of Christina Rossetti and William Michael
Rossetti at 5 Endsleigh Gardens and 30 Torrington Square, respectively.
George Robinson's fame as an architect helped to establish him as a fa-
mous host, and his house, in Pennell's words, was "one of the most inter-
esting in London."[23] Among the regular *saloniers* were William Michael
Rossetti and his wife Lucy Rossetti, Richard Garnett, William Sharp and
Elizabeth Amelia Sharp (the editor of *Women's Voices: An Anthology of the
Most Characteristic Poems by English, Scotch, and Irish Women* [1887] and
Women Poets of the Victorian Era [1890]), Robert Browning, Madox Brown,
William Morris, Walter Pater, William Holman Hunt, Edward Burne-
Jones, Wilde, Whistler, Gosse, Moore, and Symons, to name but a few.

This particular aesthetic set admired the poetry of Republican activist
James Thomson, as Robinson informed Symonds. They were particularly
influenced by French literature, not Molière or Hugo but "the divine"
Villon and Marot, Gautier and Baudelaire being their "daily bread and
butter." And in relation to painting, Robinson noted that they all admired
Whistler and Manet for their "sincerity," and that the more advanced of
the set, including herself, thought that one could not see real art but in
the impressionists' studios of the rue de Le Pelletier.[24]

The commitment of this group to the aesthetics of impressionism
can be easily recognized in a particular "aesthetic event" that Wilde
arranged. He rented two or three large octagonal rooms in an old hotel on
Salisbury Street, where he had opened the large windows onto the
Thames, the scene enchanting because of its colors. Of course, all those
present described the scene as a "Whistler"—it was all very "aesthetic."[25]
Robinson was "the shining light" of the group, as Pennell observes:

That description of Miss Robinson is good—And when she greets you in the morning with "Hello" and seems to sail towards you like a little Botticelli figure, if you are a great clumsy lout like me you dont [sic] know what to do with yourself—and then she tells you in such a charming way of something she has just seen—I dont [sic] wonder she was a shining and a burning light among the Rossetti set. She told me a good thing about Oscar— poor Oscar—who has just likened the moon "to a yellow seal upon a blue envelope"—see new book beginning to appear— Oscar asked her what he should do to escape the world and his hosts of followers—and the *Mademoiselle* said "Go to Paris." Collapse of the incarnation of beauty (a fact).[26]

The literary connections within this network were used to help other poets, as was the case for Marston. It was Robinson who first wrote to Madox Brown asking him to participate in the formation of a three-year fund that she and William Sharp were creating to help Marston, who was going through a particularly difficult period.[27] And it was through Madox Brown that Robinson met the poet Mathilde Blind, who later became a regular at the Robinsons' salon. Madox Brown was a great admirer and a good friend of Robinson,[28] and he was the first artist to paint her (fig. 30).[29]

FIGURE 30. Ford Madox Brown, *Mary Robinson* (1881). Courtesy of Institut Pasteur, Paris

One of the most important figures in this group was the aesthete Vernon Lee (to whom *The New Arcadia* was dedicated). Robinson met Lee (born Violet Paget) in 1879, and they became inseparable companions (figs. 31 and 32). Together, Lee and Robinson expanded their aesthetic circle by nourishing a community of women writers and poets.[30] Such authors included Louisa S. Bevington, Elizabeth Chapman, Louise Chandler Moulton, Margaret Veley, Emily Pfeiffer, Augusta Webster, and Amy Levy—most of whom have attracted attention in recent anthologies of Victorian women poets.[31] Indeed, young and well-established poets, writers, novelists, and dramatists used Mary Robinson's salon to establish important literary connections. For instance, it was at the Robinsons' house that William Sharp encountered Walter Pater:

> I first met Walter Pater fourteen years ago, at the house of Mr. George T. Robinson in Gower Street, at that time a meeting-place for poets, novelists, dramatists, writers of all kinds, painters, sculptors, musicians, and all manner of folk, pilgrims from or to the only veritable Bohemia. The host and hostess had the rare faculty of keeping as well as of winning friends, and were held in affectionate esteem by all who knew them; but the delightfully promiscuous gatherings, where all amalgamated so well, were due in great part to the brilliant young scholar-poet, Miss A. Mary F. Robinson (Madame Darmesteter) and to her sister, now the wellknown novelist, Miss Mabel Robinson.[32]

In 1883, however, the Robinsons took the important decision to move from Bloomsbury to Kensington. The new location was certainly "a great improvement," and a huge social success. As Pennell's memoirs reveal, the Kensington location revitalized the Robinsons' salon, attracting well-established writers and poets to the drawing rooms of the new house and reactivating A. Mary F. Robinson's literary career and fame: "I remember hearing [disabled poet William Ernest Henley] announced once at the Robinson's in Earl's Terrace, but Miss Mary Robinson, as she was then . . . left everybody in the drawing-room while she went to see him downstairs, because of his lameness she said, but partly, I fancied, because she wanted to keep him to herself to discuss a new series of articles."[33] Another celebrity who lived in Kensington was Robert Browning, a great

FIGURE 31. John Singer Sargent, *Mary Robinson* (1881). Courtesy of Adelson Galleries, New York.

These two portraits by John Singer Sargent were painted in 1881. Lee's was painted at Robinson's house at 84 Gower Street. Lee wrote to her mother that Sargent "was much struck & charmed with [Mary], and asked leave . . . to do her likeness." Richard Ormond and Elaine Kilmurray suggest that Robinson's portrait was most probably painted in the autumn of 1881 while Mary, who was on her way to visit Lee in Florence, was staying in Paris. They also remark that "Sargent gave the sketch to Vernon Lee as a companion to her own portrait" (John Singer Sargent, *The Early Portraits*, vol. 1 of *Complete Paintings,* ed. Ormond and Kilmurray [New Haven, CT: Yale University Press, 1998], 76–77).

FIGURE 32. John Singer Sargent, *Vernon Lee* (1881). Courtesy of the Tate Gallery, London

admirer of Robinson's work, who lived next door to John Millais. Living on the same street as Browning was Henry James, who, after the success of his *Portrait of a Lady* (1881) and *Portraits of Places* (1883), took a lease on a flat at 34 De Vere Gardens.[34] Pater, after the publication of *Marius the Epicurean* (1885), moved to 12 Earl's Terrace, very close to Frederic Leighton (perhaps Kensington's most famous resident), and on the same street as the Robinsons. Here is another of Pennell's illuminating descriptions of the Robinsons' parties at Kensington:

> *Tuesday, December 22nd* [1885]. In the afternoon to the Robinsons, found the house crowded, up stairs and down. Met Miss Prestor and Miss Dodge just going away. Dr. Garnett came in almost at the same time and, as usual, began the conversation by asking me if there was nothing he could do for me at the Museum. . . . Mrs. Oscar Wilde in olive plush lined with red and blowsy hair sat in the middle of the room talking to a young man with a bang and violets in his buttonhole & unexpressible eyes. George Moore talked most of the time to young ladies. Saw the Glazebrooks, Lemons, Sharps, Miss Dunn and her friend Miss Osborn. W.M. Rossetti there and Mrs. Francillon and the Paters, the Stillmans [fig. 33].[35]

It was also on Earl's Terrace that in 1885 A. Mary F. Robinson met Michael Field. Bradley and Cooper first contacted Robinson early in 1884, when they sent her *Callirrhoë and Fair Rosamund* (1884). Having broken all relations with Bradley's former mentor, Ruskin, Michael Field were trying to enter the London poetic world by sending a copy of their book to Browning and his friend Robinson. The response that Bradley and Cooper received was so encouraging that they finally decided to go to London and meet their "dear Browning" and London's most famous and fashionable poet at Kensington.[36] Robinson helped them by writing a rather long review of *Callirrhoë* and by advising them on how to publicize their work: "At the London Library today I saw an *exceedingly* good review of your book in the *Spectator* for this week (Tuesday, May 21st). Mine is not so dazzlingly but more explanatory. And as I prefer Callirrhoë & your spectator critic Fair Rosamund, a judicious publisher should be able to make a good advertisement."[37]

FIGURE 33. Lisa Stillman, drawing of A. Mary F. Robinson, n.d., frontispiece, *The Collected Poems: Lyrical and Narrative of Mary Robinson* (London: T. Fisher Unwin, 1902)

In 1888, however, the aesthetic circle that congregated at the Robinsons' home in Kensington suffered unexpected consequences when Robinson decided to marry James Darmesteter, in spite of Lee's staunch opposition. Her marriage took place on the eve of the publication of *Songs, Ballads and a Garden Play,* which she dedicated to her sister, Mabel. This turn of events marked a drastic change in Robinson's career. She notoriously broke up with Lee and, perhaps more crucially, left London for Paris, where she remained until her death in 1944. In 1901 she changed her name once more, after her marriage to Emile Duclaux, the director of the Institut Pasteur. Thus when Bradley and Cooper saw Robinson's photograph at Fountain Court, the poet known as A. Mary F. Robinson was no more—at least in name.

At this juncture, it is useful to turn to Eduardo Cadava's discussion of photography. He suggests that in a photographic image "the essential relation between death and language flashes before us." Indeed, "what takes place in any photograph" is "the return of the departed." As he explains:

> Photography is a mode of bereavement. It speaks to us of mortification. Even though it still remains to be thought, the essential relation between death and language flashes up before us in the photographic image. "What we know that we will soon no longer have before us." . . . Like an angel of history whose wings register the traces of this disappearance, the image bears witness to an experience that cannot come to light. This experience is the experience of the shock of the experience, of experience as bereavement. This bereavement acknowledges what takes place in any photograph—the return of the departed. Although what the photograph photographs is no longer present or living, its having-been-there now forms part of the referential structure of our relationship to the photograph. Nevertheless, the return of what was once there takes the form of a haunting.[38]

Cadava's insights help us to appreciate Michael Field's glance at Robinson's portrait. In Symons's drawing room, Robinson returned to Bradley and Cooper in an ethereal form. Moreover, the once intimate relations between Robinson and aesthetic culture flashed up before them through the spectral image. The photograph registered not Robinson's presence but the traces of her disappearance from London's literary culture. More important, the photograph's presentation of Robinson's "having-been-there" served a further purpose: it formed part of the referential structure of the fin de siècle.

In what follows, I explain why Robinson's capacity to return to Michael Field as a ghost belongs to a central component of fin-de-siècle aesthetics, which we can best understand through a close exploration of Robinson's poetic interest in immateriality. Cadava compellingly argues that the possibility of the photographic image requires that there be such things as ghosts, and he quotes Robert Desnos's notice of the photographer Atget's death: "Atget is no more. . . . His ghost, I was going to say, 'negative,' must haunt the innumerable poetic places of the capital." This quotation encapsulates Robinson's literary position within the 1890s: it was the immateriality of her negative that haunted literary circles of late-Victorian London. Her early poetry, dating from 1878 to 1888, assists us in understanding why this was the case.

III

In one of the defining critical statements of the fin de siècle—the essay titled "The Decadent Movement in Literature," which appeared in *Harper's New Monthly Magazine* in 1893—Symons offered British and American readers a definition of what was originally a French term:

> Taking the word Decadence, then, as most precisely expressing the general sense of the newest movement in literature, we find that the terms Impressionism and Symbolism define correctly enough the two main branches of that movement. Now Impressionist and Symbolist have more in common than either supposes: both are really working on the same hypothesis, applied in different directions. What both seek is not general truth merely, but *la vérité vraie*, the very essence of truth—the truth of appearances to the senses, of the visible world to the eyes that see it; and the truth of spiritual things to the spiritual vision.[39]

Symons had written before on some of the poets discussed in "The Decadent Movement in Literature" but this essay proved to be more than a critical review of new poetry emanating from England, France, and elsewhere. As many literary historians have observed, his groundbreaking discussion also took a leading step toward what would later become known as modernist thought. Significantly, the principles that he outlines in this essay underwent revision six years later. In 1899 he redrafted and expanded the essay, dispensed with the term "Decadence," and published his discussion as *The Symbolist Movement in Literature,* which he dedicated to W. B. Yeats. Richard Ellmann directly links *The Symbolist Movement in*

Literature to Freud's *Interpretation of Dreams* (also dating from 1899) because both were interested in the inward world of the mind, a world that had little to do with exterior reality.[40] It is also worth remembering here the enormous influence this work had on modernist poetry, particularly that of T. S. Eliot, who read it in 1908, when he was at Harvard.[41]

The notable transition between the 1893 and 1899 versions of Symons's essay can help us focus on how some key transformations in fin-de-siècle aesthetics illuminate a number of preoccupations in Robinson's poetry. In the 1893 essay, Symons places emphasis on seeking "truth": both the truth perceived by the senses and spiritual truth (best represented by "Impressionism" and "Symbolism"). By 1899, however, Symons had rejected the word "Decadent"—mainly because the 1895 trials of Oscar Wilde stigmatized the Irish author, in William Ernest Henley's words, as the "High Priest of the Decadents."[42] Symons also claims, in the later essay, that "after the world had starved its soul long enough in the contemplation and the re-arrangement of material things, comes the turn of the soul."[43] Adapting the French term *Symbolisme,* he concentrates his attention on a literature "in which the visible world is no longer a reality, and the unseen world no longer a dream."[44]

The visible and unseen worlds appear in Robinson's poetry not as dialectically opposed, but as linked by symbols that function as linguistic passages leading from palpable reality to sensorial disembodiment. Her lyrics frequently transition from an outward vision of city life to an inward contemplation of an abstract idea or the interiority of the self. Robinson's earliest reviewers quickly identified this aspect of her poetry. Critics generally praised *A Handful of Honeysuckle* both for its lyric musicality and its affecting tendency to explore the unreal. Andrew Lang, for instance, wrote in the *Academy:* "The collection is infinitely superior to most handfuls of lyrical honeysuckle. Many of the verses are spontaneous; the musical expression of dreams and delicate fancies. . . . They are so natural sometimes with their faults and their freshness that they affect one like voices out of the early years. . . . One may hope that Miss Robinson will write more lyrics."[45] The *Athenæum* described the poems as "[a]ltogether fantastic and unreal. . . . Still there are quaint picturesque touches every here and there in these poems which recall the touches of early poets."

"Song of a Stormy Night" (1888) is a good example of Robinson's subtle use of the natural world symbolically in order to evoke affect.

Song of a Stormy Night

In my pale garden yesternight
The statues glimmered ghostly-white,
The brooding trees that haunted me
Flapped dusky wings despairingly.

Both air and sky death-heavy were,
But oh my heart was heavier,
For life (I said) is useless grief,
And death an undesired relief.

Then the wind rushed up
    Clad in darkness and hail,
Whirling the rain
    As a rent white veil,
But my heart, my heart,
    Was glad of the gale.

The roar of the wind
    Grew hoarser and higher,
Till the thunder spoke
    And its voice was fire.
But my heart was freed
    From the storm of desire.

My lilies passion-sweet are dead,
Love's purple, royal roses shed,
But heart and garden are besprent
With flowers of patience and content.[46]

Graham R. Tomson's "In a London Garden" (1891) and Olive Custance's "The White Statue" (1897) would later echo this perfectly symbolical poem. In his insightful study of rhetoric, Paul de Man offers a very useful examination of the symbol in nineteenth-century literature. He remarks that "the symbol is founded on an intimate unity between the image that rises up before the senses and the supersensory totality that the image suggests."[47] This definition helps us understand Robinson's use of the symbolic imagination. In this poem, the subjectivity of the experience is expressed in the unity between the image of the garden in the storm and the powerful, overpowering emotion that this image suggests. Further, the use of aesthetic words such as "pale," "lilies," and "royal roses," and phrases such as "statues that glimmered ghostly-white," or "the brooding trees that haunted me," speak of the heart's "undesired relief." To glimmer is "to shine faintly" (*OED*). This is exactly what this symbolic garden does: it projects light, meaning, out of itself into the feelings of the speaker's self.

This inward world of emotions is re-created and further stimulated by Robinson's expert use of rhyme, meter, and stanza. Here Robinson follows S. T. Coleridge's dictum that in the symbolic imagination "such as the life is, such is the form."[48] The poem starts with two regular quatrains rhyming *aabb ccdd*. The metrical pattern of the lines is also typically regular: four accents per line. There are, however, two important exceptions to this rule: line four has five accents, while line six has three. In line four, the iambic rhythm changes through the use of a trochee at the beginning of the line: "Flapped dusky wings despairingly." This rhythm produces an important visual and aural effect, and, more significantly, it draws our attention to the word "flapped" in its two meanings: to "swing or sway about" and (colloquially) to "become agitated or panicky" (*OED*). Thus Robinson's use of rhythm is equally expressive of the material perception of the landscape, on the one hand, and the speaker's state of mind, on the other hand. In line 6, Robinson slows down the soothing rhythm of the quatrains for a similar reason: to make clear the analogy between the garden and the self. In this way Robinson disrupts the serene beauty of the landscape by projecting the speaker's own anxiety onto it.

This feeling of uneasiness anticipates and prepares the reader for the arrival of the storm. Robinson uses the spiral intensity of the sestet to replicate linguistically and graphically the fierceness of the gale. The change in meter (from four to three to two accents per line) and rhyme, particularly in the second sestet, increases the speed of the poem until it reaches climax—a climax in which both the storm and the self are released from desire. Once the climax has been attained, both self and garden achieve a state of equilibrium, which is expressed in the last stanza in the form of a regular quatrain with a single rhyme. This poem offers an excellent example of Robinson's use of symbolism, for indeed in these lines, as Yeats would have put it, "[a]ll sounds, all colours, all forms . . . evoke indefinable and yet precise emotions"—they "call down among us certain disembodied powers, whose footsteps . . . we call emotions."[49]

Although most of Robinson's contemporary reviewers acknowledged her talent and pointed to her clear debt to the poetry of the Pre-Raphaelites, they were preoccupied with her easy access to the realm of fantasy.[50] Dante Gabriel Rossetti warned her of this tendency in a letter written in May 1879:

> 16, Cheyne Walk, 31st May
>
> Dear Madam,
>
> Allow me to thank you for the gift of your "Honeysuckle." I see you have some command over what belongs to fantasy, though the extremes to which you carry form seem to hamper you sometimes; and indeed the simpler poems please me best. If you mean to pursue poetry, I would suggest you taking up some subject which should deal with realities and see what you could make of that. This test should always be resorted to when the natural tendency lies strongly in the other direction.
>
> Yours very truly,
> D.G. Rossetti.[51]

How Robinson reacted to this letter remains unknown, but in *The Crowned Hippolytus*, published in 1881, her flight into the realm of the unreal is more controlled. This is partly because her representation of urban landscape in the three lyrics brought together as "London Studies" allowed her to think about the ways in which art might produce closer connections between a world of external appearances and an inner, unconscious world. In this respect, it is helpful to compare Robinson's "London Studies" with Levy's "A London Plane-Tree" (1889), because both poets constitute the city as a symbol of the poet's urban identity. Interestingly, both Levy and Robinson depict an organic element, a tree, in order to represent their speakers' desires in an urbanscape (the city, the square). But while Levy's poem expresses an outward enthusiasm for the plane tree's capacity to flourish in urban space, Robinson's lyric sequence turns inward in order to contemplate a yearning for abstract beauty. "London Studies" anticipates what Virginia Woolf would later call "moments of being," in which the cityscape is transformed into a subjective experience, whether in "A Square in November," "Outside the Museum," or "After the Storm in March." These poems also resonate with the most famous formulations that Pater, the founding theorist of aestheticism, makes in his widely read conclusion to *Studies in the History of the Renaissance* (1873). Pater memorably argues that the whole of human physical life is "but a combination of natural elements to which science gives their names," and that these elements are not limited to the human body: "[W]e detect them in places most remote from it. Our physical life is a perpetual motion of them—the passage of blood, the waste and repairing of the lenses of the eye, the modification of the tissues of the brain under every ray of light and sound. . . . Like the elements of which we are composed, the action of these forces extends beyond us."[52] In line with late-Victorian theories of entropy, which claimed that the energy of the human body and mind and the energy of the world were forever dissipating, Pater draws on physics to describe the organic unity of the fluctuating self and the world. His conclusion, however, goes further. Pater suggests that not only physical life is in a state of perpetual flux. He contends that the "hard, gem-like flame" of the inner world of thought and feeling is even more eager and devouring (189).

For Robinson, the outer and inner entropic worlds that Pater theorizes in the conclusion to *Studies in the History of the Renaissance* coexist, one superimposed on the other, as a kind of archeological layering. The literary technique she uses to bring such worlds into linguistic discourse is impressionism. In "A Square in November," for example, what first draws our attention is the poem's impressionistic technique and the use of quatrains to replicate the city's square:

> Down the street the wind looks black;
>   Underfoot the leaves are shed
>   Spoiled and dead; overhead
> All the sky is dark with rack.[53]

The dominant color here is black, and the overall perception is one of death and darkness. The adverbs "[u]nderfoot" and "overhead" locate the speaker in between the blackness of the sky and the deathliness of the ground. The second stanza depicts the urban scene in a similar vein: "Winter-ruined leaves exhale / Chilly vapours thin and blue." But by the eighth line the speaker has begun to question the relationship between outer reality and inner being, for she observes "[t]rees that *look* unreal and frail" (emphasis added). At that moment, the outside world takes an inward turn:

> How they reach their branches out!
>   Groping in the lifeless air
>   Blind and bare, for some fair
> Long-since-vanished May, no doubt.

> So my life, as bare and blind,
>   Towards some beauty unattained,
>   Lost or waned, stretches strained
> Helpless aims that never find.

In "A Square in November," the death of the urban landscape is symbolic of the death of the poet's creativity. Here it helps to refer to Paul Verlaine's definition of his poetic technique as "sincerity, and the impression of the moment followed to the letter."[54] Verlaine's definition is particularly useful for an analysis of the poems contained in "London Studies." The same interest in capturing "impressions of the moment" later influenced Tomson in poems such as "Nocturn" (1895) and "London in October" (1895), and Alice Meynell in her collection of essays *The Colour of Life*, appositely subtitled *On Things Seen and Heard* (1896).

In her next collection of poems, *The New Arcadia*, Robinson made an important attempt at social criticism, which most reviewers found disagreeable. Her following book, *An Italian Garden* (1886), however, returned to the immateriality that had come to characterize her lyrics. Symons believed that this third volume was Robinson's greatest achievement. According to Symons, in *An Italian Garden* "[t]he dreamer has fallen back into the circle of dreams. But the dreams can never again be of that mere heaven in arabesque and embroidery. There is a human note in them, a note of sincerity . . . a pensiveness, a gentle melancholy—in this nature which has come through art to take an interest in life."[55] In a letter to Robinson, Lee describes the collection in similar terms. After reading the manuscript of *An Italian Garden,* Lee writes that she is struck "by what [she] can only call the *soprano* quality of these poems: a certain charmness, youthfulness, childlikeness—a negation of all that's of the flesh & blood . . . a quality of voice rare, aetherial, singing in an altogether higher stratum of atmosphere, coming out of what seems an immaterial throat."[56] She adds:

> One asks oneself to what extend is all this true, whether these are not the experiences of some soul that cries far away and distant from the writer's body; it is all fantastic, unreal, yet every now and then—especially in the Rispetti—a note comes, so real that it brings the tears into my eyes. You are a stray creature, Mary, & I feel that were I to clutch you never so close, I should clutch you thus a phantom, or rather that the real thing would elude me, volatile, distant. I ask myself to what extent is all this real-real experience, like the flesh & blood experiences of my own heart as tangible, if I may say so, as hunger or a headache.[57]

In this letter, Lee articulates quite perceptively the core philosophy of Robinson's aesthetics: the negation of physical experience in favor of the disembodied soul. This is an important statement, particularly in view of Robinson's use of urbanscapes. For indeed what Lee is suggesting is that Robinson's subjective perception brings into question their physical reality. They are after all a mirage of the real. And yet, it is precisely in their immateriality that they truly come alive, stimulating real and profound emotions. Robinson recognized this in the preface to her 1888 volume of verse, *Songs, Ballads and a Garden Play.* Here, as a response to her sister's interest in realism and the naturalist novel, she notes that "[t]he only real things, you know, are the things that never happen."[58]

In such poems as "The Ideal" and "Venetian Nocturne" Robinson takes some of the ideas already present in "London Studies" in a new direction. While the urban landscape remains crucial for Robinson's entry into interior modes of being, here she radically reduces her impressionism. In "The Ideal," she interiorizes the street so that it instantly becomes a metaphor of the "Soul":

I walk along the byways of my Soul,
    Beyond the streets where all the world may go,
Until at last I reach the hidden goal
    Built up in strength where only I may know.[59]

Here the search for truth, as Symons put it, focuses on "the truth of spiritual things to the spiritual vision." This statement is also true of "Venetian Nocturne," whose title is reminiscent of Whistler's paintings; in this poem, however, Robinson's experimentation with immaterial poetics takes her further than in "The Ideal." She eliminates the relationship between the urbanscape and consciousness. In other words, and paraphrasing de Man, material perception and symbolical imagination are continuous no more. The street is purely figural. What Robinson seeks to capture by using figural language is the immateriality of the self:

Venetian Nocturne

Down the narrow Calle where the moonlight cannot enter
    The houses are so high;
Silent and alone we pierced the night's dim core and centre—
    Only you and I.

Clear and sad our footsteps rang along the hollow pavement,
    Sounding like a bell;
Sounding like a voice that cries to souls in Life's enslavement,
    "There is Death as well!"

Down the narrow dark we went, until a sudden whiteness
    Made us hold our breath;
All the white Salute towers and domes in moonlit brightness,—
    Ah! could this be Death?[60]

The poem asserts the disembodiment of the self by transforming the physicality of those footsteps into ghostly, phantasmic sounds. This represents a key moment in Robinson's poetics, for she has now moved truly into figurative language, away from her previous impressionistic technique, in her search for a language that will allow her to look into the soul. It is at this point that Robinson's urban immateriality becomes truly modern. In *The City in Literature,* Richard Lehan makes the useful observation that

> [b]oth the modernist self and impressionism were urban phenomena: impressionism discovered the landscape quality of the city and depicted the world through the subjective eyes of the city dweller, reacting to the external impressions with the overstrained nerves of modern technical man or woman. . . . As the impressionistic view became more intense, the ability to see the city objectively became paradoxically more difficult, and the intensity of personal feeling often was accompanied by a more opaque sense of one's surroundings.[61]

In keeping with Lehan's remarks, Robinson's poems from *An Italian Garden* show how the truth of the world of the senses is now secondary to an "intuitive truth" that dwells in the realm of the inner being. The collection ends with the powerful sestina "Pulvis et Umbra":

> Along the crowded streets I walk and think
> How I, a shadow, pace among the shades,
> For I and all men seem to me unreal:
> Foam that the seas of God which cover all
> Cast on the air a moment, shadows thrown
> In moving westward by the Moon of Death.[62]

Robinson's spectral city is populated with unreal, disembodied humans. Though the tone of the poem is certainly ghostly, it nonetheless offers a positive articulation: for thoughts to be free, they must transcend the prison of the body, its physicality:

>   . . . As I think,
> From one surmise upon another thrown,
> My very thoughts appear to me as shades—
> Shades, like the prisoning self that bounds them all,
> Shades, like the transient world, and as unreal.[63]

This is a fantastically modern poem. It is not about the interiorization of the urban landscape and the urban crowd but about the disembodiment of the urban modern poet in the unreal city, which would be the main subject of T. S. Eliot's *The Waste Land* (1922).

I began this essay by conjuring up Robinson's photograph in Arthur Symons's drawing room. This photograph—or, more precisely, Michael Field's perception of it—has not only helped us to reinscribe Robinson's footsteps in the poetic world of fin-de-siècle London but has also been a means to reconsidering the essential rapport between Robinson's poetics and fin-de-siècle culture. Finally, by focusing on Robinson's interest in immateriality, and on her move from impressionism and symbolism to the spectrality of modernist urban poetics, I hope to have brought back to life the sheer modernity of Robinson's immaterial poetics.

Notes

I am grateful for the assistance provided by the staff at the Adelson Galleries Inc., New York; the Arts and Social Sciences Library, University of Bristol; Bibliothèque Nationale de France; the Bodleian Library; the British Library; Special Collections, the Miller Library, Colby College; Institut Pasteur; the National Art Library; and the Tate Picture Library. My thanks are also due to Joseph Bristow and to the audience of "The Fin-de-Siècle Poem" conference, February 22–23, 2002, at the William Andrews Clark Memorial Library, UCLA. I am also grateful to the European Social Funds and the Junta de Extremadura for a postdoctoral fellowship at Birkbeck College, University of London; and to Birkbeck College for a small travel grant to visit the archives of the Bibliothèque nationale de France and the Institut Pasteur.

1. Edmund Gosse, "A Ballade of Poetesses." Bibliothèque nationale de France, Fonds Anglais 251.f.41–42.

2. Michael Field, journal entry, 28 February 1891, British Library, Add. MS 46779f.20–20v.

3. Michael Field was fascinated by Whistler's paintings. They wrote in their journal: "Truly, Solomon, there is nothing *quite* new under the sun . . . & yet, forgive me, great Pessimist, there is—a room of Whistler's Nocturnes." Michael Field, Journal, British Library, Add. MS 46780f.62v (1892). Their journal contains an extensive record of their visit to Whistler's 1892 exhibition in London: Michael Field, Journal, British Library, Add. MS 46780ff.63–64 (1892).

4. Karl Beckson, *London in the 1890s* (New York: W. W. Norton, 1992).

5. For discussions of Arthur Symons, see, for instance, Karl Beckson, *Arthur Symons: A Life* (Oxford: Clarendon Press, 1987); and R.K.R. Thornton, "'Decadence' in Later Nineteenth-Century England" in *Decadence and the 1890s*, ed. Ian Fletcher, Stratford-upon-Avon Studies, 17 (London: Edward Arnold, 1979), 15–29. On George Moore see John Lucas, "From Naturalism to Symbolism," in Fletcher, *Decadence and the 1890s*, 131–48; and Adrian Frazier, *George Moore, 1852–1933* (New Haven, CT: Yale University Press, 2000). On George Meredith, see Gillian Beer, *Meredith: A Change of Masks; A Study of the Novels* (London: Athlone Press, 1970); Susan Payne, *Difficult Discourse: George Meredith's Experimental Fiction* (Pisa: Edizioni ETS, 1995); and Richard D. McGhee, *Marriage, Duty and Desire in Victorian Poetry and Drama* (Lawrence: Regents Press of Kansas, 1980). On Sarah Bernhardt, see Elaine Aston, *Sarah Bernhardt: A French Actress on the English Stage* (Oxford: Berg, 1989); and Arthur Gold and Robert Fizdale, *The Divine Sarah: A Life of Sarah Bernhardt* (New York: Knopf, 1991). For discussions on Olive Schreiner and New Woman fiction and feminism, see Ann L. Ardis, *New Women, New Novels: Feminism and Early Modernism* (New Brunswick, NJ: Rutgers University Press, 1990), and Sally Ledger, *The New Woman: Fiction and Feminism at the Fin de Siècle* (Manchester: Manchester University Press, 1997). Recent studies of the late-Victorian dissatisfaction with domesticity include Lori Anne Loeb, *Consuming Angels: Advertising and Victorian Women* (New York: Oxford University Press, 1994).

6. There is a vast literature on this subject. See, for example, Janet Wolff, "The Invisible *Flâneuse:* Women and the Literature of Modernity," *Theory, Culture and Society* 2, no. 3 (1985): 37–46; and "The Artist and the Flâneur: Rodin, Rilke and Gwen John in Paris," in *The Flâneur*, ed. Keith Tester (London: Routledge, 1994), 111–37. See also Griselda Pollock, "Modernity and the Spaces of Femininity," in *Vision and Difference: Femininity, Feminism and Histories of Art* (London: Routledge, 1988), 50–90; Jenny Ryan, "Women, Modernity and the City," *Theory, Culture and Society* 11, no 4 (1994): 35–63; Erika D. Rappaport, "'The Halls of Temptation': Gender, Politics and the Construction of the Department Store in Late Victorian London," *Journal of British Studies* 35 (1996): 58–83; Lynne Walker, "Vistas of Pleasure: Women Consumers of Urban Space in the West End of London, 1850–1900," in *Women in the Victorian Art World*, ed. Clarissa Campbell Orr (Manchester: Manchester University Press, 1995), 70–85; and Elizabeth Wilson, *The Sphinx in the City: Urban Life, the Control of Disorder, and Women* (London: Virago, 1991). See also Lynda Nead, *Victorian Babylon: People, Streets and Images in Nineteenth-Century London* (New Haven, CT: Yale University Press, 2000).

7. See M. Lynda Ely, "'Not a Song to Sell': Re-Presenting A. Mary F. Robinson," *Victorian Poetry* 38, no. 1 (2000): 94–108. See also Angela Leighton and Margaret Reynolds,

eds., *Victorian Women Poets: An Anthology* (Oxford: Blackwell, 1995); Isobel Armstrong and Joseph Bristow with Cath Sharrock, eds., *Nineteenth-Century Women Poets* (Oxford: Clarendon, 1996); and Linda K. Hughes, ed., *New Woman Poets: An Anthology*, Lost Chords, 1 (London: The Eighteen Nineties Society, 2001). There is, however, a growing interest in Robinson's work. See, for example, Yopie Prins, "Ladies' Greek: *The Crowned Hippolytus* of A. Mary F. Robinson" (paper delivered at the "Women Poets and the Fin de Siècle" conference, London, 2002), and Martha Vicinus, "'A Legion of Ghosts': Vernon Lee (1856–1935) and the Art of Nostalgia," *GLQ: A Journal of Gay and Lesbian Studies* 10, no. 4 (2004): 599–616. I am very grateful to Yopie Prins and Martha Vicinus for sharing this material with me. See also Helen Groth, *Victorian Photography and Literary Nostalgia* (Oxford: Oxford University Press, 2003).

8. Amy Levy to Katie Solomon, 18 July 1882, in Linda Hunt Beckman, *Amy Levy: Her Life and Letters* (Athens: Ohio University Press, 2000), 242.

9. Talia Schaffer, *The Forgotten Female Aesthetes* (Charlottesville: University Press of Virginia, 2000), 6, 7.

10. E[dmund] W. Gosse, "Some of the Younger English Poets," *Century Illustrated Monthly Magazine* 26, no. 6 (1883): 954. Gosse must be referring here to Rennell Rodd.

11. Sylvaine Marandon, *L'Oeuvre poétique de Mary Robinson* (Bordeaux, France: Imprimerie Pechade, 1967), 26.

12. See Phyllis Grosskurth, *John Addington Symonds: A Biography* (London: Longmans, 1964), 222. When Robinson's *The New Arcadia* was badly reviewed in the *Spectator*, Symonds wrote to her: "I think you are suffering from what success at the beginning always brings—a certain cruel & spiteful reaction—which is also not unjustified" (Symonds to A. Mary F. Robinson, 6 October 1884, Arts and Social Sciences Library, University of Bristol, Special Collections, MS.202/C/15).

13. See Robinson to Countess Ballestrein, 1 December 1879, Bibliothèque nationale de France, Fonds Anglais 252.ff.4–5.

14. Marandon, *L'Oeuvre poétique*, 22.

15. Susan Brown, "The Victorian Poetess," in *The Cambridge Companion to Victorian Poetry*, ed. Joseph Bristow (Cambridge: Cambridge University Press, 2000), 183.

16. The American critic Edmund Clarence Stedman, for instance, linked her to Elizabeth Barrett Browning because she was, "like Mrs. Browning, an enthusiastic student of Greek" ("Some London Poets," *Harper's New Monthly Magazine* 64 [1882]: 887).

17. William Sharp, "Some Personal Reminiscences of Walter Pater," *Atlantic Monthly* 74 (1894): 801.

18. John Addington Symonds discussed extensively this collection with Robinson. Walter Pater may also have had some influence on Robinson's choice. As William Sharp

notes, Pater had "great faith in scrupulous and sympathetic translations as a training in English composition" ("Some Personal Reminiscences," 806).

19. Eric S. Robertson, *English Poetesses: A Series of Critical Biographies with Illustrative Extracts* (London: Cassell, 1883), 376.

20. Arthur Symons, "A. Mary F. Darmesteter," in *The Poets and the Poetry of the Century*, 2nd ed., ed. A. H. Miles (London: Hutchinson, 1892–97), 8:521.

21. All biographical details on Robinson's childhood are taken from Robinson's letter to Countess Ballestrein (see note 13).

22. See George Moore, *Confessions of a Young Man* (London: Swan Sonneschein, 1888), 283. Here he notes how he could use the plot of one of Mabel Robinson's novels on Ireland for his own novel.

23. Elizabeth Robins Pennell, *The Life and Letters of Joseph Pennell*, 2 vols. (London: Ernest Benn, 1929), 1:117.

24. Marandon, *L'Oeuvre Poétique*, 25; translations from the French are mine.

25. See Robinson to J. A. Symonds, 10 November 1879, in Marandon, *L'Oeuvre poétique*, 26; translations from the French are mine.

26. Pennell, *The Life and Letters of Joseph Pennell*, 1:94.

27. National Art Library, London MSL/1995/14/88/1.

28. An example of their close relationship is that when Lucy Rossetti was diagnosed with a carbuncle, it was Mary Robinson who immediately wrote to Lucy's father, Ford Madox Brown, to inform him of the doctor's results. Madox Brown was one of the very few people who supported Robinson's decision to marry Darmesteter (National Art Library, London, MSL/1995/14/88/6).

29. George Robinson to Ford Madox Brown, 1881, National Art Library, MSL/1995/14/89/6.

30. For further discussion, see Ana Parejo Vadillo, "New Woman Poets and the Culture of the *Salon* at the *Fin de Siècle*," *Women: A Cultural Review* 10, no. 1 (1999): 22–34.

31. On 11 January 1884, Vernon Lee wrote: "I am delighted you have settled for the Arcadia, & glad it is Ellis, who seems more the day than Kegan Paul. At a remote period you mentioned dedicating that volume to your humble slave; but should you prefer Miss Amy Levy or Miss Beavington [*sic*], padrona" (Lee to A. Mary F. Robinson, Bibliothèque nationale de France, Fonds Anglais 245.f.148).

32. Sharp, "Some Personal Reminiscences," 801.

32. Elizabeth Robins Pennell, *Nights: Rome, Venice in the Aesthetic Eighties; London, Paris in the Fighting Nineties* (Philadelphia: J. B. Lippincott, 1916), 129.

34. See *The Correspondence of Henry James and the House of Macmillan, 1877–1914*, ed. Rayburn S. Moore (London: Macmillan, 1993), 120, 122.

35. John Lawrence Waltman, *The Early London Journals of Elizabeth Robins Pennell* (PhD diss., University of Texas, Austin, 1976), 101.

36. See Robert Browning to Edith Cooper, 8 June 1885, in *Works and Days: From the Journal of Michael Field*, ed. T. and D. C. Sturge Moore (London: John Murray, 1933), 9. After reading Katharine Bradley and Edith Cooper's first coauthored book of poems, *Bellerophôn* (1881), which they published under the names "Arran and Isla Leigh," John Addington Symonds wrote to Bradley and Cooper encouraging them to read Robinson's *The Crowned Hippolytus* for a better use of the Greek myth. See *The Letters of John Addington Symonds*, ed. Herbert M. Schueller and Robert L. Peters, 3 vols. (Detroit: Wayne State University Press, 1968), 2:675–77. I would like to thank Yopie Prins for bringing this information to my attention.

37. The first letter from A. Mary F. Robinson to Michael Field is dated 16 May 1884. Robinson thanks Field for sending their play *Callirrhoë* and offers her advice on how to improve the play (Bodleian Library, MS.Eng.letts.e.32.ff.95–98).

38. Eduardo Cadava, *Words of Light: Theses on the Photography of History* (Princeton, NJ: Princeton University Press, 1997), 11.

39. Arthur Symons, "The Decadent Movement in Literature," *Harper's New Monthly Magazine* 87 (1893): 859.

40. Richard Ellmann, introduction to *The Symbolist Movement in Literature*, by Arthur Symons (New York: Dutton, 1958).

41. Richard Lehan, *The City in Literature: An Intellectual and Cultural History* (Berkeley and Los Angeles: University of California Press, 1998), 76.

42. [William Ernest Henley], "Notes," *National Observer*, 6 April 1895, 547.

43. Symons, *Symbolist Movement*, 2–3.

44. Symons, *Symbolist Movement*, 2–3.

45. This extract from the *Academy* was later used in *The Crowned Hippolytus* as a selling point; see frontispiece in A. Mary F. Robinson, *The Crowned Hippolytus: Translated from Euripides with New Poems* (London: C. Kegan Paul, 1881).

46. A. Mary F. Robinson, "Song of a Stormy Night," in *The Collected Poems, Lyrical and Narrative of A. Mary F. Robinson* (London: T. Fisher Unwin, 1902), 72.

47. Paul de Man, *Blindness and Insight: Essays in the Rhetoric of Contemporary Criticism*, 2nd ed. (London: Methuen, 1986), 189.

48. S. T. Coleridge, quoted in de Man, *Blindness and Insight*, 191.

49. W. B. Yeats, "The Symbolism of Poetry," in *W. B. Yeats: The Major Works*, ed. Edward Larrissy (Oxford: Oxford University Press, 2001), 360.

50. The following letter from Robinson to Maurice Barrès explains her indebtedness to the Pre-Raphaelites: "Quand j'étais, moi, une jeune fille, folle de poésie et de

Platon, j'avais un grand ami que je n'avais jamais un: l'historien J.A. Symonds. Il habitait à Davos, condamné par la tuberculose aux neiges à perpétuité; moi, jeune fille fêtée, je vivais dans un petit monde préraphaélite, à Londres" (When I was a young girl, mad about poetry and Plato, I had a great friend as I have never had one: the historian J. A. Symonds. He lived in Davos, sentenced by tuberculosis to dwell in the snow for life; a vivacious young girl indeed, I lived in a small pre-Raphaelite world, in London.) Mary Duclaux et Maurice Barrès, *Lettres échangées, précédé de Les trois Mary par Daniel Halévy* (Paris: Editions Bernard Grasset, 1959), 61; my translation.

51. Reprinted in Marandon, *L'Oeuvre poétique*, 43.

52. Walter Pater, *The Renaissance: Studies in Art and Poetry; The 1893 Text*, ed. Donald L. Hill (Berkeley and Los Angeles: University of California Press, 1980), 186; further page reference appears in parentheses.

53. Robinson, "London Studies: I. A Square in November," in *The Crowned Hippolytus*, 157.

54. Quoted in Symons, "Decadent Movement," 867.

55. Symons, "A. Mary F. Darmesteter," 523–24.

56. Vernon Lee to Mary Robinson, 8 February 1886, Bibliothèque National de France, Fonds Anglais 246.ff.147–48.

57. Lee to Mary Robinson, 8 February 1886. In a letter to Symonds, Robinson explains that the rispetti were "all written in two days of great excitement." She writes that for two years she had been "ridiculously (though silently) jealous" of Vernon Lee's friendship with Mrs. Alice Callander: "The songs are addressed by me, ill & neglected, to Vernon who has already (only in the verses) outgrown her affection. They are the utterances of a jealous dying woman who feels herself forgotten before she is dead.— Thank Heaven, I don't believe it now—but I did at the time to a passionate & tragic extent" (Robinson to J. A. Symonds, 17 January 1886, Bibliothèque Nationale de France, Fonds Anglais 248. f.137).

58. A. Mary F. Robinson, *Songs, Ballads, and a Garden Play* (London: T. Fisher Unwin, 1888), 6.

59. A. Mary F. Robinson, "The Ideal," in *An Italian Garden: A Book of Songs* (London: T. Fisher Unwin, 1886), 11.

60. Robinson, "Venetian Nocturne," in *Italian Garden*, 16.

61. Lehan, *City in Literature*, 78–79.

62. Robinson, "Pulvis et Umbra," in *Italian Garden*, 100.

63. Robinson, "Pulvis et Umbra," 100.

PATMORE'S LAW, MEYNELL'S RHYTHM

Yopie Prins

I do not know which to prefer,
The beauty of inflections
Or the beauty of innuendos,
The blackbird whistling
    Or just after
—WALLACE STEVENS, "THIRTEEN WAYS OF LOOKING AT A BLACKBIRD"

"At rare intervals the world is startled by the phenomenon of a woman whose qualities of mind and heart seem to demand a revision of its conception of womanhood and an enlargement of those limitations which it delights in regarding as essentials of her very nature," Coventry Patmore writes in his 1892 tribute "Mrs. Meynell: Poet and Essayist."[1] His idea of womanhood had been enlarged by "a very small volume of very short essays" published late in 1892, called *The Rhythm of Life* and culled from the literary journalism of Alice Meynell over the past decade. Meynell's *Poems* had also just appeared, most of them previously published under her maiden name of Alice Thompson in *Preludes* (1875): another very small volume of very short poems that try to "breathe, in every line, the purest *spirit* of womanhood, yet they have not sufficient force of that *ultimate* womanhood," Patmore concludes (762). Eager to "admire the poetess still more than her poetry" (763), Patmore considers the poems reprinted from *Preludes* a prelude to Meynell's later, greater work: if not in poetry, where she seemed to have fallen silent, then in prose.

But during the final decade of the century Meynell returned to publishing poetry, for which she received renewed critical acclaim. She became a much admired poetess of the fin de siècle: in 1895 she was proposed for poet laureate, and she continued writing poems from time to time until the year of her death, 1922. In "The Rhythm of Life," the essay that gives its title to her collection, she announces the periodic return of her muse. "If life is not always poetical, it is at least metrical," she begins her essay, insisting that "periodicity rules over the mental experience of man."[2] Even more, it would seem, periodicity rules over the experience of woman. Ending her essay with a meditation on "the rhythmic pangs of maternity," Meynell turns giving birth into a trope for poetic creation, the articulation of life experienced as "intervals between aspirations, between actions, pauses as inevitable as the pauses of sleep" (6). While "few poets have fully recognized the metrical absence of their Muse" (4), according to Meynell these recurring, seemingly vacant intervals of time measure the course of creation, in poetry and in life.

Not only was Meynell the "phenomenon of a woman" that appeared (at least to Patmore) at rare intervals, and not only did her poetry appear in publication at rare intervals, but the poems themselves mark the appearance of rare intervals, in highly refined forms of versification associated with the New Prosody toward the end of the nineteenth century. Meynell was influenced by Patmore's "Essay on English Metrical Law," first published in 1857 and circulating in different versions alongside Patmore's poetry. In his essay, Patmore defines meter as "the function of marking, *by whatever means,* certain isochronous intervals," and although accents might be the most obvious means of counting meter in English accentual-syllabic verse, he prefers to imagine meter as a temporal measure that "*has no material and external existence at all,* but has its place in the mind, which craves measure in everything, and wherever the idea of measure is uncontradicted, delights in marking it with an imaginary 'beat.'"[3] This idea (or idealization) of an imaginary beat led to an abstraction of meter, variously schematized and quantified in late-Victorian metrical theory and prosodic practice. Increasingly, meter was theorized as a principle of spacing that could formalize temporal relations between abstract quantities, mentally perceived in the act of counting and not necessarily audible.

The compulsion to measure poetry in "isochronous intervals" was part of a broader impulse toward the temporal and spatial demarcation of time in fin-de-siècle England. Of course the counting and recounting of days to the end of the century could be the mark of any fin de siècle, as Elaine Scarry points out in "Counting at Dusk (Why Poetry Matters When the Century Ends)." She speculates that a pronounced interest in poetic meter at the ends of centuries may have something to do with "the etymological identity of *meter* with *measure,* the intimacy between poetry and the act of counting, and hence the heightened poetic attention to numbers at the moment when the calendar turns over."[4] The poetry and prosody of the late-Victorian period in particular mark a turn toward forms of measurement and quantification that formalize the trope of counting, as George Saintsbury remarks in his *History of English Prosody:* looking back on "the *polymetric* character of the century," he surveys many poets experimenting with "fancy prosodies."[5] Alice Meynell contributed to these metrical experiments at the end of the nineteenth century, and (not unlike Saintsbury) looked back on them in the early twentieth century in a poem entitled "The Laws of Verse." Here, as we shall see, Meynell's "fancy prosody" gives us insight into the heightened sense of periodicity and periodization that makes the fin de siècle a distinctive period—simultaneously an ending and a beginning—in English literary history.

Writing in the wake of Christina Rossetti and Elizabeth Barrett Browning, Meynell was part of a generation inventing new measures for new women poets. Like Mathilde Blind, Amy Levy, Graham R. Tomson, Michael Field, A. Mary F. Robinson, Mary E. Coleridge, and other poetesses living in fin-de-siècle London, Meynell aspired to musicality in her versification. She is introduced in A. H. Miles's influential anthology *The Poets and the Poetry of the Century* with reference to "the memorable passage in which Mr. Pater speaks of poetry . . . aspiring towards the condition of music," because the distinction between matter and form "is all but obliterated" in her poems: "[F]ew of our generation have exhibited . . . more finely balanced harmony."[6] But while Walter Pater may have provided a general aesthetic frame for reading the poetry of female aesthetes such as Meynell, the theoretical frame for her prosody came from Patmore, who argues in "Essay on English Metrical Law" that "the relation of music to language ought to be recognized as something more than that of similarity" (17) and who develops a theory of meter to account for the musical effects of poetic language in particular.

Patmore's relation to Meynell has been treated biographically as an older man's fixation on a younger poetess, whom he worshipped as another "Angel in the House" after his wife's death. He gave to Meynell a manuscript of *The Angel in the House* (1854–63) and *The Unknown Eros* (1878), and he dedicated a series of light verses to her; in one he recalls a visit to her house when he brought his review of her poetry: "I read her praise while, sweet / She smiles in contemplation / Of her fame and her small feet."[7] If we shift the emphasis from biographical to formal analysis of this poetic relationship, then we see that Patmore's praise of Meynell's "small feet" is more than personal. What he admired in her verse was its delicate pacing, the deft manipulation of subtle intervals according to his own prosodic theory. In his "Essay on English Metrical Law" he writes that "the language should always seem to *feel*, though not to *suffer from*, the bonds of verse" (8), a sentiment that Alice Meynell took to heart, as she writes in a notebook: "All true poets love the bonds of prosody, and, in lyrics, of rhythm: because all true poets have something of the wild at heart that looks for bonds."[8] Willingly, Meynell submitted to Patmore's metrical law, allowing her language to feel the bonds of verse, and herself to love them.

A Poetics of Pauses

Like Patmore, Meynell was especially interested in the metrical value of pauses. According to the theory of isochrony developed in Patmore's "Essay," the measuring of a poetic line into "equal or proportionate spaces" assumes "an 'ictus' or 'beat,' actual or mental" (15) that can be heard in accents but might also be counted in pauses: "The marking of the measure by the recurrent ictus may be occasionally remitted, the position of the ictus altered, or its place supplied by a pause, without the least offence to a cultivated ear, which rather delights in, than objects to, such remission, inversion, or omission, when there is an emotional motive" (22). To give a "much fuller consideration of the element of pause than has commonly been given to that subject," Patmore treats catalexis (the absence of a syllable from the beginning or end of a line) and caesura (a pause in the middle of a line) more systematically than other analysts of modern meter, to whom such pauses "appear rather as *interruptions* than *subjects* of metrical law." For Patmore, on the contrary, forms of interruption such as catalexis and caesura are an integral component of English metrical law. The very structure of this law as he conceives it is the measuring of poetry (by analogy to music) into isochronous units that can be filled either with sound or with silence. This principle of spacing makes it possible to feel the beat even if the accent has been withdrawn from a syllable ("remission"), or if the accent has been placed on another syllable ("inversion"), or if there is no syllable to carry the accent ("omission"). In fact, "a cultivated ear" might take special delight in those silent intervals, as Patmore goes on to write: "We must reckon the missing syllables as substituted by an equivalent pause; and, indeed, in reading catalectic verse, this is what a good reader does by instinct" (23).

Meynell was a good reader of Patmore, turning his theory into a poetics of pauses that would appeal to cultivated ears. In an early poem from *Preludes,* entitled "To the Beloved," she meditates on the musical effect of metrical pause as her own *ars poetica.* The first stanza is addressed to a nameless beloved, a "thou" whose subtle presence is felt in silence:

> Oh, not more subtly silence strays
>   Amongst the winds, between the voices,
> Mingling alike with pensive lays,
>   And with the music that rejoices,
> Than thou art present in my days.

The beloved is heard in the intervals between sound ("[a]mongst the winds" and "between the voices") and also resounding ("mingling alike") in music: by analogy to the temporal experience of music, the presence of this unnamed beloved one emerges over time, made "present in my days." The regularity of the verse—iambic tetrameter, with musically mingling rhymes—suggests a harmonious alternation between what is heard and not heard, measuring the space between the presence and absence of the beloved.

In the following stanzas, the poem goes further in presenting the beloved as a form of silent music, measured in stanza 2 by "the pauses" of breath and the "hush" of melody, compared in stanza 3 to "silence all unvexed" and "unperplexed," and then invoked in stanza 4 as a "most dear pause":

My silence, life returns to thee
   In all the pauses of her breath.
Hush back to rest the melody
   That out of thee awakeneth;
And thou, wake ever, wake for me!

Thou art like silence all unvexed,
   Though wild words part my soul from thee.
Thou art like silence unperplexed,
   A secret and a mystery
Between one footfall and the next.

Most dear pause in a mellow lay!
   Thou art inwoven with every air.
With thee the wildest tempests play,
   And snatches of thee everywhere
Make little heavens throughout a day.

In the pauses "[b]etween one footfall and the next," Meynell's poem is also presenting the rise and fall of its own metrical feet as a musical interplay between sound and silence. According to Patmore's prosody, there is not much room for counting pauses in tetrameter: for him the basic unit of iambic verse is the "dipode" (a double foot of four syllables, with a minor and a major accent), and in a line of four iambic feet (or two dipodes) the syllables are all filled with sound.[9] But while it is possible to scan Meynell's lines this way, she leaves room for variation. For example, in the line "Between one footfall and the next," does the accent fall exactly where it should, or might it fall between the feet?

The space between this line and the next stanza must give us pause as well, since Meynell goes on to invoke the very pause she inscribes in the poem: "Most dear pause in a mellow lay!" The stanzaic break has already created a silent pause in the melody of the poem, and if we scan this line in isochronous intervals of two dipodes, as Patmore would suggest, we would also have to imagine a silent beat before "Most." Thus we hear a pause even before it is voiced, making it "inwoven with every air"; "thou" is felt in the "air" or breath of the spoken word, and in the "air" of melodious song, and even dissolving into empty air. As the object of address is diffused into "snatches of thee everywhere," the comparison of "thee" to music gradually proves to be an address to the lovely music of pausing itself.

While "To the Beloved" begins with an intimate address in the second person singular (a form that Meynell hoped the English language would retain[10]), it concludes with a formal apostrophe ("O pause"):

> Darkness and solitude shine, for me.
> For life's fair outward part are rife
> The silver noises; let them be.
> It is the very soul of life
> Listens for thee, listens for thee.
>
> O pause between the sobs of cares;
> O thought within all thought that is;
> Trance between laughters unawares:
> Thou art the shape of melodies,
> And thou the ecstasy of prayers!

In these final stanzas, Meynell's poem turns away from the outward sounds of life and "[l]istens for thee" internally. The reiteration of "Listens for thee, listens for thee" produces a caesura, or pause, in the middle of the line that allows us to listen for a sound within. Listening for the pauses "between" and the "thought within" each of these lines makes it possible to think about the beloved as an abstract form: "Thou art the shape of melodies," the poem concludes, turning "thou" into a musical performance or the formalized "ecstasy" of silent prayer.

The invocation of the beloved as a formal abstraction makes "To the Beloved" a curiously impersonal poem, less concerned with addressing a person than apostrophizing a metrical effect. Nevertheless this is a relation of love, articulated as a relationship between sound and silence. The *Pall Mall Gazette* referred to Meynell as "the prophet of silence and dejection, the herald of abstention and pause." Yet this prophetic pausing is not a form of self-silencing or abstaining from communication with others, but rather, as Maria Frawley argues, the projection of a mental experience.[11] Frawley traces "a trajectory of Meynell's thinking about thought," an ongoing effort to give form to the movements of the mind in poetry and in prose. Measured in the silent music of her meters, thinking was a metrical performance for Meynell, beginning with early poems like "To the Beloved" and continuing periodically throughout her life as a poet. Although she outlived the fin de siècle, her poetry recalls the past century as a period when prosody was regularly used for the regulation of thought. To imagine meter as a living, embodied form thus became Meynell's poetic calling.

A More Vital Union

Reviewing Meynell's *Poems* of 1892, Francis Thompson writes that "the footfalls of her Muse waken not sounds but silences."[12] As Meynell's friend and admirer, he considered her the "foremost singer of a sex which is at last breaking the silence," paradoxically because she was giving new forms to silence. In Thompson's prediction, "[S]he will leave to her successors a serener tradition than masculine poets bequeathed to men," for "she has given them the law of silence." Her calling, in Thompson's view, is to transform English metrical law through the rhythms of women's poetry: "That high speech must be shod with silence, that high work must be set forth with silence, that high destiny must be waited on with silence—was a lesson the age lacked much. Our own sex has heard the nobly tacit message of Mr. Coventry Patmore. But by an exception rare as beautiful, the woman's calm has been austerer-perfect than the man's" (191). Indeed, the poetry of the woman might surpass the theory of the man, making his "tacit message" into her poetics of pauses, turning Patmore's law into Meynell's rhythm.

Included in Meynell's *The Rhythm of Life* is an essay titled "Mr. Coventry Patmore's Odes," which examines some points of convergence, but also divergence, in the poets' metrical practice.[13] Although Meynell admires the octosyllabic stanza of Patmore's earlier poetry (as in *The Angel in the House*) for demonstrating "a composure which was the prelude to the peace of the Odes" (96), and although she praises some of the later odes (as in *The Unknown Eros*)—for "a truer impetus of pulse and impulse English verse could hardly yield" (95)—nevertheless she raises some questions about Patmore's versification in these odes. His use of pauses to fill up a measure seems to her, at times, an arbitrary enforcement of his own metrical law: "[H]e rather arbitrarily applies to liberal verse the laws set for use," she protests (94). The free iambic verse of these odes "can surely be bound by no time measures—if for no other reason, for this: that to prescribe pauses is also to forbid any pauses unprescribed" (95). Without altogether rejecting his "principle of catalexis," Meynell resists an artificial imposition of isochrony that tries to prescribe pauses: she prefers a more natural variation according to a more natural measure of time.

Meynell locates such "natural" measures in a different experience of rhythm. In "The Rhythm of Life"—published in the same collection as "Mr. Coventry Patmore's Odes"—metrical law is redefined as a "law of periodicity" that is made manifest in various cycles and orbits and seasons: in the return of each day and in "the tides of the mind," in the recurrence of sorrow and in disease "closing in at shorter and shorter periods toward death," in the "metrical phases" of the moon and in the "sun's revolutions," and finally (as noted earlier) in "the rhythmic pangs of maternity." So Meynell projects the metricality of verse into the universe, as a universal rhythmic experience that cannot be precisely measured but is felt inside and outside the body. According to Meynell, "Thomas à Kempis knew of the recurrences, if he did not measure them" (2), and Shelley was able "to guess at the order of this periodicity"; these two writers are singled out because "no deliberate human rules, infractions of the liberty and law of the universal movement, kept from them the knowledge of recurrences" (2–3). Implicit is a critique of English metrical law as formulated by Patmore: as an imposition of "deliberate human rules" on verse, his theory may work to limit "the liberty and law of the universal movement," and "the knowledge of recurrences."[14]

Although Meynell's essay may be read as an attempt to naturalize and perhaps even feminize rhythmic experience, it proceeds by a recurring series of associations that function as figures for meter. Rather than rebelling against Patmore's metrical law, she turns his argument about meter to her own purposes by insisting that life is "at least metrical." In "The Unit of the World" (another essay published in *The Rhythm of Life*), Meynell again insists that nature is best understood as a metrical phenomenon: "[L]et me assert that though nature is not always clearly and obviously made to man's measure, he is yet the unit by which she is measurable."[15] By the same logic, we may assert that though Meynell's poetry was not always clearly and obviously made to Patmore's measure, he was yet the unit by which her poetry is measurable. She had learned much from Patmore, as her daughter would later recall:

> Even after my mother had given her immeasurable praise to Coventry Patmore's poetry, the full extent of her feeling remained unexpressed, and in a letter to him she breaks off suddenly to say: "I have never told you what I think of your poetry. It is the greatest thing in the world, the most harrowing and the sweetest. I can hardly realize that he who has written it and who is greater than his words is celestially kind to me and calls me a friend." As far as his teaching, his "gospel," was concerned, she was docile, receptive, impressed.[16]

Along with his Catholicism, Meynell shared in Patmore's "gospel" of poetry, giving "immeasurable praise" to the metrical law that had made an impression on her own ideas about rhythm, in theory and in practice.

Meynell wrote about Patmore's poetry on multiple occasions and edited selections for publication, proving through her praise that she owed much to him.[17] In a later and longer essay, simply titled "Coventry Patmore," Meynell comes closer to associating his law with her own sense of rhythm than in her earlier review, "Mr. Coventry Patmore's Odes." She explains that "a mind trained in the less obvious measures and restraints both of thought and of verse is needed to recognize the law of *The Unknown Eros*," and she identifies herself as just such a reader.[18] By setting an example for how to read his odes, she hoped to show how "any reader should pause upon the mere intervals in poetry so profound and penetrating as, in a hundred passages, shakes the metre with a hand of control" (104). Here Meynell is more able and willing to appreciate the musical pauses in Patmore's free iambic verse: "When he wrote the Odes, and used thus a free metre because he knew himself at liberty by his very knowledge and love of law, that heart beat in the sensitive line, and he caught rapturous breath, or sighed, as a spirit blowing whither it will" (100). In these figures of rhythmicized embodiment (like rapturous breathing, and the beating of the heart), Meynell rationalizes the versification of his odes in language reminiscent of her own meditations on meter. She read his odes to reiterate her own conviction that poetry "is to be figured . . . by a more vital union: mind and body, where tidal thought and feeling are quick with the blood and various with the breath of life, give a juster as well as a simpler and a human image of a vital poem" (96).

This "image of a vital poem" with "a more vital union" of mind and body has a long history in nineteenth-century women's verse, in which Victorian poetesses measure the pulse of their poetry by the quickening of blood and breath. The impulse, or aspiration, to give new life to the rhythms of poetry is articulated by Aurora Leigh, the prototype for the poetess in Elizabeth Barrett Browning's novel-poem:

> O life, O poetry,
> —Which means life in life! Cognizant of life
> Beyond this blood-beat, passionate for truth
> Beyond these senses!—poetry, my life.[19]

Throughout *Aurora Leigh*, Aurora struggles to unify mind and body in poetry, extending beyond the "blood-beat" of her own heart into a song that will capture "the full-veined, heaving double-breasted age" (book 5, 216). To embody the spirit of the age, the poetess must transform the rhythmic figure of the body into the rhythm of the poem, the rhythmic figure of the poem into the rhythm of history, and the rhythmic figure of history into the rhythm of nature: the heart beating in the verse of the poetess could then be understood, at least in its ideal form, as a law of the universe. So Meynell, who praised Elizabeth Barrrett Browning for "the continuous impulsiveness of her passion for truth," was also eager to transform the impulsive figure of the Victorian poetess into a universal pulse: "[S]uch impulses are those of perpetual motion; they are flights like the flight of planets," she writes in one of several introductions to the poetry of Elizabeth Barrett Browning.[20]

In Meynell's reading of Elizabeth Barrett Browning, we can see how Patmore's law and Meynell's rhythm are juxtaposed and transposed through the medium of women's verse. Meynell was a passionate collector and editor of Elizabeth Barrett Browning's poetry, and although she was aware of faults in some of the poems that came from "a too conscious and too emphatic revolt against her time, a too resolute originality," nevertheless she admired this revolutionary impulse. Even if the blank verse of *Aurora Leigh* seemed at times so "defiant" that "the reader should keep his own composure in order to feel the value," Meynell knew enough about the composition of meters to value "the leap of the spirit" in *Aurora Leigh;* she also valued "Lady Geraldine's Courtship" in which Elizabeth Barrett Browning "relaxes the rush of her manner and gathers herself in to a shape of gravity," and she admired "a pause of style" in "The Sea-Mew" and "Sonnets from the Portuguese" (163) as well. In these sonnets Meynell discovered a poetics of pauses not unlike her own: "Mrs. Browning is strictly Petrarchan in rhymes though not in pauses," Meynell observes, locating "the noble impulse of her thought" as much in the pauses of the sonnets as in their audible pulse: "Every sonnet of the series has a subject fit for it, a thought with a close. As you come to the last line, and the heart of the poem that has throbbed strongly, subsides, you acquiesce in the last word" (166). The sonnets of Elizabeth Barrett Browning are figured by Meynell as a more vital union of mind and body, with thought embodied in the throbbing heart of each poem.

Meynell wrote another essay about Elizabeth Barrett Browning, on "The Art of Scansion," in which she praises the poetess "in her quieter moments, when she is not marching, in doublet and hose, the march of her blank verse, but pacing softly in the strictest measure of the bonds that all true poets so love—the bonds of numbers, stress, quantity, rhyme and final shape."[21] Echoing the entry in Meynell's notebook that claims "[a]ll true poets love the bonds of prosody," the essay on scansion follows Patmore while also proposing a woman's response to his "Essay on English Metrical Law." Meynell reiterates a commitment to "strictest measure" and suggests, through the example of Elizabeth Barrett Browning, that women poets are best heard "pacing softly." The implicit gendering of English metrical law as a feminine form becomes explicit at the end of Meynell's essay, when she refers to Patmore by name, simultaneously deferring to his authority and using it to authorize the vocation of the poetess: "Coventry Patmore held poetry to be the gravest among the undertakings of man, and Elizabeth Barrett Browning—child, maid, and wife—took her vocation with gravity, passion and delight" (ix). Here the vocation of poets in general is transformed into the specific example of a poetess who wrote as "child, maid, and wife": a passionate undertaking not only for Elizabeth Barrett Browning, but for Meynell as well. Thus, while following Patmore's directive "to *feel*, though not to *suffer from*, the bonds of verse," Meynell also follows in the footsteps of poetesses who were expected to embody this feeling as the passion of their poetry.

Dear Laws

To *feel* the bonds of verse, Meynell incorporated English metrical law into the rhythms of her poetry, most succinctly in a late poem entitled "The Laws of Verse." Composed in 1921, the year before her death, and published posthumously in *Last Poems* (1923), this short lyric looks back on a life dedicated to poetry. Like Elizabeth Barrett Browning, who "took her vocation with gravity," Meynell invokes the laws of verse in order to feel their weight:

> Dear laws, come to my breast!
> Take all my frame, and make your close arms meet
> Around me; and so ruled, so warmed, so pressed,
> I breathe, aware; I feel my wild heart beat.
>
> Dear laws, be wings to me!
> The feather merely floats. O be it heard
> Through weight of life—the skylark's gravity—
> That I am not a feather, but a bird.

The rising and falling accents sustain the hypothesis of this poem, namely, that its lyric subject comes to life through rhythmic beats like those of a heart or of a bird's wings. In the first stanza, this rhythm is figured as a weight bearing down on "my breast," measuring "all my frame" in a pattern of stressed syllables that animate the poem "so ruled, so warmed, so pressed" into a living body: the reiteration of "so" is a rhythmic marker, allowing the stress to be felt on "ruled" and "warmed" and "pressed" in a series of iambs. The stanza ends "aware" of the rhythmic pulse of its own breath, and able to "feel" a wild heart that beats within the regularity of its iambic pentameter lines. Thus metrical law is embodied in a "more vital union" of mind and body, perfectly illustrating a point made by Patmore (in his "Essay on English Metrical Law," paraphrasing Hegel): that "art, indeed, must have a body as well as a soul; and the higher and purer the spiritual, the more powerful and unmistakable should be the corporeal element" (7).

Against the weight of this corporeal element, the second stanza rises toward a spiritual element, more abstract and less human. Here the accents that weigh down the first stanza, allowing its metrical "frame" to be read as an embodied form, lift this body upward and transform it into the figure of a bird in flight. In the alternation of stressed and unstressed syllables in Meynell's iambic lines, it is possible to hear a rising movement. The poem is momentarily suspended in the strong caesura before the vocative "O" ("The feather merely floats. // O be it heard") and also in the dramatic enjambment between this line and the next ("Through weight of life—the skylark's gravity—"). In moving from "O be it heard" and "Through weight of life" the poem moves down through the weight of its own stresses and up toward the skylark, hovering between dashes that suspend the phrase in midair. In "—the skylark's gravity—" the poem upholds its own metrical law, taking wing in the iambs of the final line, with the proclamation "[t]hat I am not a feather, but a bird." The gravity of this bird illustrates another point made by Patmore in his "Essay" (again borrowing from Hegel), on the "counterpoise afforded by metre to the high spirituality of poetic thought" (41). Poised in the measured pauses of the poem, the skylark is a figure for the meter, simultaneously rising and falling in controlled flight.

Like "To the Beloved," with its interplay of sound and silence "inwoven with every air," this late poem is an invitation to listen for the pauses ("O be it heard") as the metrical figure of the bird soars through the air. The formal principle of this rhythmic interplay, addressed in the earlier poem as "most dear pause," has been abstracted and multiplied in the later poem as an address to "[d]ear laws." The apostrophe gives form to something absent, calling on the laws of verse to manifest their presence in the outlines of a melody that moves beyond the lines of the poem itself. The shape of the melody may be seen, if not heard, in the first line of each stanza: before "Dear laws" there is a blank space, an indentation that is not audible at first; but with repeated reading these empty intervals can be understood more abstractly as rhythmic spaces. While the invocations to "[d]ear laws" fall short of iambic pentameter, thus violating the metrical law that rules the rest of the poem, the silent beats we feel before and after each invocation seem to fill out the line. Without adhering exactly to Patmore's principle of isochronous intervals (according to which every pentameter line should have an extra silent foot to complete the dipode), Meynell invokes this principle of spacing in her poem to make it seen and heard: "O be it heard" marks the conversion of something seen into something heard, a mental apprehension of meter in the mind's eye and the mind's ear.

Meynell also articulated this formal principle in "Symmetry and Incident," published in *The Colour of Life, and Other Essays on Things Seen and Heard,* a volume (not incidentally) dedicated to Coventry Patmore.[22] Linking repetition and interruption of pattern in the visual arts (specifically, in Japanese compositions) to symmetry and variation in musical compositions, Meynell points out the value of empty space: "But as time, not silence, is the subject, or material, of contrast in musical pauses, so it is the measurement of space—that is collocation—that makes the value of empty intervals" (145). Her argument about formal patterning proceeds not simply as a comparison of temporal and spatial forms, but also as a conversion of one into the other through the law of rhythm. Although things heard and things seen take different material forms, they all depend on symmetry (literally, a "measuring together") as their basic law. But symmetry depends in turn on "incident," an interruption that allows the law to materialize in a particular medium and to be felt precisely in its absence: that is the value of empty intervals.

For Meynell the best example, and indeed the very definition, of symmetry is the law of meter, for in poetry we have the convergence of what is seen and what is heard, in patterns marked by interruption. This understanding of meter defined by metrical variation is drawn from Patmore, quoted by Meynell at the end of her essay in order to conclude her meditation on symmetry and incident. According to Patmore, "Law . . . should be the poet's only subject"; the poet should demonstrate how "the music of verse arises, not from infraction but from inflection of the law of the set metre . . . in correspondence with feelings and passions." Indeed, it is the inflection of meter that produces passion, as "law puts a strain upon feeling, and feeling responds with a strain upon law" (151). This mutual restraint defines the lyric strains of Meynell's poetry, bending the bonds of verse without breaking them, creating inflection without infraction.

Following Patmore's claim that "the poet's only subject" should be "law," Meynell made the laws of verse the subject of her poem "The Laws of Verse." But in versifying the argument of Patmore's essay, Meynell reverses his claim into a question about what it would mean to make metrical law into her poem's object. Is the title of her poem announcing the law of versification or the versification of the law? Should we read "The Laws of Verse" as subjective or objective genitive? The poem does not simply propose a grammatical inversion or pose a rhetorical question; it suggests the possibility of reading meter nonmimetically and nonexpressively: not as the metrical embodiment of its meaning, not as the metrical expression of the poet's feeling, but as the performance of affect produced by formal abstraction.

The intimacy of address to "[d]ear laws" suggests a passionate attachment to form itself, variously interpreted by recent critics as Meynell's expression or repression of personal feeling. In her feminist recovery of Meynell as "poetess among poets," Beverly Schlack approaches "The Laws of Verse" as a poem of "erotic abandon" that also "gives poignant expression to woman's insecurity as artist,"[23] while Vanessa Furse Jackson emphasizes the irony that "one of [Meynell's] most passionate, even sensuous poems, should be devoted to an expression of her poetics."[24] Despite the difference in perspective, both critics read the poem expressively, assuming that its lyric subject can be referred back to a person, and identifying Meynell with the desire to be the bird in the poem.

But what if we read the first-person pronoun as a metrical mark, another "empty interval" that is present only to mark an absence? The first-person singular is introduced gradually in the poem, first as a possessive pronoun ("all my frame"), next as a direct object ("around me"), and only then as a grammatical subject in "I breathe" and "I feel." If we scan this line, the "I" is an unstressed syllable, and it is not until the second stanza that the pronoun is a stressed syllable: first, as a direct object of the imperative ("be wings to me!"), and more emphatically in the final line: "That I am not a feather, but a bird." Here "I" emerges as the subject, grammatically and rhythmically speaking, except that it is identified with a bird that must be read as a metrical figure and not a human being. The detachment of the pronoun from the person makes it difficult, then, to read the poem as self-expression.

This detachment has led other critics to understand "The Laws of Verse" as repression rather than expression of personal feeling. In Angela Leighton's reading of Meynell, "[T]hose laws, of metricality, impersonality, exactness, but also of a certain meager and precious dispassionateness, became a lifelong poetic creed," a self-imposed faith not only in poetry but in the law of the father and of the Catholic church.[25] To reinforce the feeling of constraint and self-restraint, Leighton mentions a familiar description of Meynell as a "tethered angel" behind the bars of a cage, quoted from the novelist Phyllis Bottome: "The sense of this disciplined self-control was so severe, and yet so impassioned, that it hurt me. I wanted to break down the bars and I knew that I never could. A.M. meant never to have the bars broken down."[26] From this, Leighton concludes there must be "an unbreakable imaginative bar to passion," except perhaps when "Meynell's poetry risks becoming impassioned *about* the bars" (247). But the "risk" of "becoming impassioned *about* the bars" might be the primary reason for reading her poems metrically, not as a bar to passion but as the performance of passion *through* these metrical bars. Meynell's attachment to the "[d]ear laws" of verse is a formal relation best understood as a detachable form of intimacy: not her own passion, but a disciplined affect that produces passion as its effect.

While Leighton considers "The Laws of Verse" a poem of personal "dispassionateness," its impersonality could be considered the mark of Meynell's passionate style as a female aesthete. In *The Forgotten Female Aesthetes,* Talia Schaffer emphasizes Meynell's construction of "an inviolable public persona, behind which she could hide her private self," a self so private that even her daughter recalled that "with her children she had always preserved the privacy and formality of a stranger in her personal things."[27] Yet the formality of her self-presentation created a kind of intimacy, within the family and in public, so that Meynell was widely read as a woman of letters who revealed true womanhood, in poetry and in prose. Already as a girl, Meynell recognized the literary conventions of such self-revelation: she wrote in her diary that any girl who "thrills through every nerve and fibre of her intense self-consciousness" might "if her nerves are tolerably in tune with one another" grow into "a great woman—a writer, say, famous for laying bare the melancholy secrets of the female heart to the curious gaze of material-minded man."[28] Toward the end of her life, when she had indeed grown into "a great woman," she would write "The Laws of Verse" as if to lay bare the secret rhythms of the female heart: "I feel my wild heart beat." But what the poem reveals to "material-minded man" is the spiritualization of meter: the rhythm of the woman's wild heartbeat has been transformed into the metrical form of her poem, intensifying its effect (and its affect) through a formalization rather than personalization of passion.

An Inverse Flight

The spiritualization of literature was part of a fin-de-siècle aesthetic urged by Arthur Symons in his manifesto *The Symbolist Movement in Literature* (1899). With the French symbolist poets as his inspiration, Symons writes about their perfection of form as a necessary annihilation of traditional poetic forms: "It is all an attempt to spiritualise literature, to evade the old bondage of rhetoric," he claims, adding that "the regular beat of verse is broken in order that words may fly, upon subtler wings."[29] But for Meynell, verse did not need to be broken in order to fly on subtler wings; she preferred "the skylark's gravity" to the free-floating feather of free verse, as we have seen, following Patmore's insistence, in his "Essay," on "the necessity of the material counterpoise afforded by metre to the high spirituality of poetic thought" (41). Instead of turning to the example of French poetry in order to break the regular beat of verse, she returned to the English metrical law exemplified in Patmore's odes. At a time when meters were breaking up in English poetry, Meynell was one of last readers to feel the difference between bending and breaking metrical law, between feeling the bonds of verse and (no longer) suffering them.

Meynell's late essay "Coventry Patmore" can be read as a response to Symons and his contemporaries. Although Patmore's odes might have looked and sounded like free verse to many, Meynell knew their irregular meter had been written in accordance with his theories to demonstrate the power of inflection without infraction of the law. To recognize the law at work in Patmore's poetry required not only "a mind trained in the less obvious measures and restraints both of thought and of verse," as we have already noted, but also "liberty, flight, height, courage, a sense of space and a sense of closeness, readiness for spiritual experience, and all the gravity, all the resolution of the lonely reader of a lonely poet." It seems that Meynell alone was still able to read *The Unknown Eros* with a sense of gravity. Reaching the height of language by feeling its weight, Meynell tried to trace the "profound flight" of Patmore's odes, showing how he went "far in an inverse flight—intimately into time and space, remotely into the heart of hearts."

Or perhaps this inverse flight was hers. Even more than showing us how to read Patmore's odes, her essay suggests a way of reading "The Laws of Verse" as a poem that performs his law in verse. Flying "remotely into the heart of hearts" is an apt phrase for her poem's revelation of a heart beating, and flying "intimately into time and space" is an equally apt phrase for the poem's identification of, and with, a bird in flight. Figured in "the skylark's gravity" is the temporal and spatial movement of Meynell's poem, an abstract pattern that is perceived in the rise and fall of its meter and is, as I have suggested, simultaneously remote and intimate. Despite the final proclamation, "I am not a feather but a bird," the formal abstraction of the poem makes it difficult to identify Meynell personally with this bird.

Easier to identify within the poem is the skylark of Percy Bysshe Shelley. In his "Ode to a Skylark," the bird is invoked as a figure for the poetry that the poet has projected into nature:

> Hail to thee, blithe Spirit!
> Bird thou never wert—
> That from Heaven or near it
> Pourest thy full heart
> In profuse strains of unpremeditated art.[30]

Meynell's poem aspires to embody in the first person the "blithe spirit" addressed by Shelley in the second person, with full knowledge that "[b]ird thou never wert." But rather than treating this figure as an inspiration for "unpremeditated art," Meynell's poem is artfully premeditated to feel its own lyric strain: not "in profuse strains" but as a brief meditation in carefully measured pauses, not "full" with sound but better heard in moments of silence. While Shelley appeals to the skylark to teach its skills—"better than all measures / Of delightful sound"—to man, Meynell's bird has already incorporated those measures as a man-made (or woman-made) discipline.

In "The Laws of Verse," Meynell therefore seems to reverse the movement of Shelley's ode, by performing the trope of the skylark in an inverse flight: rather than invoking nature as a figure for poetry, she invokes poetry as a figure for nature. Despite these different points of departure for their flights of fancy, Meynell shares common poetic ground with Shelley in trying to project the laws of verse as a universal phenomenon. As we recall from "The Rhythm of Life," Shelley was singled out by Meynell as one of the few who have knowledge of "recurrences" in nature:

he is mentioned as a poet who refused "deliberate human rules" when these proved to be "infractions of the liberty and law of the universal movement" (3). Meynell considered Shelley a poet of inflections and not infractions, attending to the laws of the universe even when he seemed to rebel against the human rules of verse. At the end of his "Ode to a Skylark," Shelley has become an intermediary for the skylark's song, projecting his own poem into the future so that "the world should listen then, as I am listening now." In listening to Shelley's skylark, Meynell's poem does not echo its song but reiterates the lesson that Meynell read in his poetry: refiguring the laws of verse as the rhythms of nature, she can claim, as she does in "The Rhythm of Life," that if life is not always poetical, it is at least metrical.

And often life did appear to Meynell in a metrical form. She notes the daily song of a blackbird, more mundane than that of a poetical skylark:

> The blackbird is generally in the major, but he knows the minor scale, and now and then sings a more than usually lovely phrase in it. . . . By listening you may hear the same phrase for several successive days, especially from such a tree at such an hour; but it is not certainly, though it is probably, the same bird every time. He comes while the dawn is still dark and cool, and sings his few and intelligible notes aloud, in their definite shape and form. Other kinds of birds are still whispering, without rhythm or rest. He is the only singer of perfect and valued pauses.[31]

Although it is "not certainly" the same bird every time, Meynell carefully measures the timing of its song. With the same phrase heard on successive days, in the same tree at the same hour, in the same definite shape and form, the regularity of this song makes the blackbird sound metrical: a "singer of perfect and valued pauses" not unlike the pauses that Meynell cultivated in her poetic meters. The phrase she admires in particular is in the minor scale, heard in more subtle intervals by a more subtle ear as a variation on the major key: another exercise in symmetry and incident, a formal pattern defined by interruption that is heard but not seen.

Increasingly, the blackbird sounds like an embodiment of English metrical law, and indeed in her "Coventry Patmore" essay, Meynell mentions that hearing "the blackbird at dawn . . . brought him in full the message of the wild suggestion that never left poet's heart at rest" (100). That wild suggestion of song, never leaving any poet's heart at rest, stirs in the heart of her own poems as well; given her claim to be "not a feather but a bird" it is possible to place Meynell within a long tradition of identifying poetesses with birdsong. Thus, not long after her death, she was remembered for "a bird-like quality to her writing, which is at once intense but detached."[32] But insofar as Meynell's writing was "bird-like," it also performed its detachment from that traditional trope for spontaneous song: her poems took the form not of singing but of listening for the pauses, incorporated, as we have seen, in the silent music of "To the Beloved" and in the metrical impulse of "The Laws of Verse." In such poems we are startled by a phenomenon that is neither bird nor woman but meter itself, perceived in rare intervals by poets at the end of one century and the beginning of the next: in the beauty of inflections and innuendos, in the silence heard just after.

Notes

1. Coventry Patmore, "Mrs. Meynell: Poet and Essayist," *Fortnightly Review*, n.s., 41 (1892): 761; further page references appear in parentheses.

2. Alice Meynell, "The Rhythm of Life," in *The Rhythm of Life and Other Essays*, 6th ed. (1892–93; reprint, London: John Lane, 1897), 1; further page references appear in parentheses.

3. Coventry Patmore, *Essay on English Metrical Law: A Critical Edition with a Commentary*, ed. Sister Mary Roth (Washington, DC: Catholic University of America Press, 1961), 15; further page references appear in parentheses.

4. Elaine Scarry, "Counting at Dusk (Why Poetry Matters When the Century Ends)," in *Fins de Siècle: English Poetry in 1590, 1690, 1790, 1890, 1990*, ed. Scarry (Baltimore: Johns Hopkins University Press, 1995), 8.

5. George Saintsbury, *A History of English Prosody* (London: Macmillan, 1923), 3:317, 345. See also Yopie Prins, "Victorian Meters," in *The Cambridge Companion to Victorian Poetry*, ed. Joseph Bristow (Cambridge: Cambridge University Press, 2000), 89–113.

6. James Ashcroft Noble, "Alice Meynell," in *The Poets and the Poetry of the Century*, ed. Alfred H. Miles (London: Hutchinson, 1898), 8:421–22.

7. The friendship between Patmore and Meynell began in 1892. Their initial intimacy and later estrangement is described by June Badeni in *The Slender Tree: A Life of*

Alice Meynell (Padstow, UK: Tabb House, 1981), chap. 11. According to Badeni, the gift of Patmore's manuscripts to Meynell "acknowledged both his love for her and her love for his poetry" (105); Badeni reprints two of Patmore's poems written in praise of Meynell (105–6). See also Derek Patmore, *The Life and Times of Coventry Patmore* (London: Constable, 1949).

8. Alice Meynell's notebook entry, quoted by Badeni in *Slender Tree*, 243.

9. On "dipody," see Patmore, *Essay on English Metrical Law*, 26. For further discussion of Patmore's metrics, see Frederick Page, *Patmore: A Study in Poetry* (London: Oxford University Press, 1933); J. C. Reid, *The Mind and Art of Coventry Patmore* (New York: Macmillan, 1957); Robert M. Pierson, "Coventry Patmore's Ideas concerning English Prosody and *The Unknown Eros* Read Accordingly," *Victorian Poetry* 34, no. 4 (1996): 493–518.

10. In her essay "The Second Person Singular," Meynell laments the improper use of this grammatical form. "Must we needs, as we go on, grow so lax?" she wonders, and concludes it would be worthwhile "to recall, responsibly, the second person singular" to "make our language again more various and more charming" (Alice Meynell, *The Second Person Singular, and Other Essays* [Oxford: Oxford University Press, 1922], 138–39). I am grateful to Emily Harrington for stimulating conversation about various forms of address to "you" in Meynell's poems.

11. "Throughout Meynell's work, silence reveals not so much her beliefs about the status or predicament of women in her society, as it does her assumptions about 'the mental experience of man,' to use a phrase she invoked in her essay 'The Rhythm of Life.'" Maria Frawley, "'The Tides of the Mind': Alice Meynell's Poetry of Perception," *Victorian Poetry* 36, no. 4 (1998): 63. On Meynell's poems driven by thought, see also Vanessa Furse Jackson, "'Tides of the Mind': Restraint and Renunciation in the Poetry of Alice Meynell," *Victorian Poetry* 36, no. 4 (Winter 1998): 444–45. The review of Meynell in the *Pall Mall Gazette* is from a publisher's advertisement, cited in Frawley, "'Tides,'" 65.

12. Francis Thompson, "Mrs. Meynell's Poems," *Tablet*, 21 January 1893, reprinted in *Literary Criticisms by Francis Thompson*, ed. Terence L. Connolly (New York: E. P. Dutton, 1948), 187–91; further page references appear in parentheses.

13. Alice Meynell, "Mr. Coventry Patmore's Odes," *National Observer*, 25 July 1891, reprinted in *Rhythm of Life*, 89–96; further page references appear in parentheses.

14. Meynell's theory of meter as a "universal movement" that is also a measure of thought corresponds to the work of E. S. Dallas, one of the nineteenth-century prosodists reviewed by Patmore in his "Essay on English Metrical Law." I wish to thank Adela Pinch for sharing with me her work on forms of metrical thinking in Dallas and Patmore.

15. Alice Meynell, "The Unit of the World," *Scots Observer*, 2 February 1889, reprinted in *Rhythm of Life*, 29–35.

16. Viola Meynell, *Alice Meynell: A Memoir* (New York: Scribner's, 1929), 110.

17. Alice Meynell edited selections of Coventry Patmore's poetry for *Poetry of Pathos and Delight* (London: Heinemann, 1896); she edited *The Victories of Love*, together with *The Angel in the House*, for Muse's Library (London: Routledge, 1905).

18. Alice Meynell, "Coventry Patmore," *Outlook*, 10 November 1906, rewritten and reprinted in *Second Person Singular*, 94; further page references appear in parentheses.

19. Elizabeth Barrett Browning, *Aurora Leigh*, ed. Margaret Reynolds (New York: W. W. Norton, 1996), 1:915–18.

20. Alice Meynell, "Elizabeth Barrett Browning," first published as the introduction to her edition of *Prometheus Bound and Other Poems* (London: Ward, Lock and Bowden, 1896), reprinted in *The Wares of Autolycus: Selected Literary Essays of Alice Meynell*, ed. P. M. Fraser (London: Oxford University Press, 1965), 163; further page references appear in parentheses. Meynell also published an essay on "The Letters of Elizabeth Barrett Browning" in the *Pall Mall Gazette*, 3 November 1897, and a brief introduction to her selection of *Poems by Elizabeth Barrett Browning* for the Red Letter Library (London: Blackie and Son, 1903). She included some parts of this writing in her entry on Elizabeth Barrett Browning for the eleventh Encyclopedia Britannica; see Gillian Thomas, *A Position to Command Respect: Women and the Eleventh Britannica* (Metuchen, NJ: Scarecrow Press, 1992), 107.

21. Alice Meynell, "The Art of Scansion" (London: privately printed by Clement Shorter, 1916), vii; further page references appear in parentheses. The essay is a preface to a letter on prosody, written by the young Elizabeth Barrett in April 1827 to Sir Uvedale Price.

22. Alice Meynell, "Symmetry and Incident," *Fortnightly Review*, November 1894, reprinted in *The Colour of Life, and Other Essays on Things Seen and Heard* (London: John Lane, 1896) and in *Essays by Alice Meynell* (London: Burns and Oates, 1914), 142–51; further page references appear in parentheses.

23. Beverly Schlack, "The 'Poetess of Poets': Alice Meynell Rediscovered," *Women's Studies* 7 (1980): 122.

24. Furse Jackson, "'Tides,'" 455–56.

25. Angela Leighton, *Victorian Women Poets: Writing against the Heart* (Charlottesville: University Press of Virginia, 1992), 246; further page references appear in parentheses.

26. This reminiscence of Meynell is quoted by Leighton in *Victorian Women Poets* from Phyllis Bottome, *The Challenge* (London: Faber, 1952), 364.

27. Talia Schaffer, *The Forgotten Female Aesthetes: Literary Culture in Late Victorian England* (Charlottesville: University Press of Virginia, 2000), 173. On the public circulation of Meynell's privacy, see also Jerusha McCormack in this volume, and Ana Parejo Vadillo's major reconsideration of Meynell in chapter 2 of *Women Poets and Urban Aestheticism: Passengers of Modernity* (Basingstoke, UK: Palgrave Macmillan, 2005).

28. From the diary of Alice Thompson in 1865, quoted in Badeni, *Slender Tree,* 28.

29. Arthur Symons, introduction to *The Symbolist Movement in Literature* (1899; reprint, New York: E. P. Dutton, 1908), 8.

30. Percy Bysshe Shelley, "To a Skylark," *The Complete Works of Percy Bysshe Shelley,* ed. Roger Ingpen and Walter E. Peck (New York: Gordian Press, 1965), 2:302.

31. Quoted from "The Wares of Autolycus," Alice Meynell's column in the *Pall Mall Gazette,* in Badeni, *Slender Tree,* 208.

32. Osbert Burdett, "The Poems of Alice Meynell," in *Critical Essays* (New York: Holt, 1926), 132.

ALIEN HOMELANDS

Rudyard Kipling, Toru Dutt, and the Poetry of Empire

Tricia Lootens

I

"Alien Homelands": the phrase seeks to evoke fin-de-siècle poetry's concern both with the dislocations of empire—with evocations of home as alien site—and with the refiguring of alien territory, including poetic territory, as homeland. Beyond this, it may also suggest our need to rethink the "home sites" of the poetry of empire. For such poetry's passionate national attachments exceed as well as shape any direct, exclusive bonds between Great Britain and particular colonies—or, for that matter, between Britain and its colonies altogether.

Within scholarly discussions of the early nineteenth century, to address relations between imperial centers and peripheries is often to engage with Katie Trumpener's 1997 *Bardic Nationalism;* and indeed, among the alien imperial homelands of the nineteenth century's close, bardic nationalism remains a powerful and disquieting presence. "English literature, so-called," Trumpener argues, "constitutes itself in the late eighteenth and early nineteenth centuries through the systematic imitation, appropriation, and political neutralization of antiquarian and nationalist literary developments in Scotland, Ireland, and Wales"; and it does so "under the sign of the bard."[1] A communal figure whose art seeks to bind "the nation together across time and across social divides" (xii), this original bard enacts the "resistance of vernacular oral traditions to the historical pressures of English imperialism," bringing "the voices of the past into the sites of the present" (33): his poetry seeks to reanimate "a national landscape made desolate first by conquest and then by modernization, infusing it with historical memory" (xii). His eventual English counterpart, in contrast, is "inspired, isolated, and peripatetic" (6). Committed to "cultural fragmentation and aesthetic autonomy," the English bard practices a "dislocated art," claiming the national literatures of Scotland, Ireland, and Wales as if they were so much "movable, transferable property" (xv, 6, 34). In the process, paradoxically, he ensures that early nineteenth-century English literature's very "notions of collective and individual memory" come to "have their origins in the cultural nationalism of the peripheries" (xi).

What, then, of bardic nationalism some hundred years later? The "peripheries" have expanded; but what of the process? One way to begin addressing such questions is to consider that great late-century testimony to the appropriative power of "English literature, so-called," Edmund Clarence Stedman's groundbreaking 1895 *A Victorian Anthology*. "[T]he poetry of the English people, and of the English tongue, that knight peerless among languages," is Stedman's self-proclaimed subject; and in his introduction, that poetry seamlessly incorporates writings by "the colonial pioneers of life and literature in a new land."[2] In the table of contents, however, the project of identifying "the poetry of the English people" with that of "the English tongue" becomes more challenging. For under "Colonial Poets: India—Australasia—Dominion of Canada," where authors, poems, and page numbers should appear for India, one finds the following lines instead: "See Toru Dutt, Rudyard Kipling, in the preceding division of this Anthology. See also, in the second division, Sir Edwin Arnold, Sir Alfred Lyall, poets of English birth, and sometime resident in India" (xxxviii).[3] Turn back, and sure enough, there they are: Kipling and Dutt under "Close of the Era (Intermediary Period): Recent Poets of Great Britain" (xxxvii, xxxv), and Arnold and Lyall under "The Victorian Epoch": "Composite Idyllic School" (xxvi).

That Arnold and Lyall should even enter Stedman's note might merit an essay in itself. Most suggestive here, however, is the joint evacuation of Dutt and Kipling. What does it mean to class the Indo-Anglian Dutt as one of the "recent poets of Great Britain"? Is she thus simultaneously claimed by empire and blocked from poetic cultural authority? Certainly as a Bengali, Dutt could scarcely claim a place among the introduction's celebrated colonial "pioneers": for her, the "life and literature" of India were scarcely those of a "new land." Still, having thus disqualified the Indo-Anglian Dutt, why exclude the Anglo-Indian Kipling as well? Had Kipling somehow forfeited colonial status by pursing a successful career outside the "new land" of his birth? Or does Stedman merely evacuate the category of "Indian poetry" in order to do honor to Dutt and Kipling, elevating both poets to a transcendent category of Britishness? Whatever its sources, Stedman's category crisis underscores the problems of attempting to anthologize a poetry at once "English" and "imperial." It reminds us that for fin-de-siècle imperial patriotic poets, the empire was "English"—often by right of (increasingly purified, "Anglo-Saxon") capital-*B* "Blood," and always with reference to Thomas Babington Macaulay's "imperishable empire" of the English language, with its intimate, occluded, and fraught relations to raw political power. What relation might this imperial English bear to "the" English? That question, which may yoke Dutt and Kipling in Stedman's note, also connects both poets to the alien homelands of late nineteenth-century bardic nationalism. In Kipling, it may help catalyze a major creative crisis; in Dutt, it seems to serve as a source of inevitably politicized poetic inspiration.

II

Let me begin with Kipling, the poet we know—or think we know—or, some might claim, know only too well. Without rehearsing long-standing arguments about Kipling's disturbing and ambiguous position as unofficial "Poet Laureate of Empire,"[4] it may be useful to note that for certain of Kipling's critics, the turn of the century—and more specifically, the turn of the Boer War—coincides with a poetically and politically disastrous movement, whereby Kipling turns away from the messy materiality of imperial experience toward an increasingly abstract, racist, vitalist imperial fantasy realm. For M. van Wyk Smith, for example, the Boer War, and with it, the turn of the century, arrived just as Kipling's "celebration of the colourful characters of empire" had "given way" to the "worship of a vast and ultimately nebulous panorama of imperial ideology."[5] Paula M. Krebs sees a clearer causal relationship: the increasing abstraction and desperation of Kipling's attempts to "flatten the whole of the British empire into a unity," she writes, arose in great part from the poet's alienation from

African or Afrikaner cultures, which rendered him incapable of conceiving of "South Africa as a country with a history, or histories."[6] Certainly from my perspective as well, this moment may mark the intensification of implicit conflicts between Kipling's ambitions as a bard of imperial soldiery and his performance as empire's popular, unofficial poet laureate. Attempting to speak at once for a Romantically imagined quasi nation of working-class soldiers; for the loyal, native-born "English" of individual colonies; and for an elegiacally conceived British empire itself, Kipling's poetry during this period repeatedly tests the limits of bardic nationalism. This is a lengthy, conflicted process. Here, I would like to sketch out some of the levels on which it works, based on three poems: "The Flowers," "The Native-Born," and "Chant-Pagan."

Written during Kipling's Vermont years (1892–96),[7] "The Flowers" and "The Native-Born" both speak, albeit in different registers, to a project that Trumpener associates with the paradigmatic novels of Sir Walter Scott: they "underline . . . the ideological capaciousness of empire," arguing for "the continued centrality of national identity as a component of imperial identity" (xiii). In "The Flowers," for example, the songs of bard and laureate harmonize as an interestingly feminized, Anglicized flower-girl speaker counters a dismissive epigraph attributed to the *Athenæum*. "To our private taste," that epigraph reads, in part, "there is always something a little exotic, almost artificial, in songs which, under an English aspect and dress, are yet so manifestly the product of other skies. They affect us like translations . . . the dog's-tooth violet is but an ill substitute for the rathe primrose."[8] "Buy my English posies!" the speaker's refrain responds. To colonial customers, she offers the likes of blood-root, clematis, and kowhai, from "home / Half the world away" (11–12); on Britons, who already have their "own" flowers, she urges the wisdom of buying exotic colonial "English" blooms for a "brother's sake, / Overseas, alone" (59–60).

> Weed ye trample underfoot
>> Floods his heart abrim—
> Bird ye never heeded,
>> Oh, she calls his dead to him!
>
> (61–64)

With this defense of colonial posies—and poetries—as the genteelly de-politicized, interchangeable properties of an overarching "English" empire, Kipling's speaker explicitly turns the apolitical politics of sentimentality to the service of imperial loyalties. She closes with an overt warning concerning the public implications of domestic empires of love. "Far and far our homes are set round the Seven Seas," she insists; and, "Woe for us if we forget, we that hold by these!" (65–66).

"The Native-Born" is an edgier poem, imaginatively grounded not in some English street, but in a symbolic colonial space somewhere in the Southern Hemisphere. Here, the familial associations of empire are more dangerous; they may even be the shoals on which bardic nationalism founders. This is a drinking poem: one should not be surprised if it becomes more belligerent as it goes on. Still, the precise moment of the shift into aggression is telling. By the time the poem opens, its speakers have already had a few: they have "drunk to the Queen"; their "mothers' land" (not, interestingly, their "motherland"); their absent English "brother" who "does not understand"; and the "wide creation" (1–5).[9] Now, they proclaim, it is time for the "[l]ast toast, and of obligation": "A health to the Native-born!" (7–8). "They change their skies above them, / But not their hearts that roam!" (9–10): thus comes the expected reassurance of unchanged Englishness. Even by the next lines, however, the tone shifts: "We learned from our wistful mothers / To call old England 'home'" (11–12). Already suggestive, the quotation marks around "home" become even more significant once one learns that these same mothers have "passed with their old-world legends— / Their tales of wrong and dearth—" (17–18). With such a heritage, no wonder the "Native-born" ultimately locate their now-singular, collective "heart" where their mothers "rocked our cradle": that is, on colonial ground (21).

Enjoined to a "good pride" that "shall teach us / To praise our comrade's pride" (31–32), the drinkers now return to the bardic task of unifying empire through toasts to a parallel series of idealized, sensuously realized imperial landscapes, punctuated by calls to *"Let a fellow sing o' the little things he cares about, / If a fellow fights for the little things he cares about / With the weight of a single blow."* (Fairly quickly, the "fellow" moves from a "single" to a "two-fold blow" [43–45, 56–58].) The crescendo of this call to harmonious Englishness as the heart of expanding empire comes, suitably, with a movement from the African landscape to "the last and the largest Empire, / To the map that is half unrolled!" (73–74).

At this, however, apparently out of nowhere, comes another, unannounced toast:

> To our dear dark foster-mothers,
>> To the heathen songs they sung—
> To the heathen speech we babbled
>> Ere we came to the white man's tongue.
>>> (75–78)

It is as if the toastmaster has lost his place. These may be African nurses; but it is hard to forget Kipling's own Indian childhood—and impossible to overlook how this evocation of dear, dark motherhood, and of primal memories of "heathen" babble and song, threatens to effect a definitive dissolution of the "Native-born"'s claims to unchanged English hearts. Peripheral "[b]ardic nationalism," Trumpener writes, "insists on the rich fullness of national knowledge, on the anchoring of discursive traditions in landscape, in a way of life, in custom. The English, in comparison, have only borrowed words" (34). Here, this assertion takes on new meaning. Alienated at once from the old world's "tales of wrong and dearth," and from their own first "heathen songs," Kipling's "Native-born" have two mothers and none, two mother tongues, or ancient national literatures, and none. For them, to attempt the bardic task of infusing national landscapes with historical memory is thus to risk dislocating or even dissolving their own imperial claims to any homeland at all—unless it be a free-floating, abstract racial homeland of imperial possession and dispossession.

Not surprisingly, perhaps, at this point the poem's attempts at concretely, historically imagined unity break down. What emerges now is a different kind of toast: an oracular paean to an aggressive and almost purely symbolic England whose "dread high-altar," like her "Bank of the Open Credit" and "Power-house of the Line," bespeaks brute—and abstract—imperial force (85, 89–90). Bardic performance has faltered; in its place arises the performance of a laureate of empire. One foot on the table, the "Native-born" now seem drunk enough to imagine an English brother who *will* "understand" (93–94)—and disturbed enough, perhaps, by the memory of "dear dark foster-mothers," to unite with that brother under the sign of white warriorhood. The poem ends with the following italicized toast:

> A health to the Native-born! (Stand up!),
>   We're six white men arow,
> All bound to sing o' the little things we care about,
> All bound to fight for the little things we care about
>   With the weight of a six-fold blow!
> By the might of our cable-tow (Take hands!),
>   From the Orkneys to the Horn,
> All round the world (and a little loop to pull it by),
> All round the world (and a little strap to buckle it),
>   A health to the Native-born!
>   (99–108)

On their feet, hands interlocked, Kipling's drinkers are now bound both to one another and to paralleled singing and fighting. What is more, in a metaphorically violent enactment of combined military and technological power, their bonds, as literalized by the "might" of the "cable-tow," now claim the earth as an abstract possession. Traversed by telegraph cables, the globe now has a "little" imperial "loop to pull it by," a "little strap to buckle it," and "six white men" to do the job.

Anger is reserved for the laureate voice.[10] Still, there is an emotional undercurrent even in this poem's opening reference to the English brother who does not understand. And indeed, many of Kipling's dramatic (or half-dramatic) monologues seem fueled by the rage and desire of speakers for whom love of country and love of empire can't be reconciled. If "The Native-Born" brings bardic nationalism into crisis by evoking British imperial subjects who *can't* be English, "Chant-Pagan" offers a British imperial subject who may no longer want to be.

With "Chant-Pagan," I come to my first direct instance of Kipling's working-class imperial soldier, a figure who is often, at once, quintessentially English, too wild for England, and too good for the civilian and governmental English whose interests he defends. Tommy Atkins fights for his country; but he also makes that country nervous. Even in a poem such as "The 'Eathen," in which imperial military discipline succeeds at transforming indigenous urban rabble into the "saved," the potential threat of a military "Cockney nation" seems clear.[11] In "Chant-Pagan," however, things go further: Kipling comes close to presenting an imperial soldier capable of deliberately, explicitly condemning England itself. Through this "ambivalent imperial narrative," Kipling drives the possibilities of bardic imperialism to, and perhaps beyond, their limits.[12]

Here, attachments to a vulnerable, beloved vernacular focus not on the "dear dark" mothers' heathen songs, but on a different product of quasi-national oral tradition: the "pagan" chant of an "English Irregular" soldier whose vital (and no doubt vanishing) speech draws at once on urban dialect, military slang, Afrikaans, and echoes of Yeats.[13] "Chant-Pagan" marks the coming to consciousness of a speaker whose heroic service to the British Empire can't extend to being England's bard. To be sure, like Trumpener's peripheral bards, this speaker represents "the resistance of vernacular oral traditions to the historical pressures of English imperialism."[14] In this case, however, the resistant vernacular traditions in question *are* explicitly imperial. At once an English and, in some sense, an antiquarian bard, Kipling's common soldier/speaker can only occupy his alien homeland; the culture he defends is one of imperial exile. Against the historical pressures of an empire represented by respectable (and often feminized) civilian, military, or religious authorities, not to mention reporters and politicians, the speaker of "Chant-Pagan" defends a defiantly borrowed "native language": a rich, vulnerable vernacular whose origins may lie in the world of urban music halls, but whose power has taken form in the imperial encampment or on shipboard. "Me that 'ave been what I've been," the poem begins—

> Me that 'ave gone where I've gone,
> Me that 'ave seen what I've seen—
>   'Ow can I ever take on
> With awful old England again . . . ?
>
>   (1–5)[15]

Even if one reads the revision of "merry old England" as jocular, the point is clear. The speaker may no longer belong in England; and this is so, not merely because of where he's "gone" and what he's "seen," but because of what he's "been." He has become a part of all that he has met; and his meditation on this truth may be read as a condensed imperial version of William Wordsworth's *The Prelude*—a progression of intense, localized memories whose force and specificity convey an irreversible coming to consciousness. That this consciousness is in part poetic, even bardic, seems clearer to us than to him; that it encompasses an acute new awareness of class is undeniable. The touching of the hat to "parson an' 'gentry,'" in house-lined streets or on hedge-lined lanes; the rolling of the squire's lawns; the walk, "almost / As much as a mile, to the post," having been reminded to bring back the change (8, 31–33): one can't miss the raw irony of juxtaposing these current scenes and duties with the speaker's acute and isolated memories of fighting in South Africa. Such tension reaches its culmination in his assertion that

> I am doin' my Sunday-school best,
> By the 'elp of the Squire an' 'is wife
> (Not to mention the 'ousemaid an' cook),
> To come in an' 'ands up an' be still,
> An' honestly work for my bread,
> My livin' in that state of life
> To which it shall please God to call
>   Me!
>   (43–50)

For this speaker, to do his "Sunday-school best" is to surrender, hands up. He seems to face two choices: that of accepting his original "state of life" as a subjected citizen of the less powerful of England's famous "Two Nations," or that of leaving the nation-state of his birth. In Latin, "paganus"—which, as Ralph Durand points out, first meant "villager" or "rustic"—came in time to mean an irregular soldier, a development that foreshadows the speaker's own.[16] From rustic (or Cockney), to soldier, to skeptic: the seemingly inexorable linguistic progression links Kipling's soldier-bard to an ancient conceptual "nation" of his own—the mobile, ambiguous, alien homeland of the hard-bitten soldier of empire.

Infusing the South African landscape with intimate memories at once historical, individual, and sublime—to use irresistibly Wordsworthian language—the speaker of "Chant-Pagan" traces the growth of a working-class imperial "singer's" mind. Having seen "'arf a world / 'Eave up all shiny with dew, / Kopje on kop to the sun" (11–13); having heard the guns answer *"Are ye there? Are ye there? Are ye there?"*; and having known "the silence, the shine an' the size / Of the 'igh, inexpressible skies," the speaker dreams of returning to a landscape of transfigured conscious- ness (18, 29–30). He is, of course, no traditional bard. Homesick for battlefields, he voices a longing for land rendered beloved by bloodshed rather than blood ties.[17] Still, he seeks—and, for his readers, creates—a place with a local habitation and, presumably, an unspoken name: *"I* know," he says—and the emphasis on "I" counts, given how often he has said "me"—

> . . . *I* know of a sun an' a wind,
> An' some plains and a mountain be'ind
> An' some graves by a barb-wire fence;
> An' a Dutchman I've fought 'oo might give
> Me a job were I ever inclined,
> To look in an' offsaddle an' live
> Where there's neither a road nor a tree—
> But only my Maker an' me
>
> (70–77)

Although the speaker does not (yet) say so, it seems clear that military empire, in its demand for raw nerve, both shared and solitary, has joined with the sensuous, spiritual presence of material empire ("the silence, the shine an' the size" of its "'igh, inexpressible skies") to save him from spiritual defeat by England. He knows now that he need not submit "'ands up an' be still." Thus, though in one sense "Chant-Pagan" is a deeply Wordsworthian poem, a poem thoroughly invested in the revela- tory power of landscapes of memory, in another sense, this poem offers a "pagan" response to England's claims on the sublime. With its "pale" sunshine and "stale" breezes, this speaker's England seems to have "gone small" (67–69). Crucially, moreover, even when the speaker imagines re- turning to South Africa, it is not to join British colonists, but to work for the "Dutchman." The speaker of "The Flowers" may hope to re-place, or relocate, Englishness throughout the empire; but the Englishness of the speaker of "Chant-Pagan" may well be "replaced" in the more usual sense of the word. "I will arise an' get 'ence" (64): the tribute to W. B. Yeats's

"The Lake Isle of Innisfree" (1890) is parodic, but it is also deeply seri-ous.[18] The speaker of "Chant-Pagan" hears a song of Africa, and he hears it in the deep heart's core.

III

If South Africa catalyzes disquieting imperial nostalgia for war in Kipling, then England serves as a difficult site of desire for Toru Dutt. It is tempt-ing, when dealing with Dutt, to offer an extended consideration of the poet's biography. And indeed, in most contexts, one cannot address the full implications of Dutt's career without giving some sense of her life. Born in Calcutta in 1856, Dutt grew up in an intellectual, English-speaking Hindu family whose official conversion to Christianity took place when she was six years old.[19] In 1869, she traveled to Europe with her sister Aru and their father—poet Govin Chunder Dutt—becoming one of the first Bengali women to make such a journey.[20] After studying French at a Nice *pensionnat* until spring 1870,[21] and visiting London, Toru and Aru Dutt traveled in 1871 to Cambridge, where they attended the "Higher Lectures for Women."[22] Both sisters began working on a project of translating re-cent French poetry into English. Within a year of their return to Calcutta in 1873, however, Aru was dead of tuberculosis.[23] Toru herself would live only four more years. She left behind the completed translation project, an ambitious 1876 volume entitled *A Sheaf Gleaned in French Fields*, whose achievement Edmund Gosse termed "simply astounding";[24] new translated poems in the *Bengal Magazine;* essays on Leconte de Lisle and Henry Vivian Derozio;[25] translations of French legislative debates;[26] a completed novel in French, *Le Journal de Mademoiselle d'Arvers;*[27] an unfinished novel in English, *Bianca, or The Young Spanish Maiden;*[28] and finally, a series of original poems, as well as narratives drawn from the *Ramayana* and the *Mahabharata,* and from the *Vishnu Purana.*[29] These last, published under the emphatically, if somewhat incongruously, bardic title *Ancient Ballads and Legends of Hindustan* (1882), established Dutt's claims as a fin-de-siècle poet.[30]

Given all this, it is no wonder, perhaps, that Dutt should stand as a complex, conflicted figure for national poetry, be it Indian, English, or French. That she should also be an interesting figure in terms of bardic nationalism is both her own doing and that of her admirers, including Edmund Gosse. For Gosse, who wrote the often-quoted "Introductory Memoir" to *Ancient Ballads and Legends of Hindustan,* attempted to package Dutt as a bard of a very particular sort; and he did so within a volume already oddly associated with bardic tradition. "I never heard the old song of Percie and Douglas, that I found not my heart moved, more than with a trumpet," reads the Philip Sidney epigraph of *Ancient Ballads and Legends,* "and yet it is sung but by some blinde crowder, with no rougher voice, than rude style."[31] The choice seems ambiguous. Are we to identify Dutt with the rough, rude "blinde crowder" or the moved listener? Both, Gosse's essay suggests; and, perhaps, neither.

"The poetess seems in these verses," Gosse writes, of Dutt's actual recounting of Hindu stories, "to be chanting to herself those songs of her mother's race to which she always turned with tears of pleasure" (xxiv). Her poems on Hindu topics "breathe a Vedic solemnity and simplicity of temper" tellingly "devoid of that littleness and frivolity which seem, if we may judge by a slight experience, to be the bane of modern India" (xxiv). These are complex, significant claims. On one level, they constitute Dutt as a form of appropriative "English bard," in Trumpener's sense; on another, as an authentic "native informant." As a "pure Hindu" who preserved "her appreciation of the poetic side of her ancient religion, though faith itself in Vishnu and Siva had been cast aside with childish things" (xi), Gosse's Dutt appropriates and Anglicizes her culture's traditions, even as she ratifies attempts to cast Hinduism—and with it, perhaps, other ongoing, independent vernacular cultural traditions—as archaic. At the same time, however, Gosse's "Hindu poetess" lacks the agency and potential influence associated with "real"—and masculine— English bards. Rather than write or declaim, for example, she is "chanting to herself" (xv, xxiv).[32] Privately rehearsing the domesticated and desacralized "songs of her mother's race," she seems to channel bardic poetry without assuming bardic power. In her sequestration from the "littleness and frivolity" of cultural life in "modern India," moreover, Dutt herself seems somehow archaic—almost, indeed, her own portable living "ancient," or at least antiqued, legend of "Hindustan." "[M]ellow sweetness," Gosse concludes, "was all that Toru lacked to perfect her as an English poet, and of no other Oriental who has ever lived can the same be said. When the history of the literature of our country comes to be written, there is sure to be a page in it dedicated to this fragile exotic blossom of song" (xxvii).

This final phrase was to become iconic within Dutt studies for over a hundred years. At the very least, like Stedman's inclusion of Dutt among "recent poets of Great Britain," Gosse's transformation of the poet's work into a "fragile, exotic blossom" renders her a portable national treasure, fit to be laid in the pages of Great Britain's literary history. At most, as when echoed by Stedman himself, the characterization fixes Dutt's work as souvenir rather than living art, equating it to the "pressed leaves of a tropic flower that, striving to adapt itself to an atmosphere not its own, exhaled some fragrance ere it died."[33] This is not to suggest that Dutt's work remained neatly pressed into national place, however. European critics might merge doomed poetess and bard in a dream of fragile blossoms; but Indian critics have often sought more vital botanical tropes. "[I]n Ancient Ballads," K. R. Ramachandran Nair writes, for example, some hundred years after Gosse's introduction, Dutt "rediscovered her roots. . . . Like Walter Scott, who immortalised the ancient past of Britain in his historical novels, Toru Dutt through her ballads and legends gave a habitation and a name to the hoary past of our ancient land."[34] Moreover, even the blossoms of literary empire might be under dispute. After all, only a year after Gosse's introduction, critic James Darmesteter insisted that Dutt had "the right to a line in the history" of French literature—not least as "a frail and sweet image of what the Hindu genius might have produced under the wing of France."[35] Whose ancient ballads were these? Like her career itself, Dutt's reception seems calculated to dramatize the instability of national affiliations and appropriations.

If English bards are imitation Welsh, Scottish, or Irish bards, what is an Indian bard? A female Indian bard who writes in English? In French? What might it mean to be a bard whose "nation" was already being moved to seek unity, in part, through processes of translation—including translation into an originally imperial language which was, as Malashri Lal puts it, neither "indigenous nor alien"?[36] Produced, in Alpana Sharma Knippling's words, "not from the site of a monolithic 'truth' and 'native' authenticity, but from the infinitely more fascinating site . . . of reinvention and improvisation," Dutt's work inhabits a "risk-ridden, in-between, yet productive space in the international arena of textual production and reception."[37] This may be nowhere clearer than in Dutt's most famous original poem, "Our Casuarina Tree."

As little analyzed as it has been frequently cited in discussions of the poet's career, "Our Casuarina Tree" first appeared as one of the *Ancient Ballads and Legends of Hindustan*. Rendered doubly archaic, both by its status as honorary "ancient ballad" and by Gosse's influential suggestion that it celebrates the poet's childhood in a lost "mystical retirement more irksome to an European in fancy than to an Oriental in reality" (xi), "Our Casuarina Tree" helps inscribe Dutt's career in thoroughly posthumous, sapphic terms.[38] Strip off the antiquing, however, and what emerges is a very different autobiographical meditation on an adult poet's cosmopolitan, fin-de-siècle family garden outside Calcutta.[39] Because the poem can be difficult to find, I offer it here:

Our Casuarina Tree

Like a huge Python, winding round and round
    The rugged trunk, indented deep with scars,
    Up to its very summit near the stars,
A creeper climbs, in whose embraces bound
    No other tree could live. But gallantly   5
The giant wears the scarf, and flowers are hung
In crimson clusters all the boughs among,
    Whereon all day are gathered bird and bee;
And oft at nights the garden overflows
With one sweet song that seems to have no close,   10
Sung darkling from our tree, while men repose.

When first my casement is wide open thrown
    At dawn, my eyes delighted on it rest;
    Sometimes, and most in winter,—on its crest
A grey baboon sits statue-like alone   15
    Watching the sunrise; while on lower boughs
His puny offspring leap about and play;
And far and near kokilas hail the day;
    And to their pastures wend our sleepy cows;

And in the shadow, on the broad tank cast   20
By that hoar tree, so beautiful and vast,
The water-lilies spring, like snow enmassed.

But not because of its magnificence
    Dear is the Casuarina to my soul:
      Beneath it we have played; though years may roll,   25
O sweet companions, loved with love intense,
    For your sakes, shall the tree be ever dear!
Blent with your images, it shall arise
In memory, till the hot tears blind mine eyes!
      What is that dirge-like murmur that I hear   30
Like the sea breaking on a shingle-beach?
It is the tree's lament, an eerie speech,
That haply to the unknown land may reach.

Unknown, yet well-known to the eye of faith!
    Ah, I have heard that wail far, far away   35
    In distant lands, by many a sheltered bay,
When slumbered in his cave the water-wraith
    And the waves gently kissed the classic shore
Of France or Italy, beneath the moon,
When earth lay trancèd in a dreamless swoon: 40
    And every time the music rose,—before
Mine inner vision rose a form sublime,
Thy form, O Tree, as in my happy prime
I saw thee, in my own loved native clime.

Therefore I fain would consecrate a lay   45
    Unto thine honour, Tree, beloved of those
    Who now in blessed sleep, for aye, repose,
Dearer than life to me, alas! were they!
    Mayst thou be numbered when my days are done
With deathless trees—like those in Borrowdale,   50
Under whose awful branches lingered pale
    "Fear, trembling Hope, and Death, the skeleton,
And Time the shadow;" and though weak the verse

That would thy beauty fain, oh fain rehearse,
May Love defend thee from Oblivion's curse.[40]   55

"Our Casuarina Tree": the title already raises the question "Who are 'we'?" This is, then, a poem about possession, identification, affiliation; and though a number of possibilities emerge, "our" identity never becomes entirely clear. "Like a huge Python, winding round and round": metrical and symbolic surprise unite in this first, crucial phrase (1), as Dutt's vine opens a lesson in the difficulties of reading. The slow power of that winding embrace, the strength of that scarred, up-reaching trunk, mark the rest of the poem, as does the tense, dangerous, fruitful symbiosis that follows. How should we read the gallantry with which the tree transforms its strangling creeper into a scarf, a fertile bearer of crimson clusters, a source of life—and, it is suggested, a source or home for "one sweet song that seems to have no close" (10)? Surely this song is akin to that of Keats's nightingale or Wordsworth's Solitary Reaper; but how and why should it overflow from this strangling botanical python?

In a Western context, Dutt's powerful, ambiguous opening image inevitably calls up the serpent in the Tree of Knowledge of Good and Evil—or, perhaps, the Tree of Life, which takes on intimate, enigmatic form elsewhere in Dutt's work. Given Dutt's admiration for William Makepeace Thackeray, it may even draw strength from Dobbin's gallant support of Amelia, the "tender little parasite" of the novelist's 1847 *Vanity Fair*.[41] Still, another resonance seems inescapable, not least because of frequent critical recourse to metaphors of rootedness in addressing Dutt's own national and cultural positions.[42] Might the tree represent India itself? One critic has suggested as much.[43] Certainly, in such contexts, one cannot help but remember the sort of popular patriotic verse in which Anglicized "ordered Freedom" grows "to a great tree where'er / In either hemisphere, / Its vital seeds are blown."[44] And indeed, it is deeply tempting to assign the python-like vine's heavy—and fertile—"crimson" embrace to British rule of India, arguing that if the Casuarina tree reaps life and beauty from the dangerous embraces of its creeping counterpart, this is because it is strong enough to wear the would-be strangler as a dashing ornament. Those scarlet blooms: might they not be associated with red coats, with the red of Great Britain's possessions on late-century world maps, or even with blood? Perhaps. Still, it is best to pause here.

For one thing, at least one Indian critic, C. D. Narasimhaiah, has traced the vision of the tree wearing the python as a scarf to Indian literary antecedents.[45] For another, this vine is surely too ancient, too intimately connected to its bearing tree—and, quite simply, too tropical—to assume such a stable allegorical weight. Indeed, this may be part of the point. Ultimately, the Casuarina, like "Our Casuarina Tree" itself, is not *about* England.

This is not to deny, however, that Dutt's poem is in some sense about English poetry. Indeed, at many points, the emphatically Indian garden of "Our Casuarina Tree" seems so uncannily steeped in Romantic nostalgia as to call forth a new form of what Dutt herself terms "eerie speech" (32). English poetic tropes saturate this evocation of an Indian garden—and are, in the process, subtly transformed. As the Keatsian darkling song of the first stanza gives way to the morning scene of the second, for example, the Romantic, courtly "casement" is thrown open; the familiar "delighted" eye rests—and the speaker perceives, of all things, a gray baboon (12–15). For a Western reader, this is a moment of culture shock, and one that intensifies as the statuelike animal assumes the classic visionary's position, paralleling and perhaps not quite parodying the speaker's own stance. Silent on a tree in Calcutta, the baboon stares at the sunrise, as the speaker stares with and at him. T. H. Huxley famously claimed that "he was not ashamed to have a monkey for his ancestor"; the Darwinism he defended in 1860 was apparently hotly debated in English-speaking India.[46] Might this be an ancestor figure, older even than bardic mossy altars or ancient ballads and legends? If so, the word "puny," used to describe the baboon's offspring at play below (17), is particularly disturbing, especially given the existence of a poem in which Dutt's father describes his young daughter Toru as "puny and elf-like."[47] Unsentimental, even derisory, in its characterization of physical frailty, "puny" thus effects a crucial break in the stanza's tone. At this point, however, that break is only momentary: as "our" sleepy cows wend their way to pasture, and darkling song gives way to that of the kokilas, those cuckoos who sing of desire in the poetry of India, the stanza quickly resumes its movement from playfulness to serenity, to close with a quietly dazzling, almost visionary layering whereby the Casuarina's shadow, falling over the garden's water tanks, floats on white lilies that seem to lie, in turn, like "snow enmassed" on the bare branches of a very different winter tree (22).

Quickly, however, both the tree and its poetic associations become more explicitly personal and painful. The Casuarina is dear, we learn, "not because of its magnificence," but because the speaker once played beneath it with her lost "sweet companions" (23–27)—perhaps Toru Dutt's sister Aru and their brother, Abju, who died in 1865, at age fourteen.[48] Even as this stanza disturbingly parallels the "puny" young baboons with the lost companions, it reshapes the poem's earlier celebration of blended living and imaged trees, as the speaker promises both that she will henceforth see the Casuarina in memory, blended with the faces of those she has lost, and that, as this visionary tree arises, it will blind her with "hot tears" (29). Her promise to love the tree "for your sakes" may remind us of "Tintern Abbey"; but when, as if already blinded, she asks, "What is that dirge-like murmur?" her answer moves, for one brief and essential moment, into another era (27, 30). No religious doubt is spoken; indeed, with the next line, she asserts that this same "eerie speech" may "haply" reach the "unknown land" of those she has lost—a land "unknown, yet well-known to the eyes of faith" (32–34). Still, after Matthew Arnold's "Dover Beach" (1867), this "tree's lament," with its sound "like the sea breaking on a shingle-beach" (31), cannot help but bring the eternal note of sadness in. And indeed, that very note carries over to the next stanza, as the Casuarina undergoes yet another metamorphosis. "Ah, I have heard that wail far, far away" (35), the speaker says; and one has to wonder where. Near some deep romantic chasm, perhaps? The "distant lands" to which this wail has already reached are technically earthly; significantly, given Dutt's other projects of decentering British cultural power, their names are "France" and "Italy" (36, 39). With their slumbering cave-housed water-wraith, and kissing waves, however, such lands also seem to be those of poetry. Here, where the waves kiss rather than break as dirges; where the water-wraith sleeps; and where a moonlit Keatsian earth lies "trancèd in a dreamless swoon," what should one make of this memory of the tree's eerie wail (40)? It is hard to know—and hard to know, too, whether the "music" that rises toward the stanza's end is itself the wail or the sound of kissing waves (41). What *is* clear is that in response to this music, a visionary Casuarina Tree once arose to embody the speaker's memories of home. At that point, the tree bore no images of loss: rather, it appeared, as it now appears, in the form of a simultaneous symbol of the speaker's own lost "happy" youth and of her own "loved native clime" (43–44). Arising against an alien, "classic" landscape (38), the transfigured Casuarina has thus become at once a tree of homesickness and of visionary home.

"Therefore I fain would consecrate a lay": with this revelation of bardic ambition, the speaker opens a final stanza devoted to laying bare her own creative ambitions (45). Now, almost shockingly after such a wealth of echoing, ambiguous intertextuality, comes an explicit literary reference, to Wordsworth's 1815 "Ewtrees." With the evocation of Wordworth's "deathless trees," "under whose awful branches," in Dutt's words, "lingered pale, / 'Fear, trembling Hope, and Death, the skeleton, / And Time the shadow,'" the later poem's ambiguities become both newly acute and differently focused (50–53). Lingering—or loitering—palely, the shapes of Wordsworth's actual poem, as proffered by Dutt, seem less to haunt the trees above than to be held in thrall by them. As such, they complete a triad of presences. The puny baboons; then the sweet companions; then Fear, trembling Hope, Death, and Time: even as this progression intensifies earlier meditations on home, memory, and mortality, it invests those longings with explicitly bardic significance. For the Casuarina's alien and inalienable connections to a personal, familial home now extend, as the poet seeks to align her own tree with Wordsworth's.

Standing single in the midst of its own darkness, the opening "venerable" yew of Wordsworth's poem is at once a material defender and a metaphoric embodiment of nation.[49] Having been "[n]ot loth to furnish weapons for the bands / Of Umphraville or Percy," or boughs (bows) for the battles of "Azincour . . . Crecy or Poictiers," the yew's life, "[p]roduced too slowly ever to decay; / Of form and aspect too magnificent / To be destroy'd," now produces a metaphor for the slow, triumphal growth of Englishness itself.[50] In the mid-1970s, "Ewtrees" sparked a well-known debate between Michael Riffaterre and Geoffrey Hartman on the uses and limits of structuralism.[51] What is striking, at this distance, is that neither critic addresses the poem's shift midway through—its bizarre, quiet, midline move from a solitary, almost sinisterly independent tree of slow-grown, implicitly martial Englishness, to the four trees of Borrowdale, whose sinuous connections and ghostly force seem not only to exude, but also, possibly, to exceed Englishness, at least if one thinks of Englishness as human and historical. Haunted by "Shapes," Borrowdale's forbidding "Fraternal four," whose looks "threaten the profane," are at once more sensually, materially realized than the poem's initial tree, and more intimately connected to abstraction (26, 15, 21). Each "a growth / Of intertwisted fibres serpentine, / Up-coiling and inveterately convolved" (17–19), Borrowdale's trees create a pillared, primal site on which Fear, Hope, Silence, Foresight, Death, and Time may materialize to worship or lie and listen in "mute repose" (26–33). Far from seeking to reanimate Trumpener's "landscape made desolate first by conquest and then by modernization," "Ewtrees" infuses landscape with memory that is precisely not historical. The shapes who "[m]ay" haunt these shades at noontide—who "celebrate . . . [u]nited worship" at their "altars undisturbed of mossy stone"—are pre-Roman, pre-Christian, pre-nation-state: indeed, if "Death" weren't a skeleton, one might be tempted to claim, pre-human (27, 29–32). They offer an archaeology of English landscape poetry, back beyond Englishness in any conceivable political sense, to a thoroughly localized, pagan gothic sublime.[52] "Ewtrees" thus moves into and through patriotic Englishness, out to what may be, in some sense, some other side; and this movement may be part of what renders the poem so important for Dutt.

This is not to suggest, of course, that "Ewtrees" manages some step outside, say, Edward W. Said's "worldliness": indeed, one could even argue that in some sense, those four trees' primal bond parallels that of the "four nations" of Great Britain, rendering "Ewtrees" a powerful and perhaps in some sense coercive imagining of ancient origins for the internal British empire.[53] What it *is* to suggest is that whereas Kipling's turn to abstraction marks an aggressive deracination of the poetry of empire, Dutt's evocation of haunting Wordsworthian abstractions may tend in precisely the opposite direction. Indeed, the point at which Dutt cites Wordsworth—and thus evokes an emphatically and yet ambiguously English model—may be that at which she definitively marks the "we" of "Our Casuarina" as specifically "Indian"—and, perhaps, Bengali. For even that appropriative "English" bardic tradition which Dutt claims through Wordsworth can itself be deeply localized. Borrowdale is—and eerily is not quite—England; Baugmaree, Dutt's family home near Calcutta and the inspiration for her poem's garden, may stand in a somewhat analogous relation to the more abstract concept of India.

To the national and pre- or preternational images of Wordsworth's solitary and fraternal yews, Dutt adds another sort of image, then: one of passionate, dangerous intimacy, of conflicted joint fruition. She links her tree to Wordsworth's; but she does so through a bardic project that is at once passionately localized and thoroughly cosmopolitan. The darkling song of Dutt's garden might call up Keats's nightingale; but when morning breaks, equally resonant voices of longing sound from the kokilas of Hindu narratives. "[F]ain, oh fain" would Dutt's poetry claim the Casuarina's place among the "deathless" trees of English bardic poetry (54, 50). Still, even in voicing this ambition, Dutt does not give up the tree's—or her own—intimate creative ties to Baugmaree or to the "classic shore / Of France or Italy" (38–39). If part of a family garden outside Calcutta can arise, transfigured by memory, in these non-British lands of poetry, then any claims as to the inevitability of primary literary relations between "center" and "periphery" must break down. An "English bard," in the sense of one who deracinates and appropriates earlier bardic nationalist writing, Dutt simultaneously renders her own linguistic "Englishness" a matter of more or less explicit choice. In this, as in other ways, she confronts Wordsworthian national trees with an intransigently ambiguous colonial counterpart. Whose tree is this? Dutt's speaker's, perhaps; a Bengali garden's; English poetry's—but England's? Surely not. Even as Dutt's bardic performance honors Wordsworth's, then, it also seeks, in some sense, to haunt the earlier poem—to infuse a once-familiar homeland with the "eerie speech" of an English poetry whose "imperishable empire" can no longer be controlled by "the" English.

Notes

1. Katie Trumpener, *Bardic Nationalism: The Romantic Novel and the British Empire* (Princeton, NJ: Princeton University Press, 1997), xi–xii; further page references appear in parentheses. Many thanks to Monica Smith for her help in locating sources, as well as to Anne Williams, for our discussions of Toru Dutt and Romantic poetry.

2. Edmund Clarence Stedman, ed., *A Victorian Anthology, 1837–1895* (Boston: Houghton Mifflin, 1895), ix, xiv; further page references appear in parentheses.

3. Only the Indian section is vacant. Fourteen poets represent Australasia; twenty-two represent Canada.

4. For the most extensive and ambitious discussion of Kipling's poetry to date see Ann Parry, *The Poetry of Rudyard Kipling: Rousing the Nation* (Buckingham, UK: Open University Press, 1992).

5. M. van Wyk Smith, *Drummer Hodge: The Poetry of the Anglo-Boer War (1899–1902)* (Oxford: Clarendon Press, 1978), 98.

6. Paula M. Krebs, *Gender, Race, and the Writing of Empire: Public Discourse and the Boer War* (Cambridge: Cambridge University Press, 1999), 173, 167.

7. Kipling composed "The Native-Born" in September 1895. Encouraged by his American friend Charles Eliot Norton, he sent the poem to the London *Times*. Its appearance on 14 October 1895, which marked the *Times*'s first publication of a poem not written in response to a specific event, also inaugurated a series of some twenty public poems, for which Kipling accepted no payment (Charles Carrington, *Rudyard Kipling: His Life and Work* [London: Macmillan, 1955], 213, 258–59); "The Flowers" was begun in November 1895 (213, 226–27).

8. Rudyard Kipling, "The Flowers," in *The Seven Seas* (London: Methuen, 1896), 111–14, reprinted in *Kipling's Verse: The Definitive Edition* (New York: Doubleday, Doran, 1940), 189–91; line references appear in parentheses.

9. Kipling, "The Native-Born," in *The Seven Seas*, 49–54, reprinted in *Kipling's Verse*, 191–94; line references appear in parentheses.

10. "The displacement of political anger into cultural expression," Trumpener writes, was "a central tenet of bardic nationalism from its beginnings" (11).

11. Kipling, "The 'Eathen," *The Seven Seas*, 210–16, reprinted in *Kipling's Verse*, 449–51; line references appear in parentheses. Although it is far from the dominant note of the later volume *The Five Nations* (London: Methuen, 1903), the disillusionment of "Chant-Pagan" surfaces in other "Service Songs" in this volume as well. See, for example, "Stellenbosh" (lines 194–96) and "'Wilful-Missing'" (lines 204–5), reprinted in *Kipling's Verse*, 480–81, 475–76. For a discussion of the volume and its reception, see Parry, *Poetry of Rudyard Kipling*, 79–106.

12. Krebs, *Gender, Race*, 171.

13. For an explicit comparison of Scott's and Kipling's bardic uses of vernaculars, see Carrington, *Rudyard Kipling*, 348–49. Smith captures the nostalgia behind the "Service Songs" of *The Five Nations* when he writes that "these are mostly thinly camouflaged eulogies of various branches of the armed services" (*Drummer Hodge*, 107).

14. Trumpener, *Bardic Nationalism*, 33.

15. Kipling, "Chant-Pagan: English Irregular; '99–'02," in *The Five Nations*, 159, reprinted in *Kipling's Verse*, 459–61; further line references appear in parentheses.

16. Ralph Durand, *A Handbook to the Poetry of Rudyard Kipling* (Garden City, NY: Doubleday, Page, 1914), 251.

17. Kipling's South Africa, Krebs writes, "is indeed historically specific, but it is specific to only the Boer War" (*Gender, Race,* 168).

18. W. E. Henley's *National Observer* first published Yeats's poem on 13 December 1890 (Henry Merritt, "Rising and Going: The 'Nature' of Yeats's 'The Lake Isle of Innisfree,'" *English* 47 [1998]: 103–9, 103; see also Peter D. McDonald, "A Poem for All Seasons: Yeats, Meaning, and the Publishing History of 'The Lake Isle of Innisfree' in the 1890s," *Yearbook of English Studies* 29 [1999]: 202–30); as well as Mark Mossman's connection of Yeats's speaker to "a nationalized physicality or body that represents all of Ireland" ("W. B. Yeats and Salman Rushdie: Political Advocacy and an International Modernism," in *W. B. Yeats and Postcolonialism,* ed. Deborah Fleming [West Cornwall, CT: Locust Hill Press, 2001], 176).

19. "An enthusiastic pupil of English literature," Toru Dutt's grandfather Rasamoy Dutt "had a splendid collection of English books" (Padmini Sen Gupta, *Toru Dutt* [New Delhi: Sahitya Akademi, 1968], 17–18). The Dutt family's formal conversion in 1862 was led by male family members. Despite initial resistance, Toru's mother, Kshetramoni Mitter, eventually acceded, going so far as to publish a Bengali translation of a book entitled *The Blood of Jesus* with the Tract and Book Society of Calcutta (Gupta, *Toru Dutt,* 18–19; see Harihar Das, *The Life and Letters of Toru Dutt* [London: Oxford University Press, 1921], 7–11).

20. Das, *Life,* 19. In 1870, in London, Govin Chunder Dutt published *The Dutt Family Album,* the "first anthology of English verse by Bengalis" (Gupta, *Toru Dutt,* 14–15). See Rosinka Chaudhuri, "The Dutt Family Album and Toru Dutt," in *A History of Indian Literature in English,* ed. Arvind Krishna Mehrotra (New York: Columbia University Press, 2003), 51–69.

21. Here, Toru, in her diary, claimed the status of "an indomitable and steadfast French woman" (Gupta, *Toru Dutt,* 27).

22. Das, *Life,* 39.

23. Das, *Life,* 43.

24. Edmund W. Gosse, "Toru Dutt: Introductory Memoir," in *Ancient Ballads and Legends of Hindustan,* by Toru Dutt (London: Kegan Paul, Trench, 1882), xvi; further page references appear in parentheses.

25. Das, *Life,* 43.

26. One of these translations, "A Scene from Contemporary History," focuses on Victor Hugo's July 1851 speeches before the National Assembly; it is immediately followed

by Dutt's scathingly satirical translation of a Hugo poem on Louis Napoleon (*Bengal Magazine* 3 [1875]: 510–24).

27. Published by Didier in Paris in 1879, the book apparently received good reviews (Das, *Life*, 320–22). For Dutt's translations, see Meenakshi Mukherjee, "Hearing Her Own Voice: Defective Acoustics in Colonial India," in *The Perishable Empire: Essays on Indian Writing in English* (New York: Oxford University Press, 2000), 113.

28. Installments appeared in the *Bengal Magazine* 6 (1878): 264–75; 279–94; 325–31.

29. Harihar Das, "The Classical Tradition in Toru Dutt's Poetry," *Asian Review* 27 (1931): 695–715, 696.

30. Indeed, at least some of this final work was translated back into Dutt's native language: see, for example, Mukherjee, "Hearing," 106. "In Bengal," wrote Dipendranath Mitra in 1966, "perhaps more people have read" Dutt's "*Jogadhya Uma*" in Satyendranath Dutta's beautiful Bengali rendering than the original in English" ("The Writings of Toru Dutt," *Indian Literature* 9 [1966]: 33–38, 37–38).

31. Dutt, *Ancient Ballads*, iv; Philip Sidney, "The Defence of Poesy," in *Sir Philip Sidney: A Critical Edition of the Major Works*, ed. Katherine Duncan-Jones (Oxford: Oxford University Press, 1989), 231; the punctuation in Dutt's epigraph differs slightly from that in Duncan-Jones's text.

32. Why so private an act should transpire in English is not quite clear. Gosse himself suggests, somewhat inconsistently, that Dutt despaired "of an audience in her own language" ("Toru Dutt," xiii). Mukherjee's comments on private writings by other late-century English-educated writers usefully contextualize Dutt's actual (and unknowable) relations to English as an intimate language ("Hearing," 8–12).

33. Edmund Clarence Stedman, *Victorian Poets*, 28th ed. (New York: Houghton Mifflin, 1895), 470.

34. K. R. Ramachandran Nair, *Three Indo-Anglian Poets (Henry Derozio, Toru Dutt, and Sarojini Naidu)* (New Delhi: Sterling Publishers, 1987), 78.

35. James Darmesteter, "Miss Toru Dutt," in *Essais de Littérature Anglaise* (Paris: Librairie Ch. Delagrave, 1883), 269–92, 292; my translation. See Gosse, "Toru Dutt," xii. National and imperial literatures' claims to Dutt are often framed in terms of "rights"; see, for example, H. A. L. Fisher's foreword to Das's standard *Life and Letters* (vii), as well as Das, *Life*, 313–15. As Mukherjee argues, even many readings of Dutt as an "Indian" poet remain in some sense problematic ("Hearing," 88–115).

36. Malashri Lal, *The Law of the Threshold: Women Writers in Indian English* (Shimla, India: Indian Institute of Advanced Study, 1995), 4. For a brief description of the "law of the threshold," as Lal derives it from a reading of Indo-Anglian novels by women, see 16–21.

37. Alpana Sharma Knippling, "'Sharp Contrasts of All Colours': The Legacy of Toru Dutt," in *Going Global: The Transnational Reception of Third World Women Writers*, ed. Amal Amireh and Lisa Suhair Majaj (New York: Garland, 2000), 209–28, 217, 213.

38. See Yopie Prins, *Victorian Sappho* (Princeton, NJ: Princeton University Press, 1999), 13, 179, 199.

39. Suggesting that Dutt's "faculties" seem to have "slumbered," perhaps like Cinderella's, until her removal to Europe, Gosse presents "Our Casuarina Tree" as devoted to Dutt's "earliest memories, the circling wilderness of foliage, the shining tank with the round leaves of the lilies" ("Toru Dutt," xi–xii). Ironically, the frail exotic blossoms in the case were the same lilies: "I hope Mamma will succeed in her attempt to introduce English plants in India," Dutt wrote a friend on December 19, 1873. "Our tanks look very pretty with white water-lilies and blood-red lotus!" (Das, *Life*, 56). Suggestively, even Casuarina trees may be colonial imports from Australia.

40. Dutt, *Ancient Ballads and Legends of Hindustan*, 137; line references appear in parentheses.

41. William Makepeace Thackeray, *Vanity Fair: A Novel without a Hero*, ed. John Sutherland (Oxford: Oxford University Press, 1983), 871. On Dutt and Thackeray, see Das, *Life*, 193, 203, 208–9.

42. See, for example, E. J. Thompson's controversial early characterization of Dutt's *Ancient Ballads* as "not deeply-rooted"—a claim associated with his suggestion that Dutt's mind might not have been "primitive" enough for her subject matter ("Supplementary Review," in Das, *Life*, 343). In contrast, see K. R. Srinivasa Iyengar, *Indian Writing in English* (New York: Asia Publishing House, 1973), 60, 63. See also the nonbotanical metaphors of Meena Alexander's sympathetic account ("Outcaste Power: Ritual Displacement and Virile Maternity in Indian Women Writers," *Journal of Commonwealth Literature* 24 [1989]: 15).

43. See Elena J. Kalinnikova, "The Ganges' Child: Toru Dutt," in *Indian-English Literature: A Perspective*, ed. K. K. Sharma, trans. Virenda Pal Sharma (Atlantic Highlands, NJ: Humanities Press, 1982), 37.

44. Lewis Morris, from "A Song of Empire" (1887), in *The White Man's Burdens: An Anthology of British Poetry of the Empire*, ed. Chris Brooks and Peter Faulkner (Exeter, UK: University of Exeter Press, 1996), 260.

45. C. D. Narasimhaiah, *The Swan and the Eagle: Essays on Indian English Literature* (Shimla, India: Indian Institute of Advanced Study, 1987). The image, Narasimhaiah asserts, recalls Kalidasa's *Sakuntala* (28).

46. Leonard Huxley, from *The Life and Letters of Thomas Henry Huxley*, in *The Norton Anthology of English Literature*, 7th ed., ed. M. H. Abrams et al. (New York: W. W. Norton,

2000), 1, 693. Darwinism, Gupta writes, "directly influenced India, and in particular, Bengal" (*Toru Dutt*, 12).

47. Das, *Life*, 11.

48. Das, *Life*, 11; Gupta, *Toru Dutt*, 22.

49. William Wordsworth, "Ewtrees," in *"Poems, in Two Volumes"' and Other Poems, 1800–1807*, ed. Jared Curtis (Ithaca, NY: Cornell University Press, 1983), 606.

50. Wordsworth, "Ewtrees," lines 4–5, 7–8, 11–13; further line numbers appear in parentheses. See, for example, Gene W. Ruoff, "Wordsworth's 'Yew-Trees' and Romantic Perception," *Modern Language Quarterly* 34 (1973): 150–51.

51. Michael Riffaterre, "Interpretation and Descriptive Poetry: A Reading of Wordsworth's 'Yew-Trees,'" *New Literary History* 4 (1973): 229–56; Geoffrey H. Hartman, "The Use and Abuse of Structural Analysis: Riffaterre's Interpretation of Wordsworth's 'Yew-Trees,'" *New Literary History* 7 (1975): 165–89. For a useful historicist reading, see Eric C. Walker, "Wordsworth's 'Haunted Tree' and 'Yew-Trees' Criticism," *Philological Quarterly* 67 (1988): 63–82.

52. Hartman's reference to a cancelled line on "Druid oaks" underscores this point ("Use and Abuse," 188n11).

53. Edward W. Said, *The World, the Text, the Critic* (Cambridge, MA: Harvard University Press, 1983), 34–35.

"DAMNABLE AESTHETICISM" AND
THE TURN TO ROME

John Gray, Michael Field, and a Poetics of Conversion

Marion Thain

I

In 1900, on his deathbed, Oscar Wilde might have become the most famous convert of the fin de siècle. But, during this period, writers as diverse as Aubrey Beardsley, Alfred Douglas, Lionel Johnson, Frederick Rolfe (Baron Corvo), and Renée Vivien also looked to Rome. Recent criticism has amply demonstrated that Catholicism was associated in the late-Victorian mind with homosexuality and paganism, and so it is no coincidence that it appealed to Decadent writers who practiced one or the other, if not both.[1] In his major 1997 study, *Decadence and Catholicism*, Ellis Hanson argues that Catholicism could ultimately be an acceptable container for homosexuality: a suitable stage on which gay men could perform their desire.[2] Further, what Maureen Moran recognizes as the "cold limbo" inhabited by British Catholics, "mistrusted and scorned by family and friends and the nation at large,"[3] must have seemed like a good way of legitimizing (as well as protecting) the space occupied by homosexual men after the Wilde trials in the spring of 1895.

Perhaps the best representative of this fin-de-siècle climate is John Gray. The author of that most exquisite Decadent volume *Silverpoints* (1893),[4] Gray became a Catholic priest in 1901 after a drift back to the Church of Rome following Wilde's imprisonment for committing acts of "gross indecency." Gray wrote a volume titled *Spiritual Poems* (1896) as if to compensate for his Decadent works, but he soon dried up poetically, as

Jerusha McCormack observes: "[He had] written nothing since he had sent his poem 'The Emperor and the Bird' to the 'Michael Fields' for Christmas 1908. He had not actually published anything of substance since 1905. The silence held until 1921, and, then, abruptly, was broken by a rush of essays and poems which were to continue until his death."[5] This long silence was no doubt partly the result of the difficulty Gray had in negotiating a relationship between his new religious identity and his previous Decadent lyrics. Both Hanson and McCormack chart this struggle from *Spiritual Poems* onward. Nowadays Gray's religious lyrics command scant attention in comparison with *Silverpoints,* which remains of strong interest to scholars of Wilde. The Decadent John Gray, after all, has frequently been considered as the prototype for Wilde's protagonist of *The Picture of Dorian Gray* (1890, revised 1891). Most critics of fin-de-siècle poetry concur that Gray's poetic career had run its course by 1896.

By contrast, Michael Field—the aunt and niece Katharine Bradley and Edith Cooper, whose involvement with Gray's poetic career McCormack identifies above—never stopped writing poetry after their conversion, and their religious lyrics were seamlessly integrated into their oeuvre of eight books of poetry.[6] Nonetheless, for those scholars who have revived interest in Michael Field's large body of writing, it is the poetry that Bradley and Cooper produced before their turn to Rome that appears to hold the most value. At this point it is Bradley and Cooper's relationship as "[p]oets and lovers" that is central to their poetic design. In particular, their 1889 volume, *Long Ago,* has been the focus of several excellent inquiries into the ways in which aunt and niece (both of whom were trained in the classics) developed an erotic language in their poetic adaptation of Sappho's fragments.

It was not until 1907 that Bradley and Cooper rediscovered religion and entered the Church of Rome, having lived in a free, pagan spirit for most of their lives together. This conversion was partly the result of Cooper's ill health, which encouraged her to reflect on religious faith, but the main cause was undoubtedly the death of their beloved pet dog, Whym Chow, in 1906, and all that it symbolized. The dog, from the time of its arrival, had represented many aspects of pagan desire for the two women. It died at a time when that desire was suffering under the strain of being "defined" by the new normative categories of sexology. Their outpouring of grief is documented in *Whym Chow: Flame of Love* (1914). But their shift away from sensual abandon to spiritual devotion—iconized, no less, in a dead pet—has been a source of embarrassment to many critics. Angela Leighton, for example, writes that Michael Field's Catholic writing appears "flaccid and flowery." "Faith," she writes dismissively, "did not re-energise" their creativity.[7]

It would, however, be a mistake to let any exploration of Michael Field's Decadent sexuality stop at the point when, at the start of the twentieth century, it challenges—and is challenged by—newfound religious belief. The dialectic between religion and sexuality in the conversion poetry produces a dynamic as exhilarating as that found in their earlier work. In this chapter, I show how Bradley and Cooper's conversion crisis results in a provocative manipulation of religious imagery that attempts to integrate a Decadent symbolism charged with homoerotic desire. In this regard, it helps to bear in mind Hanson's leading claim that "[a]ll the great works of decadent literature are conversion narratives" (10). Michael Field's poetry is no exception. Moreover, it is essential to my reading of these poems to see the story of Bradley and Cooper's Catholic faith within the context of John Gray's conversion, and thus to reveal the crucial links between their little-discussed spiritual crisis and his emblematic one.[8]

II

While Gray lost his poetic voice, according to McCormack, from 1905 to 1921, it was during this period that he was helping Bradley and Cooper to cope with their transition from fin-de-siècle poets to Catholic converts. And, even if Gray produced no poetry during this time, his letters to Bradley, together with his theological advice, enabled the two women to find a voice for their transition, and to integrate it with their literary past. John Gray and Michael Field had known of each other's work for some time, and Charles Ricketts, a mutual friend, had tried to foster this connection.[9] Yet Bradley and Cooper didn't meet Gray until January 1906, in London. At this point they were still joyously pagan, devoted to their dog and each other, while Gray was already a priest, and had sublimated his relationship with Marc-André Raffalovich—with whom he collaborated on several projects, including a homosexual play, *The Blackmailers* (1894)—into a close but formal friendship.[10] This meeting proved timely, because it was on their return home after this very trip that Bradley and Cooper discovered their beloved dog was dying, and their own spiritual crisis began. This turn of events drove Bradley and Cooper to seek out further communication with Gray, and soon he and Bradley were exchanging letters on a very regular basis (some letters from Cooper also survive, but are much less numerous; and Bradley claimed to write for both).[11] Some months after Whym Chow died, Bradley wrote to Gray describing her conversion in response to his own spiritual crisis: "There! I have told you of my intercessor, as simply & bravely as you confide to me; & I shall never forget [?]them—the story of yours." The similarities between the two stories are apparent. Like Gray, Michael Field was an 1890s poet, and like him Michael Field was involved in the expression of homoerotic desire. Moreover, when Gray and Michael Field converted to Catholicism the coauthors shared an anxiety to leave behind, cover up, or transform a past of which they were ashamed.[12]

But, as McCormack writes, it is specifically Bradley's "struggle with 'heretic blood'" that reenacts Gray's "history of spiritual crisis and reconciliation" (209). In the letters between the two, Bradley's and Gray's shared, troublesome trajectory—from "damnable aestheticism" to Catholicism—becomes readily apparent. McCormack asserts that Bradley was one of the few people in Gray's later career who connected his past life with his present; her hybrid nickname "Father Silverpoints" could come only from one who shared this particular paradox (210). Through their correspondence between 1906 and 1914, Gray exerted a huge influence on the poetry of Michael Field, and he helped the collaborative women poets to avoid the silence into which he had fallen. That this was a painful process for Gray, and one through which he relived his own past, is clear from a letter he wrote to Bradley in January 1907: "You cause me a start when you allude to my conversion: you make me remember the ecstacy [sic] of those days when I wrestled with the Father of the angels."[13] Yet in providing them with his own most comforting elements of doctrine, he gave Bradley and Cooper theological tools and a framework that they then used in their poetry to accomplish their own reconciliation of their perverse, pagan poetic past (and their desire for each other) with their newly found Catholic faith.

Scholarship on Gray's movement toward the priesthood belongs to a gathering body of research that enables us to trace the historical development of links between Catholicism and homosexuality through the second half of the nineteenth century. Much of this criticism examines the poetry of Gerard Manley Hopkins (1844–89). Maureen Moran, for example, considers how Hopkins appropriates aspects of the muscular Christianity propounded by well-known midcentury figures such as F. D. Maurice and Thomas Hughes and applies them to his innovative interpretation of a bodily Catholicism. Moran sees the differences between Anglican and Catholic theories of Incarnation as responsible for the much greater difficulties Catholics had in holding bodily ideals. Hopkins, however, "by recasting notionally perverse or effeminate pleasures of the body in language usually associated with a popular expression of English Protestantism . . . adapted the discourse of Protestant Christian manliness" in order to give a voice to his own homoerotic Catholic discourse (65, 72). By comparison, Richard Dellamora examines how Hopkins's Catholic conversion permitted the poet "to conserve and to celebrate" his attraction to other men.[14] The intense atmosphere of religious discussion, shared worship, and joint observance of ritual in an all-male environment "stimulated homoerotic feeling, valorized it, and provided it with a convenient alibi." Dellamora continues, "[B]y focusing desire on the real but transcendent body of Christ," Hopkins aimed to allay the problem of illicit desire (47). If Hopkins can be seen, to some extent, as a bridge from midcentury ideas of muscular Christianity to fin-de-siècle Decadent obsessions with Catholicism, then this moment at the very end of the century, inhabited by John Gray and Michael Field, looks less isolated, and its sexualized religious discourse has some precedent.

Yet neither Moran, nor Dellamora, nor Hanson presents us with any evidence that there could be such a rapprochement between *female* same-sex desire and Catholicism. Further, the props and narratives that Catholicism appears to have offered male homosexual poets (including Christ as an emblem of the desirable and desired male body) are much less obviously beneficial and plausible for figuring desire between two women.

To be sure, other—expressly feminine—tropes were available to Bradley and Cooper within the church. Ruth Vanita, in her account of Michael Field's work in *Sappho and the Virgin Mary*, claims that Bradley and Cooper's conversion "occasions a shift from Sapphic to Marian imagery, but the content does not alter substantially" (133). In *Same-Sex Desire in Victorian Religious Culture* Frederick S. Roden builds on Vanita's brief account, devoting much of his important chapter on Michael Field to Marian imagery, the feminization of Christ through Mary, and poems celebrating biblical women and female saints.[15] But while female imagery is one important means for women writers like Bradley and Cooper to reconcile their gender and their desire with their newly found Catholicism, the aim of the present discussion is to contextualize Michael Field's work within the influence of one of their great male mentors. Vanita observes astutely that modern critical histories of Victorian gender and sexuality— which are often concerned with tracing lesbian or masculine networks and communities—"almost completely elide the importance of relationships between homoerotically inclined men and women" (4). Yet she does not pursue these relationships in the context of Michael Field's later work.

In what follows, I trace the influence of John Gray's homoerotic affiliation with Catholicism on Michael Field's spiritual poetry. This task is best achieved through a close reading of two critically neglected poems in light of Bradley and Cooper's correspondence with Gray. This female erotic religious discourse needs to be situated, at least partly, within—as well as growing out of—a more established and more visible male homosexual theological language.

III

The imagery of "Blessed Hands"—taken from the posthumously published volume *The Wattlefold* (1930)—demonstrates well the combined religious and erotic charge that occupies much of Michael Field's Catholic poetry. Since the poem will not be familiar to most readers, I quote it in full.

I

Virginal young finger-tips
Offered eager to my lips
To confer more blessing of the Chrism
Filtered down from God's abysm!

What of dew, kissed as it shone,
Wild rose I have fed upon—

Flesh that fortifies and wins,
Finger-tips forgiving sins!

Flesh that bears of sin no trace
Flesh that is of Mary's grace,
Bough from Heaven let down that we
Kiss of Paradise the tree.

Lovely and incarnate things,
Clean as violets at their springs—
Let us touch them, kiss them, pray
For our Resurrection-day!

II

Hands just blessed and consecrate
  Blessing my low head—
   Then each one outspread
With joined tips as on a bed
Of sea-sand the sea-shells mate
Shining valve with valve rose-red.
From God's sea, O priestly hands
Ye are shining and so sweet,
Held to me, my homage is complete
And the kiss I fall on you
Is softer than a Bridegroom ever knew.
Soft as that brine that swathed you in its bands,
That moves your young and shell-like finger-tips
Up to the softest motion of my lips.[16]

    "Blessed Hands" can initially be read as the story of the narrator receiving religious blessing from her priest. The "priestly hands" rest, outspread, on her head, and touch her lips in an offering of benediction. Biographically, the narrator could be either Bradley or Cooper—or both if we take seriously their claim to write as one—receiving the church's blessing. All we know about the bearer of those holy hands is that he is "young." Gray would seem to be good candidate to fill this role. He was one of Bradley and Cooper's favorite priests. He was younger than both of them, and considerably younger than Bradley. Yet the unmistakable erotic charge to these hands seems quite inappropriate as part of a narrative about the women and their male priest, and it certainly does not fit with the tone of their interaction with Gray in their letters.

The inability of the explicit narrative of the poem to entirely account for the poem's imagery highlights the existence of a less literal dimension to the verse: the "Blessed Hands" that title the poem are also implicitly the wounded hands of Christ nailed to the cross. Bradley's correspondence with Gray points to Christ's figuration in the poem; in an undated letter, she describes her station at the "blessed feet," dripping with blood, of Christ on the crucifix. While this extract from her letter does not fully explain the erotic core of "Blessed Hands," it helps to shift our understanding of what at first appears to be a literal encounter between priest and supplicant.

The conceit of hands touching in prayer like the kiss of lips is a traditional device with a long heritage. In a well-known dialogue in *Romeo and Juliet*, Shakespeare's star-crossed lovers act out just such a motif.[17] Here Shakespeare has the touch of the hands in prayer modulate to the touch of lips in erotic union: "O then, dear saint, let lips do what hands do / They pray; grant thou, lest faith turn to despair" (act 1, scene 5, lines 102–3). It is this same conceit that Michael Field deploys in the above poem. Hands and fingers in prayer kiss and are kissed; the poem is simultaneously devotional and erotic. And it is worth remembering that the "holy palmer's kiss" that Romeo figures is an excuse to legitimize sexual contact. Already, then, there are clues that for Michael Field the sacred context of "Blessed Hands" provides legitimacy for their intimacy. But, importantly, Michael Field's poem moves away from the traditional heterosexual setting of the "holy palmer's kiss" of *Romeo and Juliet*.

In fact, since Cooper converted to Rome before Bradley, leaving Bradley anxious to join her, we might read "Blessed Hands" as a work that describes Cooper's hands as "priestly." This reading suggests a narrative in which Bradley receives a sexualized blessing from Cooper. Moreover, that the "youth" of the blesser is stressed in the poem accords with Bradley's denotation of Cooper elsewhere as "Child" (even when the niece was in her forties and the aunt sixteen years older). In this light, we can understand more fully the significance of the hands that touch the supplicant.

As many critics have recognized, hands and fingers hold a special place in current lesbian symbology. The lesbian hand is sexy and stimulating. Judith Roof has written of lesbian films in which the problem of imaging women's desire for other women is solved by "providing a fetishistic hand that stands in for—is a metaphor of—what exactly cannot be seen in the scene."[18] Teresa de Lauretis, who engages closely with Roof's research, quotes from a conversation in which the hand again signifies lesbian eroticism: "[E]roticizing her need that I feel in her hands as she touches me . . . [I] begin to imagine myself being the *woman that a woman always wanted.* That's what I begin to eroticize. That's what I begin to feel from my lover's hands."[19] "Erotic power, wound, need, hands," writes de Lauretis, "these are the signifiers of [lesbian] desire" (296).

It seems likely that hands could signify female homoerotic desire in the nineteenth century also. Writing specifically about lesbian codes in Victorian poetry, Virginia Blain has warned us "not to overlook the importance of *hands* as signifiers of erotic power."[20] Blain's observation is relevant to a number of poems by Bradley and Cooper in which hands feature significantly. There is, for example, a poem in *Underneath the Bough* that describes an uncanny encounter with the fairies and that focuses on the touch of their "strange little hands" ("The Iris Was Yellow," 111–12). The poem contains echoes of Christina Rossetti's "Goblin Market" (1862), a work renowned for its striking images of women's sensual intimacy. Elsewhere, Bradley describes Cooper as "of the fairies."[21] Together, Michael Field's poem and Bradley's memorable description of Cooper suggest that the "little hands" were central to the erotic intimacy between the two women who wrote as Michael Field. It is worth remembering here that one of Bradley's pet names for Cooper, "Onycha," drew into their intimate vocabulary the image of the fingernail. This erotic significance must not be lost in our understanding of the hand and shell imagery in this poem.

The sexual charge of hands in "Blessed Hands" is apparent in the very first line. How could fingers be virginal unless there was the possibility of their being otherwise? Offered to the lips, this is no innocent kiss, but an erotic union of lips and fingertips:

> What of dew, kissed as it shone,
> Wild rose I have fed upon—

Flesh that fortifies and wins,
Finger-tips forgiving sins!

In the final stanza of part I, the acts of touching hands and then kissing them are connected with acts of prayer and devotion. Thus the sexual connotations of the hands are sanctified, and the flesh remains free from sin because these acts of love are performed in a spirit of devotion.

Part II of "Blessed Hands" elaborates the conceit of hands touching in prayer as an image of erotic contact between two like beings. Here the fingertips that rest on one another in the act of prayer are likened to mollusks with shells half-open on the seabed. The simile is complex. First, it conjures the image of a double shell, slightly open, yet with each half still in contact with the other; the meeting of fingertips provides the hinge that combines the two halves. But there follows a line that dismisses the image of the one shell with two halves and introduces instead an image of two separate, but identical, sea creatures bonding—"Shining valve with valve rose-red"—in an unmistakably erotic union. This image reminds us of the bipartite Michael Field: two poets who merge in a single identity with two mirroring halves. Moreover, Bradley often talks of Edith's shell-like beauty. For example, in "A Picture" (in *The Wattlefold*, 194), written by Bradley in 1913 while Cooper was ill, Bradley muses on Cooper's beauty, thinking of her face appearing "[a]s a shell under water, secret, keen." In this context, the intimate meanings of the "rose-red" valves at the end of "Blessed Hands" grow in intensity. The poetic voice observes the sea lifting "your young and shell-like finger-tips / Up to the softest motion of my lips." Here the fingertips—which are literally shell-like because the fingernails share some of the texture and opalescence of the seashell—carry a remarkable female homoeroticism. Thus the poem, which is ostensibly about a devout woman receiving the church's blessing, also articulates Bradley and Cooper's heretical, pagan desire for each other. In "Blessed Hands" Catholic devotion and a shared female eroticism co-exist—not crudely but in a careful and sophisticated manipulation of literary and theological images. In short, the idea that the kiss that the "I" gives to "you" is "softer than a Bridegroom ever knew" might denote not only the touch of the Holy Spirit but also the embrace that is unknown to men because it happens between two women.

In a letter to Gray, Bradley writes about Cooper's recent acceptance into the church: Cooper was found by the clergy to be "already full + entire Catholic on the central doctrine of the Blessed Sacrament," while Bradley waited at the door wanting to be allowed in to make "true confession." "It cost much for us—who are one poet—thus to break in twain," Bradley observes. "For me, I must wait, til you know whether you can open the door." In this letter, Bradley worries that she is "too wild for the Fold": "I love all that is pagan in the Church so dearly. I love the Paschal Candle with a great hugging love. I want to [?]sing the bees who make the wax. I love all about the lights. . . . Is it that once I was a torch-bearer on the hills?" Here Bradley declares that she identifies with the liturgy and emblems of the church, but, then, she celebrates through these parts of Catholic ritual a pagan desire that is anything but sacred. The same transmutation is responsible for the double narrative of "Blessed Hands": hands that touch in prayer become an image of sensual desire between women.

But that is not to say that Gray's priestly presence is irrelevant to the eroticism between the two women that is at the core of this poem. The integration of pagan and Catholic in "Blessed Hands" parallels the work of male poets who concentrated on the sensual body of Christ within Catholicism—from Hopkins to the likes of Gray and Raffalovich in the later nineteenth century. In his long tract on homosexuality, *Uranisme et unisexualité* (1896), Raffalovich identifies "superior" or "sublime" inverts who are able to sublimate their sexual desires through religion, among other things. When Raffalovich brings together religion and homosexuality, the result is a naturally noble being. Raffalovich's description of "the love of the virginal uranist for his 'young God, naked and bleeding, disfigured and transfigured, wounded and wounding'" shows a powerful system of imagery at work—one that was shared with Bradley and Cooper, as well as with Gray.[22]

In *Uranisme et unisexualité* Raffalovich points to the writings of Angelus Silesius, Friedrich von Spee, St. John of the Cross, and St. Teresa (30–31)—all examples from a narrow range of the more exotic Christian texts—in order to make this comparison between the earthly lover of Christ and the lover that Richard von Krafft-Ebing describes in *Psychopathia Sexualis* (1886) as the homosexual. In particular, the fetishization of the wounded male body (whether Christ's or St. Sebastian's) is such an important emblem of male Catholic homoeroticism at this time—one expressed most clearly by Raffalovich—that Michael Field's "Blessed Hands" must be read in light of it. For Bradley and Cooper, it seems the wounds of Christ are also central to their articulation of desire, but in this poem the "blessed hands" that bear the stigmata manifest the "wound" that is the mark of femininity, and a specifically female suffering. Again we see that cluster of "[e]rotic power, wound, need, hands" that de Lauretis identifies as the "signifiers of [lesbian] desire" (296). In her essay "'Mighty Victims': Women Writers and the Feminization of Christ," Julie Melnyk identifies a persistent androgynizing or feminizing of Christ during the nineteenth century that might be seen to offer a form of "empowerment" to Victorian women. She concludes, however, that this avenue turned out to be "an ideological dead-end" because not one woman writer was able entirely to leave behind the context of social powerlessness and suffering that the identification brought with it.[23] This does not hold true for Bradley and Cooper, who, quite exceptionally among women, but not so unusually among the men with whom they associated, identify with Christ's suffering not as a form of social powerlessness, but as a form of erotic transcendence.

Once we recognize the femininity of the "wound" that exists only implicitly within the poem, we can understand how "Blessed Hands" resonates with Gray's homoerotic references to Christ's stigmata in *Spiritual Poems*. While many of the poems in Gray's volume are translations, they are no less Gray's works for that. As Hanson writes, Gray's "art is not only in the translation, but in the selection" (314). For example, "Saint Bernard: To the Stabbed Side of Jesus"—a translation from the German of Paulus Gerhardt—is an unflinching fetishization of the wound:

> Save in thy wounded Side, for me
> There rests no consolation.
> O precious Wound, be thou adored . . .
> . . . .
> Conceal me, Wound; within thy cave
> Locked fast, no thing shall harm me;
> There let me nestle close and safe,
> There soothe my soul and warm me.[24]

Just as Gray and Raffalovich use Christ's body and his wounds as an erotic interface between sexuality and religion, Michael Field also engage with this discourse. Bradley and Cooper, however, transform it to signify female homoerotic desire by concentrating on only the "hands" of Christ, which image, in "Blessed Hands," a specifically female sexuality. Of course, Bradley and Cooper's writing of their desire for each other within religious passion is not limited to their subtle exploration of the protolesbian and Christlike hands. In their poetry, Michael Field also respond to Gray's teaching by reconciling their passion for each other and their Catholic devotion in their distinctive figuration of the Holy Trinity.

IV

Because the duality of Michael Field's authorship has been so central to commentary on Bradley and Cooper's poetry, the importance of the Holy Trinity in their joint work tends to be neglected.[25] But the Holy Trinity is not only a point of reconciliation between Bradley and Cooper's sexuality and religion but also a point of continuity between Michael Field's earlier pagan and later Catholic poetry. Michael Field configured a pagan trinity in honor of Bacchus, with Whym Chow as the third party, in order to symbolize their love for each other. At the time of their conversion, this threesome underwent a rapid and ingenious translation into a Holy Trinity of their own. Rather than leave their triadic intimacy behind as a part of their old life, Bradley and Cooper carefully adapted its meaning to their new faith, in a manner characteristic of their personal mythology, if eccentric to any observer.

Their attachment to Whym Chow cannot be overestimated. They were nearly deserted by their good friends Charles Ricketts and Charles Shannon at the time of the dog's death because of their loud and interminable grieving.[26] Writing to Bradley and Cooper from his new house in Holland Park on 9 April 1906, Charles Ricketts asserts: "I am quite unable to face an interview with this excessive and dolorous lamentation still in your ways of speech."[27] In her recent study of human devotion to pet dogs, Marjorie Garber writes of the death of the family dog—presumably purchased as a puppy for very young children and so in its old age when they reach their teens—as symbolizing, for the maturing children who love it,

the end of their own childhood: "[W]hat is lost is both the canine companion and a sense of one's own youth and innocence."[28] There is a sense in
which Bradley and Cooper, too, came of age when their dog died, only in
their case the loss of innocence was a result of the aging of a century that
was categorizing desire and defining sexual norms. There is no doubt
that the death of Whym Chow acquired a much greater significance for
the two women than it might initially seem to have merited because it
came to symbolize a crisis in their identity.

Many of the poems that appear in *Whym Chow: Flame of Love* address
the dead dog as either a muse figure or a beloved. Such works may be open
to the charge of bathos. But Bradley and Cooper's reference to Whym Chow
as a figure within a trinity helps them to overcome significant anxieties
about their erotic relationship in the context of their Catholic conversion.
Take, for example, the poem simply called "Trinity":

> I did not love him for myself alone:
> I loved him that he loved my dearest love.
> O God, no blasphemy
> It is to feel we loved in trinity,
> To tell Thee that I loved him as Thy Dove
> Is loved, and is Thy own,
> That comforted the moan
> Of Thy Beloved, when earth could give no balm
> And in Thy Presence makes His tenderest calm.
>
> So I possess this creature of Love's flame,
> So loving what I love he lives from me;
> Not white, a thing of fire,
> Of seraph-plumèd limbs and one desire,
> That is my heart's own, and shall ever be:
> An animal—with aim
> Thy Dove avers the same . . .
> O symbol of our perfect union, strange
> Unconscious Bearer of Love's interchange.[29]

Here Whym Chow is an otherworldly presence, with his shaggy legs seen
as "seraph-plumèd limbs," and his russet coat declaring him a "creature

of Love's flame." He is almost a red-colored Cupid, figuring forth the women's unity: a "symbol of our perfect union, strange / Unconscious Bearer of Love's interchange." However, the comparison in which Whym Chow stands to Bradley and Cooper as the dove stands to God is certainly striking, if not bizarre. The dove as Holy Spirit—the ineffable unifying spirit that forms the Holy Trinity with God and Christ—is the third member of the triad that also remains present within the other two. Similarly, Whym Chow is a unifying spirit that binds the two women in the trinity. In this complex figuration, Bradley and Cooper would seem to be reconciling their carefully crafted erotic union with their Catholic faith by finding a new way to image their unity.

Many of the letters between Bradley and Gray discuss Trinitarian doctrine, and the women were clearly thinking about the issues in sophisticated terms. In "Trinity," Bradley and Cooper theorize their desire for each other along the lines of the Trinitarian doctrine of St. Augustine. By the end of the nineteenth century, the legacy of the Oxford Movement's interest in the early church fathers generated considerable interest in Augustinian thought. Augustine's *De Trinitate* was translated and published in 1887, and it would seem to have exerted influence on Bradley and Cooper's conversion poetry. Edmund Hill explains that in *De Trinitate* Augustine attempts direct or intellectual contact with God. God is love, Hill muses, "so when we love and see our love and ourselves loving with it, surely we see God."[30] Eventually, however, Augustine decides that we cannot penetrate directly and immediately into the inmost being of God. We can, however, perhaps become more thoroughly acquainted with the divine mystery by looking at it indirectly, through its reflection or image in ourselves. The image that Augustine suggests we know God by is that of the trinity of love, lover, and beloved.[31] This structure therefore helps us comprehend Bradley and Cooper's interest in their dog. If they are lover and beloved respectively, then Whym Chow is pure love. Together, the three of them comprise the image of the Holy Trinity by which Augustine believes we can apprehend God. Thus, Augustine gave Field a way of allowing body and soul, sensuality and spirituality to come together in an image that celebrates their intimacy on earth as a route to understanding God.

Hill suggests we interpret Augustine's notion of the Holy Spirit as "the relationship of being Gift, the relationship of 'giveness' if you like":

"[H]e is the gift of both the Father and the Son."[32] Similarly, for Bradley and Cooper Whym Chow features as the gift given by Bradley and Cooper to each other. As such, the gift that is Whym Chow enshrines love: "I did not love him for myself alone: / I loved him that he loved my dearest love." The line "So loving what I love he lives from me" makes little sense unless placed within this doctrinal context, which sees Whym Chow/Holy Spirit as a gift of love that goes out from one to the other—not only as something that is a part of the giver but also as a gift with an independent existence that becomes a part of the recipient. Thus Whym Chow for Bradley and Cooper, like the Holy Spirit for Augustine, is "a kind of inexpressible communion or fellowship of Father and Son"[33]—or, in Michael Field's case, of the aunt and the niece.

At this point, we need to turn to Bradley and Cooper's correspondence with Gray once more in order to show how Michael Field figured out this particular trinity. In an undated letter to Gray, Bradley describes the period of mourning that followed Whym Chow's death and her temporary despair:

> I was quietly told of Heaven; that we three Henry, Whymmie, + Michael were accepted—to reflect as in a dark pond—the Blessed Trinity.
>
> It is our Mystery—*it is our secret.* In return for our blasphemy—Whymmie returned to us to be our guardian angel . . . + little living Flame of Love. He is my little Fellow, as Henry is my Fellow.[34]

Michael Field thus conceived that the blasphemous pagan trinity should be translated and accepted as their own earthly reflection of the Holy Trinity. That is to say, Whym Chow could reflect back to the poets their identity as lovers and the union of their dual authorship, which now existed within a sanctified Trinitarian space.

Of course, it is no coincidence that in this Holy Trinity the two women occupy the positions of the Father and the Son, a not inappropriate metaphor for an aunt and niece, who also share a special bond with each other. By seeing themselves as parts of the Holy Trinity, Bradley and Cooper image their special, much-proclaimed unity by reference to the ultimate distinctness yet oneness of the Father and Son.[35] Yet how might readers view the sensual intimacy between an aunt and niece within the Trinitarian unity that Father and Son enjoy? White examines Michael Field's ability to use diverse sources for their language of love "but never noticeably the language of blood-relatives" (202). Recent critics rarely pay attention to the potentially incestuous aspect of Bradley and Cooper's relationship, and for good reason. In the letters, diaries, and poetry of Michael Field the issue simply does not arise. But if there is any hint of repressed incest anxiety, then it is located in this identification with Father and Son. This is a familial identification that neutralizes and legitimizes the intense erotic bond between aunt and niece: "O symbol of our perfect union."[36]

But if we can detect some plausibility in Bradley and Cooper figuring themselves in the roles of God and Christ in "Trinity," what might we make of their portrayal of Whym Chow as the Holy Spirit? This question might initially be thought to elicit nothing but bathos: any sense in which dog and God are comparable risks conflating the sub-propositional with the super-propositional. In order to answer this question in a meaningful way we need to turn once more to the homoerotic Catholicism that Gray communicated, and represented, to Michael Field. More specifically, we need to focus on what is arguably Gray's most treasured biblical figure: St. John of the Cross. It is no coincidence that St. John of the Cross was also obsessed by the Trinity,[37] but his work appealed to both Gray and Michael Field particularly because he wrote mystic love poetry as sensuous as the Song of Songs. He exemplified the perfect reconciliation of luxurious poetry and religious doctrine.[38] In *Spiritual Poems*, Gray translates a number of poems attributed to this saint. In the letters sent to Bradley between 1906 and 1914, it becomes apparent what an important role St. John played in his own journey of conversion, as he remembers that painful period of his past. In November 1908 he writes of his "invincible love of S: John of the Cross," explaining that St. John "made a hole in the covering which I had woven about myself to hide me from God."[39] Hanson observes that "[t]he image of the hole in Gray's covering, rendering him vulnerable to God, is especially suggestive given that, in Gray's hands, the translation of [St. John of the Cross's] 'The Obscure Night of the Soul' reads more than ever like a decadent and homoerotic love poem" (325).

If, however, one looks to other letters in which Gray refers to the importance of St. John, then one sees that the saint, at least in Gray's retrospective memorializing, is part of a discourse of assimilation as well as penetration. In January 1908, Gray writes of a time when he "used to lie in bed, having at the time a brown eiderdown + brown bed curtains reading a brown book—works of St. John of the Cross."[40] St. John seems, in this quotation, to be blended into the embracing environment of the bedchamber, enabling him to be equated with sensuous protection as well as to be the means by which Gray is made exposed and vulnerable. This combination is also to be found in Michael Field's work, in which St. John is connected with a terrifying baring of the soul, but is at the same time assimilated into Michael Field's domestic world through another color connection—this time, as we shall see, involving the russet red of their Chow dog. For both Gray and Michael Field, St. John marks an erotic tension between, on the one hand, self-exposure and, on the other hand, a sensuous assimilation of the self imagined through the experience of lying in a curtained bed and of touching the fur coat of a beloved dog.

Michael Field's identification with St. John is clear throughout *Whym Chow: Flame of Love*. The title marks a personal reference to the pet dog's flame-colored coat, while simultaneously alluding directly to St. John's *The Living Flame of Love*: his most sensual and personal poem, which Gray partly translated but eventually rejected from *Spiritual Poems*. Bradley's letters record her asking Gray specifically for the loan of this volume:

Jan 24th Feast of St. John

Then of S. John of the Cross! Oh that I could read him with quiet heart! . . . (Will you—can you lend me his Spiritual Canticle + "Living Flame of Love." . . . I cannot speak of the new life I am getting from St. John—perhaps this is best—not a drop of the precious emotion is wasted—it is all wanted for the Spirit to use.)

The *Living Flame*—the most sublime account that St. John gave of the spiritual life—is addressed to a woman, Doña Ana de Peñalosa: a rich widow who placed herself under his direction. There is also a prose commentary written to accompany the poem, which speaks of the Holy Spirit as a purgatory flame and the gradual operation of fire on the soul: "The soul feels itself to be at last wholly enkindled in Divine union, its palate to be wholly bathed in glory and love. . . . The soul addresses this flame, which is the Holy Spirit."[41] As Robert Sencourt explains, "[T]he *Living Flame* becomes a long argument for the mystery, the freedom, and the splendor of God's direct action upon the soul" (168):

> O love with living flames that climb
> Profound and dear the sear sublime,
> Thine ardour has begun.
> Since thou'rt no longer hard to please,
> Devour with thine imperial ease
> The web our meeting spun.
>
> O scald and sear of purest love,
> O wound enjoyed all ease above,
> O delicate, soft touch
> Of hand which every ransom pays
> And savours of eternal days
> And slaying, quickens much![42]

How, then, does this reference to St. John's *Living Flame* affect our reading of "Trinity"? For a start, Gray's advocation of the teaching of St. John explains Field's repeated description, in correspondence with Gray, of the loss of the dog as their "sacrifice," which brought them nearer to God. Bradley writes: "I knew nothing of sacrifice till I offered one. It has been accepted. To my dear Henry the pain was worse—for she loved him most and from this I have learnt all I know of the sacrifice in the bosom of the Trinity, and the search light you must cast—in on my *blasphemy*— and God rewarded *that*—so!" St. John repeatedly "insists on the needs of sacrifice, of effort, of suffering, of generosity," according to Sencourt (167); indeed, his capacity for suffering is one of the most notable features of his story. Correspondingly, Bradley and Cooper's suffering, together with the sacrifice of the dove (or dog), places them firmly on St. John's preferred road to God, and thus assures Gray's approval.

It is also important that "Trinity" is addressed, potentially blasphemously, to an object of earthly love. Michael Field's engagement with *The Living Flame of Love* provided Bradley and Cooper with a further opportunity to legitimize their quest to incorporate their earthly love into an apprehension of the divine. Moreover, St. John's poem enabled the presence of Whym Chow in the trinity to be fleshed out in sacred terms, with the nice conceit of the russet-colored dog becoming a metaphor for the purgatorial flame that would cleanse the two women of blame for their previous blasphemy. To quote St. John's commentary: "The soul is completely absorbed in these delicate flames, and wounded subtly by love in each of them, and in all of them together more wounded and deeply alive in the love of the life of God, so that it can see quite clearly that that love belongs to life eternal, which is the union of all blessings."[43] This extract helps us see why Michael Field's "creature of Love's flame" figures forth the Holy Spirit. Whym Chow is not the Paraclete or white dove but John's flame— "a thing of fire." Bradley and Cooper have absorbed the male homosexual discourse of Catholic desire that Gray communicated to them but they have also twisted it in unexpected ways in order to integrate it with their own personal mythology and to make it reflect a love between women.

Bradley and Cooper were not without moments of doubt about the extraordinary reconciliation of pagan and Catholic love that I have explored in these two poems. This anxiety is shown in "Trinity" itself, of course, by the lines: "O God, no blasphemy / It is to feel we loved in trinity." Similarly, in an undated letter to John Gray, Bradley tellingly adds a postscript that reads, "I am a little scared at our invocation of the Trinity. . . . you will know what is right—in this 'supernatural life' one must of course perpetually invoke the Holiest." Yet, the strategy does seem to have enabled them to manage the process of conversion while keeping their carefully crafted identity intact. For rather different reasons, the reader, too, may be forgiven for moments of doubt about the appropriateness of such doggy elegy—and, for that matter, my serious consideration of it. There is no denying that the poetry of this later period, even when it is as complex and well-wrought as "Trinity," has a deliriously camp quality to it. In order to understand this poetry it is necessary to appreciate that Bradley and Cooper were at some level aware of, and in control of, this quality, while also being absolutely sincere about their grief and their feelings for the dog. I am not sure whether we are seeing Michael Field gently laughing at Bradley and Cooper's seriousness, or Bradley and Cooper having a wry smile at Michael Field's effusions, but I am convinced that the camp quality in work such as this is not entirely unselfconscious. How else could *Whym Chow* have ended up covered in russet suede that mimicked the dead dog's coat? This textual taxidermy is more aware of its status as the last of a long line of Victorian pet elegies than we might initially credit, and Bradley and Cooper are more knowing taxidermists than we might want to believe.

V

I wish to conclude this chapter by reflecting a little more on how both Gray and Michael Field managed their conversions poetically. All three individuals wanted to deny their past lives, while allowing that past to live on, somehow, in their Catholic present and future. McCormack tells us of a statuette that stood on Gray's mantelpiece "shrouded from head to foot" because this commission from Eric Gill (supposed to depict a man weeping for his sins) was deemed, on arrival, to be too fleshly for general display. McCormack also reports how Gray kept his Decadent first editions still on his shelves, but with their spines "mysteriously turned toward the wall." If a visitor picked up one of these books, "it would without comment be gently lifted from his hand and replaced" (219).

Bradley clearly identified with this need. Her letters to John Gray express a similar terror of "those eighties, & their damnable aestheticism" but at the same time admit "there have been moments when" she has "cursed it, & its lovely void." Although Bradley concedes that she "did seek to flee" the fin de siècle, she also acknowledges "the work of those eighties & early Nineties—the good & vital work of Oscar—rising up from the folly—the good & the harm of Pater—your work—ours!" Her mixed condemnation of the era of aestheticism, combined with a sense of not being able to leave it entirely behind, characterizes Michael Field's desire to reveal and acknowledge the past, while also rewriting its meaning.

Michael Field appears to have managed such a task of rewriting much more successfully than Gray, and for Michael Field this certainly seems to be a more deliberate aesthetic strategy. Bradley and Cooper explicitly state that they will create the double narratives I have examined in "Blessed Hands" and "Trinity." In "A Palimpsest" the narrator declares: "The rest / Of our life must be a palimpsest— / The old writing written there the best." Here, on the cusp of their conversion, Bradley and Cooper proclaim their desire to mask the narrative of their former life, while not erasing it: "Let us write it over, / O my lover, / For the far Time to discover."[44]

In a sense, Gray's letters to Michael Field helped Bradley and Cooper succeed where he had failed—in constructing an artful whole in which imagery and symbolism of past poetry was rewritten and given new meaning within Catholicism. It is worth remembering that while Gray spent the rest of his life on the quest to buy up and destroy copies of the limited edition of *Silverpoints,* Michael Field took an altogether different approach that signals their greater poetic adaptability. It is intriguing to discover there is a copy of *Wild Honey from Various Thyme* (1908)—the women's conversion volume, and the only volume to straddle pagan and religious phases—that contains the handwritten dedication, inscribed by Michael Field in 1911: "To the Very Revd, the Prior of Holy Cross— / in autumn / Michael Field."[45] If one opens up this volume, one discovers that Bradley and Cooper have either crossed out or pasted new Christian poems over the top of the most explicitly pagan contents.

This act of postpublication editing to befit the volume for a new audience is typical of Michael Field's palimpsestic process of adaptation, and quite different from Gray's wish to destroy his past poetry. In a letter to Gray, Bradley writes of her shame at their earlier poetry: "[W]hat hot cheeks for the religious!! poems in Wild Honey. Is there nothing to erase them?—all, save the envoi. With lay hands they touch the things on the altar, they offend." Yet, while sharing Gray's shame, Michael Field ultimately chose to transform rather than destroy—to write over rather than "erase" completely. The poems I have examined invite us to misconstrue them: in misreading them as stories of an erotic encounter between Bradley and Cooper, or misreading them as stories of a religious encounter, we discover the fluidity of a poetic identity that interlaces past and present, as well as self and lover, to create a personal mythology that is not only governed by its own logic but also strives for a coherent interface with the cultural concerns of the age. The more established discourses of male homosexuality within the Church of Rome (as well as Marian narratives) were essential to their ability to achieve this end, and their friendship with Gray provided a crucial context for this process.

Notes

I gratefully acknowledge the Trustees of the National Library of Scotland, and the Dominican Chaplaincy, Edinburgh, for their permission to reproduce quotations from the letters of Michael Field to John Gray. For permission to reproduce passages from the letters of John Gray, I thank the Berg Collection of English and American Literature, The New York Public Library, Astor, Lenox and Tilden Foundations, and St. Dominic's Priory, London.

1. Ruth Vanita explores these issues in chapter 1 of *Sappho and the Virgin Mary: Same-Sex Love and the English Literary Imagination* (New York: Columbia University Press, 1996); further page references appear in parentheses. See also E. R. Norman, introduction to *Anti-Catholicism in Victorian England,* ed. Norman (London: George Allen and Unwin, 1968); and Walter L. Arnstein, *Protestant versus Catholic in Mid-Victorian England: Mr. Newdegate and the Nuns* (Columbia: University of Missouri Press, 1982).

2. Ellis Hanson, *Decadence and Catholicism* (Cambridge, MA: Harvard University Press, 1997), 24; further page references appear in parentheses.

3. Maureen Moran, "'Lovely Manly Mould': Hopkins and the Christian Body," *Journal of Victorian Culture* 6 (2001): 72; further page references appear in parentheses. The phrase "cold limbo" is a quotation from Gerard Manley Hopkins's father, and is referenced by Moran to the *Further Letters of Gerard Manley Hopkins including his Correspondence with Coventry Patmore,* ed. Claude Colleer Abbott, rev. ed. (1956; reprint, London: Oxford University Press, 1970), 435.

4. Joseph Bristow writes about Gray's *Silverpoints* in the introduction to the present volume.

5. Jerusha Hull McCormack, *John Gray: Poet, Dandy, and Priest* (Hanover, NH: Brandeis University Press, 1991), 225; further page references appear in parentheses.

6. Indeed, when Bradley and Cooper write (in their poem "It Was Deep April") that, as "[p]oets and lovers" they are "[a]gainst the world," they might as well be writing of their later Catholic identity as well as their sexual identity (Michael Field, *Underneath the Bough: A Book of Verses* [London: George Bell, 1893], 79; further page references appear in parentheses).

7. Angela Leighton, *Victorian Women Poets: Writing against the Heart* (Hemel Hempstead, UK: Harvester Wheatsheaf, 1992), 223.

8. This relationship has previously been discussed very little, and only by writers whose primary interest is in John Gray: see McCormack's *John Gray;* and Ruth Z. Temple's "The Other Choice: The Worlds of John Gray, Poet and Priest," *Bulletin of Research in the Humanities* 84 (1981): 16–64.

9. See Temple's "Other Choice," 40.

10. See Temple, "Other Choice," for further analysis of this relationship.

11. The letters from Michael Field to John Gray are held in the National Library of Scotland, Edinburgh. Most are undated and are not indexed, but are known to have been

written between 1906 and 1914. All those referred to in this paper are from the bundle Dep 372, no. 17. Hereafter quotations from these letters will appear in the text without further reference.

12. Christine White examines the "[c]omplicated shifts" that took place in Bradley and Cooper's conception of their own relationship when they converted to Catholicism ("'Poets and Lovers Evermore': Interpreting Female Love in the Poetry and Journals of Michael Field," *Textual Practice* 4 [1990]: 208–9; further page references appear in parentheses).

13. John Gray to Michael Field, 26 January 1907. The letters of John Gray to Michael Field are held in the Henry W. and Albert A. Berg manuscript collection, in the New York Public Library. Further references to John Gray's letters will be identified by date alone; they are all from this archive.

14. Richard Dellamora, *Masculine Desire: The Sexual Politics of Victorian Aestheticism* (Chapel Hill: University of North Carolina Press, 1990), 17; further page references appear in parentheses.

15. Frederick S. Roden, *Same-Sex Desire in Victorian Religious Culture* (Basingstoke, UK: Palgrave, 2002), 190–225.

16. Michael Field, "Blessed Hands," in *The Wattlefold: Unpublished Poems by Michael Field,* collected by Emily C. Fortey, with preface by Fr. Vincent McNabb (Oxford: Basil Blackwell, 1930), 66–67; further page references appear in parentheses.

17. The famous speech in Shakespeare's *Romeo and Juliet* occurs in act 1, scene 5 (see the Arden edition, ed. Brian Gibbons [London: Methuen, 1980], 118–19).

18. Judith Roof, *A Lure of Knowledge: Lesbian Sexuality and Theory* (New York: Columbia University Press, 1991), 62.

19. Teresa de Lauretis, *The Practice of Love: Lesbian Sexuality and Perverse Desire* (Bloomington: Indiana University Press, 1994), 294; further page reference appears in parentheses.

20. Virginia Blain, "Sexual Politics of the (Victorian) Closet," in *Women's Poetry, Late Romantic to Late Victorian: Gender and Genre, 1830–1900,* ed. Isobel Armstrong and Virginia Blain (Basingstoke, UK: Macmillan, 1999), 137.

21. A manuscript copy of "The Iris Was Yellow" is held in the Huntington Library, San Marino, California, dated circa 1890. With it is a letter from Bradley to Frances Power Cobbe (also dated circa 1890), which contains this reference to Cooper's fairy ancestry.

22. Marc-André Raffalovich, *Uranisme et Unisexualité* (Paris: Masson, 1896), 30; further page references appear in parentheses. I have used the translation given by Hanson in his excellent discussion of this work (*Decadence and Catholicism,* 320–23).

23. See Julie Melnyk, "'Mighty Victims': Women Writers and the Feminization of Christ," in *Victorian Literature and Culture* 31, no. 1 (2003): 153.

24. *The Poems of John Gray*, ed. Ian Fletcher (Greensboro, NC: ELT, 1988), 110–11; John Gray, *Spiritual Poems* (London: Ballantyne Press, 1896).

25. Vanita's work provides a brief, but notable, exception (*Sappho*, 120, 230).

26. It is true that Victorian women writers seem to have had a particular penchant for pets and often invested much in them (see, for example, Elizabeth Barrett Browning, Emily Brontë, Emily Dickinson, and their pet dogs), but Michael Field is still an extreme case.

27. *Letters from Charles Ricketts to "Michael Field" (1903–1913)*, ed. J. G. Paul Delaney (Edinburgh: Tragara Press, 1981), 19–20.

28. Marjorie Garber, *Dog Love* (New York: Simon and Schuster, 1996), 245.

29. Michael Field, *Whym Chow: Flame of Love* (London: Eragny Press, 1914), 15.

30. Edmund Hill, *The Mystery of the Trinity* (London: Geoffrey Chapman, 1985), 79.

31. St. Augustine, *The Trinity*, trans. and intro. Edmund Hill, ed. John E. Rotelle (New York: New City Press, 1991), bk. 8, chap. 5, sec. 14, 255.

32. Hill, *Mystery of the Trinity*, 93, 109.

33. St. Augustine, *The Trinity*, bk. 5, chap. 3, sec. 12, 197.

34. "Henry" was one of Bradley's nicknames for Cooper.

35. "In a wonderful way therefore these three are inseparable from each other, and yet each one of them is substance, and all together they are one substance or being, which they are also posited with reference to one another" (St. Augustine, *The Trinity*, bk. 9, chap. 1, sec. 8, 274–75).

36. One only has to look at sexological writings of the time to see that, although Bradley and Cooper's relationship was in many respects a long way from the cases that were cited in textbooks (which detailed mainly fathers preying on their daughters, or intimacy between brothers and sisters), there would inevitably have been a certain amount of anxiety about their familial bond. Identification with the Trinity appears to have been at least partly a defensive gesture.

37. St. John's version of the Trinity was one based, again, on Augustine (and Aquinas's fine-tuning of Augustine's thinking), albeit mediated through Denys the Carthusian, whom St. John studied, and who then held immense influence in Spain (Robert Sencourt, *St. John of the Cross: Carmelite and Poet* [London: Hollis and Carter, 1943], 36; further page references appear in parentheses).

38. Sencourt writes: "The crude Freudian would say that this passion for the unseen lover was but an ebullition or at best a sublimation of the carnal in his nature. . . . But the Freudian explanation is soon refuted by the technical treatises: they make it

perfectly clear how the flesh of the mystic was subdued to the spirit: his impulses of love were both ordered and exalted" (*St. John of the Cross*, 140).

39. John Gray to Michael Field, 24 November 1908; this letter is also quoted in Mc-Cormack, *John Gray*, 169.

40. John Gray to Michael Field, 20 January 1908.

41. St. John's commentary on *The Living Flame of Love*, from the translation in Sencourt, *St. John*, 165.

42. St. John, stanzas 1 and 2 of *The Living Flame of Love*, from the translation in Sencourt, *St. John*, 165.

43. St. John's commentary on *The Living Flame of Love*, from the translation in Sencourt, *St. John*, 171.

44. Michael Field, *Wild Honey from Various Thyme* (London: T. Fisher Unwin, 1908).

45. Thanks are due to R. K. R. Thornton (a private collector) for sharing this discovery with me, and for advising on the transcription of some of Michael Field's letters.

SELECT BIBLIOGRAPHY

Alford, Norman. *The Rhymers' Club: Poets of the Tragic Generation*. London: Macmillan, 1994.

Armstrong, Isobel. *Victorian Poetry: Poetry, Poetics and Politics*. London: Routledge, 1993.

Armstrong, Isobel, and Virginia Blain, eds. *Women's Poetry, Late Romantic to Late Victorian: Gender and Genre, 1830–1900*. Basingstoke, UK: Macmillan, 1999.

Armstrong, Isobel, and Joseph Bristow, with Cath Sharrock, eds. *Nineteenth-Century Women Poets: An Oxford Anthology*. Oxford: Oxford University Press, 1996.

Beckson, Karl, ed. *Aesthetes and Decadents of the 1890s: An Anthology of British Poetry and Prose*. 2nd ed. Chicago: Academy, 1981.

———. *London in the 1890s: A Cultural History*. New York: Norton, 1992.

Bristow, Joseph, ed. *The Cambridge Companion to Victorian Poetry*. Cambridge: Cambridge University Press, 2000.

Burdett, Osbert. *The Beardsley Period: An Essay in Perspective*. London: John Lane, 1925.

Charlesworth, Barbara. *Dark Passages: The Decadent Consciousness in Victorian Literature*. Madison: University of Wisconsin Press, 1965.

Cronin, Richard, Alison Chapman, and Antony Harrison, eds. *A Companion to Victorian Poetry*. Oxford: Blackwell, 2002.

Dellamora, Richard. *Masculine Desire: The Sexual Politics of Victorian Aestheticism*. Chapel Hill: University of North Carolina Press, 1990.

Dowling, Linda C. *Aestheticism and Decadence: A Selective Annotated Bibliography*. New York: Garland, 1977.

———. *Language and Decadence in the Victorian Fin de Siècle*. Princeton, NJ: Princeton University Press, 1985.

Evans, B. Ifor. *English Poetry in the Later Nineteenth Century*. 2nd ed. London: Methuen, 1966.

Fletcher, Ian, ed. *British Poetry and Prose, 1870–1905*. Oxford: Oxford University Press, 1987.

———, ed. *Decadence and the 1890s*. London: Edward Arnold, 1979.

Hanson, Ellis. *Decadence and Catholicism*. Cambridge, MA: Harvard University Press, 1997.

Hough, Graham. *The Last Romantics*. London: Duckworth, 1949.

Hughes, Linda K., ed. *New Woman Poets: An Anthology.* Lost Chords, no. 1. London: Eighteen Nineties Society, 2001.

———, ed. "Whither Victorian Poetry?" *Victorian Poetry* 41, no. 4, and 42, no. 1 (2003–2004).

Jackson, Holbrook. *The Eighteen Nineties: A Review of Art and Ideas at the Close of the Nineteenth Century.* New York: Alfred A. Knopf, 1913.

Kermode, Frank. *Romantic Image.* London: Routledge and Kegan Paul, 1957.

Le Gallienne, Richard. *The Romantic '90s.* New York: Doubleday, Page, 1925.

Leighton, Angela, and Margaret Reynolds, eds. *Victorian Women Poets: An Anthology.* Oxford: Blackwell, 1995.

———. *Victorian Women Poets: Writing against the Heart.* Hemel Hempstead, UK: Harvester-Wheatsheaf, 1992.

Muddiman, Bernard. *The Men of the Nineties.* London: Henry Danielson, 1920.

Murdoch, W. G. Blaikie. *The Renaissance of the Nineties.* London: De La More Press, 1911.

Nelson, James G. *A Checklist of Early Bodley Head Books: 1889–1894.* Oxford: Rivendale Press, 1999.

———. *The Early Nineties: A View from the Bodley Head.* Cambridge, MA: Harvard University Press, 1970.

———. *Elkin Mathews: Publisher to Yeats, Joyce, Pound.* Madison: University of Wisconsin Press, 1989.

———. *Publisher to the Decadents: Leonard Smithers in the Careers of Beardsley, Wilde, Dowson.* University Park: Pennsylvania State University Press, 2000.

Perkins, David. *A History of Modern Poetry: From the 1890s to the High Modernist Mode.* Cambridge, MA: Harvard University Press, 1976.

Prins, Yopie. *Victorian Sappho.* Princeton, NJ: Princeton University Press, 1999.

Psomiades, Kathy Alexis. *Body's Beauty: Femininity and Representation in British Aestheticism.* Stanford, CA: Stanford University Press, 1997.

Schaffer, Talia. *The Forgotten Female Aesthetes: Literary Culture in Late-Victorian England.* Charlottesville: University Press of Virginia, 2000.

Schaffer, Talia, and Kathy Alexis Psomiades, eds. *Women and British Aestheticism.* Charlottesville: University Press of Virginia, 1999.

Showalter, Elaine. *Sexual Anarchy: Gender and Culture at the Fin de Siècle.* New York: Viking, 1990.

Smith, Timothy d'Arch. *Love in Earnest: Some Notes on the Lives and Writings of English "Uranian" Poets from 1889 to 1930.* London: Routledge and Kegan Paul, 1970.

Stetz, Margaret D., and Mark Samuels Lasner. *England in the 1880s: Old Guard and Avant-Garde.* Charlottesville: University Press of Virginia, 1989.

———. *England in the 1890s: Literary Publishing at the Bodley Head*. Washington, DC: Georgetown University Press, 1990.

———. *The Yellow Book: A Centenary Exhibition*. Cambridge, MA: Houghton Library, 1994.

Sturgis, Matthew. *Passionate Attitudes: The English Decadence of the 1890s*. London: Macmillan, 1995.

Temple, Ruth Z. *The Critic's Alchemy: A Study of the Introduction of French Symbolism in England*. New York: Twayne, 1953.

———. "Truth in Labelling: Pre-Raphaelitism, Aestheticism, Decadence, Fin-de-Siècle." *English Literature in Transition (1880–1920)* 17 (1964): 201–22.

Thesing, William B. *The London Muse: Victorian Poetic Responses to the City*. Athens: University of Georgia Press, 1982.

Thornton, R. K. R. *The Decadent Dilemma* (London: Edward Arnold, 1983).

Thornton, R. K. R., and Marion Thain, eds. *Poetry of the 1890s*. Harmondsworth, UK: Penguin, 1997.

Vadillo, Ana Parejo. "New Woman Poets and the Culture of the *Salon* at the *Fin-de-Siècle*." *Women: A Cultural Review* 10 (1999): 22–34.

———. *Women Poets and Urban Aestheticism: Passengers of Modernity*. Basingstoke, UK: Palgrave Macmillan, 2005.

White, Chris, ed. *Nineteenth-Century Writings on Homosexuality: A Sourcebook*. London: Routledge, 1999.

NOTES ON CONTRIBUTORS

LINDA HUNT BECKMAN is the author of books and essays on nineteenth-century literature (some of them written under the name Linda Hunt). Her first book was *A Woman's Portion: Ideology, Culture, and the Female Novel Tradition* (Garland, 1988), and in 2000 Ohio University Press brought out *Amy Levy: Her Life and Letters*. Her articles on Amy Levy have been published in *Studies in the Novel* and *Victorian Literature and Culture*, and she wrote the entry on Levy for the *New Dictionary of National Biography*. Professor emeritus in the English Department at Ohio University, Linda Hunt Beckman is now writing and teaching in Philadelphia.

JOSEPH BRISTOW is a professor of English at the University of California, Los Angeles, where he edits *Nineteenth-Century Literature* (University of California Press). His recent books include an edited collection of essays, *Wilde Writings: Contextual Conditions* (University of Toronto Press, 2003), and the Oxford English Texts edition of Oscar Wilde's *The Picture of Dorian Gray* (Oxford University Press, 2005).

NICHOLAS FRANKEL teaches English at Virginia Commonwealth University, Richmond, Virginia. He is the author of *Oscar Wilde's Decorated Books* (University of Michigan Press, 2000) as well as of various essays on the relationship between late-Victorian literature and graphic design. He is currently writing a history of Victorian ideas about decoration and ornament titled "The Discourse of Decoration: Design and Visual Mediation in Victorian Britain."

LINDA K. HUGHES, the Addie Levy Professor of Literature at Texas Christian University in Fort Worth, works on Victorian poetry, fiction, and periodicals in the context of gender and publishing history. Her recent work includes the biography entitled *Graham R.: Rosamund Marriott Watson, Woman of Letters* (Ohio University Press, 2005); "Women Poets and the Contested Spaces of *The Yellow Book*," *SEL: Studies in English Literature* 44, no. 4 (2004); and an edition of *Elizabeth Gaskell's Shorter Tales*,

1859–1865 (Pickering and Chatto, forthcoming). She is also the author of a study of Tennyson, *The Manyfacèd Glass: Tennyson's Dramatic Monologues* (Ohio University Press, 1987), and coauthor, with Michael Lund, of books on serial literature and Gaskell's publishing career.

HOLLY A. LAIRD, a professor of English at the University of Tulsa, is the editor of *Tulsa Studies in Women's Literature* and the author of *Women Coauthors* (University of Illinois Press, 2000)—on late nineteenth-century to contemporary women literary collaborators—as well as numerous articles on Victorian and modern writers.

As editor and author, JERUSHA MCCORMACK has published four books on the life and work of Oscar Wilde and that of his disciple, John Gray. Now retired from University College, Dublin, she has been appointed Professor at Beijing Foreign Studies University, where she teaches culture studies (including the first course in the People's Republic of China on gender). She is currently working (as coauthor) on the first textbook in the world on *Western Civilization with Chinese Comparisons*, to be published in China in September 2005, which will form the basis for this course to be taught at BASE. Thereafter, it is hoped to adapt this course to teaching Chinese Civilization in the West, as no such bridge course yet exists.

JEROME MCGANN is the John Stewart Bryan University Professor, University of Virginia. His edition of Algernon Charles Swinburne's prose and poetry, which was published by Yale University Press in 2004, follows his edition of Dante Gabriel Rossetti's literary works (Yale University Press, 2002).

YOPIE PRINS is an associate professor of English and comparative literature at the University of Michigan. She is the author of *Victorian Sappho* (Princeton University Press, 1999) and has published various articles on Victorian poetry, classical literature, and nineteenth-century Hellenism. Currently she is working on two projects: a book entitled *Ladies' Greek*, and a series of essays about Victorian poetry and prosody, tentatively entitled *The Fetish of Meter*.

JULIA F. SAVILLE is an associate professor of English at the University of Illinois at Urbana-Champaign. She is the author of *A Queer Chivalry: The*

Homoerotic Asceticism of Gerard Manley Hopkins (University Press of Virginia, 2000) and various essays on Victorian poetry, painting, and fiction. Her current book-length project is entitled *Bathing Boys: An Aesthetics of the Male Nude in Victorian Literature and Culture.*

MARION THAIN teaches at the University of Birmingham, England. She has published primarily on late nineteenth- and early twentieth-century literature, particularly poetry and poetics. She is the general editor of a series of reprinted fiction, Late Victorian and Early Modernist Women Writers (University of Birmingham Press), and she coedits the Victorian section of Blackwell's online metajournal, *Literature Compass.*

ANA PAREJO VADILLO teaches in the School of English at the University of Exeter, United Kingdom. She was previously a European Social Funds and La Junta de Extremadura Post-doctoral Research Fellow at Birkbeck College, University of London. Her monograph *Women Poets and Urban Aestheticism: Passengers of Modernity* will appear from Palgrave Macmillan in 2005. She is also coediting, with Marion Thain, "Michael Field: An Anthology" for Broadview Press.

INDEX